# LETTERS ·FROM THE CRIMEA.

# LETTERS

## FROM

# THE ARMY IN
# THE CRIMEA

BY 'A STAFF OFFICER' WHO WAS THERE
LT. COL. SIR ANTHONY CONINGHAM STERLING

**The Naval & Military Press Ltd**

published in association with

**FIREPOWER**
**The Royal Artillery Museum**
Woolwich

Published by
## The Naval & Military Press Ltd
Unit 10 Ridgewood Industrial Park,
Uckfield, East Sussex,
TN22 5QE England
Tel: +44 (0) 1825 749494
Fax: +44 (0) 1825 765701
www.naval-military-press.com

*in association with*

**FIREPOWER**
**The Royal Artillery Museum, Woolwich**
www.firepower.org.uk

*In reprinting in facsimile from the original, any imperfections are inevitably reproduced and the quality may fall short of modern type and cartographic standards.*

# CORRIGENDA.

PAGE

viii  line 18 from top, *for* "1854" *read* "1855"

     Add to foot-note as follows :—

xvii    "Lord Rokeby was appointed to Command 1st Division   13 Aug. 1855.

      Colonel Ridley (a Guardsman) to 2nd Brigade, 1st Division, (Line Brigade)   13 Aug. 1855.

      Colonel Drummond (a Guardsman) to Brigade of Guards   11 Aug. 1855.

      The latter was superseded in this Command by General Craufurd, also a Guardsman.   29 Oct. 1855."

     In the note *for* "Crawford" *read* "Craufurd"

4    line 10 from top, *for* "waning Crescent" *read* "pale waning"

15   line 4 from top, *for* "baggage, animals" *read* "baggage-animals"

36   line 23 from top, *for* "known" *read* "know"

81   line 14 from top, *for* "faits" *read* "fait"

143  *after* "fired a shot" *the words* "FOURTH DIVISION" should be introduced, as on the next page.

174  line 19 from top, *for* "Cossack" *read* "body"   In the following line, *for* "latter gentry" *read* "Cossacks"

401  in the note, *for* "Crawford" *read* "Craufurd" and add to note " see note at page xvii of Preface."

408. line 2 . for "junior" read "senior"

# PREFACE.

———◆———

WHILE in Turkey and in the Crimea my time was too much occupied to permit my attempting to keep a regular register of events ; these Letters were generally written in the night, at hours stolen from sleep. There has been so much spoken and written, there have been so many " Inquiries," that the subject of the Crimean War may be considered to be rather threadbare. However, the nation has been so excited on this subject, and has, after all, had so little satisfaction to its curiosity, that I decided, when I had looked over what Letters it was possible to recover, that I would put them together, and present to my friends a picture of what was passing in the mind of a working Officer of that Crimean Army, the subject of so much praise and blame, for which so many tears have been shed, and on which so much national sympathy has been expended.

It will appear, on perusing this work, that occasionally personal remarks have been made, which in truth I have endeavoured as much as possible, consistently with the matter in hand, to modify; and where I thought the original phrases were tinged with any thing of an unjust asperity, I have expunged them. Still I am sensible that many persons will be annoyed by my remarks; for which I am sincerely sorry. There is, however, nothing set down here which I do not consider to be perfectly true; and if the people of England wish to have that truth,—a wish which has been continually expressed by them,—here it is, in a form of minute detail not hitherto attempted, and touching on parts of our military system which have escaped the ken of Commissioners.

There are two subjects to which it appears to me that the national attention should be directed in case of another war being undertaken.

One of these is the manner in which our Press affects our military affairs; and the other, the manner in which the system prevailing in the regiments of Guards has acted upon, and will act upon, the interests and efficiency of the rest of the British Army. As to the Press, in these Letters I found many angry passages (which have been excised), evidently brought forth by the constant stream of attacks and sarcasms directed against us, day after day, in the columns of the newspapers, which reached the camp twice a week with very great regularity.

The newspaper press of England was required by the nation to supply perpetual information about military movements, and perpetual gossip about the routine in the camp. The gentlemen sent for that purpose did supply all this, to the best of their ability; but unfortunately the British people could not receive this information and this gossip without providing it also for the use of the enemy and for the amusement and astonishment of our continental neighbours. The English, as a nation, are peculiarly insensible to ridicule; and not being naturally a military people, they appear not to have comprehended the feeling of many officers, whose professional pride was hurt by a public *exposé* of all our blunders and sufferings, which was no doubt translated into Russian for the benefit of the Russian Army; these statements of course encouraged the enemy. It never seemed to strike the public as rather monstrous, that a gentleman should be permitted to reside in camp, and to draw rations, while his pen was employed in attacking Lord Raglan's military conduct, and in laying open the whole Army to the ridicule of the universe. As a friend of mine remarked: " If the British nation chooses to have its Army governed by the newspapers, the result must be, that by degrees all the officers who reflect will, as it becomes possible, get out of the service. No army can succeed with such spies in its camp. No general can command when his character and conduct are canvassed openly by editors, and while their remarks upon both are sown broadcast among the soldiers. I do not believe that the outcry in the papers did any good. There is no doubt in my mind that the evils complained of would have been remedied as soon as possible, whether the newspapers had taken up the question or not. If the correspondents had been really competent judges, they, who were with the Army, and who had nothing else to do, ought to have discovered the defects and published their opinions long before the mischief which occurred in January 1857 had risen to such a pitch as to excite all England, and to fill the swelling heart of the people with pity and indignation."

It is to be considered now what has been the result of such an outcry. Names were brought forward; but as far as I can see there has been no conviction arrived at, except that our military system was a bad one; while it remains doubtful whether the fatal blots have been hit, or even noticed. It is known, however, that

Gortschakoff had an officer employed in doing nothing else than collating the English newspapers, and that he considered the *Times* equal to half a dozen good spies. Still the editors congratulate themselves on the good they have done, and honourable gentlemen admit the same. Folly on every side. As my friend says: " It is really provoking that the practical English nation should be so stupid as to insist on giving the best information to their deadly enemy."

With respect to the accuracy of the intelligence so supplied, we know from the character of the gentlemen employed that it was as accurate as they could make it, considering that they had small access to officers of rank, and that the position of such officers as were well-informed was one which rendered it impossible, or at least exceedingly improper, for them to give information. What I mean to maintain is, that although usually the facts published in the papers were correct, yet still there was a considerable exaggeration on many occasions, and also a misrepresentation, no doubt unintended, of the general tone of feeling in the Army. The most remarkable blunder made by the Government at home was in not appointing Sir Colin Campbell to command when Lord Raglan died. Long after that event the newspapers con-

tinued to attack and to sap Sir Colin's military
reputation, assisted by letters from officers circu-
lated in the London fashionable coteries. If the
correspondents had been competent judges of military merit, they would have joined in turning
public attention to the great qualities of this officer,
and in pointing him out to the nation as the man
whom they should look to. Even now it probably
is not understood that the insult offered to the
most distinguished soldier and to the most skilful
general now serving in the Queen's Army, by
placing over his head to command him a junior
officer, who had no claims and no experience, is a
part of our military system. In fact, that the latest
improvement in that system,—viz. the warrant
which established promotion by selection for merit,
—was the very measure which made it possible to
accomplish such an act of ingratitude and of folly.
It may be granted that the editors acted as well as
they could, and that they believed conscientiously
that they were performing a public duty by their
writings. Military officers usually do not think it
becoming to write to the newspapers accounts of
the war they are engaged in. I myself was applied
to by one of the most respectable of the magazines
to write for it before I joined the Army; but I
declined, purely on this ground. That I had the

leave about eight months in the year. All the company duty done by officers of the Guards is done by the subalterns; and the discipline of each regiment of Guards is maintained by the commanding officer, his adjutant, and the sergeants. From this statement it is evident that the military education of an officer of the Guards does not put him in contact with his men, and that he has not the opportunity of acquiring a knowledge of the interior economy, which the regulations require that all captains of the Line shall have, and which they are compelled to have by a strict commanding officer, and by the general officers who inspect them. If a lieutenant-colonel of the Line were to exchange with a captain and lieutenant-colonel of the Guards, as sometimes happens, he would be surprised to find, that though nominally commanding a company, he would be allowed to have little or nothing to do with its management.

The public may from this explanation perceive that from youth upwards the habits of officers of the Guards must lead them to suppose that the officers should be spared as much as possible. I therefore consider that any officer who has spent the first fourteen or fifteen years of his life in the Guards is likely to have imbibed a fixed idea that the officers should be spared; and as he has seen the companies of the Guards managed without the assistance of the captain, so he will naturally feel that it is a hardship to call on any captains to meddle with such work. Early custom will prevent him from seeing the propriety of what is an established maxim in the opinion of the best practical soldiers, viz. that the sergeants should be made responsible for nothing, and that the whole onus should be thrown on the officers, who should never leave their men, whether on fatigue or under arms; and that every captain should have all the particulars concerning each soldier in his company at his fingers' ends.

Where a brigade of Guards takes the field, it forms part of a division; this division is provided with an assistant-adjutant general; and each of the two brigades composing it has a brigade-major. In the Crimea I was brigade-major to the brigade which was in the same division with the Guards, and I was afterwards assistant-adjutant-general to the division of which the Guards formed one brigade. I mention this to show that I had an opportunity of seeing something of the working of such a division.

When an army advances to battle, in the brigade of Guards, as in all other brigades, each captain, although a lieutenant-colonel, marches at the head of his company; but in the trenches, in our army, it was not so. In the Line, when a captain is a brevet-major, or a brevet-lieutenant-colonel, he receives 2s. a day extra pay. He does all his company work, and besides that is liable to do duty as a field-officer. It is not so in the Guards. All the captains are lieutenant-colonels, and they are put on the roster of field-officers. No captain of the Guards took trench duty at the head of his company—he went in as a field-officer; instead of being in the trenches every third day, he only went in about once a fortnight, and then as a field-officer.

The result of this was, that the lieutenants and ensigns of the Guards, who had rank respectively of captains and lieutenants, had to do all the duty done in regiments of the Line by the whole of the captains, lieutenants, and ensigns of each regiment; so that these officers were overworked. The duty of the trenches was taken by detachments; a certain number of men, in proportion to the strength of the division, was sent into the trenches with officers, that is, captains and subalterns, in the proportion of two officers to every hundred men. When the companies were weak, if all the officers had gone with their companies, the proportion would probably have been two officers to

thirty or forty men; which it would have been
impossible for the Guards to furnish, as none of
their captains were really captains; they were all
lieutenant-colonels. This I imagine to have been
the cause of so anomalous and objectionable a
manner of taking trench duty. When Sir Colin
Campbell was sent up to the siege with his division,—in the middle of June 1855,—he found this
system existing, and of course he had no power
to alter it; but he did make a demonstration, for
at the same period the division of the French
Army commanded by General Canrobert came to
the siege, and took the trenches immediately on
the right of our attack. In the French Army the
trench duty was taken by divisions; and General
Canrobert, who had been Commander-in-Chief,
took himself his turn of the trenches every third
day. One of his two brigades took the advanced
trench, and the other was in reserve—alternately.
This was the division which afterwards stormed
the Malakoff. When Sir Colin Campbell found
this, he also took his turn in the trenches, instead
of detailing a brigadier. He did so three times;
but the example was deemed contagious, and an
order came out directing the generals of division
to remain in their camps in reserve, with the
cooks. I do not know the precise date of this

order; for the printed general orders which I had were all destroyed when my hut was burned down. But I perceive that in one of my Letters it is mentioned that, in August, there were then in the ·Army a commander-in-chief, a chief of the Staff, three generals of division, and three generals of brigade, all Guardsmen,*—total eight; and only twelve of the Line.

Now I think it surprising that some of these gentlemen, who had all been brought up together in the same corps, did not suggest to the Commander-in-Chief the propriety of imitating the French, who sent into the trenches a division complete, with its general, its brigadiers, and every staff-officer, as well as the lieutenant-colonels, majors, captains, and subalterns of each regiment.

The importance of having a large number of officers present with the men in the trenches was immense; for the soldiers were almost all young, some of them not three months from their homes; and the example of officers was very necessary for them.

When in a division one of the brigades is a brigade of Guards, detachment duty is only taken

---

| * Simpson. | Bentinck. | Crawford. |
| Barnard. | Rokeby. | Ridley. |
|  | Codrington. | Windham. |

by the other brigade. This was unfolded to us in Bulgaria, where the Highland Brigade furnished a detachment of two companies to head quarters; and when Sir Colin Campbell applied to have it relieved, he heard the remarkable fact, that the Guards did not take that sort of duty.

Having explained, as well as I can, how the example of the Guards is likely to act upon and to spread through the Army to the detriment of discipline, I will just touch upon the point of the tremendous privilege, that every ensign in the Guards is a lieutenant, *ipso facto*, in the Army, every lieutenant a captain, and every captain a lieutenant-colonel.

I will here introduce a Letter on this subject, which my friend A. wrote to Lord —— from the Crimea, and which enters very fully into the question.

" Camp before Sebastopol,
8th April, 1856.

" A printed memorandum, signed by Colonel James Lindsay, of the Grenadier Guards, has been circulating here among the commanding officers of regiments of the Line; it is a sort of commentary on the Memorial lately presented by the officers of the Guards on the subject of their promotion. Colonel Lindsay does not advert to the fact, that petitioning at all is a breach of military discipline. Had the officers of the Line petitioned,—as they might well have done,—with a view to their being put on a footing of equality with the Guards, they would have been immediately called mutinous, and would have been punished for such a combination. The prayer of the Guards Memorial having been refused, Colonel Lindsay, by this memorandum upon it, is doing worse than petitioning; for he is agitating after a refusal, which is a most unmilitary proceeding. Colonel Lindsay begins by admitting that the former arrangement was unjust, and that the new one had for its object to repair this injustice. He only complains that it does this too effectually; he thinks that all the captains and lieutenant-colonels of the Guards, who had served three years in that rank at the period fixed by authority for the introduction of the new system, should have been made full colonels, as were those officers of the Line who had commanded regiments for that length of time—taking no account of the different degrees of military knowledge possessed by men who had commanded battalions of the Line, compared with that of those who had only commanded companies of the Guards.

He talks of the higher price of commissions in the Guards; but he does not mention what

the difference of the price is; *that*, in the rank
of lieutenant-colonel, I beg to record; it is just
260*l.*,—no such mighty matter, considering that
their pay is much larger than that of lieutenant-
colonels commanding battalions of the Line, and
that the officers of the Guards, on an average,
which I once struck, attain that position in about
fourteen years; while the average in the Line was
twenty-five years. I have no books or documents
here; but the averages I quote I remember were
struck from a Blue-book which contained the average length of service completed by officers of the
Guards and of the Line before they got command
of battalions; the average length of time before
the Guards officers became captains and lieutenant-colonels was omitted; but I thought it of
consequence, and found it to be about fourteen
years.

The average, if taken now, after this active
war, will, I suppose, be lower in both services;
some young officers of the Guards have lately become captains in their regiments, and lieutenant-
colonels in the Army, in seven or eight years'
service.

Colonel Lindsay does not take any account of
the bad climate, and the banishment to the Colonies, which is the lot of the Line; in fact, he calls

out that the Guards have a right to a vested in-justice. I, who have served in the Crimea and in the trenches with the Guards, have seen the consequences of this rank of lieutenant-colonel being held by the captains of the Guards. These officers, instead of doing captains' duty, were put on the roster of field-officers: they were senior in rank to all majors of the Line; and I have seen a youth of eight years' service detailed to command 2000 men in the trenches for twenty-four hours, and before such an enemy as the Russians. This practice became so notoriously improper, that the commanding officer of the brigade of Guards was obliged to break the roster, and put older officers on duty out of their turn; which is quite contrary to the custom of the service. The real remedy is to take away from the Guards the absurd and monstrous privilege of holding the rank of lieutenant-colonel while they are in reality only captains, and captains of companies for the discipline of which they are not responsible. Colonel Lindsay says nothing about this rank qualifying the captains in the Guards to hold certain staff-appointments, which lead, in three years, to the rank of full colonel; while lieutenant-colonels commanding battalions of the Line cannot hold them without going on half-pay; and

*b*

he overlooked the condition of this Army,* in
which there are at present three battalions of the
Guards, and about fifty battalions of the Line,
out of which the Guards furnish the Commander-
in-Chief, the Chief of the Staff, the general officers commanding two divisions and two brigades;
total, six general officers, besides numerous other
staff-appointments.  They also furnished the previous Commander - in - Chief.  There are seven
battalions of the Guards altogether, and  they
have about 80 officers of or above the rank of
lieutenant - colonel;  while the whole 112 battalions of the Line have not, at the outside, more
than about 190.  A common rule-of-three sum
will show that the proper proportion which seven
battalions of the Guards ought to  have would
be only twelve officers of this rank.   These 80
field-officers compete with the 190 of the Line for
all staff-appointments, and with the greater success, because so many officers of the Guards are
highly connected, and are known to the authorities
from their being always in London; besides which
the Guards form a clique,—they are banded together by the strongest ties of self-interest and
personal friendship; and, from their wide-spread

* viz. the Army in the Crimea.

relations with the all-powerful British aristocracy and plutocracy, they compose a very formidable political body, combining as one man in defence of their privileges, and blinded by habit to the injustice of their possessing any such advantages.

As to Colonel Lindsay's second point, viz. that, from the average he goes upon, the future lieutenant - colonels of the Guards will have to serve ten years at least as captains and lieutenant-colonels before they become full colonels, I am contented to hear that is the case. They will become captains and lieutenant-colonels in about fourteen years; ten more will make them full colonels: total, twenty - four years' service; — whereas the lieutenant-colonels of the Line will, on an average, only obtain the rank of lieutenant-colonel after twenty - five years' service, after which they must serve three years to become full colonels: total, twenty - eight years' service, all over the world; while the officers of the Guards will have spent their time, when not on leave, or on active service before the enemy, in parading at St. James's or Windsor.

If I could hope to bring the case fully and clearly, and in a popular form, before the nation, I should consider that I had laid the axe to the root of this enormity. It will not bear looking into. The Guards have committed an act of folly in preferring their petition. The difficulty is the want of a soldier in the House who knows the details and the working of the system; one who at the same time has the ear of the House, and who does not care for court favour. An attack on the Guards will be construed, however unjustly, into an attack on the Queen, as it certainly is one on the aristocracy."

The sufferings of the Army were at one time very great, and it is now decided to lay them on the system; and that, I think, is the most generous and most manly view to take of the case. Let us try to do better next time. But, in order to show that sufferings are not unusual in war, I will here print some extracts from an interesting old letter in my possession, dated New York, 20th November 1780, written by Lieutenant Colin Campbell, of the 74th Highlanders, who was afterwards killed by the Red Indians. He had been engaged to my grandmother; and his Letter has thus been preserved.

"New York, 20th November 1780.

\* \* \* " I embarked about the beginning of June last at Charlestown for this place with his Excellency General Clinton, the British Light

Infantry, the Hessian Yaggers, the British and
Hessian Grenadiers, the 42d Regiment, Queen's
Rangers, &c., amounting to 5000 men, in transports convoyed by Admiral Arbuthnot. We had
fine weather and an agreeable passage. Whenever
we landed here, I was obliged (on the 21st of
June) to get a billet and retire to sick quarters in
this town, where I have remained ever since. I
informed Kitty in my letter above mentioned that
I had a violent attack of the fever and ague about
the conclusion of the siege of Charlestown. I was
twice cured of it in South Carolina, once in the
passage from thence hither; and I have had so
many relapses since, that I have been cured no
less than nine times in all of the same disorder in
the course of this season; three times of a flux,
two of them bloody; and, to conclude the catalogue
of my calamities, I am now lately recovered of a
smart high fever, which lasted only ten or twelve
days. I was so harassed with the continual returns of these different ailments, that you can
easily believe I had been at one particular time
extremely reduced; but neither my doctor, myself,
or my friends ever despaired of my recovery; and
since the cold weather has set in, I have recruited
so fast that I might already join the battalion and
do duty with them, which at present is very easy,

as they have gone into winter quarters at Bedford,
in Long Island, about a mile and a half from the
village of Brooklyn, immediately opposite to this
town, which gives its name to the ferry from thence
to Long Island.   I remain here only a few days
longer, till my health and strength are perfectly
established, which I may say is already the case.
I would not consent that any of my friends who
wrote to Isla should mention my being sick till I
had it in my power to inform you of my perfect
recovery : it could answer no purpose but to make
you uneasy.   I flatter myself that my friends still
entertain so much regard for me that the knowledge of such an event would give them a little
concern.   I did not wish to put any of them to
the trial; it would be an ungenerous experiment.
Though I had the misfortune of being very much
indisposed both last year and this for a long series
of time, I cannot help congratulating myself on
the uncommon good luck of its happening at times
when the Light Infantry, and consequently the
whole Army here, were quite unemployed and dis-
engaged from field service.   The campaign (1779)
was short, and ended early in August.   It was
not till our Army was ordered within our lines at
King's Bridge that I was taken ill (as I formerly
wrote home).   The embarkation for South Caro-

lina occasioned the first movement of our troops.
I got well in time enough to accompany them, and
not much sooner.   I never was better than during
that very fatiguing expedition, and till about the
end of the siege of Charlestown ; but in traversing
the woods of that country for six or eight weeks,
without bed, tent, or any other cover than a great-
coat against the cold dew and sometimes frosts of
the nights, or against the excessive rains or scorch-
ing heat of the days in that climate ; and for near
six weeks more at the siege lying in the open air,
except the last fortnight only, at which time we
got tents, and then, as well as before, twenty-four
hours on duty in the trenches for every forty-eight
hours we were off duty, whether cold, hot, wet, or
dry, all of which we frequently experienced in the
extreme before we were relieved,—this was too
much for most constitutions to bear unhurt ; mine,
I confess, was not proof against it, as I have already informed you.   I may also declare that for
ten weeks after landing in South Carolina the 11th
February last, I had neither my clothes or side-
arms off, except while shifting, or never lay down
to sleep without my fuzee stretched alongside of
me, or within my arms, ready to start up with it
to the first sound of the bugle horn, which the
Light Infantry use instead of a drum.   It re-

sembles a huntsman's horn, and by different notes, easily distinguished, loudly expresses the different words of command, to be heard at two miles distance; twelve or fifteen of them together make the most lofty warlike music in the world. With these I have known the whole Light Infantry roused at one o'clock in the morning on a sudden alarm, formed, and ready for action within the short space of three minutes from the time of their being in a profound sleep after a fatiguing march; and to the honour of these brave fellows be it told, not one man of a company in the whole battalion missing. The pleasure, the happiness of being on actual service with such delightful fellows is inexpressible. Toil and hardships alongst with them lose those names, and are softened into agreeable amusements. A man's constitution may not always be equal to support a variety of such diversions often repeated; but his inclination can never fail him. Some time after our arrival from the southward in this province, it was known that a small squadron of French ships of the line, with 4000 or 5000 men, had taken possession of Rhode Island. It seemed to be the resolution both of Admiral Arbuthnot and of General Clinton, with the fleet here, and with a considerable part of the army, to make a vigorous attack upon them and their rebel allies in that post. Our fleet sailed directly, and are still stationed in view of that place. The troops designed for this service also embarked; the Light Infantry were a part of them; but I was so ill of the fever and ague I could not attempt to leave my sick quarters, and for the first time had the mortification to be left behind when the battalions of Light Infantry were going upon any expedition. But kind Providence favoured me beyond my expectations. I heard in a few days that the expedition was countermanded, and that the troops had disembarked. I supposed it was for the good of the service, or it would not have happened so; and I could not help being extremely well pleased. Now, God be praised! I am able to accompany them wherever they go, if their first movement should take place to-morrow; and I have had such a thorough seasoning last year and this one, both to the northward and southward of this extensive continent, that I have reason to hope that the severest service or the most intemperate climate cannot hurt me during the continuance of this war." * * *

At this period (1780), there were not, I suppose, means of communicating so easily home as we have now, and the Press had not such a circulation as to spread alarm and despair over the whole country. We have now arrived at a new order of things, which we cannot alter; and I have said so much about the Press, in the hope that in future wars the correspondents will be considerate of the consequences of their communications, and that during the military operations they will refrain, and endeavour to restrain the curiosity of their readers, from insisting on so much publicity to our disasters, if we should unfortunately have any; and, above all, that they will look to the danger of attacking the conduct of a general while at the head of his army, and conducting operations in the field. I have said enough to show that I myself am a military reformer. There is now a new plan, I am told, nearly ready, whereby it will be secured that all the officers of the Army shall be educated for their profession. This is a step in the right direction. Many years ago — more than twenty years ago — I had occasion to wait upon Lord Fitzroy Somerset, afterwards Lord Raglan : he was then Military Secretary. Lord Fitzroy was a very clever man, and one of the most polite and urbane gentlemen in Europe. In the course of conversation, I took the opportunity of stating to his Lordship that the officers of the English Army required to be educated. He differed with me altogether on this point, and said they were sufficiently examined before they got their commissions. As I knew more than one who could not write a decent letter, I stuck to my opinion, and Lord Fitzroy got rather angry and dismissed me. Who can say how much might have been accomplished during these twenty years if I had then been listened to? I have lived to see an order that all officers shall be examined for their commissions and for their promotions; it has indeed been hitherto very imperfectly carried out. I believe that his Royal Highness the Duke of Cambridge, the present Commander-in-Chief, is impressed with the necessity of educating the officers, and of forwarding many army reforms; but he will require to be backed by public opinion.

Routine must ever rule in offices and among heads of departments, who cannot help feeling a disinclination to change. Besides which, there are questions which do not precisely come under the head of education, nor strictly under that of reform. The very existing regulations require to be more faithfully attended to. The officers, besides being instructed, must be forced to work; and the whole tone of the Army must undergo a complete change before this ugly dull word, "work," will be looked upon as the mainstay of the profession. It is not flaunting about in a red coat which makes the officer; it is an earnest attention to very minute and tiresome details connected with the soldier's welfare. Truly there is a mighty field for reform, on which many a contest will take place before the reform itself will be attained.

On a careful examination of our regiments, there will be found generally a specious outward show, but which, when thoroughly looked into, will prove to be only a mask for constant and provoking idleness, and disregard of the most essential portions of interior economy. Many of the officers know nothing, or next to nothing, of their profession, or even of the first rudiments of drill. The provisions of the Circular Memorandum of the 4th July 1851 have been a dead letter, even as to military instruction; and no machinery has existed, till this year, for carrying out the educational parts of that memorandum.

In order to induce the younger officers to pay attention to this instruction, it will be advisable that the examination previous to promotion should be made a *bonâ fide* test of the officer's knowledge, which it certainly has not been hitherto, at least in all cases; as I lately met a lieutenant who did not know the length of a pace, or the number of paces taken per minute in quick time; who, in

short, knew nothing at all. Of course his examination for promotion to captain, which he had
passed, must have been a mere pretence; such
officers should be kept at drill and instruction till
they are able to pass a strict examination; and
should they, after a fixed period, fail to make themselves competent, it is to be considered that the
matters upon which they are required to be thoroughly informed are of such a nature, that they
may be comprehended by any one who can comprehend any thing; and that being the case, a persevering disregard of instruction may justly, in the
end, entail on the officer guilty of it the penalty of
losing the commission, which he did not think it
worth while to qualify himself for holding.

The fact is, that her Majesty's regulations are
as nearly perfect as any code we can hope to see;
the real difficulty is, to have them strictly and faithfully attended to.

For the most part our young officers do not
obey the regulations with real zeal, as if they took
an interest in the performance of the duty; their
main endeavour seems to be to avoid trouble; they
do just enough to save their consciences, and to be
able to say that they performed their task, caring
not how badly, or with how little benefit to the
service. These officers require to be taught that

they hold their commissions for the good of the
service; that they are placed in the Army to be
made a convenience of, and to instruct themselves
with a view to their becoming fit to be worked
for the advantage of their men.

Those who read these pages, if they judge
aright, will perceive that the writer was writing
the truth; that his object has been to give honest
information, and to assist so far as he could the
amelioration of our Army, by explaining in simple language many matters which must otherwise
remain dark to unmilitary persons. For this object he has ventured to make statements which may
expose him to the animosity of the most powerful
people in the country. His only aim has been the
hope of doing some good, and of improving the
profession to which he belongs, and which he loves.
The people who sent so many Commissioners to
the Crimea, where they were of no use whatever,
should be thankful for the endeavour.

With respect to the commissariat, which has
been sufficiently abused, I have to say, that whenever and wherever a really good commissariat
officer was met with, he was always treated with
respect,—and there were many such sent into the
Army; but there were others as bad as the first
were good. The gentlemen who held the superior

situations, such as Mr. Drake, Mr. Carpenter, and Mr. Young, were, I am certain, both liked and respected by every one who knew them, or who had to transact business with them. As a friend of mine remarks with great truth :

" The commissariat is the stomach of the Army. Without it, or with an inefficient one, the Line and the Artillery (the limbs) are worthless. Therefore it ought to be the aim of every sensible officer to support the commissary, to claim for him aid and respect, instead of running him down. With the commissariat there should be included all the non-combatant branches of the service. At present it is the fashion for fighting men to sneer at these, as if they were troublesome servants, unendowed with the pluck on which they, the fighting men, build up their claims to honour and reward. Now there is no reason why a commissary should not have as much pluck as a lieutenant of the Line; and there is very good reason why he should be better educated. In fact he ought, for the efficiency of the public service, to be the best animal of the two."

So says my friend, and so say I. But it is to be remarked, that if there were sundry unprofitable lieutenants, so there were also unprofitable commissaries; and there did not exist equal means of keeping them in order. Why, I have known a commissary accuse a regiment of being troublesome because they objected to his unsound wares; and I have known a commissary threaten a quartermaster who refused his meat, that he would not show him any favour again. Favour from a commissary! The very idea is disgraceful. To favour one, he must rob another. What we wanted with our Army was not merely accomplished accountants, but also a number of young, active, skilful underlings, provided with butchers and drovers not picked out of the regiments, but belonging to the commissariat corps. The commissaries invariably complained that they could procure no men of this sort on whom they could rely, except from the Army. Now our Army is not numerous enough to furnish all these civilians. It is only a question of giving pay enough: the precious estimates would appear to run up; but the commissary never calculated what the soldier whom he took out of the ranks had cost, and was costing the country.

In addition to this very brief introduction, I have thought that the following Letters would in some places be elucidated by a few explanatory remarks, which I have made as short and simple as I possibly could.

*London, October* 1857.

# CONTENTS.

c

# LIST OF PLANS.

# LETTERS FROM THE CRIMEA.

It is to be borne in mind that the author of the following Letters had virtually retired from military service on the 28th November 1843, when he resigned his staff-appointment of Deputy-Assistant Adjutant-General in Dublin.   He came to London, having purchased from his brother John the lease of a house in South Place, Knightsbridge. This house he expended cash upon for various improvements; and in the garden thereof finally, in 1851, he built the *White Cottage*, which became a reception-room for hebdomadal meetings of his literary friends.   He was thus unemployed in the military way for about ten years, viz. from 1844 to 1854, or from his thirty-ninth to his forty-ninth year.   In the spring of 1853, his relation Sir Colin Campbell, the " C." of the Letters, came back from India with a high military character ; and in February 1854 this officer, still only a colonel, with forty-five years of active service, was offered the rank of Brigadier-General, and a command in the expedi-

B

tion then planning for a war in the Levant. C. and
S. had become intimate by this time; and it was pro-
posed by C., and accepted by S., that, if the military
authorities agreed to it, S. should go out as Aide-de-
Camp or Brigade-Major. After due negotiations at
the Horse Guards, it was finally settled that Captain
Sterling should be Brigade-Major to Brigadier-General
Sir C. Campbell. From memoranda extant in certain
pocket-books, it appears that Sir C. Campbell and
his staff, viz. his brigade-major and his aide-de-camp
—Captain Shadwell, son of Sir Lancelot—went to
Woolwich on the 3d April 1854, and embarked with
their servants and horses on board the Tonning, a
steamer with Morgan's feathering paddles; the said
vessel had been plying from Hull to Tonning for the
conveyance of cattle; and the cabins, which had been
constructed for the cattle-dealers, were now used for
general officers and their subordinates. Sir Colin and
his Brigade-Major shared a very small one between
them. Brigade-Generals Eyre and Pennefather had
their passage in the same vessel, which started from
Woolwich at 2 A.M. on the 5th of April (Wednesday).
The Morgan's paddles came to grief, and the larboard
one struck work altogether, on Easter Sunday, 16th
April, two days before the Tonning entered Malta harbour. It is only fair to the said Morgan that it should
be remembered that his principle was good; the failure
was in the details: the points or ends of the rods

belonging to the eccentric or feathering apparatus (technically, bearings) were at first made too short. In the recently-constructed paddles these bearings have been lengthened, and such accidents as occurred to the Tonning are now, it is understood, not to be apprehended.

This Letter I. notices one from Malta, which it seems was lost in the post-office. It probably gave an account of the voyage with and without paddles, and distances run, as well as the touch at Gibraltar and delay there of twenty-four hours.

At Gallipoli, on the European side of the Dardanelles, the engineers were contriving a safe retreat, in case of the Russians advancing by Adrianople on Constantinople, and driving back the Allies, by making a line of fortification from the Gulf of Saros (ancient Melas) to the Dardanelles. This idea was apparently soon abandoned. The immense barrack spoken of was afterwards turned into an hospital ; and it is probable that Miss Nightingale occupied the very turret in which Sir C. Campbell and his staff were lodged during their sojourn at Scutari. The barrack was calculated to hold comfortably 5000 men, but would have given cover, if necessary, to double the number.

## LETTER I.

Barracks, Scutari, Saturday, 29th April 1854.

I WROTE to you, I think from Malta, a hurried note. We were only there for a few hours, and were towed out of the harbour by the Trent at 8 o'clock P.M., our paddles being quite *hors de combat.*

On Friday we reached Cape Matapan, and came among the Cyclades, and poor Haidee was mourned over by the poetical part of the company. The weather was perfect. At 3 A.M. on Sunday morning (23d), I found myself near Tenedos; a waning ~~crescent~~ moon, the poor remnant of the moon we left England with, hung over the Trojan shore.

At daylight we were quite close to Tenedos, and Ovid's contest between Ajax and Ulysses for the arms of Achilles rose again in memory : " *Est in conspectu Tenedos,*" &c. We then saw the tumuli of Homer's heroes, and Sigæum, all dear to classical scholars.

Entering the Dardanelles very striking. The castles of Europe and Asia, Abydos, &c., all these lying before us.

Gallipoli! Most picturesque; wretched houses and miserable streets, with a motley population of Turks, French, and English. Here we received our orders to drop Brigadier Eyre and his staff, and proceed, as soon as we could get out their horses, on to Stamboul.

It appears that the French are to make a tremendous fortification, I believe to be revetted with
brick, across the Chersonesus, about three miles long,
situated one mile west of Boulahar, from the Gulf of
Saros to the Dardanelles. This will make for the
allies an impregnable fortress, as we shall have the sea
on both sides entirely in our possession ; and in case of
retreat, it will do for the Russians what the lines of
Torres Vedras did for the French. We were much
amused by the commanding officer here, who is a
great disciplinarian, writing to C. and mentioning that
he observed that some of the staff-officers were nour-
ishing mustachios, which he wished should be done
away with. The only two guilty were officers of cavalry,
who had a right to wear them ; one was a nice lad
named ——— : and C., who enjoys a joke, after laughing heartily at the order, pretended he was going to
shave the youth, who was desperately frightened, till
he found it was only in fun.

The English are to keep 5000 men for the present
on the lines which are in process of construction at
Gallipoli ; and the remainder of the army, it is believed, will be employed in digging trenches about
fifteen miles from Constantinople.

We departed from Gallipoli at 10 A.M. on Monday (24th), and entered the Sea of Marmora ; on
Tuesday morning, at daylight, we found ourselves
nearing the Bosphorus. The surpassing beauty of the

approach to Stamboul I need not enlarge upon ; it is
the proper situation for the capital of the world.

Old C. found me very attentive to him on the voyage, and the soldiers who were employed as a guard
with us to keep order found Major S. very troublesome. C. heard one of them saying to the other, " He
is a wonderful ould man ; he only sleeps two hours,
and smokes the other twenty-two." It was necessary
to be vigilant with a vessel full of hay. We lost three
horses on the passage ; all the rest are pretty well.

On Wednesday morning we landed the horses and
ourselves, and came into barracks, where I had scarcely
arrived when I found our brigade—viz. the 1st Brigade,
consisting for the present, that is, till Lord Raglan
arrives, of the 7th and 23d Fusileers, and the 33d
regiment—was in orders for all the duties of the camp
and garrison ; and instead of being able to get my
matters in any way arranged, I was forced to sit on a
stone to write orders, and by night was fagged to death.
Fancy being here within a mile (of water) from Stamboul, and not having yet been able to go to see its
wonders ! The day after our horses landed, instead
of allowing the poor things to rest and recover from
their three weeks' standing, a field-day was ordered
for the Seraskier, and we had to gallop about and
leap over ditches.

The army gets drunk, I am sorry to say, and has
committed a few robberies. The food is good, that is

to say, 1 lb. of tough beef and 1½ lb. of brown acid bread; that is the diet of men and officers, with the exception of our lot; for that provident "ould" officer Major S. brought with him a quantity of preserved provisions from his yacht, the Viking, and has thus enabled his chief to distinguish himself by feeding the hungry. Strange to say, none of us have received our private letters or our newspapers, and we know of nothing about those who are so dear to us in our distant home.

The Terrible came in here yesterday from Odessa with the news of the bombarding there. I should much wish to have gone aboard, but had no time; a ship just after an action coming to repair damages must be a curious sight. My life is very odd; I am tired every day with walking and standing, so that my feet are quite sore. I am never, or scarcely ever, alone, and never safe from a demand for an order for some duty to be performed by the 1st Brigade; day and night all come to me, so that I may be called the providence of 2500 men.

In a few days it is very probable we may be moved into tents. Very soon we must know our fate, as I have just heard of Lord Raglan's arrival here.

Nothing can be more picturesque than the situation of our camp. An immense and beautiful barrack (square 230 yards to the side) crowns a hill close to the sea; from this hill a sloping, undulated, grassy

descent leads down to a brook, which enters the Sea
of Marmora about half a mile down the coast ; on the
other side of the stream the ground again rises, and
the view is closed by a green elevation, on which the
Brigade of Guards is encamped, and behind their tents
far off snowy Olympus of Asia Minor makes a silvery
distance. On the right hand is the sea, with an island
or two, and Stamboul, variegated and brilliant as the
Arabian Nights. On the left, a long Turkish cemetery
in a cypress grove, with its white Moslem tombstones
upright, and mixed among the russet stems of the
trees.   The encampment stretches along the side of
this space next to the sea, and all sorts of Oriental
creatures go wandering and wondering at the Ferin-
ghis.   If perpetual worry and bodily fatigue be good
for the soul, which may be doubtful, mine ought to be
in prime condition ; but I do not enjoy it, and long
to lie down and be at peace—a hopeless hope, alas !

BUJUC CHECMAJEE is a village at the entrance of
a small bay on the south coast of Thrace, 18 miles
west of Stamboul.   Unkiar Skelessi is a village in
Asia Minor, about half a mile north of Beicos Bay in
the Bosphorus.   At Unkiar Skelessi, in the spring
of 1833, 16,000 Russian troops, under command of
General Mouravieff, were encamped, to defend the

Porte from Ibrahim Pasha's attack. In May of that year Egypt was given up by the Sultan ; and on the 8th July 1833, the defensive alliance Treaty of Unkiar Skelessi was concluded between the Russians and Turks, which was considered to be a great blow to the English and French diplomatists ; for one condition of the treaty was, to bind the Turks to shut up the Dardanelles, in case of Russia being attacked by any European power. At the period when the 2d Letter was written every one supposed the Russians would try to advance in overwhelming numbers by Silistria, Schumla, and Adrianople, on Constantinople itself. It will be observed that the author repeatedly refers to the impossibility of the army advancing for a long time. This was from want of transport mainly, which difficulty and the remedy had been very early pointed out to the Government by Mr. Layard, who had recommended purchasing animals in Asia Minor. Before the army embarked from Varna there had been collected a very fair proportion of animals, which were in charge of the brigades to which they belonged, but most of which remained in Bulgaria. The reference at the end of the letter to the French army having come provided with transport, and having baked bread within twenty-four hours after landing, is very significant.

Letter III. is very short, and mentions the arrival of the 93d Highlanders, and that fifteen officers were sleeping in Sir C. Campbell's quarters,—it may be supposed only till they could get their tents pitched.

---

## LETTER II.

Scutari, 4th May 1854.

MAIL after mail comes in, and no letters, nor even newspapers, which seems even more surprising than the fact of my being here. Since I wrote to you, the army has been definitively organised by Lord Raglan, who arrived on the 2d with his staff. Among other changes from Sir G. Brown's temporary arrangements, C. and Major S., his Brigade-Major, have been appointed to the Highland Brigade, which is considered complimentary to C., but is really a great disadvantage, as he will only be third in rank in the division, whereas in any other division he would have been second. The Highland Brigade is composed of the 42d, 79th, and 93d, the latter of which is at Gallipoli; the other two not arrived from England, but expected daily. They will be the 2d Brigade of the 1st Division; the Guards forming the 1st Brigade of the same under Prince George,—the Duke of Cambridge, I mean,—who no doubt will find C., from his great experience in the field, a most useful subaltern. As our brigade is not here, we shall have a day or two to make our arrangements in Constantinople with regard to tents, &c. Prince Jerome is here, but no

French soldiers as yet. Lord Raglan has a house in a small village close to the camp ; and I suppose will shortly give him a field-day. The engineer officers are hard at work surveying the ground at Bujuc Checmajee, where the lines are to be formed, about 18 miles west of Constantinople, to extend from the Sea of Marmora to the Black Sea ; the idea is, that the army, as soon as it is ready to move, will march to Unkiar Skelessi and camp there, sending a portion over into Europe by divisions, to camp on the lines and dig the entrenchments ; and I have reason to think that the Guards and Highlanders will go first. Meantime we have no news at all, except what comes round by Paris *viâ* Marseilles. We hear that Austria is about to occupy Servia ; if so, that will add much to Nicholas's difficulties, for it will disengage the Kalafat* troops. In fact, I do not see how it is possible, with an Austrian army on his right flank, and our fleet on his left, with an allied French and English army in his front, he can advance at all, whatever be his numbers. He will therefore have to keep on the defensive, and let us do our worst. We cannot advance for a long time yet. It is understood that a portion of the French army will move up to Constantinople, on the European side of the Bosphorus.

* Kalafat, a fortified Turkish camp on the left bank of the Danube, opposite Widdin.

5th May, early in the morning.

Last night I got a letter, the first I have received from England. While lying awake I observed a tremendous fire in Stamboul, which illuminated the whole sky. To-day we shall probably hear what mischief was done, but too late for the post, which goes off at 11.

I heard yesterday the probable reason why my papers do not come ; it is that the mail-bags are all opened at the Custom-house, and the poor letters maltreated in the most Turkish manner, previously to sending them to the post-office. This will be remedied in the Turkish manner by a firman giving power to an agent appointed by us to seize the bags before they go to the Custom-house, and bring them away at once to the army. We sat about for a considerable time yesterday at Stamboul in the bazaar; the place where we were was dedicated to saddlery, leather bags, &c. What struck me most was the cheerful contented look of the people who were in the shops, and the total absence of beggars or of any appearance of misery. I also underwent the Turkish bath, and, on the whole, consider it the sight of Stamboul. The building being constructed for the purpose, I mean that in which I was, had in addition to its conveniences, a great deal of architectural beauty ; it was more like a handsome church

with chapels off it, than what we should call baths ;
and the gentleness and graceful manners of the attendants made the hour pass away in a very pleasing
sort of dream.   Strictly speaking, at a Turkish bath
there is no bath ; but warm water is splashed over
you out of a saucer in a very hot room : I imagine
it is a legacy left them by the luxurious Romans.
The people in England are, I dare say, disappointed
at the army for not having already taken Nicholas, or
at least for not having hit him a hard blow somewhere.   From what I can see, I do not think it possible we can take the field for these two months ;
during which interval he may advance, if he dare.
The further he moves from his supports the weaker
he will be ; but I do not delude myself with the idea
that the contest, should it really begin, will be a
short one.

The artillery horses are just beginning to arrive ;
they seem to lose about four or five per cent ; there
are 250 landed, and gone into barracks about three
miles up the Bosphorus.   The cavalry seem to be
very slow in coming forward ; there is a want of decision somewhere, and negligence too ; in truth, our
army has never been kept on a proper establishment.
The French Algerine army landed here with tents and
transport and corn-mills, and baked bread for themselves within twenty-four hours.   We have nothing
to complain of in the conduct of our men while they

are sober ; when drunk they knock the Turks about ; so we flogged a man the other day to make an example.

---

## LETTER III.

Scutari Barracks, 10th May 1854.

STILL here, as you will perceive from the date. The troops are gradually dropping in ; some horse artillery having arrived, also one of our Highland regiments (the 93d*), and the Rifles. We have had two days' rain ; and the kilted men and Rifles are all lying about the passages, and our quarters filled by fifteen officers sleeping on the floors. We were all asked to a grand ball at Pera at the French ambassador's last night. I could not go, having too much to do ; but C. went, and has not yet returned. The strange part of this business to me is, that I am never alone, and never have time to do any thing I want ; the wants of my army being constant day and night. We know nothing here whatever ; our papers from London give us the only authentic news, and they have all gone astray for some reasons unknown. Our military prospects remain blank ; but I cannot help hoping still that something decisive will take place before the summer is over. The army, how-

* The 93d landed on the 9th of May.

ever, is quite unfit to move at present; and if the newspapers are attacking Lord Raglan for inactivity, they are doing him injustice. He cannot move without baggage, animals, and artillery and cavalry, none of which to any amount has he got as yet. The Turks are very civil, but we cannot say much to them. Perhaps that may account for it.

THE author dilates in this letter, and also in a later one, on the expense of servants. Of course those who were poor could not hire such an extravagant *valetaille;* therefore he exaggerates when he states that it was impossible to get on without a dragoman at 9s. per diem. This dragoman, in fact, was borrowed by other people very often, who were themselves either too poor or too economical to hire a man of their own. Eventually there were interpreters attached to every regiment and brigade; one of these was very amusing, for he could not speak Turkish, and he used to jabber gibberish with plenty of action, and then explain to us what it was about.

## LETTER IV.

Scutari, 15th May 1854.

I HAD hoped ere this to have received a letter from you, as I am left in the dark about every thing in

England ; either my letters are lost, or you did not write. If you did not, it's a great shame. Our army is very anxious to advance ; but I do not find that the Commissariat is procuring baggage-animals very rapidly ; and without means of conveying ammunition and sick, a move inland is impossible. The officers are mostly provided with animals, which they purchase, and receive forage for ; the price of these ponies has risen enormously, also the pay of dragomans or interpreters. I have one who acts as my valet, and receives sixty piastres a day, or about nine shillings. Ruinous ; yet to get on without him is impossible in a place where I have to send hither and thither to procure requisites for marching, and where I am tied to the barrack by the duty I have undertaken. In fact, the whole of my military pay will just about pay my different servants' wages. If I had time to go about, this neighbourhood would be well worth exploring ; the short distances I have gone as yet have shown me the most lovely views imaginable. If the interior of Asia Minor be like its coast, Eden ought to have been there. The climate, however, is very variable, and the spring very late. We had a storm of wind and rain yesterday, and the nights are still cool —in fact, in tents cold would be the word. I am still in the barrack ; only one regiment of our brigade having arrived. It is not probable that the Highland Brigade will be complete till the 10th of June. The

English soldiers are behaving very well, and the camp is full of natives offering change for a sovereign; they are quite unmolested. The life in a camp is most monotonous, especially here, where there are few resources by way of amusement; walking about in Constantinople is miserable, from the steepness of the ascents and the badness of the pavements. The young regimental officers, who have little to do, ride about on their ponies, and see a good deal of the country, having the advantage moreover of youth on their side. Fancy my having an opportunity of being present at the Sultan's visit to the Duke of Cambridge, and not going; but in truth I take no interest in any thing going on here, and perform my dull duties with attention, merely out of a remnant of military pride.

We are all pretty well in health, this not being the season for sickness; no doubt when that begins we shall have a fearful list.

## LETTER V.

Scutari, 20th May 1854.

AFTER my letter of the 15th went off, I received one from you. Since then, as you may guess, there has not much occurred to break the monotony of this existence. The wonderful beauty of the place remains as great a wonder as ever; but of the people one

C

knows nothing. I went yesterday, which was Friday, to the Valley of Sweet Waters ; the Golden Horn stretches up some four miles, and at last becomes a river, running through a narrow valley, closed in on both sides by two bare hills. Here the whole population, or at least many thousands of Turks, Turkesses, Greeks, Armenians, and strangers of all nations congregate ; they go some in carriages from Stamboul, but most in caiques by water. The scene is very curious : the women have their heads wrapped in fine thin muslin, leaving only the eyes uncovered ; but their outer cloaks are of the gayest colours. No one speaks to them, so far as I could observe. They sit by the water-side in groups, with their children ; and the ladies of rank go in carriages, very much after Rotten-Row plan ; there was a sultana, too, with a number of carriages full of young girls, who, some of them, seemed very pretty. The river has two tumbling-bays* across it, made with white marble, in broad steps, scalloped out into fanciful patterns, with the Sweet Waters running over them in a shal-

---

* This word has given rise to many queries. A bay in one sense is a dam; and a tumbling-bay is a phrase which I have heard applied in my youth to a dam over which the water tumbles. It may be a Hertfordshire provincialism. It is used in a parliamentary report upon the Serpentine; applied also to the rush of water in the weirs on the Thames. There are two at least near Eton.

low stream. There were, I should guess, seven or eight hundred carriages, and two miles of crowd ; no drinking except coffee and lemonade, and scarcely any eating except ices. A quieter and apparently a more happy and contented set I never saw, although they were not Christians, and the women had no souls. With regard to public matters, I believe there is no doubt the army will go to Varna as soon as it is ready to move. Lord Raglan went there the night before last : St. Arnaud went with him, and the Admiral ; and they are to meet Omar Pasha, and hold council as to ulterior measures. The Russians are lying quiet ; but they are only five hours from Silistria, and their next move will be the investment of that fortress, which, if they attempt it, will cause our advance, with the French and Turks, to relieve it. The English army continues healthy ; the artillery is arriving ; I believe there are as many as twenty-four guns complete. The head-quarters of the 17th Lancers has come ; but our 2000 dragoons will have a poor chance against 27,000, which, it is asserted, the Russians have in the Dobrudscha. The lines in front of Stamboul are not spoken of any longer. Perhaps the intention of making them is given up. As to my own position—my dragoman receives sixty piastres a day (about 9s., which is the amount of my staff-pay) ; my English groom has 5l. a month, his food and clothes ; I have besides one soldier and one native muleteer; so that it is an expensive job. I have five horses and two mules, and the forage allowance for them nearly feeds them. I live with C. After all requisites for marching are completed, my only expenses will be washing and servants' wages, which is not a small item : dragoman 170*l.* ; groom 60*l.* ; soldier 6*l.* ; and muleteer 36*l.* = 272*l.* My staff-pay and field-allowance is 13*s.* per diem, or about 230*l.* a year ; half-pay about 120*l.* : total 350*l.* My outfit for this expedition has cost about 900*l.* You see officers are cheap articles when they serve as I do with no pay. How poor men manage I cannot say. My newspapers do not come, so that we know little of home. Yesterday a young officer of the 93d was drowned in the small watercourse just beyond the barracks. A sudden storm made a torrent of what was usually dry, and he was swept down into the sea.

## LETTER VI.

Scutari, 28th May 1854.

RUMOURS of all sorts presage a start. The Light Division, consisting of seven regiments, was ordered to embark, and their horses and baggage-animals are now on board ; but a stop took place, for reasons which are not known; either a difficulty about the commissariat, or that the merchant-steamers would

not go without a convoy. Varna is the point, as I
believe, and this division is to move about 20 miles
west, to Devna, stretching a hand towards Schumla.
Silistria is invested, but not closely. There I expect
we shall meet the Russians, so soon as the French are
up, and drive them into or over the Danube. One of
our Highland regiments, the 79th, arrived yesterday.
Lord Raglan has been to Schumla, and has seen Omar
Pasha. The Turks are very anxious to see us in front;
but it is useless moving till our arrangements for feeding the troops are complete. We, belonging to brigades, have little means of knowing what is going on
in the way of preparation. Our business is to obey
orders and keep our powder dry. We are changing
our firelocks for Minié rifles, which is an untried arm
for large bodies of men. The prudence of the change
at this moment may be doubted ; our advantage has
been, and always will be, in closing rapidly with the
enemy : when you are near enough, the old gun is as
good as the new one. We knew yesterday, what you
must have heard long ago, that the Greeks have killed
3000 Egyptian troops somewhere in Thessaly. I suppose Otho will be dethroned ; meantime his manœuvres have withdrawn a certain number of French
troops from the field to occupy Athens.* Our army

* Eventually there was an English regiment stationed at
Athens.

is quite healthy, and in high spirits, longing to be at them. The principal weak point is a want of experience on the part of the staff-officers of the Quartermaster General's department. I never heard of Lord De Ros having served any where except as Brigade Major to the cavalry in England. He is Quartermaster General; but I do not know who is responsible for his being selected to hold his present most important situation. They have appointed a number of young men, who learned a dose of mathematics and how to sketch ground at Sandhurst. Now that is mere cram ; a good clear understanding and methodical habits will do without them. The sketching is indeed useful, but it is very soon acquired, and in fact all officers ought to know how to make a rapid rough sketch of country.

I am in good health, although my spirits remain as much depressed as ever ; the mainspring, youth, is gone out ; the old wheels still go round with the *vis inertiæ*,—come here, go thither, order that. Weary life ! Faults and blunders are daily committed, which I see, but cannot prevent, on account of the routine of military matters. We, I mean C. and staff, intend to move out under canvas to-morrow or the next day. At present we live among fleas in large barrack-rooms, and our servants buy our food at Pera. We have not yet begun a regular camp life. We shall have a large marquee for the General, two Turkish tents for the

Aide-de-camp and Brigade Major, and two bell-tents for the servants; all this we have to carry on our animals on the march, besides beds and books and clothes. My horses cost 300*l.*, my two mules 72*l.* : see what an expense officers are put to! Letters come few and far between. My time is so broken up by duties that I never can call an hour my own, nor attempt to write any thing such as we talked of. When we meet the enemy, I augur nothing but success; such a body of men, led on by the chivalry of England, must succeed. It is impossible to fancy any thing more creditable to our country than the conduct of every one. The natives roam about the camp offering change for a sovereign more safely than they could in Hyde Park. The Turks appear to have the most perfect reliance on our honesty. When we get into Bulgaria, I hope the Greek population may not be roused against us by Russian intrigue ; that is our only risk. With a friendly population, if the commissariat do their duty, our supplies are certain, as the country teems with grain. I will tell you a story of a job. The Rev. Heliogabalus Balm of Gilead is a poor curate, and is related to General Geoghegan Gilhooly, who at the beginning of the job is on the staff at home. The Rev. Virtuosus Speciosissimus, when he goes his round of inspection, puts up with General Gilhooly for bed and board. Gilhooly asks him to appoint Balm of Gilead a chaplain to the forces in Turkey, which is managed.

After which Speciosissimus asks Gilhooly to appoint young Diabolus Speciosissimus to a situation on the staff at home. " But," says Gilhooly, " I am off the staff; I am going to Turkey." " Then," says Speciosissimus, " you will appoint Diabolus as your Aide-de-camp or Brigade Major." " No, I cannot," says t'other ; " I have given away the appointments to two of my brother officers." Whereupon Speciosissimus flares up ; " I only appointed your relation chaplain because I expected you would pay me back with an appointment for Diabolus." There's a man of God !

## LETTER VII.

Camp, Scutari, Highland-Brigade Office,
4th June 1854.

WE are now in camp under canvas, so that I have not so far to go to see my soldiers, and I much prefer it to the fleas in the barracks, the number and voracity of which is inconceivable. My tents are two, viz. a round Turkish tent, red inside and green out, about twelve feet diameter, and a small tent which I brought from England, on which I have painted in large letters " Highland-Brigade Office." To-day the thermometer in the officers' bell-tents stood at 96°, in mine at 80° ; just after ascertaining which the servant knocked down the thermometer and broke it. We are momentarily expecting to be ordered on to Varna, nine miles west of which town Sir G. Brown is encamped with seven regiments behind the Devna Lake. I have no doubt that the moment the commissariat say they are ready with transport for ammunition, &c., we shall advance in company with the French, join the Turks, and drive the Russians over the Danube. It is not likely that they will retire without an action ; if I survive, I will write you an account of it. My health, in spite of the constant work and exposure to the sun, is very good, and I have recovered my old power of walking and enduring fatigue ; but I suppose I am much thinner. Our time is now principally spent in trying to get our servants to practise packing our baggage on the animals, and to see after their health. The English grooms cannot at present conceive that a fine mule, which perhaps cost 40l., is worth looking after ; while, in fact, very often the efficiency of the officer depends on this beast bringing up his baggage. The utter thoughtlessness and selfishness of the civil servants is beyond belief. They never look out for any thing, and talking to them is about as effective as whistling jigs to a milestone.

All our division has been provided with Minié rifles. I hope it will turn out to be a wise measure. My horses, after whose health —— inquires, are all right, in spite of chopped straw and barley. I never go away from the lines of the camp, and am in fact on duty always. Our 42d regiment not come yet. I shall leave Constantinople without having seen one sight. I have never been in a mosque, or seen the Seraglio, or Therapia, or any one single thing in Stamboul; and I do not care to see them. Here I am called off to write a letter complaining of the contract-bread supplied to the men, which is the same that I eat myself; it is mixed rye and wheat, with a good deal of sand, and very wholesome I dare say.

That is done, and the orderly despatched with it. The men of our division have been allowed to go without their stiff leather stocks to-day, and at church parade this morning many of them had coloured handkerchiefs on, which hurts the military eye. Poor soldiers! they have many masters. To-morrow we are all, I mean our division under the Duke of Cambridge, ordered out at 5 A.M., to march on routes to be pointed out by some staff-officer. God knows how long we may be out. The Light Companies of the three battalions of Guards and those of the two Highland regiments are ordered to cover the battery of artillery under the command of the senior captain, that is to say, of the five captains of these companies. But three of the captains are Guardsmen, consequently lieutenant-colonels in the army, so that this command will not fall to the senior captain in the service, but to a young gentleman probably years his junior in age and experience, but who is only nominally a captain, being in fact a lieutenant-colonel. If this order is given before the enemy, the commanding-officer of these Light Companies will have a fair claim to promotion. Here come the privileges of the Guards into direct collision with the rights of the Line officers. I do not know if you will understand this ; but it is a great shame.

THE matter is simply this, that a regiment of the Line would have the same privilege as the Guards if all the ten captains were suddenly made lieutenant-colonels, and told they had no longer any charge of their companies except appearing with them on parade. It is incomprehensible how such an arrangement can stand in these reforming days. Here it seems that some officers must have excited the ire of the author, those whom he thinks are not " very wise." He scrupulously refrains from mentioning names where it is possible to avoid doing so. His remarks on the composition of the staff are worthy of consideration. This was the moment to consider, for the army had not yet begun the campaign. The next Letter (the 9th) takes the 1st Division to Varna, not more than a week's march from the Danube and from the Russians, and at this time (16th June) nothing was ready for moving or taking the field in earnest. Now would have been the time for the newspapers to cry out for transport, and to turn the attention of the nation to our manifold deficiencies.

## LETTER VIII.

Camp, Scutari, 10th June 1854.

THE post goes out to-day, and although I have nothing new to tell you, I cannot refrain from sending a line. We have had very strong reports of the intention of sending the Guards and Highlanders to Varna directly. The latter brigade is now complete ; but I imagine that the French who are marching by land are so much behind, that it is considered useless to move any more of our troops up to Varna than the seven regiments already there. When the French get up, we can be very rapidly got into line by steamers. It would never do for Lord Raglan to be with all, or nearly all, his men at Varna, and yet find himself too weak to move on and relieve Silistria.

Some of our officers are not very wise ; themselves totally without experience, they yet imagine they can instruct old war-worn officers in their business. I am quite worried with perpetual returns, notes, &c. every half-hour all day. I generally rise at three, and go to bed at ten. My health is good. I never go out of camp, now that I am under canvas, unless ordered

out to a field-day. When I consider the composition of our staff, the prospect looks dubious. In the
Quarter-master General's department there is only
one officer who ever served in that department before ; he is a young man who was Deputy-assistant
Quarter-master General at the Cape. How they are
all to become in a moment expert at their work is
a mystery. I am not in that branch now, although
I served in it in Canada, under a Colonel Mackenzie
Fraser, who is dead, but who gave me an idea of
what a quarter-master general ought to be, certainly
very unlike any I see here. The Adjutant-General is
a very amiable man, a perfect gentleman and a good
Christian, but as innocent of the meaning of discipline as a sucking-baby. Some one must be responsible for the selection of the staff ; the ultimate
responsibility of course must fall on the Commander-
in-chief, who, however capable, as I believe him to be,
cannot do every one's work and his own too.

THIS picture of landing a party of staff-officers at
Varna, with all their horses and baggage, on a lonely
beach at nightfall, miles away from their troops, and
with no assistance from any one, is very pregnant.
Where was the hurry ? Six hours longer on board
the steamer would have made all the difference. It
was said the steamer was going for Lord Raglan ; but

his Lordship did not arrive for several days afterwards. One Navy-Captain said the party was not to land till the next morning ; then came some other authority, which ordered it ashore instanter. But two hours of daylight were lost by this misunderstanding. The place where the troops were encamped was proverbially unhealthy, with a swamp and lake close by. The village of Aladeen, where the Light Division was at this time encamped, lies at the head of the lower Devna Lake, on its northern shore ; so that there was water-communication to and from Varna, which probably was partly the reason for taking up that ground ; but the vicinity of a lake in the heat of summer is a questionable good.

## LETTER IX.

Camp, near Varna, Friday, 16th June 1854.

AFTER expecting the order to move for so long a time that we almost thought we should not move at all, it came suddenly ; and last Monday our horses were embarked on board a steamer in the Bosphorus, and ourselves on Tuesday 13th, that is to say, the division of the army under the Duke of Cambridge, General Bentinck, and C. The two Brigadiers who command the Guards and Highlanders, with their staff-officers, servants, &c. were put on board the City of London, which vessel conveyed us to the Bay of

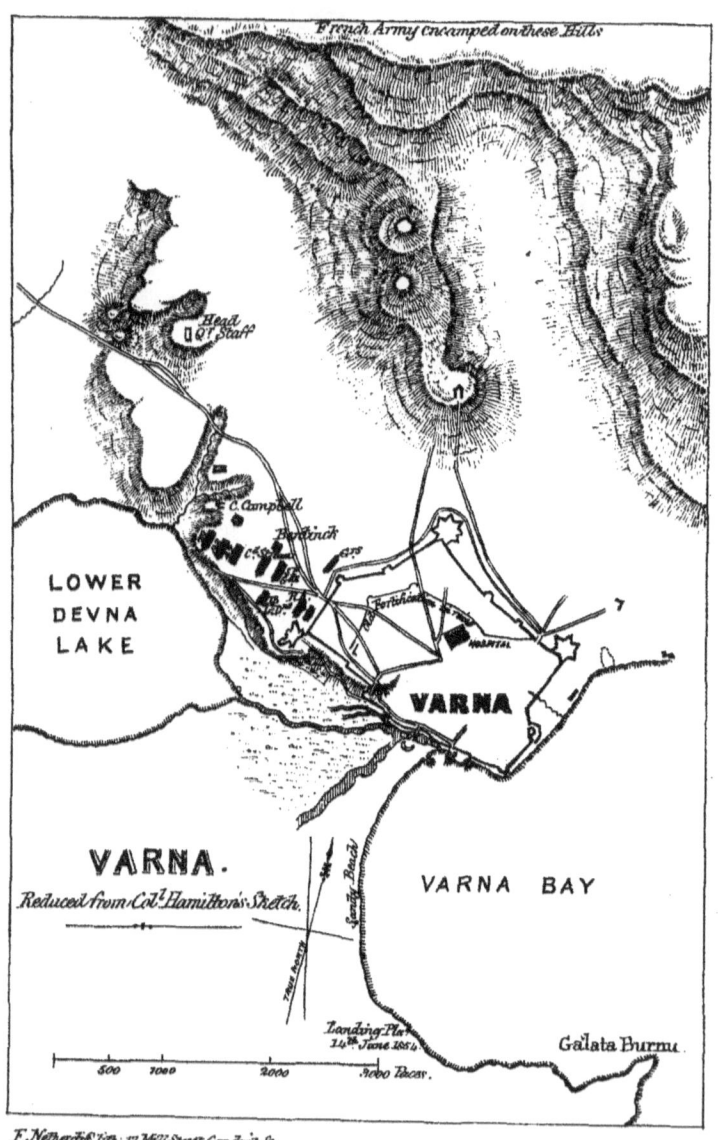

French Army encamped on these Hills

Head Qr Staff

C. Campbell.
Bentinck
C.K.S.H.
Light Div

Fortificon

HOSPITAL

LOWER
DEVNA
LAKE

VARNA

VARNA.
*Reduced from Col.l Hamilton's Sketch.*

500    1000    2000    3000 Paces.

VARNA BAY

Sandy Beach

Landing Place
14th June 1854

Galata Burnu

F. Netherclift lith. 17 Mill Street, Conduit St.

to face Page 31.

Varna in about 24 hours, towing two transports at the same time. The passage of the Bosphorus is very pleasing; the Turkish houses and forts on either hand being so picturesque. At the extremity of the strait or entrance to the Black Sea we saw the blue Symplegades or Cyanean Rocks, which are enshrined in classic memory. I am sorry to say they are not blue, but black and yellow. On reaching our anchorage, we heard that the Russians were retiring from Silistria, which I do not believe. However, our ship was to sail again in three hours, to bring up Lord Raglan ; so we, Brigadiers and tail, were all shot ashore, just at dark, on the beach, about four miles from the town of Varna, horses, bag, and baggage. Our soldiers six miles off, and no one to help us but our servants. These were about ten in number. To add to the scene, it began to rain ; we had eighteen horses and mules to picket and feed, and Bentinck's lot as many. The confusion was wonderful, for they were landing out of the ship at the same time commissariat stores, tents, &c., all of which had to go to a different side of the bay from our landing-place. The result was the loss of our two Brigadiers' tents, two most essential spades belonging to Major S., and a very superb large mallet for driving tent-pegs, which we had procured at Scutari. At last we got all the horses secured, one tent up, and our Brigadier's bed in it ; the rest of the baggage lay scattered over the beach in most admired disorder under a pouring rain. I was wet through, and dog-tired, so I threw myself down on the ground under the tent, and slept for three hours. As soon as daylight came, we proceeded to gather up our dispersed properties, and count up our losses; we then loaded the animals and carts. Our road lay along a deep sandy shore round the Bay of Varna. Behind that town, on the slopes of a country something like the Brighton Downs, we found our three Highland regiments, as well as the Guards. The soil here is light and sandy; grass and small shrubs spread over it furnish a sufficient land-scape. The Devna Lake is in our rear; a brigade of French about two miles in our front; and the Light Division (English) at Aladeen, about eight miles to the left. We have some cavalry and artillery up, and fully expect to advance very shortly. Yesterday af-ternoon rain set in, and my bed got wet, as the tent is not perfectly watertight in all parts; so that during the last two days some of the hardships of war have come to my lot. It is now 5 A.M., and the ground is steaming; a thick fog scarcely allows the sun to be seen; and considerable discomfort prevails in my family, small as it is, viz. one! The material sun will, however, prevail, and take away the fog and dry up the ground, and nature will look triumphant.

## LETTER X.

Camp, Varna, 21st June 1854.

You will be surprised at finding us still lingering here ; but in truth the commissariat arrangements are so incomplete that we may still be detained some days.   We have now one division (the Light one) encamped nine miles off, west of Varna, at the head of the Lake, and the first and second divisions encamped here.   Two regiments of Dragoons, the 5th and 13th, are gone on about fifteen miles to Devna. We understand that there will be forty-five miles to get over without water, which we shall find to be a great obstacle ; and yet to save Silistria we must do it. Lord Raglan is expected here with the head-quarters this morning ; every thing about us shows a tendency to advance,—the inclination without the power.   Nothing so helpless as an army without transport ; and our Government has either been grossly deceived, or has been very neglectful of this important matter. The French have a division encamped about three miles off, and I saw Canrobert reviewing them,—very fine troops indeed.   I have also ridden to see the camp of the Light Division, which is very prettily situated, with a view of the lake, in a country more wooded than this is.   We are told that the trees disappear a little further on ; so, with no shade and no

D

water, our advance to give battle will be any thing but a luxury. We staff-officers know nothing of the plan of campaign ; Lord Raglan, very wisely thinking that it should be a secret, does not tell it to any one, except perhaps to St. Arnaud. The Turks are making a brilliant defence of Silistria, which is partly, and perhaps unjustly, ascribed to the presence of some English officers who have entered their service.

I observe that you quote a book called ——————, which, as I understand you, libels the character of the English officers. Among them, no doubt, as in other professions, there may exist some " unmitigated black-guards," as you say ; but believe me, they rarely hold their ground. The officers as a body are rather com-monplace, and many of them not a little idle ; but a body of men who are ready at any moment to lead their soldiers into fire, and die in performance of extremely irksome duties, is not to be written down by a novelist.

THE retreat of the Russians from Silistria, and their gaining the left bank of the Danube, settled at once the question of the Allies moving up to the banks of that river, which on the 25th June must have been frightfully unhealthy, as was too soon discovered when the French went to the Dobrudscha. The author takes for granted that Lord Raglan could not help the inactivity of his army, because it had no transport. It seems probable that at this period the power of the Commander-in-chief as to controlling the Commissary was but ill defined. The chaplains were sent to the army with good pay ; but they were not entitled, like military officers, to have a soldier as a servant, and they had great difficulty in procuring any decent man to attend upon them. With respect to the name " Tomi," Bayle calls it " Tomes." On the maps of the Society for the Diffusion of Useful Knowledge it is called Tomi, and is placed at the eastern or Black-Sea end of the Roman wall, close to Kostenjee, ancient Constantiana. Ovid was banished thither in the year of Rome 761, and died there in 771, at about sixty years of age ; one of his verses begins, " Cur aliquid vidi ?"

It has been suggested that Ovid detected Augustus in the commission of incest ; but it seems unlikely, if that was the case, that he would have referred to it in his verses, which he sent to Rome with piteous prayers for pardon. There is a similar story told of an Italian painter in the times of the Medici, who was on a scaffold painting a ceiling : he, however, prudently feigned sleep ; the prince tried him with a candle, and a dagger in his hand, but was deceived by the painter's nerve.

Marshal St. Arnaud, whom the author only saw

on this occasion, and then on horseback, was a short-
ish and rather stout person, with a light complexion.
He seemed immensely pleased with the applause he
received. This approbation would probably have been
very much modified if the soldiers had known any of
his antecedents. St. Arnaud, among other ways, not
so respectable, of gaining his livelihood, came to London to teach fencing; and when he found that the
English did not want to learn fencing, he became a
dancing-master, and it is said a marker at a billiard-
table. He was a most unscrupulous person, and this
quality raised him to the top of his profession; for
when Napoleon was meditating his *coup-d'état*, he
looked out for a proper instrument to command the
army, and he speedily heard of St. Arnaud,—a dashing soldier, of buccaneering nature, *criblé de dettes*,
who would be willing to risk his head for a million of
francs. At this moment he was in Algiers; and the
first step taken was to send him on an expedition
against the Kabyles, from which he came back successful; and with this feather in his cap he was
brought to Paris, and there transacted his master's
business, with the fortune we know of. Marshal St.
Arnaud was born in 1798. There has been published
a collection of his letters, beginning in 1831. In the
year 1815 he became a *garde du corps* in the company commanded by the Duke de Grammont; and
the best thing known about him, as a man, besides

his affection for his family, is a letter which he wrote
to the Duchesse de Grammont, when he got the command of the Eastern army, in which he said, that although *il avait fait des farces*, yet that he could not
forget the kindness he had received from herself and
from her husband, his old commanding-officer, and
he hoped she would allow her son to become his aide-
de-camp.　None are all evil, and this touch of kind-
liness ought to be taken into the account which pos-
terity will hold of the dead St. Arnaud.

## LETTER XI.

Camp, Varna, 25th June 1854.

THIS morning we heard of the Russians' retreat
from Silistria, which is very fortunate for Lord
Raglan, as we are not yet ready to advance, and
now perhaps we shall not do so at all.

The climate of the valley of the Danube is so
very bad that I cannot help thinking that so soon
as there is no longer any risk of a direct attack by
the Russians on the line of the Balkan, we shall turn
our attention towards Sebastopol.　They say the Russians suffered much loss in recrossing the Danube.　If
they are wise, they will evacuate the Principalities,
which would relieve Austria from the necessity of
acting.　Our plain here where we are encamped is
getting quite filled up with troops ; French and Eng-

lish arriving every day. At this moment about 5000
Turks are firing a *feu de joie* half a mile from my tent;
no doubt in honour of the success obtained against
the Russians. I know Lord Raglan expected Silistria
would fall every day, and he would have been much
blamed for a loss which he could not help. I suppose
the Russians suffered terribly from disease, and were
also perpetually fearing our advance. Had we got
them on this side of the Danube, they would have
lost a great many prisoners, who could not have
crossed the bridge under our fire. Thank —— for
his letter. I read Kossuth's speech with admiration
at its eloquence. I do not feel so furiously as some
people about these foreigners, but I always abominated
the partition of Poland. The poor Turks I think I
like better than any of them, perhaps because I know
less about them. I believe they are improving, but
they have a fine long march to make in that direction
before they can be said to be perfect. The most ridiculous part of our position here is the way we are
treated by the native servants, Armenians, Greeks,
&c. They get money to buy clothes, and then run
away. We caught one of them afterwards, tied him
neck and heels, and sent him to the Pasha, who, by
way of punishment, ordered him back to Constantinople. My English groom is in hospital with fever,
and my five horses and two mules are looked after by
one soldier and two savages. The Presbyterian minis-

ter has just been relating his woes. He is paid 16s.
a day and his rations, but is not entitled to a soldier-
servant, and talked of being left behind, and that his
position required certain appearances, &c. &c. ! I remarked that the Apostles got on remarkably well without servants, so far as I knew; and that if all my own
horses died, and servants too, I should go on upon
foot. In the middle of my writing, I am forced to
get up to settle my tent-pegs ; a squall of wind and
rain having set in, threatening the overturn and
swamping of my whole establishment. There is a
brevet coming out, I understand, which will make me
a lieutenant-colonel from length of service.

27th June.

The post goes, we hear, to-morrow. We now believe the Russians have entirely abandoned this side
of the Danube, and are retreating towards the Pruth.
This Varna is, I believe, the ancient Tomi to which
Ovid was banished, for seeing something wrong done
by Augustus ; he alludes to it in his *Tristia*, which
were written here, and are filled with rather unmanly
lamentations over his hard fate. Yesterday Marshal
St. Arnaud rode through the camp escorted by twenty
wild Arabs of the Desert, all decorated with the Legion
of Honour. The English troops turned out and treated
him to a loud and hearty cheer. He passed through
again this morning, and I had a good look at the

Arabs, who are dressed in their own country dress, viz. a red cloak, and a white cloth over their heads, tied round with a coloured shawl. At a little distance they look like women; they carried their swords under their thighs, to prevent the jingling which our cavalry make from the scabbard hitting against the spur and stirrup. In spite of my opinion to the contrary, people say we are going to advance so soon as the commissariat report themselves able to feed us. I do not believe we shall advance much into the interior, if at all, unless they propose to let the army winter at Bukarest. The report may be spread to mislead the Russians, as our game is evidently Sebastopol. I see Kossuth does not relish the Austrians joining us; it upsets all his schemes, but gives far the best chance of peace. Some of the cavalry under Cardigan are gone scouring after the retreating enemy, so that we shall soon get certain intelligence of their whereabouts.

---

## LETTER XII.

Camp, Aladeen, 4th July 1854.

SINCE I wrote to you last our division has marched from Varna here, about ten miles west. Our camp is on the spur of a hill just over the narrow river which joins the two Devna lakes : said river flows through

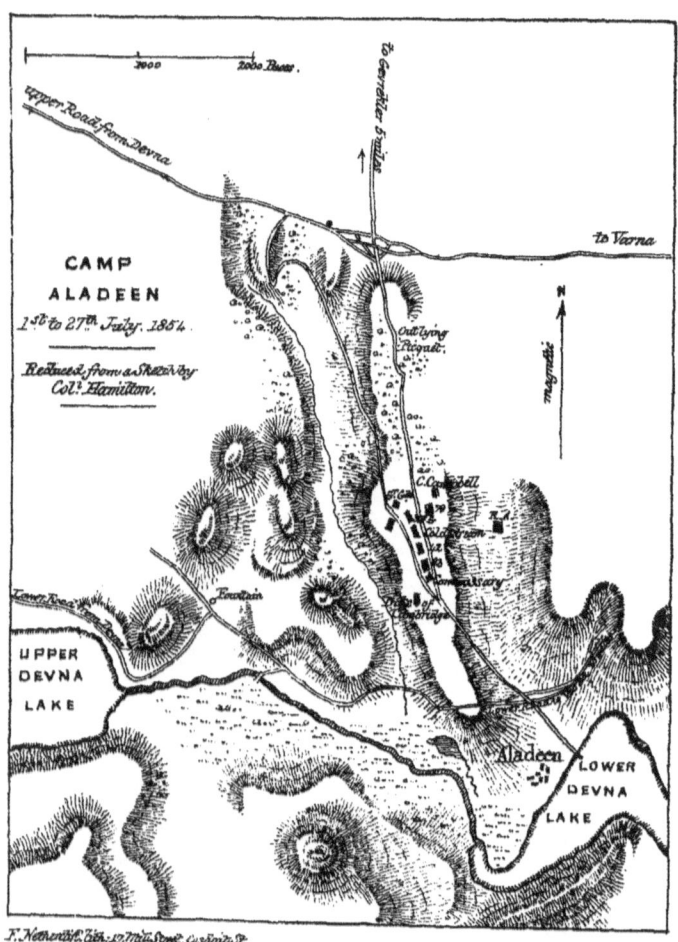

**CAMP ALADEEN**

1st to 27th July, 1854.

Reduced from a Sketch by Col. Hamilton.

Upper Road from Devna

to Varna

To Gevrekler 5 miles

UPPER DEVNA LAKE

LOWER DEVNA LAKE

Aladeen

Fountain

a swampy bottom, which as to its salubrity is doubt-ful. The Duke of Cambridge has gone to Constanti-nople, and left us to our own devices. We have no forage for our horses except barley—no straw or hay. I have to send our servants and mules all round the country to cut grass. The preparation for marching, viz. packing baggage on mules, striking tents, &c., is very hard work, especially with our indigenous hired servants, to whom we cannot speak. My Eng-lish groom is gone home sick with fever, and the unbreeched gentry who form our brigade have no skill in horse-management; so that I am in a mess, as you would say, if you could see. It is now half-past three in the morning. There was a tremendous storm of hail and rain yesterday, which continued partially all day and this night, and is now going on with a truly admirable perseverance. I was absent when it began. My tent is pitched in a fine garden loam; the floor is in consequence at this present speaking a swamp. Moreover the rain was so fierce that it came through the roof and wet all my things. I am now sitting up to my ancles in mud with a pair of sea-boots on, not having of course taken my clothes off at all, nor having any prospect of being able to take up new ground till the rain stops and the sun has shone for several hours. In these circumstances, as the post goes at half-past seven, I thought I would solace myself by telling you about Omar Pasha. Yes-

terday, not being on duty, I rode forward a march
to Devna, where the Light Division is encamped. I
took the most northern road, which runs over a
sandy soil, with chalk rocks in many places, and some
singular granite pins, which look like gigantic ruins,
and seem to me to be like Stonehenge, only not in
a plain. There is a very beautiful river at Devna,
with many mills on it, and a good stone bridge, close
to which there stands a wretched khan. General
Airey commands the division in the absence of Sir
G. Brown. I rode up to his tent to call on him, and
found him in a flannel jacket and ditto trousers, only
the latter were red ; a most curious-looking general
indeed. He was waiting the arrival of a cavass to
announce the approach of Omar Pasha, who was *en
route* to visit Lord Raglan at Varna. After smoking,
drinking coffee, and feeding my horse, the cavass
arrived, and was followed by the body doctor, to say
the great man was near. We all mounted straight-
way and galloped towards the bridge, which we
reached at the same time with the Turk. He was
travelling in a German calash with four horses, the
postillions being dragoons, and a guard of dragoons ;
his wife following in another carriage. Omar Pasha
seems to be about fifty-five years old, with gray
mustaches and beard. A little red fez on his head,
a plain blue frock-coat and gray trousers, was his
garb, without decoration or ornament of any sort.

His face indicates great good sense, and he has a
very pleasing smile ; but although his figure is good,
I suppose he would hardly be called handsome. He
had with him a French Colonel Dieu, and an English engineer officer, Simmons. By their statements
it would appear that the Russians are retiring by
divisions towards Brailow, which is their nearest
point for reaching their own Bessarabia. Before
moving from Silistria, Paskewitsch issued an order of
the day to his army, informing them that in consequence of a movement on the part of Austria he was
compelled to alter the position of his army. The
Russians lost, by Omar Pasha's calculation, 10,000
killed and 6000 wounded ; and the outwork they
failed to take was of the most contemptible kind, the
ditch only twelve feet wide, so that a good horse
would have jumped it. Their conduct was most
barbarous : the whole garrison except two battalions
was in this outwork ; the inhabitants of Silistria only
numbered 11,000, so that they had no chance of
overpowering the garrison ; yet the Russians shelled
the town cruelly, killing numbers of poor women and
children. Perhaps they injured thus their chance of
taking the place, as the fire spent so brutally might,
if turned on the outwork, have forced the garrison out
of it. Omar Pasha was very unhappy for some days
before they retired, and was of course proportionately
happy when he found the attack finally abandoned.

The chief Russian engineer, General Schilders, lost
his leg, and they had three or four generals killed,
which shows that the officers must have exposed
themselves very much in driving the men to attack.
A treaty was signed at Constantinople on the 12th
ult. between Austria and Turkey, by which the
former is bound, in case Russia should not retire on
the Austrians entreating them to do so, to join the
Allies.  I do not believe the Austrian troops have
as yet moved forward; but their intention to do so
is best proved by the retreat of the Russians, whose
army would have been cut off and lost had they per-
severed in besieging Silistria.  Except from the chance
of some most unfortunate disagreement among the
Allies, this Austrian advance ought to finish the war.
If our Government can now make a treaty with
Russia of a proper kind, they will deserve much
credit ; meantime it is for us soldiers to be regretted
that we have had no opportunity to give Nicholas a
touch of our quality.  Yesterday we received a report from Varna of an armistice.  I do not think
that can be granted until the Russians shall have
crossed the Pruth.  There will be much time consumed in the arrangements, and an army of occupation will doubtless be left.  After some talk between
our generals and Omar Pasha, the troops, seven
battalions, were ordered out to show him the army :
in twenty minutes they were all under arms, and we

had a short review; the cavalry then came up and
marched about and charged. Omar Pasha asked to
be allowed to head the charge by himself, in order
that he might judge of our pace, with which he was
well pleased. We then rode back to Aladeen, and,
strange to say, had no rain till we got there, when we
found the devastation of our camp; officers and men
running about naked, having left their clothes under
the doubtful shelter of the tents while they were
making trenches round them to let off the water. I
have just been inspecting the picket, the men composing which are going to march off all wet through
to a spot in the bush about a mile and a half distant,
where they will spend twenty-four hours without
tents; this is called being on outlying picket, with
the duty of watching our left flank from any possible advance of the retreating Russians! Any thing
more thoroughly miserable than the appearance of the
camp at dawn it would be hard to conceive; and
there are some wretched women with us, poor soldiers'
wives, who have to suffer all this. The hardships
that seamen bear are a joke in comparison, for they
are dry under hatches. A fine sunshiny day would
be of monstrous consequence, but the sky looks for
rain. Now I must call up the servants and send
them off for water and forage and wood, and all the
numerous things which you good people find at your
doors.

## LETTER XIII.

Camp, Aladeen, 9th July 1854.

I WROTE to you the other day when we heard of
the retreat of the Russians, since which the English
papers show me that you knew of their discomfiture
before we did ; rumour flies slow in this Bulgaria.
You observe that I anticipated on the 4th* a collision,
while Lord Raglan wrote on the same date that there
would be no fighting.  The event shows he was right :
but I could only judge from what I could see ; he had
other sources.  It is very unfortunate for the army
that we could not give Nicholas one good kick.  The
report here is growing that he has abdicated ; which
step will, I conclude, enable the diplomatists to begin
their ridiculous manœuvres again.  Our division seems
rooted here ; it is not a very good place : the water
is about two miles off ; we send mules with leather
bottles for it, and the men have to walk with their
little canteens and cooking-pots.  Yesterday a snake
walked, or rather glided, into my tent, and we had to
bring all my boxes, &c. out to get at him.  The nuisance of a tent-life consists principally in the necessity of keeping all one's clothes, books, &c. shut up in
the boxes they travel in ; to get out a pocket-hand-

---

* Letter of 4th June (No. 7), from Scutari.  It is strange to
see how convinced Lord Raglan was that we should have no
fighting.

kerchief, a whole portmanteau must be unpacked and repacked : barring that, the life in a tent during fine weather is more endurable than life elsewhere. It is something like being in a ship, except that when you go overboard you are not obliged to swim. Your horses are all picketted round you, and you see at one glance your whole possessions. *Per contra,* the servants are very tiresome, as usual : the natives, whom we hire at exorbitant rates, are continually running away, and the soldiers getting drunk ; all which is very confusing, especially if there is any thing in the way of business to be done. The brevet promotion which reached here by this mail has produced a great fuss. Some men go home who want to stay, and others stay who would gladly have got back to England. I am to be called Lieutenant - Colonel for the future. I do not intend to return home, however ; my face is not set to that airt of the compass. The diplomatists cannot work without having an army here at present. Where shall we pass the winter ? Schumla ? Bukarest ? Scutari ? or shall we, after all, go to Crim-Tartary ? There's wale of places besides Circassia, and our own will has nothing to do in it. Three or four penmen will arrange it all. One thing is certain ;* we shall not live in tents in the

---

* Not quite certain, as it turned out. Our friend is reckoning without somebody whom the Commissioners have discovered and exposed.

winter, but either in houses or in mud-huts which we
shall construct for ourselves.  The next two months
must settle that ; for the weather sets in bad very
early in autumn, and the roads become impassable.
The post will still go, however, and affectionate
thoughts will find their way.  Even if the letters are
lost, they will still be believed in.

---

## LETTER XIV.

Camp, Aladeen, Sunday, 16th July 1854.

I RODE over on Thursday to Devna, to inquire
after ——, and found him in his tent.  He had returned two days before from an extensive patrol on
the banks of the Danube.  He saw Cossacks across
the river at Rassova, and a large force of Russians
opposite Silistria.  He described his excursion as very
interesting, though he had to sleep on the ground
without a tent all the time.  They had a great many
sore backs.*  As to our campaign, we have reason to
think from conversations with navy officers that there
is a probability we may again be embarked.  There
are three places possible, viz. Kostengi,—which is
only thirty miles from the Danube, at the east end
of Trajan's wall,—Anapa, or Sebastopol.  We have

---

* This was the cavalry-patrol under Lord Cardigan.

no means of knowing what force the Russians have in the Crimea; but Lord Raglan has probably some information. Without a large force,—that is, all the Frenchmen as well as the English,—we dare not venture there.* The risk of a catastrophe to England's only army would be too great. At the same time, it is the only way to bring Russia effectually to reason ; and if the English Minister is in earnest, he must do it sooner or later. My own idea is, that the Government are afraid of the enterprise, and still hope to negotiate. With that belief, I guess we shall be landed at Kostengi, threatening Brailow, and wintering at the mouth of the Danube ; which river, if we could clear it of Russian gunboats, and deepen the entrance, would be of wondrous use to us in conveying supplies.† The siege-train is arrived at Varna. We in camp here lead the most monotonous life imaginable, varied sometimes by scenes with the commissary. You, I suppose, know that the commissary makes contracts with natives, bakers and butchers, for the supply of the troops : these commissaries often labour under the suspicion of being too friendly with the

---

* It turned out that we had not enough in mere numbers. The common rule is three times the enemy's force for a siege: three times 40,000 = 120,000,—that is the number we ought to have taken.

† This was of course with the idea of remaining in Bulgaria.

E

contractor; sometimes they are suspected of being bribed to pass indifferent provisions—sometimes doing so out of laziness. A commissary here has been taking liberties lately. I will tell you the story. The bread is inspected by a regimental Quartermaster before it is issued; and if he should object to the quality, the regulation is that the commissary should apply for a board of officers to decide. On a late occasion, the bread being objected to, this commissary, instead of calling for a board, posted off with a loaf* in his hand, and got the General to taste, and declare the bread capital, and the complaint unfounded. (N.B. the soldier pays for it; and the duty of all officers is to protect the soldiers' interest.) Shortly after, the bread was again objected to; and a staff-officer assembled a board, armed with the proceedings of which he attacked the commissary, and forced him to make a new issue. The commissary, being ryled at this, went off to the General, and got a new board to sit and condemn the proceedings of the first one, so as to compel the troops to take the bad bread. One of our brigade-majors heard of the new board, and slipped down accidentally to the commissary's tent, and dropped into his august presence while he was entertaining the board and getting their palates into order,

---

* We afterwards discovered that there were two sorts of bread, made by different bakers! Probably it was the good bread which the General tasted.

previous to the inspection, by exhibiting cheese and brandy. The field-officer who was president of the board will not soon hear the end of his taste for brandy and cheese.

Since writing the above, I have had some reason to think that we shall attempt Anapa,—an enterprise for which I believe the English themselves are strong enough. Fairly landed in Circassia, Schamyl will, I suppose, join us. I see the Government at home is very shaky, and most likely by this time is out. I hope the war will be prosecuted vigorously, let who will be the Minister. This is England's opportunity; we shall not easily get another army to Turkey. Being here, however, this one may be strengthened; and indeed we expect immediately an addition of 600 men to this division. There is as yet but small sickness in the army; the bad season has scarcely begun, and we have not moved near enough to the Danube to feel the full force of the malaria. The heat has not been very intense except on a few occasions, and the nights are always cool. It is now 11 o'clock A.M., and the thermometer is 77° in my tent; but, *per contra*, two of my servants are ill of fever. One of C.'s mules drowned himself two or three days ago; I believe from *ennui*. The newspapers come rather irregularly, but the letters seem now safe. We have two London post-office clerks,—one at Stamboul, the other at

Varna,—and they have already organised what was
very disorganised.    If we go east, you will get earlier
news by letters than " our own correspondents" can
send, for I do not believe they will be allowed to
embark ; at least they should not do so if I had
power to stop them.    From the Danube you will
hear every thing almost as soon as ourselves, and
probably with greater accuracy.    Some of the French
who marched by Adrianople to this neighbourhood
describe the country as most beautiful ; they say that
they marched for days under the shade of large trees.
Here there are scarcely any; only dwarf acacia-bushes,
which I think must make the ground damp and unhealthy.    If we can only bring our men sound into
line opposite the Russians, I have no doubt of the
result, although who may live to tell the tale is very
questionable.    The beard-movement is making progress in this army.    Lord Raglan has made up his
mind to take no notice of hair, and so I have put by
my razors for the present.    There does not seem any
chance of the militia being called on to volunteer; to
the regret, I dare say, of the young officers, who, having
tasted the idleness and excitement of soldiering, would
like to try the real article.    The striking character of
our proceedings hitherto has been dulness ; we have
not even had any marching ; only ten miles have we
marched as yet ; and the Highlanders did that much
better than the Guards, that is to say, fewer men

fell out ; only eighteen or twenty out of 2500 did not come in together ; of the Guards, 180 dropped to the rear. The poor women are most to be pitied ; they have no carriage allotted to them ; and if they get on a baggage-wagon, it is only on sufferance and by winking ; miserable wretches, and a most depraved set too. The soldiers are behaving very well, except in the article of drink, which they cannot resist, and I must say they do not carry their liquor like gentle-men. Drink is the only Christian vice we have much chance of indulging in here ; gluttony is out of the question ; and there is not a woman visible, I suppose, nearer than at Bucharest. If we should winter in Circassia, there will, however, most likely be some transactions of which I shall keep you informed.

17th July.

Papers of the 3d are in camp. Lord Aberdeen seems to have put himself right, and more army is coming ; so I suppose we shall certainly try to do some-thing. I believe that all the fleet and all the trans-ports now in the Bosphorus are to rendezvous here on the 28th, to carry us somewhere. When I took leave of Lord Hardinge, I told him that I hoped he would let us have a try at Sebastopol. If we can but hit a blow before the winter sets in, our dear Bull will be pleased. The animal has no notion of waiting till we are ready.

THIS is the last letter from Aladeen. The march really took place on the 27th and 28th; the Guards on the first day. There had been some cases of cholera; the swamp between the lakes began to tell, and the surgeons wished to have a change for their men. Gĕvrĕklĕr was the name of the new camp; and the situation was much more healthy than Aladeen, but the seeds of disease were laid there, which broke out at the new camp. Devna also had proved very unhealthy.

## LETTER XV.

Camp Aladeen, 23d July 1854.

A VERY few words, for my time is much taken up. We march to-morrow; apparently a move towards the Danube. But it is only a blind; I think you may depend upon it that we are to embark very shortly, and to be landed somewhere close to Odessa. They have been making fascines at Varna, and preparations for entrenching. You know that in landing we shall have to do so in the face of an enemy; and as we cannot all land at first, there will be some sharp fighting till we can get ourselves entrenched. This operation will effectually compel the Russians to clear out of the Principalities and come down on us, and we shall have a great battle, that will be told of in history. It is now, I believe, certain that the news of our arrival at Varna was the cause of the raising of the siege of Silistria.

---

## LETTER XVI.

Gĕvrĕklĕr, Bulgaria, 28th July 1854.

THE place I date from is only five miles from Aladeen, from whence we marched this morning ; some cases of cholera in the camp, as well as feverish attacks, led the doctors to wish for a move. It is a flat place on the top of a hill, with nothing remarkable about it except the absence of inhabitants, and want of cultivation. A camp is a camp, place it where you will. No events have occurred to speak of; the badness, or " badderness," of our dinner seems generally what is of most consequence. If we can judge by signs, our leaders are planning some enterprise ; if we believe what we hear, nothing whatever will be done this autumn, and we shall have to look out immediately ·for winter quarters. I am inclined to think they will try something; but that is a mere opinion. It requires first that St. Arnaud should agree on a plan with Lord Raglan ; and it is quite likely the Frenchman is in no hurry, as his pay and allowances are large, and he would be a loser by concluding the war too soon, or indeed at all; doubtless he wishes it to last for the term of his natural life. I see some *Evening Mails* occasionally, and the *Leader*. We are all growing beards, and looking very wild and ragged; tattered and torn with riding through the bushes; but the army cannot be called unhealthy as yet, though we have several deaths daily in our division—out of 7000 men, that is to say. The worst season is, however, now approaching, and we have no right to expect we shall escape what has been every one's lot hitherto who has campaigned in these parts.　I send you my last composition.

### "BRIGADE ORDERS.

Highland Brigade Office, Camp Gĕvrĕklĕr, 28th July.

No. 1.—No wood is to be cut near any of the springs, as the want of shade will dry them up. This order is to be read to the men at the two next parades. No persons are to wash themselves or their clothes in the springs to the rear of the camp; neither are horses to be watered there. There is water suitable for this latter purpose in front, near some large trees. Commanding-Officers are requested to take steps to cause these orders to be strictly attended to. The 79th and 93d Highlanders will furnish a bayonet sentry each during daylight over the two springs in the rear to prevent washing or watering horses there. A bower* will be made for these two sentries by the

---

* These bowers were made by cutting down bushes and green boughs, which were stuck in the ground: the sun was thus kept off, while the breeze came through, and made a much cooler place than a tent.

above-mentioned regiments, one near each spring; and a fatigue-party from the 42d Highlanders will clear the troughs early to-morrow morning. This duty will be performed daily by the regiments in rotation. Commanding-Officers will order a bower over each of the regimental cooking-places, as well as one near each of their hospital-tents, &c. &c."

Such is soldiering; striving to keep the mere requisites for living in a decent condition. The men have to cut their own firewood for themselves with blunt bill-hooks, besides pitching tents, making ditches round them, cooking, washing their clothes, turning out clean for parade, and doing fatigue-duties continually for commissaries, engineers, staff-officers, &c. Here comes a storm of thunder and rain! Quick! drive in more tent-pegs, and shut up the tent; see all the tackle in good order for a blow; put water-decks on the horses, and do not let the rain put out the kitchen-fire. It is dripping in on my pillow; so I will put a water-deck over that.

## LETTER XVII.

Camp, Gēvrĕklĕr, 4th August 1854.

STILL motionless. It is very like a calm at sea; sweeping up the decks, and keeping the ship clean, and the men in health. I am sorry to say we have already begun to have disease,—cholera, fever, and dysentery ; not as yet very fierce, but of the cholera-cases few recover. The preparations for an embarkation still go on ; and my belief is still that we shall go to Odessa, or that neighbourhood: an army landed there would compel the Russians to retire from the Principalities, for it would be on their rear. There has been a fight between Bashi-Bazooks and Cossacks in the Dobrudscha, in which the latter were victorious, and a French colonel has been killed. The mail came in last night, bringing English papers of 17th July. We expect to have to sell or shoot our baggage-animals, and burn most of our baggage, when we embark. Perhaps the commissariat may offer 10l. a piece for mules* which I paid near 40l. each for. You see we go to war at our own charges, contrary to the ortho-dox maxims. I have been unwell ; a devil of a walk on duty, which I had in the wet one night lately, set my bile all wrong ; but it is past away, and I hope that sickness will spare me to strike a blow for old England before I quit the scene. Here there is no-thing and none to interest me. It is more solitary than being alone. None of my quondam acquaint-ances in England ever write to me ; but I see the papers, and occasionally read of your doings,—the

---

\* The author's two mules were afterwards sold to the Rus-sians in the Crimea for 4l. each.

ministerial ones, I mean,—said ministry very shaky. They are waiting for my note; so I close. We shall not embark for some days; and if I hear any thing, or indeed if I hear nothing, I shall probably write a line to show I am still on this side of the cholera.

## LETTER XVIII.

Camp, Gĕvrĕklēr, 8th August 1854.

WE have had a good deal of sickness in camp; so much that our strength in this division would be diminished for battle by 800 men, which is not far from a sixth—a serious consideration. The diseases are cholera, fever, diarrhœa, and dysentery. The days are not so very hot, but the nights are cold out of proportion; and I imagine the sudden changes of the temperature must be the proximate cause of disease; then we must remember that the men lie on the ground; and of course the recoveries are retarded by want of comfort. The note of preparation sounds all round us. I hear the gabions we are making, at the rate of 3000 a day, are sent to Varna, and embarked, which looks like a siege. We all wait in an apathetic manner for orders to move, which will come no doubt the moment the necessary preparations can be made. A number of the *Edinburgh Review* has wandered out here, containing a masterly account of the diplomatic part of the war. This is the first book I have read since I left England ; my only other one is Shakespeare, which comes to hand at all odd moments. I see some severe attacks on officers in the papers, which give me pain. Those in question seem to have been behaving like schoolboys, and I suppose are very young. We have just received an order to take mustaches into wear, with particular explanations how the beard is to be shaved,—a regular topiary work; with a special proviso that we in this army are to do as we like ; that is, not shave at all. It is very probable we may be embarked before I can write again. I hope we may do something for the honour of old England and the detriment of old Nick. I will not give up the coöperation of Austria as hopeless ; on the contrary, I believe she will advance as soon as we do. There is an article in the *Times* about Captain Butler, who died of his wounds, rather making out that he, who was on half-pay by his own wish and in search of adventures, deserves more credit than we who stick to the dull prosy work of looking after our men's health and comfort in a tiresome camp. If leave could have been had, there would have been dozens of officers at Silistria ; but they were wanted at their posts, where some of them have already died by disease,—who will get no paragraph of praise, although cool waiting for an attack of cholera shows much more true courage than behaving well before the

enemy.   No one says a word about the Turkish governor who was killed, or his successor, the responsible
person, who really saved the place, or poor Omar
Pasha, who had nerve enough not to advance, and
risk his army in a battle with the Russians.   I believe that is all I have to say, unless I were to enter
into an account of our domestic fights with the commissary, when he tries any thing we do not approve
of on our men.   These scenes are often ludicrous
enough, although sand in the bread and the sugar is
any thing but a subject for laughter.   I have invariably found the commissary disposed to defend his
contractor.

## LETTER XIX.

Camp, Gĕvrŏklĕr, 15th August 1854.

You say we are to take Sebastopol.*   It may
be so ; but I do not yet feel sure that will be our
point of attack.   Unless our leaders are performing
a gigantic sham, we certainly are going somewhere,
but not instantly, because people get leave now for
ten days ahead.   We know that the Turks are in
Bucharest ; *ergo* the Russians have continued their
retreat ; *ergo* the Austrians mean to advance ; if so,

---

* The decision of the Government to attack Sebastopol
seems from this to have been known in England at least on
the 1st August.

the Anglo-French at Odessa would be in a more
attacking position than at Sebastopol. The French
have made a most disastrous advance into the Dobrudscha, and have returned with a loss by disease
of 7000 men.* General —— was obliged to have
a guard with fixed bayonets to save him from his
own men, and it is said he has attempted suicide.
Varna has been half burned, and many stores destroyed; 300,000 lbs. of barley and 168,000 rations
of biscuit gone. Our sick increases gradually as the
season goes on, and we lose men daily by cholera and
fever; we have also lost officers, the two seniors of
the 79th Highlanders. Elliot I was rather intimate
with; he was only married a short time before he
embarked, and his poor wife, now twenty-two years
old, will be confined in December. All his money
lost with his commission, and the most she can hope
for is a pension of 80*l.* a year. We buried him on
the 13th on a woody hill looking over the lake and
the Black Sea; and I sat on a stone and made

### A Sonnet.

On far Bulgarian hills I hear the solemn strain :
From the sad Highland pipes to eastern skies

---

* The accounts of this movement were most deplorable.
The very men who were digging graves for their comrades often
fell dead in the midst of the work—in fact, dug their own graves,
like monks of La Trappe, although not from the same motive.

His native dirges mournfully arise,
Lending an echo to the distant main,
Beyond whose bounds the young bride looks in vain,
And longs and hopes, with watching tearful eyes,
Till hope be drowned in unavailing sighs,
For many a weary day of widowed pain.
Dig deep his grave in this wild woody bank,
And gather flowers to make a fragrant bed;
Stoop, kilted warriors, in a sorrowing rank
The while we scatter ashes on his head,
Bidding farewell. Comrades, his task is o'er;
While we must work till fate shall say, "No more."

I was quite touched when I looked into the grave, and saw that the poor soldiers had of their own tenderness filled it with wild flowers. We are going away from here in two or three days; the Guards march to-morrow, and we are to camp after three days' march on the south side of Varna Bay. I believe it is merely a move to divert the men's minds. Lord Westmoreland writes that Count Buol had given up hopes of peace, and declared that the soldiers must settle it; which fiat, however, does not necessarily involve any very vigorous action this autumn. The French are much dilapidated, and I can quite imagine it possible that nothing may be done till spring. The commissariat is very bad. To carry on this affair you must discard economy, especially when transport or food for the troops is in question. At this moment I see lying before me a complaint that the commissary has no straw for the sick. There are too many forms, too much time lost in obtaining any object, however important. The Guards are very much more unhealthy than we are, and do not march as well. When we marched from Varna to Aladeen, only twenty of the Highlanders who started with the column did not march in with it ; of the Guards one hundred and fifty at least were behind. Now I hear on this new march the Guards are to have their packs carried for them,—a most fatal blunder, and the beginning of blunders. We shall refuse for our men, as they are perfectly fit to carry their packs, and do not wish to be separated from their property. I am afraid we shall have to leave some sick behind in this camp—only seven or eight. The French pillaged cruelly during the fire at Varna, as did some English who were drunk, but others behaved very well, and stuck to the powder-magazine and saved it.* So many officers, staff and others, are going home sick, that it is not unlikely I may be offered some other situation ; but I cannot leave C. It is very strange how the English public

---

* Mr. M'Bean, now Adjutant of the 93d, behaved so well, and saved so much Turkish property from plunder, that the Turkish Government sent him the order of the Medjidie, which he was not allowed to accept, as it was not gained before the enemy, that being the condition upon which British officers are allowed to wear foreign orders.

persuaded themselves we were on the Danube; I never thought we should go there from the moment the Russians abandoned this bank, which I believe they did from the dread of fighting us with the river behind them; they would have all been taken prisoners had we won the day. Strategically speaking, the capture of Sebastopol would not affect the campaign; the troops in the Crimea cannot go any where by sea, nor march by land, to assist the rest of the Russian army. If the Austrians attack in front, and we roll up their left wing, we should do them much more mischief; and Sebastopol can always be taken when the time can be spared for the operation. No doubt it would affront the Czar and give us a good port; but I shall not believe we are to try it this autumn till I find myself landed there. It looks more as if we were waiting here till the Austrians have advanced so far that the two attacks shall be simultaneous. If they are so, the movement will be irresistible, and we shall winter in Odessa, with the Russians behind the Pruth, and the Austrians in Moldavia. You seem occupied by Mrs. —— and the rights of women. I do not think those rights practically so little respected as she maintains. It is true that drunken brutes beat their wives, and sometimes sober scoundrels use them ill; but they are drunk, and are scoundrels, and are acknowledged to be so. The young men had not much to do who drew me; they will be diverted now

P

by a new uniform, which, I hear, has been contrived
for them. Poor boys, they have not much amusement here, and are really very well-behaved.

August 16th.

I do begin to think that, after all, we shall go
to Sebastopol. The French losses are exaggerated,
1700 dead and 3000 in hospital. The expedition to
embark, as I hear, will be 45,000 French and 25,000
English. The first batch that lands any where will
have a tight battle to hold their ground; but if we
get 20,000 Englishmen ashore, they will not be
easily chawed up. Part of our division marched this
morning towards Varna.

## LETTER XX.

Camp, Gēvrĕklēr, 18th August 1854.

PART of our division marched yesterday, and with
it one of our regiments which ought not to have gone,
as Lord Raglan said when he heard of it. There has
been a great difficulty about transport, and now more
so, as the officers commanding the Guards persuaded
Lord Raglan to let them have their packs carried; and
Lord Raglan, having agreed to that, was compelled to
order all the others to have theirs carried likewise.
Our Highlanders (42d), particularly indignant, ap-

peared on parade with their packs on their shoulders. This dreadful fact was immediately reported to the Assistant - Adjutant - General, Colonel Gordon, who galloped up to the 42d, and ordered the foaming Cameron to take off his men's packs.* The regiment was delayed two hours in the sun, while stowing the packs on mules and ponies. I often think of the secret confided to me by an old brother officer of mine, Johnny Marsh, who had served in the Peninsula, and whose experience was given to me in the concrete: "Never, if you can help it, be brigaded with the Guards." The cholera has been very bad in the fleet, especially in the French one. Admiral Bruat's ship lost 153 men in sixty hours. Lord Raglan keeps his

---

* Colonel Cameron received the order to be on the appointed ground at a certain hour, and also to have the men's knapsacks packed upon mules ; but he found that if he attempted to comply with the latter order, he would be too late for the time at which he was ordered to be on the ground from whence the column was to march. He therefore decided on letting the soldiers carry their packs, not being aware of the importance attached to this scheme of employing mules. After the three battalions of Guards and the 42d marched, taking all the transport with them, which was on the 16th, Sir Colin Campbell was obliged, by his own activity and that of his interpreter, to collect native arabas, which could not be got in sufficient numbers till the 21st. Not a single cart was sent to us from Varna. Each mule could only carry six packs, or about 100 mules for a battalion of additional transport, or carts in proportion, to execute this unsoldierlike plan.

secret well, I am happy to say; somewhere we are
surely going as soon as every thing is ready. The
idea is, that the Russians are 60,000 strong in the
Crimea. If we go there with 70,000, the operation
is pretty serious; for the Russians will be strongly
entrenched, and the storming their works will be
murderous, but certain to succeed with such soldiers
as we have here. We have now 300 sick in our brigade, but we have only lost thirty-five men dead since
we came to Turkey, without counting the officers. I
see there is an amusing article in the *Times*, laughing
at our Adjutant-General's order about dress, white
collars, &c.; he does not write well, it must be con-
fessed. The fact is, that almost every one wears a
flannel shirt, red, blue, or gray, and those who dislike
shaving, do not shave at all. General Bentinck of the
Guards, who shaves, professes that he does it to look
like a gentleman. I suggested that Philip Sidney
and Raleigh, Shakespeare and Co. were very pretty
gentlemen, and yet wagged their beards. I suppose,
however, he would not call Shakespeare a gentleman,
even if shaved. The —— business is horrible, and, I
believe, in the worst intention that could be imputed.
Some fifty years ago, among the farming people of
Ireland, abduction was thought rather a joke; I suppose the poor women were used to it. I am going to
ride into Varna, where I have not been for a month,
just to look at the fire, or rather at its effects. If

this war continues, as seems likely, I shall very possibly receive a higher appointment, when all the men of interest are provided for. The only difficulty is separating from C., unless he gets promoted also, which may occur.

## LETTER XXI.

Camp, Galata, on the south side of Varna Bay,
24th August 1854.

WE have been marching for three days, and are now camped in a very beautiful spot close to the sea, but very high, with many trees. It is near, and a little to the south of, the place where we were landed on the 14th (same as described in Letter IX.). Walnuts, wild pears, and cherry-trees. There are so many troops camped about us, and so many horses, that water is hard to come by, and there is literally nothing to be bought; my breakfast is dry ration-bread made of rye and sand, with tea, but no milk. They have begun embarking the artillery guns; the men and horses bring them to the wharf, and go back to their camp, where they can get water. We cannot find out when the infantry is to embark; but that we are to embark and go somewhere is certain. It is asserted that the Russians have not more than 50,000 men in the Crimea; so that with our 60 or 70,000 French and English, and some thousand Turks, we

ought to lick them handsomely, if they give battle ;
but should they retire behind their entrenchments,
there will be some sharp fighting.   The common idea
is, that we shall land on the north side of Sebastopol,
and get possession of a fort which is situated there,
from whence we should be able to bombard the fleet
and town.   If we succeed in destroying the ships, even
should we fail in taking the town, we should effect a
good deal for Turkey ; but the thing will not be complete unless we take the town, and winter there.   I
cannot myself feel sure that we are going to Sebastopol at all ; a short time must decide it.   There is a
strong north wind blowing at present, which would
hinder a disembarkation on the west side of the
Crimea.   We have had a good many deaths among
the officers, and many have gone home sick ; all are
tired of this inactivity.   The weather has become
cooler, and they say the sickly season is nearly over ;
but I see the men pulling the wild pears and cherries
all round them, which will certainly make some of
them sick, and that will be laid to the climate.   Properly speaking, I do not believe there is any thing
the matter with the climate ; if we all lived in houses,
and had good food, I will be bound to say there would
not be more sick than in England.   Meantime the
—— regiment has been quite disorganised by the
death and sickness of officers ; there is not one remaining with the regiment who has been more than

six years in the service; a tenth of the men dead, and the rest got so frightened, that they gave up cleaning their horses. The Highland Brigade is considered healthy in the army; but the Guards are sickly and dispirited, and accordingly have lost three times as many as we have, and very likely will go on losing in that proportion, should the sickness continue. I think I told you about their marching without packs, and the Commander-in-Chief forcing us to do the same, to the disgust of men and officers. It is a bad speculation to be in the same division with the Guards; they are always on the right by virtue of their seniority; they do not take detachment-duty, which falls on the left brigade. Then the march is usually right in front. On the march, those who come last have to sweep up baggage and sick and ammunition, and have a good deal of dirty work to do; so that, in fairness, the brigades should be ordered to march day about, left and right in front. We have the resource, the native Englishman's privilege, of grumbling. If there is another post before we go, I shall write; after that event, we shall be landed in forty-eight hours, and who can tell what our lot may be? Victorious as an army, I feel convinced; but who will be able to write, is another matter, on which it is bootless to speculate.

## LETTER XXII.

Camp, Galata Burnu, 28th August 1854.

I GIVE now the proper name, which is indeed
that of the cape which makes the south corner
of Varna Bay. Preparation goes on fast and furious; embarking artillery, gabions, fascines, horses.
Those who are only waiting to embark have not
much to amuse them, except reading the papers.
Sometimes in the same paper we find we are in the
Crimea and on the Danube. Lord Raglan says
nothing, and I do not believe it is absolutely fixed
where we are to land; we shall sweep along the
Russian coast like a mighty bird of prey, and swoop
where we find a quiet place for landing. Once landed,
and the French and English in line, I have no doubt;
but I consider we are going to begin a winter campaign, including the siege, and that, even if victorious
in a short time and more easily than now seems
likely, we shall winter there. Possibly I may write
once more from on board ship, as I suppose there will
be a floating post-office. After landing I can think
that it will not be easy to write or send letters. All
the cavalry is to go, I now hear; so I hope ——— will
have the opportunity of seeing some service and of
distinguishing himself; and that all the army may,
by its carriage, wipe out the memory of the disgraces
come to light in their barrack-life. Practical jokes I

have myself always objected to. When I was young I was in a regiment where some such absurdities as we hear of took place, and I announced my intention of stopping it on the first opportunity; this soon occurred from an officer in joke pulling off my spectacles. I immediately called him out; and he was obliged to apologise before the whole mess; which transaction cured the disease completely. The peace-people have made some absurd rule, interdicting this rough practical method, and I trace to that order much of the irregularity now occurring. However, the order would come to nothing if such indignities were attempted on the right man; for he would call his insulter out, and take the chance of what might be done to him afterwards; moreover, all the sensible people in the regiment would back him. The young officers are like schoolboys, and I do not much care about their freaks; the ugly part of the matter is, that the older officers do not give straightforward evidence. Mr. —, I have no doubt, was a person whom they all wished to get rid of; he was at any rate a goose; for if he chose to take refuge in a complaint to his commanding-officer, he should have done so officially; then the colonel must have attended to him, or have left him the option of sending his complaint direct to the general officer commanding the district. The regiment ought to be broken up, and new officers appointed to it. I never had a quarrel in my life; and

in the affair I alluded to was not in the least angry :
the man meant nothing ; I acted on principle. The
poor fellow was killed at Chillianwallah, at the head
of the regiment.

THE 23d and 24th Letters were written on board
the Emeu steam-transport, commanded by Captain
Small, a most intelligent and agreeable gentleman.
The space of time embraced is from the evening of
the 29th, when the 1st Division was embarked, till
the 13th September, on which day the orders to dis-
embark in the Crimea were issued. Before leaving
Varna, there appeared a sort of proclamation or general order, stating that it was decided to invade the
Crimea ; a most unnecessary publication, which in all
probability was despatched forthwith by boat to Odessa
and to Sebastopol by Russian spies. The author was
summoned at 9 P.M., on Thursday the 28th August,
to take orders for embarking his brigade the following
morning. It would have been just as easy to give two
days' notice. The place where the orders were taken
was at General Bentinck's tent, about a mile and
a half from that of Sir Colin Campbell. General
Bentinck was the senior, and the Duke was on board ;
so there was a mile and a half to ride, a very long
and minute order to be taken down ; then a mile and

a half back, after which the order had to be read to
Sir Colin, and the adjutants to be summoned, who
had then to copy the orders, to communicate them to
the commanding-officers of their respective battalions,
occupying them half the night, for no assignable
reason. Nothing could surpass the kindness and
activity of the navy officers whose duty it was to
embark the troops. The author, in Letter XXIII.,
supposes that the troops would be disembarked and
entrenched, and that the transports would immediately return for all the animals left behind. Why
this was not done, has never been explained in a
satisfactory manner. In the 24th Letter, the author
makes his first remark upon the number of brigadiers
found by the Guards, which evil was afterwards increased ; a matter very fully entered into in this work.
It is so difficult to explain this question to civilians,
that the repetition must be pardoned, supposing the
complaint to be well founded.

## LETTER XXIII.

Steam-transport Emeu, Varna Bay,
2d September 1854.

IN my last I told you we were very near our time
for embarking. The order came very suddenly, in the
middle of the night, and a precious job they made of

it. However, the whole army may be said to be on board, with the exception of some thousand horses and mules, which are left on the hill-side to take their chance, and that but a poor one. I have left, of my own property, horses and mules to the value of 235*l.* The order to the army to invade the Crimea is out, and is now an historical fact. The fleet and transports rendezvous at Balchick Bay, some fifteen miles north of Varna, from whence 900 sail of ships, great and small, will start in a body for an unknown point of disembarkation. Among these there will be more than 100 large English steamers. The infantry will land by divisions ; first the Light Division, and then the 1st, 2d, 3d, and 4th. I make out 24,000 rank and file, besides sergeants, bands, officers, &c., and sixty guns, with five regiments of Light Cavalry. It is evident from the orders given that our leaders expect to land without any opposition. We are to carry nothing on shore with us except ammunition and three days' provisions ; and I suppose it is intended to throw up entrenchments until the ships can return and bring the remainder of the baggage, horses, mules, &c. The French army in Turkey, nominally 80,000 strong, is sadly reduced. Canrobert's division of Zouaves and Chasseurs de Vincennes amounted to 13,000 men ; it is doubted whether he can bring 4000 men into the field. The difference in the health of the two armies is very creditable to the English officers, and shows that they have attended with much care and judgment to the comfort and discipline of their men.

We are now on the crest of the wave, just going to take the plunge ; there has not been sent such an expedition from England since that unfortunate one under Lord Chatham.    Considering the distance from home, it is very well done, and the troops are full of heart.    *Prosit !*    I do not think writing will be possible ; if we fight, it will be all in the papers.    The story of England's prowess will make a page in history, which tells all but the important part, viz. the millions of thoughts, hopes, desires, and despairs, living till the last moment in the human units making up an army.    In the cold bivouac, or when the bullets are whistling round me, I shall have my share of these.

## LETTER XXIV.

Emeu steam-transport at sea, ninety miles
west of Cape Tarkan, in the Crimea,
8th September 1854.

WE are now very near our landing-place, they say ; but, indeed, no one knows.  We set out from Balchick Bay yesterday, and made a very imposing spectacle. So many ships, perhaps, never sailed together in one organised body before.    Last night there was a bright

full moon, and we saw the ships almost as plain as
by day. The look-out man on Cape Chersonese will
lift up his hands with astonishment when he sees us.

Sunday, 10th September.

At anchor about sixty miles west of Cape Tarkan,
and 110 from Cape Chersonese, that is, Sebastopol.

The whole fleet, French and English, anchored
last night, of course out of sight of land, but nearer
Odessa than any other place. The report is, that we
sail again this afternoon, and make land somewhere
to-morrow morning ; who knows in what part of Russia ? Cholera is on board ; we have lost six men by
it since we embarked, and one fell overboard in his
sleep. No one seems to be much alarmed. We are
to land without tents ; in fact, men and officers with
no more than each can carry ; sleep on the ground *al
fresco*. It sounds uncomfortable, especially if we are
under fire all the time, as is likely ; for I cannot believe that the Russians will not make a vigorous defence. However, I do not wish to be any where else
than where I am. With regard to the ⸺ regiment, about which you write, I can assure you that
the whole military society with which I am acquainted
condemns the habits prevailing in that ill-regulated
corps as much as you could do. The cowardly pre-
varication of the officers when examined is the real
blot ; all the rest is a trifle, I think. Mr. ⸺, I dare

say, was a muff of a disagreeable sort, who fell among a vulgar set of people, who took vulgar means to rid themselves of him. The result must be, that those of the officers who have committed themselves will have to retire, or stand a court-martial; and probably most of the officers will be moved into other corps, and the whole clique will be broken up. We are now going on serious business, where such fooleries would not be thought of; but no such scenes can ever occur without detection and prevention in any good regiment, like this 42d now in the Emeu with us. I am not going to proceed on the hopeless task of persuading you that all is sound in the army. Jobs of all sorts are perpetrated perpetually. There are ten brigades, three of them commanded by Guardsmen,—that is, seven battalions of Guards supply three brigadiers, and ninety-nine battalions of the Line only supply seven. That speaks volumes; and these men got their rank while walking about St. James's Street. They command companies for the discipline of which they are not responsible; and they remain posted over us, a standing provocation. Very likely, when once on shore, I shall not be able to write to you. We are to carry three days' cooked provisions with us—that is, cold pork and biscuit, and a canteen of water; and make good our ground against all comers. It is a remarkable expedition, and will have many historians to record our exploits, and recount our success or our failure. The latter I think scarcely possible ; but there is always a chance of it ; and if that chance should turn against us, the memory of the defeat will be stamped in such characters of blood as will put half England in mourning. My share will be no ignoble one. My place is at the head of the column, and the front of the line ; where danger is rifest, there must the brigade-major be. The Highlanders' plumes will wave round my path ; their wild shouts and wilder pipes will sound my triumph or my coronach ; and the glittering bayonets will flash terror and defiance wherever I go.

Monday, 11th September.

Just getting under way. We do not yet know in what direction we are to steer ; but it must be decided soon, as the whole fleet is getting ready. We waited yesterday for the French sailing-liners, which were all behind. Many dead of cholera in various transports.

Emeu, 13th September.

We have been anchoring and keeping the fleet together until now. This morning we started down the coast from near Eupatoria, and are aiming for a point very near Sebastopol ; the signal is flying, " Make every preparation for landing the troops." I do not, however, think this can be accomplished until to-morrow.

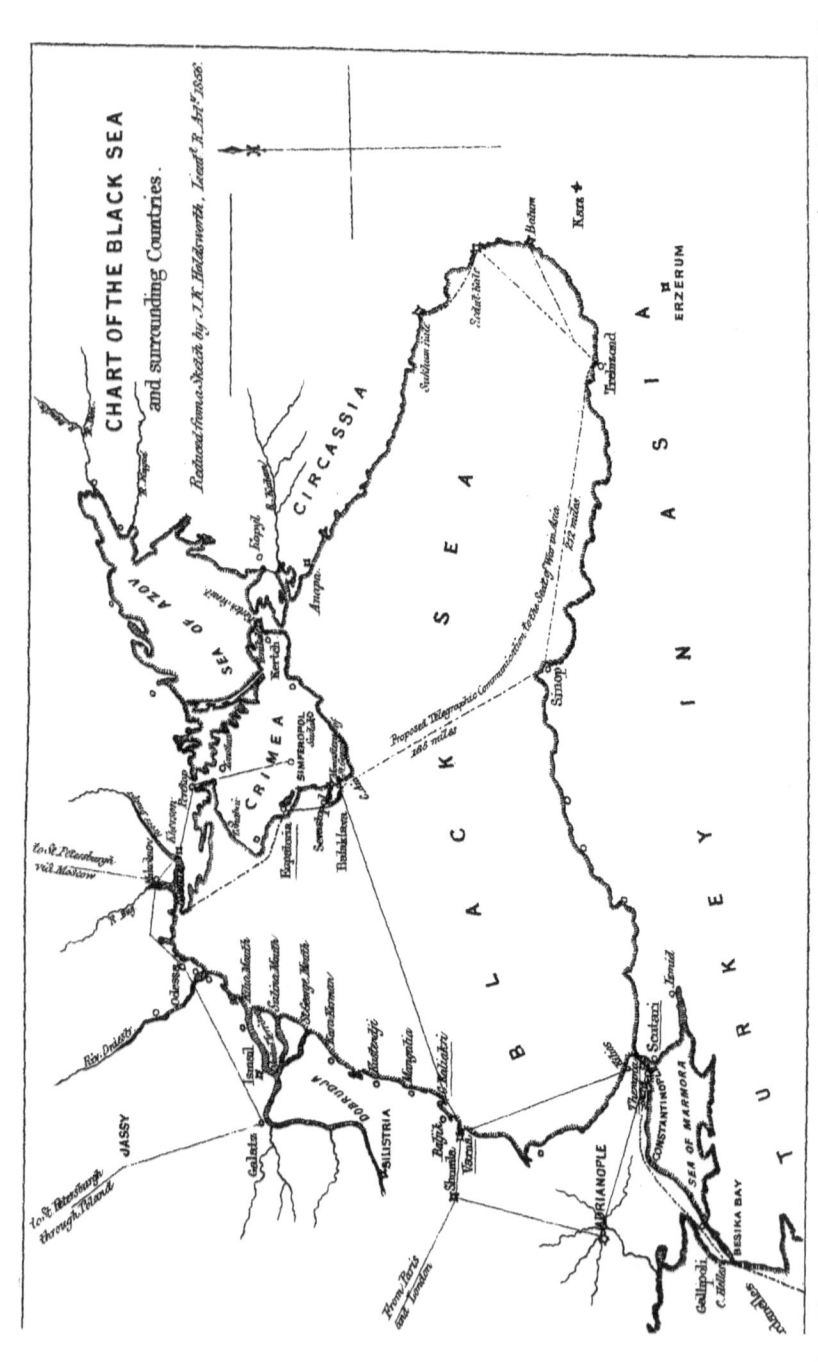

CHART OF THE BLACK SEA
and surrounding Countries.

Reduced from a Sketch by I.K. Holdsworth, Lieut.ᵗ R. Art.ʸ 1855.

IT is to be remarked, that, although most minute and precise instructions had been issued, and even a plan drawn for this disembarkation, yet the previously arranged plan was not adhered to. Probably finding no enemy was the reason; the only thing insisted on was the abandonment of the knapsacks. Such a thing was never heard of, unless for the moment of an assault. Canrobert's Zouaves threw down their packs (*sacs à terre*) before storming the heights of Alma; but a company was left to guard them, and they were recovered immediately after the action was over. St. Arnaud says significantly in his letters, speaking of the English, "J'ai le flair militaire; les Anglais n'ont pas fait la guerre depuis 1815;" as much as to say, they do not know their business.

## LETTER XXV.

Camp, near Lake Touzla,
18th September 1854.

LANDED on 14th; heavy rain all that night. Our horses were to have been landed for us, but they were not sent ashore till dark. I carried on my shoulders and about me a great deal that ought to have been on my horse; stood weighted all day; and at last had to march five miles in that state, which quite knocked me up. I had a small tent which I bought in London, and which was landed and left on the beach ; however, some of the servants were good-natured enough to bring it along ; so that our party were, I imagine, the only people who had a tent the first night. We are only twenty-five miles from Sebastopol, and shall move on to the attack the moment the artillery and reserve ammunition is up. Colonel S. and the Aide-de-camp went very early in the morning of the 15th to a village near at hand, and bought a pony, and hired two boys, with their oxen, and a barrel on wheels for water, which is likely to be of vast service to us.

We have seen no enemy as yet, but have had a false alarm at night ; I suppose not unusual with troops that have no experience in the field.

---

## LETTER *XXV.

### SIR COLIN CAMPBELL'S DESPATCH AFTER THE BATTLE OF THE ALMA.

*To Colonel the Honourable A. Gordon, Assistant Adjutant-General 1st Division.*

21st September 1854.

SIR,—I have the honour to state for the information of H.R.H. the Duke of Cambridge, commanding the division, that the division being deployed into line in rear of the Light Division, H.R.H. directed it to move forward in support of that division when it commenced its passage of the Alma. In marching across the descent, some few men of the 42d were struck down by cannon-shot. On entering the low ground, through which the stream flowed, the advance became exceedingly difficult, gardens and vineyard-enclosures breaking the order of formation most completely. The 42d and Coldstream Guards having found fewer obstacles than the regiments on the left, reached the left bank first, hastily ascended the bank and began to form on its summit; the 93d and 79th did the same as soon as they could get through. The 42d and the brigade of Guards being formed on the bank, and the 93d and 79th rapidly establishing themselves in the same position, while the attack of the troops of the Light Division on the central redoubt had failed, and the enemy had marched out in pursuit, H.R.H. determined upon an immediate attack. The 42d, somewhat in advance, was ordered to ascend the heights in front, the immediate object being to turn the redoubt while the attack in front was made by the Guards. This flank-movement was completely successful, the 42d continuing its advance with the 93d and 79th in direct echelon on its left. While the troops in this formation were moving in advance, they were exposed to the fire of five guns posted in a battery on the heights on our left front, which also contained riflemen. These guns were

withdrawn on the near approach of the Highlanders.
The 42d, being the leading regiment, gained the
heights first, and found a large body of Russian
troops, which had just quitted the central redoubt,
endeavouring to form to its front with another large
body already posted there. The 42d continued to
advance, firing in line, drove these troops before them
in confusion, and caused them great loss. On reaching the crest of the hill on the enemy's side, another
mass was met, endeavouring to support the retiring
enemy. As these troops were coming on, the 93d
arrived most opportunely, and defeated them. While
the 93d were still engaged, another body of Russians
from their extreme right moved down direct on the
flank of the 93d ; but at this moment the 79th had
reached the ground, and opened fire upon them, causing them to retreat in great confusion.

Thus the three regiments of the Highland Brigade
were formed in line on the inner crest of the enemy's
position, having driven all the large bodies of troops
which were posted there down into the valley, upon a
mass of troops which were placed in reserve on the
heights in their rear. An attempt was made by this
reserve to move in advance, forcing forward the retiring troops ; but fire being again opened, this reserve
returned to its position, evidently with a view to cover
the troops which had been driven by the three Highland regiments. At this time three guns of the Horse

Artillery, under Captain Maude, arrived on the left flank of the 79th, and three of Captain Brandling's troop formed on the right of the 42d. The fire of these guns was very effective upon the enemy in their retreat.

I have thought it right to enter into these details, in order that justice may be done to these young soldiers, who moved up to the attack under fire, led by their respective commanding officers,—Colonel Cameron 42d, Lieutenant-Colonel Ainslie 93d, and Lieutenant-Colonel Douglas 79th,—in the same order and with as much precision as if they had been on an ordinary parade. I never saw officers and men, one and all, exhibit greater steadiness and gallantry, giving evidence of the high state of their instruction and discipline, and of the noble spirit with which they are animated ; and I am happy to say that from the rapidity of their movements their loss was very small.

I beg H.R.H. to do me the favour of recommending these officers and troops to the favourable notice of the Commander-in-chief. I have also to request he will do the same for the officers of my staff—Lieutenant-Colonel Sterling, Brigade-Major, and Captain Shadwell, A.D.C., to whom I am under the greatest obligations for the services they rendered me on this and on every other occasion. Lieutenant Mansfield, extra A.D.C., who had lately joined my staff, made

himself extremely useful, and exhibited all the best
qualities of an officer.

I have, &c.

(Signed)    C. CAMPBELL.

THE Duke of Wellington said the history of a
battle was like the history of a ball.  In Marshal
St. Arnaud's letters the English are scarcely mentioned, and one would conclude, from what he says,
that they took scarcely any part.  The present author
states what he saw, with the addition of a few sent-
ences here and there, corrected by the recollections of
Lieut.-Col. Shadwell, aide-de-camp to Sir Colin Campbell at the passage of the Alma.  The author says
that some of our troops were not well handled.  The
leading troops were kept too long under cannon-fire
without advancing; the officers commanding battalions were not allowed to form after they got their
men through the river; consequently the rush against
the Russian centre battery was made in confusion,
and was unsuccessful.

In the annexed Plan the path of Sir Colin Campbell and the 42d is marked, and the 42d were where
they are shown on this Plan when the Guards got
possession of the centre battery, or breastwork, from

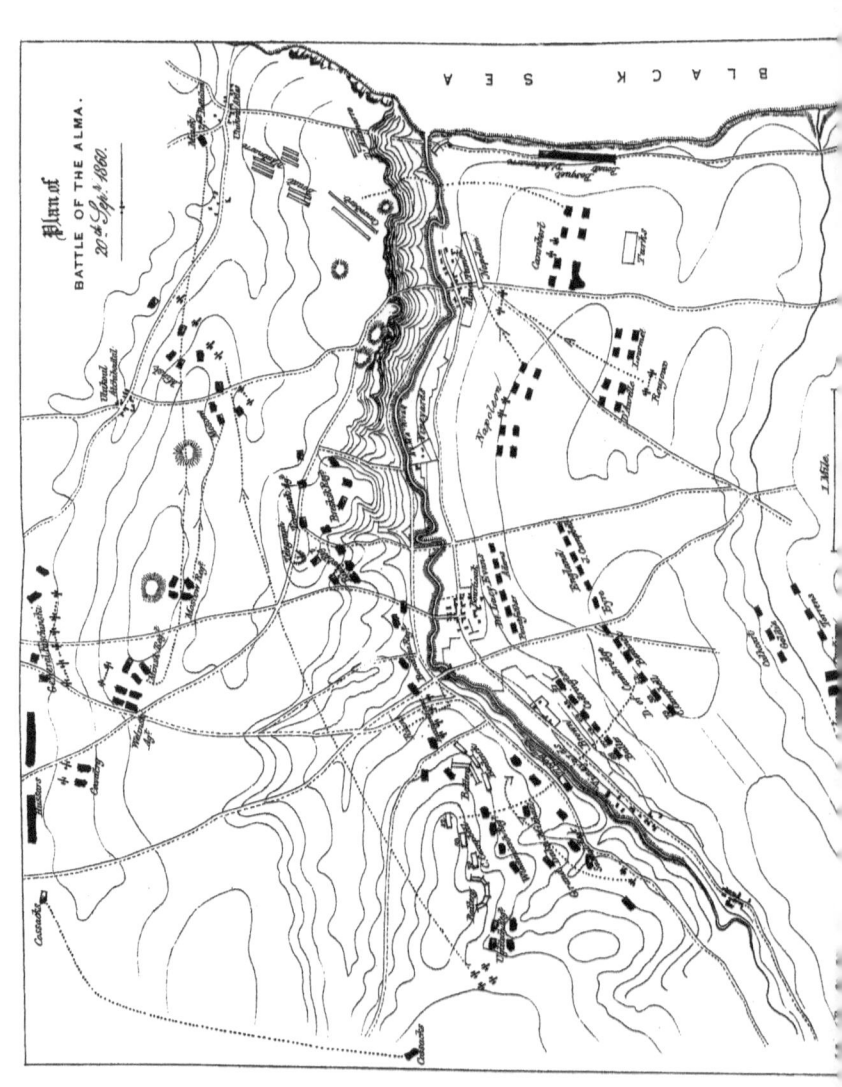

Plan of
BATTLE OF THE ALMA.
20.th Sep.r 1860.

BLACK SEA

1 Mile

which the Light Division had been repulsed. The
Russians are placed where they were on the Russian
plan, but the Grand-Duke Michael's troops were not
where they are shown when the 42d crossed the river;
those whom the Highlanders encountered were further
from the river. Buller's brigade came up behind the
Highlanders, and formed in their rear. The ground
on the right bank of the Alma was flatter than it is
shown in the Plan, and decidedly lower than the Russian position. The left bank, where the 42d forded
the river, appears correct, and the regiment formed
under the bank before advancing.

## LETTER XXVI.

Field of battle, 21st September 1854.

YESTERDAY we fought the battle which will be
called the Passage of the Alma. We advanced for
some hours across a beautiful grassy plain, in great
columns flanked by skirmishers, with the cavalry and
guns in the centre. About noon we got sight of the
Russian army, in position on the heights above the
Alma, with entrenched batteries and every preparation. Our united numbers were, including English,
French, and Turks, about 50,000 infantry; and we
estimated the enemy's force opposite to us at 40,000
of the same arm; but they had heavy guns in position,

and were very strongly posted. The French began by
attacking the left of the Russians, near the sea, and
our army attacked in front. Some of our troops were
by no means well handled, and, after taking the centre
battery, were driven back. We, who were following
them, soon got to the river, after struggling through
some vineyards. When C. got into the bed of the
river, and could see along the left bank, he perceived
that the Light Division was in a mess. " By God !"
said he, " those regiments are not moving like English
soldiers." He immediately ordered the 42d to form
as rapidly as possible on the south, or enemy's bank,
and sent orders to the 93d and 79th to do the same
as soon as they could. The Duke at this time came
up to him, and C. energetically recommended an immediate advance, saying, that "he foresaw a disaster
unless we did so." The 42d were pushed on at once
by him, marching over the 77th regiment, which was
lying down. The soldiers of this regiment called out
to us, " You are madmen, and will be all killed !" The
42d by this advance necessarily turned the Russians
out of the centre battery, and enabled the Guards, in
their second attempt, to get into it without any resistance.

The effect of his manœuvre was foretold by C.
before the 42d moved, showing the advantage of a
general with a true tactical eye. We made a deliberate parade-movement of regiments in echelon, right

in front, up the highest hill. I was sent to the left
to form the 79th in column, to be safe from the Russian cavalry. The 79th afterwards deployed. The
42d was the right regiment, and was the first formed.
I got back from the left in time to go up the hill with
it. The men never looked back, and took no notice
of the wounded. They ascended in perfect silence,
and without firing a shot. On crowning the hill, we
found a large body of Russians, who vainly tried to
stand before us. Our manœuvre was perfectly decisive, as we got on the flank of the Russians in the
centre battery, into which we looked from the top of
the hill, and I saw the Guards rush in as the Russians
abandoned it. The Guards were not moved on quite
so soon as our brigade, and suffered far more, poor
fellows. The end was, killing and wounding a many
innocent Russians and a many innocent English, and
making the Russians leave that ; but it was very
glorious; and we have to do the same thing on new
ground to-morrow, and perhaps once more before we
reach the port of Sebastopol. The feeling of a battle
is not very exciting to me, and the sight afterwards
is very horrid. I hope we shall soon be able to take
the place, and finish for the autumn; for no change
of clothes, and sleeping on the ground, is very disagreeable. C. had his horse shot under him, and we
all had plenty of bullets flying about us. I saw a
Russian skirmisher, a great big fellow, come within

forty yards, and take a deliberate shot at Colonel S.
He made two or three men on the right of the 42d
turn to their right and fire at him; but the fellows
missed him. Our brigade lost one officer, and about
one hundred men, which was very fortunate, as some
regiments lost as many as ten officers. Our getting
off so easily was mainly owing to the admirable leading of C., and the pace we went, which got us to
the top of the hill before the Russians. The dead
Russians were well fed and clothed, with very clean
linen and capital kits. Meantime they are burning
the villages, and all the horrors of war go on. J. B.
has now got the beginning of his butcher's bill; before we take Sebastopol it will make a pretty amount.
I do not know when there will be an opportunity for
sending letters, so I shall keep this one ready in my
pocket. If it does not go to day, there will be another
battle to-morrow, and perhaps it will not go at all. I
shall keep it open.

21st, in the evening.

The Fleet reports that the beaten Russians have
gone right into Sebastopol, so we shall advance to the
siege without further impediment. Our army has lost
about 2000 in killed and wounded, and we are busy
in burying the dead. I have nothing to add, except
that the Russians thought we should be three weeks
in forcing this position, and we did it in less than
three hours! Effectual people are the English.

THE last letter ends on the evening of the 21st
(Thursday). On Saturday the army marched to the
Katscha River, and passed it without any opposition.
On Sunday the 24th they crossed the Belbek, and
camped there ; and on Monday struck off by compass,
through the wild brushwood, direct for Mackenzie's
Farm, steering a course about south-east. They descended by the Mackenzie-Farm road, crossed the
Chernaya at Traktir, and very late in the night, after
a long march, finally encamped on the Feduchine
heights. During this march, it is probable that many
men were lost in the coppices, having knocked up.
These men were probably afterwards picked up by the
Cossacks. At Mackenzie's Farm the advanced troops
fell in with the baggage of a Russian column, which
had marched the same morning out of Sebastopol,
going to Bakchi Serai. If the British army had moved
off two hours sooner, there would have been another
engagement. The policy of this flank-march to gain
a new base will always remain a subject for debate.
The original plan had been, there is no doubt, to
make a *coup-de-main* against Sebastopol; and it may
be surmised that if St. Arnaud had not been dying,
this would have been attempted. The only thing
really to impede its success would have been the fire
from the Russian fleet in the harbour. Fort Sever-
naya was a poor work, very much dilapidated. The

attack upon it would have fallen to the French; the English army would have swept round the head of the harbour, bringing up its left shoulder, and would have attacked the Malakoff, at that time a simple round tower, with two guns on the top and casemates. As they had with them no battering guns, their only plan would have been to get so close that the Russian gunners would have been unable to depress their guns so as to reach the beleaguring foe; and a miner would have been attached to the wall on the first night. There is every probability that this rush would have succeeded; and whatever the loss might have been, it would have been infinitely less than what was incurred by the plan adopted. No instructed military mind can approve of an attempt to besiege without investing. At the same time it seems extremely likely that the long siege was the proximate cause of peace, as without it Russia would not have been so much exhausted. However, on Tuesday morning, the 26th, the army moved on, and got possession of Balaklava without difficulty.

## LETTER XXVII.

Bivouack, Balaklava, 28th September 1854.

I WROTE you a hurried note after the battle of the Alma, which I could not even look over. We have

since seen nothing of the Russians, except the tail
of a column which marched out of Balaklava to
meet their reinforcements from Anapa. We have
now marched completely round Sebastopol, and have
gained possession of the harbour of Balaklava, where
the Agamemnon is now moored. This becomes our
new base. They are landing the siege-train; and we
shall no doubt advance immediately to break ground
and begin. It is probable they will make an obstinate resistance; but all sieges come to an end in a
time which can be calculated. War is a horrid thing;
not merely the field of battle itself is hideous, but the
ruin of the poor helpless inhabitants. We came down
here unexpectedly; the men were not drunk, and
were quite obedient to their officers. The orders were
distinct as to not injuring property; yet the village
(Kadikoi) close to the camp of this division, where
the Duke has his quarters, was completely gutted in
half an hour. The inhabitants had run away. The
men seemed to do it out of fun; they broke boxes
and drawers that were open, and threw the fragments
into the street. The battle of the Alma must, during
its progress, have been a grand sight to spectators
who had time to admire. The cool advance of the
English under fire surprised our French allies. It is
acknowledged by them that we had much the worst
part of the position to take. Our brigade was very
lucky in not losing many officers or men. Some

other regiments suffered frightfully. The 23d lost thirteen officers, of whom nine were killed. This regiment, and the 19th and 33d, bore the brunt of the enemy's first fire from the centre battery. After passing the river, they were not allowed to form, but attacked in confusion, and were driven back; then our division, which was behind them, after some hesitation, was advanced. I believe C.'s advice, and his war-experience, were found very useful. In the Brigade of Guards, the Fusilier regiment, which was the centre one, was broken, and driven back with great loss. They got mixed with the beaten regiments of the Light Division, which retreated through them, and put them into confusion. The moment our bonnets topped the hill, on the left of the Guards, the Russians gave way. But it was pretty critical: if we had waited ten minutes, or even five minutes more, the Russians would have been on the crest of the hill first, and God knows what would have been the loss of the Highland Brigade, even if we had succeeded in pushing them back. When we got half way up the hill, I saw it was all right. We killed an awful lot of Russians; the whole ground in our front, for hundreds of yards, was strewed with dead and wounded.

## LETTER XXVIII.*

Bivouack, before Sebastopol, 3d October 1854.

I HAVE at last got a substitute for a table, and can by means of that luxury write a little more at ease. They say that a mail will go out to-day; so I must try and tell you something about us. We live a very strange life, never taking our clothes off; that is, since the 14th September, when we landed. Yesterday the officers were provided with tents; but the men still lie down on the ground without cover, but couched in such appliances of hay and straw as they can pick up. I have had a small tent all the time, except one or two nights. The difficulty about tents is the want of means to carry them; but now that we are fairly set down for a siege, I hope the soldiers will get this comfort sent up from Balaklava. I have had a good look from the heights into Sebastopol. The town is not very large, but the defences look stiff, and are increasing. We may easily be kept here some weeks. The heavy battering-guns must be all landed, and brought seven or eight miles, and batteries must be made to hold them. The ground is very unfavourable for digging; so much so, that I apprehend we shall

---

* The 1st Division, consisting of the Guards and Highlanders, with the exception of the 93d, which was left behind at Kadikoi, moved up to their camp before Sebastopol on Monday the 3d October, the day on which this letter was written.

have to use sandbags. It is said Menschikoff means to try and relieve the place, which he ought to attempt; but he will scarcely get a sufficient force up in time. We are now, you understand, on the south side of Sebastopol harbour, where the town is; but the Russians have got free ingress and egress north and east, as our army is not large enough to surround the whole place. We are just out of shot. The Russian batteries very often fire both round shot and shells at the out-picquets; doing no harm, however. Cholera continues carrying off officers and men; but our party continues healthy. The Turkish part of the population here will join us, and bring in supplies, as soon as we take Sebastopol; but they are afraid of committing themselves at present, as the Cossacks are continually roaming about, and our cavalry are not very clever at outpost duty. I am writing in the open air at half-past 5 A.M.; there has been a heavy dew in the night, and it is very sharp for the fingers; but the sun soon gets power, and then it is, if any thing, too hot. Certainly the climate is charming, that is to say, for those who dwell in houses. As to us, the common decencies, not to say comforts, of life are denied, and many of the officers grumble openly. They have no transport, and have to march loaded with heavy cloaks, besides provisions, and till yesterday had no tents. Now an officer's duty begins when the march is over; for he has then to look after his men, and he cannot do it efficiently if he is fagged. However, the excuse is the impossibility of finding transport, or food for the animals if we had them. I do not admit the excuse on the part of the commissary, for there must be lots of empty ships to send for mules and forage. We wait anxiously to hear what you think of our victory in England, and whether we had enough killed and wounded to please you.

You will have another butcher's bill at the storming of the works; and perhaps a general action when Lüders and Liprandi come up, which will make the autumn newspapers very cheerful for those who have friends out here. The sun is just rising, and shooting straight into my eyes, not a cloud any where. Peace profound! Yet advance a mile, and you will certainly be fired at.

## LETTER XXIX.

Bivouack, before Sebastopol,
4th October 1854.

I WROTE to you by yesterday's post, and just afterwards I heard of ——, who was quite well, and took an acquaintance of mine round his troop to show the miserable state of the horses, which are worn down with fatigue and want of food. We hope daily for the arrival of the French Dragoons, who will lighten

H

the work of the outposts. They are getting up siege-artillery and ship-guns as fast as they can; we hourly expect orders to begin making trenches and batteries. Meantime the only thing warlike around us is an occasional shell thrown at the infantry outlying picquets. But cholera, I am sorry to say, is increasing among officers and men. Hitherto we have not been able to get up tents for our poor fellows, who lie on the bare ground with their greatcoats and blankets; but some few tents have been distributed to-day, and I hope for more. I understand we shall have 199 heavy guns in position to batter the defences; and most likely, when once we open, the affair will soon be over. What our course will be afterwards must depend upon orders from home. I see the *Times* is inclined to make us destroy every thing, and go away. That is not my policy. I would send more troops, and keep Crim Tartary as a material guarantee and a stepping-stone next year to Georgia. Nick will not give in till he is more beaten. Our force is diminishing daily by disease, and we lost 2000 at the Alma. The Russians, it is supposed, lost from 6000 to 8000. They have an army now hanging on our flank, and talk of 40,000 more coming; so that another general action is quite likely to finish this campaign; but when they have not a strong position fortified with heavy guns, I believe we could beat double our numbers. At the Alma, so far as I could

see,* our artillery did no good at all in the way of
beating the enemy; they only pounded them a little
when they were retreating. It was the British Infantry, the invincibles, who won the battle. I have
had a great deal of trouble with the Guards; they
do not relieve our sentries in time. I spoke to their
Brigade-Major, and General ———— heard me. I
pointed out to the Brigade-Major one of our sentries
close by who ought to have been relieved. General
———— felt the reproach was just, got into a rage,
and turned upon me in the most insolent manner.
When I went back to our camp, I asked C. to protect me. He called on General ————, who would
say nothing in the way of apology—"he would be
damned if he would;" so I have only to cut him. It
is very provoking; for, away from duty, I like these
Guardsmen very much; but our division marriage is,
like some other marriages, an unhappy one. My
Highland bonnet is ready, and I shall wear it the
first time we go into fire. It will make us a very
distinguished staff, as all the others wear cocked-hats.
The existence just now is miserable; with my habits,
not to have a book at all, and to have a young fellow,
quite a stranger, living in the same tent with me.

---

* Lord Raglan brought up some guns on the British right,
which took the Russians in reverse; but this could not be seen
from the ground where the Highlanders stood.

We get little to eat here but salt pork and biscuit,—
no vegetables,—and spirits and water, tea without
milk; our baggage on board ship; most of our horses
and animals left behind, and probably lost to us for
ever. However, it is part of the war, and without
these sacrifices I suppose we could not have made this
invasion, which is a blow that will disconcert Nicholas wonderfully, especially if we succeed in beating his
army in the field once •more. One beating may be
explained away, but a second will satisfy him that we
are too much for him and his vaunted army. The
place where we are bivouacked is bare and desolate.
By riding a little forward, we can see into the town,
and watch the Russian soldiers strengthening their
works and preparing the batteries. It is supposed we
shall not fire a gun till the whole 199 are ready to
open with a grand crash, smashing ships, and works,
and town, into one everlasting ruin. The inhabitants
of Sebastopol, if the Russian generals permit it, have
free egress to the north. Now I hope the poor women
and children will be spared the horrible scene; the
men, I suppose, they will keep to work and fight for
their town. At the Alma I rode my chestnut horse,
and he behaved wonderfully, taking no sort of notice
of shot, shell, nor musketry; neither did he shy at
the dead bodies with which the ground was covered;
for though we lost few men (100), yet we killed a
tremendous number: the hill opposite, over which

the Russians fled, was quite thickly strewed with
dead and wounded, abandoned packs, and broken
arms, the work of the Highland Brigade: their
Minié's seem to shoot very strong. Lord Raglan's
eyes filled with tears when he shook hands with C. ;
and he could not speak when the brave old veteran
said to him, pointing to the killed, " Sir, it was they
who did it." And then the cheer when he asked to
wear a bonnet ! With its horrors, war has its ro-
mance.

6th October.

We are always under arms, and ready to move an
hour before daylight. This morning there was a lively
skirmish with a patrol of Cossacks just in front of us ;
the bullets came whizzing past us, and the line of
flashes from the muskets in the pale light of the
morning moon was very picturesque. We may expect something of this sort every morning till our
batteries are ready, when the attacks will be more
serious. I have now reason to believe that it is the
intention to abandon this place, and embark the army,
after destroying Sebastopol. The army has dwindled
down sadly from wounds and disease. Without large
reinforcements, I think we could not keep the field
against the enemy, who probably has much exaggerated our numbers. We have just got tents to cover
our men, so that I hope the cholera may be arrested.
What is our course to be if we go into winter-quar-

ters, having done nothing except taking Sebastopol? Nicholas will not make peace, I feel convinced; and where can we pinch him again? To make this army fit to take the field next spring with success, we must have our regiments completed, and an addition to the force of 15,000 or 20,000 men. Will England, or can England, do that? The expense will be the least part. This morning mourning has been diffused through thousands of families; for on this morning, by my calculation, the *Times* must have published the despatches with all the names of killed and wounded. An appeal must be made to the Militia. Boys will not do, they cannot stand the fatigue; bone and sinew must come, men of twenty-four or twenty-five years old; and one campaign will age many of them by a dozen years. That is war, horrible war. The fighting is nothing to the wear and tear of spirits and mind and body. In this country our soldiers can get nothing to drink, and they behave admirably. In winter-quarters they will make up for this, and we shall have to punish these splendid fellows who have this main vice. Meantime, speed engineers, get up the heavy guns. The Russian troops are no doubt streaming down from the Danube, where the Austrians have set them free; and it is on the cards that our prey may still be rescued from us. Lüders has come with a considerable force, and I daily expect to find our communications with Balaklava threatened; ano-

ther action and another list of deaths is impending.
Should we, however, take the place and then embark,
I imagine they will not molest us, having had a lesson
how we fight.  If I was England, I would send out
another 50,000 men, conquer the Crimea, and go to
Georgia, smiting hip and thigh.  But they will not
do it; half measures and hopes of peace will undo us.
Layard is here, also Kinglake, who was in the battle,
and Cayley.  The Retribution has just returned from
the Isthmus of Perekop, and reports very large bodies
of Russian troops on their march here.  Rumour
makes them 80,000 or 90,000 ; we know of 30,000
having left Odessa.  Our little army is already hemmed
round, and we just keep our communications open
with Balaklava.  This morning, at daybreak, I went
to post the outlying picquets on our right flank, with
Cameron and Shadwell.  We found the officer in command in bed in a tent fast asleep.  Conceive, on outlying picquet !  While there I saw a considerable
body of Russian cavalry in the valley below.  They
advanced, with their skirmishers in front, to within
two miles of Balaklava.  There they drove in a small
picquet of our Dragoons ; after which three regiments
of British cavalry showed themselves, which checked
the enemy, and they were finally forced to retire by
some guns which were brought up escorted by the
17th Lancers.  All this went on like a scene in a
play, just under my nose.  We must be quick in our

attack on Sebastopol, or we may be forced to embark, the thing undone, which would be very sad. The works of the place are armed with a very formidable artillery, and they have the seamen for gunners. Unless we can silence this artillery, we dare not storm ; the loss would be too frightful, besides the risk, in case of failure, of not being able to make good our retreat to the ships. It is a nervous moment for the French and English generals, and more of a toss-up than I like for the sake of my country. Large as our force was, it was not large enough. We want an army here to take the place, and another larger to beat the enemy again in the field. The post goes to-morrow, and I must keep my letter ready ; any moment may bring us into action.

---

## LETTER XXX.

Camp, before Sebastopol,
12th October 1854.

OUR preparations still go on, but we have not yet replied by a single shot or shell to many hundreds which the Russians have favoured us with. It is intended that we shall wait till all the batteries are armed. We have great working parties every night, digging approaches and making batteries ; and although the fire on the parties has been very heavy,

we have been so fortunate as to escape with very few
casualties, as they call dead and wounded men.
Whether the name softens the thing, I leave you to
judge. We are all on the alert day and night. Besides being under arms always an hour before daylight,
we are constantly turned out by alarms, real or false.
I send you a crocus which I have just gathered in the
middle of all this turmoil, mocking with its peaceful
beauty the stern and bloody aspect of war. The roar
of cannon is now unceasing, and we get but little
sleep. We are, however, all well; and the weakly
soldiers being now weeded out by disease and over-
fatigue, our men are pretty healthy. I cannot make
up my mind on the question as to our abiding here
for the winter. The baggage of some of the regiments
is come, which looks like staying; but, on the other
hand, if it did not come, or if it went elsewhere, that
would announce our intended departure after destroying Sebastopol, which it would not be wise to confide
to the enemy. The position the allied armies now occupy is immensely strong, and reinforcements, French
and Turkish, are coming, besides our own sick, as
they recover, who are sent from Scutari or Varna. I
believe the united force is nigh 80,000 men, who in
this position, Sebastopol being taken, might bid defiance to double their number, supposing them supplied
with clothing, food, and gunpowder. We are all in
rags—you never saw such figures; but the arms are

bright and the courage high. We are now told that
our guns will open in two days; but I do not think
that certain: there are so many details which must
be attended to and verified before we can be sure that
every thing is ready. This delay saves life; for what
the guns do not perform for us, must eventually be
brought about by storming with our glorious infantry,
at a frightful loss, which will read very well in the
*Gazette* no doubt, but will to the well-informed be an
index of the incapacity of our Engineers and Artillery,
and their subordinate departments. When the Duke
of Wellington in Spain made his sieges, he was not
provided with such siege-trains as we have, and he
was threatened by a French relieving army, under
French Marshals, who could not be waited for nor
trifled with. For such an attack the Russians are
very inferior stuff to the French. —— is, I believe,
near Balaklava; but I can never get away, my time
being entirely taken up with issuing orders and seeing
to their execution. I feel little excitement with all
that is going on round me, but do my duty like a horse
in a mill. The poor rank and file are wonderful:
with nothing to gain and all to lose, they submit to
the hardest manual labour, and confront the highest
perils, without a murmur, and even cheerfully; and
as they cannot get drink beyond the daily gill of
rum, there is no crime. I am called away on duty.

HERE comes a change of scene. The cavalry skirmish mentioned in Letter XXIX. as having taken
place on the 4th October, during the relief of the
outlying picquets, was only the forerunner of the approach of Liprandi with his corps towards Balaklava.
On the 14th October, Col. Steele, the military secretary, rode up to Sir Colin Campbell's tent about eight
o'clock in the morning, while he was at breakfast, and
told him Lord Raglan wished him to go and take
command of the troops at Balaklava, consisting at
that time of the 93d Highlanders at Kadikoi, a weak
battalion of invalids, picked from all the army, stationed in Balaklava, two battalions of Marines, some
Marine Artillery, and several thousand Turks. When
Sir Colin got down to Kadikoi, he found the redoubts
on the hills along the Woronzow Road already begun,
and also Battery No. 4, in rear of the 93d, already
existing. He pushed on the works with all possible
vigour. The author went down to join his chief on
the 16th October; and here they both remained until
the 18th June 1855, just eight months. The annexed Plan gives a view of the position; the same
Plan will be introduced with the additional defences
as they are added, and will also show the part of the
hills opposite Kadikoi, and the lines of Balaklava,
which were held by the Russians for several weeks
after the battle of Balaklava.

## LETTER XXXI.

Camp, in front of Balaklava,
17th October 1854.

You will be amused at the turn of events. Here I am among the Turks. You know I was very busy carrying on the siege of Sebastopol. On the 14th they became alarmed about a force said to be coming along the south coast of the Crimea to attack our rear, and drive us from Balaklava harbour ; upon which C. was suddenly ordered down here, six miles to the rear, to take charge of the defences of this place. One of our regiments (the 93d) had been left here. C., and his Aide-de-camp Shadwell, went off immediately, and left me with the 42d and 79th, under command of the senior officer (Cameron), I belonging to the Brigade. Lord Raglan afterwards wrote to C., saying that if he wished, I might join him. C. left it to me, and I decided that I could not be wrong in following such a famous soldier as C., besides loving him so much as I do. So here I am *ad interim* Assistant Adjutant-General to an Anglo-Turkish division, the Turks under command of Rustem Pasha, who speaks German, which is very convenient for me. We have two battalions of Marines, the 93d Highlanders, and eight battalions of Turkish infantry, with some artillery Turks, whom we have provided with guns to put in the redoubts which we have been ordered to make for them. We

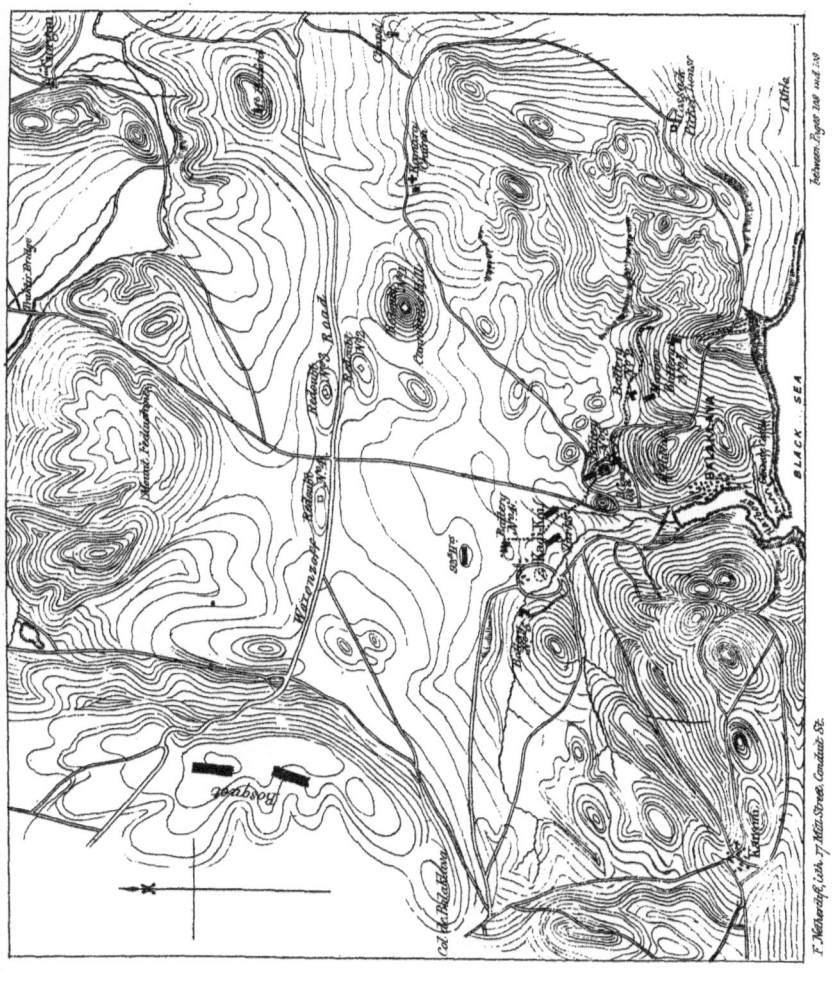

have also a battery of English artillery, and a troop
of horse artillery. There are here, moreover, two
brigades of English cavalry under Lord Lucan. The
enemy, our own particular enemy, is on the right,
about 23,000 Russians, against whom we have between 5000 and 6000. I hope we shall not be long
before we shall return to our kilted. Meantime the
English batteries opened this morning, and are pounding away hammer and tongs. So, after all the worry
of trench-making and battery-making, I shall not
perhaps have the honour of entering the place at the
head of the Highlanders. However, we may have a
battle of our own. I can well feel for the suspense
you must be in about ——. I fear this letter will go
before I can know any positive results as to the effects
of our fire on Sebastopol. Time is most important to
us, as we have Russians coming from Odessa, besides
those threatening us in the rear; and we ought if
possible to beat them in detail. At the present moment we are all standing by our arms, with the
artillery horses harnessed; the men lie down with
their belts on at night, ready to start up and fight at
any moment. You probably saw in the papers that a
young man named Nasmyth, of the Indian army, happened to be present at the siege of Silistria. Well,
this accident has been a motive sufficiently powerful
to induce the English government to transfer him as
Captain into our army, and then to make him a

Brevet-Major, and he is now *ad interim* Assistant Quartermaster-General to this Anglo-Turkish division. There is also a German engineer. These fellows take away the hard-earned rewards of our own officers, who are tied to their regiments, and worked day and night. Captain Shadwell, C.'s Aide-de-camp, was with him in three general actions in India, one of them the dreadful Chillianwallah, where C. turned the battle; and he has been since at the Alma, where C. again turned the battle; yet his Aide-de-camp has not been made a Major or an Assistant Quartermaster-General. I have just heard that Fort Pauloffsky, opposite the English right, is nearly demolished, and that four battalions of French have got behind a slight elevation, only 300 yards from Fort Nicholas, which is on the Russian right. I think it is very possible they may make a rush and get in before night. Our infantry hitherto has not moved. Depend upon it, there will be a sad account of loss both of English and French. It is now noon, and my informant himself saw eleven wounded French officers. We hear nothing of our own enemy down here. I shall not close this letter, as I shall have something more to say. The opinion is growing, that we are to stay here and keep the Crimea, which is the true policy, if we can do it. Send us more men and plenty of supplies, especially potatoes, as we eat so much salt meat. With men, food, and powder, we can do any thing.

4 P.M.

I hear the Russian fire is slackened, and Captain Peel, of the Navy, wounded. I must close. You will have a somewhat later account by the papers ; but the Correspondents have time and ways to get things off till the last moment, which are not open to me. I am tied by the leg, and dare not move away from this camp for fear of the enemy coming ; however, such is my duty.

## LETTER XXXII.

Camp, in front of Balaklava,
22d October 1854.

THE battering against Sebastopol still continues without intermission, and I do not think the British Artillery have effected quite so much as they hoped for. Sebastopol is a great arsenal, filled with guns and stores ; no sooner is a gun dismounted than they bring up another. However, I hear that Lord Raglan and his *entourage* are in high spirits about the progress, and he knows more than I do. When the ammunition brought for the siege comes near an end, they will perforce have to launch the infantry against the place and storm it, which will probably cause a great loss of life ; take it we must. Meanwhile, we of the Balaklava party are threatened continually with an attack from a very large force. It is of vital consequence to the army that we should maintain ourselves here. In about three days we expect 3000 more Turks, which will give us perhaps 6500 fighting men,—Turks, I mean, altogether,—and about 2000 British infantry, besides a battery of artillery and a troop of horse artillery. We have made lots of redoubts, but C. does not like them; and we are making batteries of position, and improving our defences daily. I feel satisfied that if we take Sebastopol, we shall remain here for the winter, with the allied armies in an immense intrenched camp. This will be a great disappointment to many of the officers who have families, and to others who only look to their own comfort, without considering their duty to England. Patriotism with the masses is but a word. When called upon to suffer fatigue and hunger, dirt and ennui, the brilliant phrase becomes dulled of its lustre, and the flesh-pots of Egypt are thought of with a sigh. The orders of Government are incomprehensible: every correspondent of a newspaper is allowed rations, without which no one can live here ; and thus, by its own arrangement, every particular of numbers of men, guns, material, ships' stores, &c. is conveyed to Nicholas in the most concise and exact manner. It is madness. The foolish officers would still do mischief enough. I have been busied making a plan of this position with our defences, and can quite imagine that if it got into the correspondents' hands, it would go straight to the *Illustrated*

*London News;* from thence, by Russian agents in London, back direct to our enemy, who is watching every opportunity to force the position and burn our ships and stores in the harbour of Balaklava. So much for our condition. About the 10th of November last year the winter set in with a cold north-east wind. We cannot inhabit tents, and shall have to construct huts, for which purpose timber must be sent over from Varna in immense quantities, and stoves and coals. Money, money! Profusion is now economy. We must also have troops. Next spring, Nicholas, if not attacked by Austria, will send every man he has to try and drive us into the sea. His numbers will only be limited by his means of feeding his men; all must be carried with them, and this is our advantage, as our ships will convey all stores to us without any difficulty. The Turkish soldiers are capital fellows, and dig better even than our own men; but we cannot speak to them further than "Buono Johnny" and "Buono Ingles." You will have racehorses called "Buono Johnny."

23d.

Some Russian officers have deserted. We hear from them that Korniloff, the governor, was killed the second day of the bombardment, and that the hero of Sinope now commands; that the inhabitants are suffering, and complaining that we burned their hospital, and have set the town on fire often, and that

the Lancaster shells have produced enormous damage
wherever they have fallen. Our artillery officers had
also discovered the merits of the Lancaster shells yesterday; they did not understand them at first, and
had their prejudices. The approaches are getting
nearer, and there is every prospect of an early possession. If we are so fortunate, I hope you will hear
that the army has turned on the Russian forces outside, who are now tormenting the Balaklava troops,
and given them a good thrashing; nothing but making Nicholas eat plenty of stick will bring him to reason. Menschikoff, the *origo mali*, is now commanding
the army opposite to us; and if he knows his business,
and dares enough, he will certainly attack us to try
and save the place. But I trust we shall beat him
back by the defences we have constructed here, where
we are in a manner besieged. In the end of this
letter I see that I give a better account of our progress than in the beginning, that is because I have
had twenty-four hours' later news. They are obliged
to make the galley-slaves work at the guns, and the
women carry earth.

THE battle of Balaklava would be called by the
Germans a "Treffen," or meeting. The Plan shows
the position of the redoubts. The garrison of only one

of them, viz. that on Canrobert's Hill at No. 1, made
any resistance at all.  As long as it was prudent to
do so, Lord Lucan made a show of supporting them
with his cavalry, but of course was obliged to withdraw his men as soon as they became exposed to
cannon-fire.  In fact, the distance of this redoubt
from any real support rendered a lengthened defence
very problematical ; the ditch and parapet, although
as deep and thick as time allowed them to be made,
were very poor defences ; the Cossacks rode over both.
The impossibility of holding these works, which it is
probable was the reason for not trying to retake them,
ought to have been a good reason for not attempting
to fortify them.  A strong picquet posted behind
Canrobert's Hill, with some cavalry videttes, would
have answered every purpose, and no guns would
have been taken ; while the Turks would have been
available to man the strong position to the east of
Balaklava, by which the Russians were effectually
stopped while flushed with their partial success.*
Captain Anitschkoff, of the Russian staff, has written
an account of the campaign in the Crimea, in which
he completely omits the mention of General Scarlett's

* *Der Feldzug in der Krim bearbeitet von Anitschkoff, Haupt-
mann im Kaiserlich Russischen General Stabe, aus dem Russischen
übersetzt von G. Baumgarten, Oberlieutenant der Königl. Sächs.
Infanterie;* Berlin, 1857, Mittler und Sohn.

charge with the heavy cavalry. He pretends that
the Russian cavalry was withdrawn, and retired in
good order. As the author saw this charge, he begs
to set the Russian officer right. The red cavalry
dashed into the middle of a far superior number of
Russians, and completely broke them; and the enemy
galloped back to the heights from whence they came,
during which flight several of our shells fell among
them. The light-cavalry charge took place on the
north side of the redoubts, betwixt them and the
Feduchine heights, and consequently the author could
not see that sad affair. To the good conduct of the
93d Highlanders, under the immediate command of
Sir Colin Campbell, the safety of Balaklava is owing.
Had the 93d been broken, there was literally nothing
to hinder the cavalry which came down on the 93d
from galloping through the flying Turks, and destroying all the stores in Balaklava. There was, indeed,
a frigate in the harbour ; but the cavalry would have
swept past her in a moment, and, once in the village,
the frigate must have fired through our own shipping,
if she could have got a spring on her cable in time to
fire at all.

Captain Anitschkoff also speaks of a "Wagenburg," which he has placed in his plan on the left of
the 93d. "Wagenburg" is a German word meaning
a fortification, or bulwark, formed by the wagons and
carriages of an army. It must be recorded that there

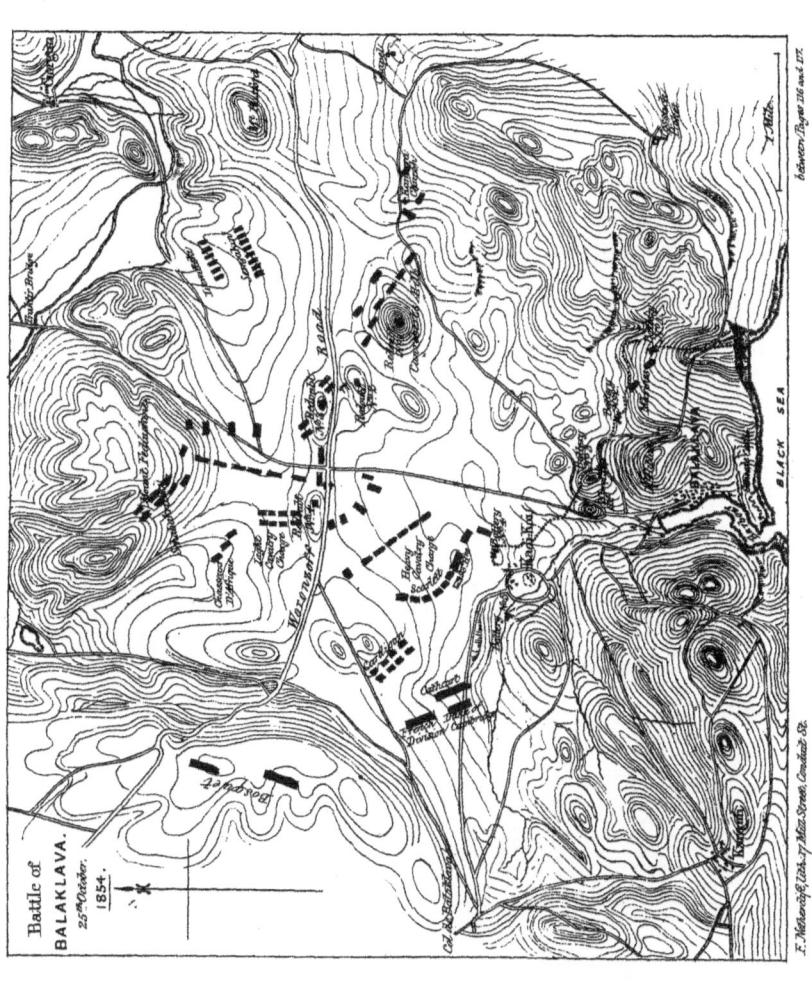

Battle of
BALAKLAVA.
25ᵗʰ October.
1854.

BLACK SEA

F. Wetherald, Lith. 27 Max Street, Cardinal St.

Edward Boyer 176 and 177.

was nothing of the kind; the only bulwark was composed of the stout hearts of 400 Highland soldiers and their indomitable leader. This imaginary wagon fortification is a salve for the Russian cavalry, but it is a pure invention. At the close of the day the 42d and 79th were added to Sir C. Campbell's force; and a brigade of the French, under General Vinoy, were placed, as shown in the Plan, behind Battery No. 5.

## LETTER XXXIII.

Camp, in front of Balaklava,
27th October 1854.

IN case no one else should write, I do so to say —— is safe, and not hurt in the action of the 25th. I have not been able to go to see him, but I have seen those who have done so. We are beleaguered here by the force which was expected from Anapa. We are in a predicament, our English force to hold this place being very small, and the courage of the Turks being mild. The defence of Silistria becomes to me more and more a mystery. On Wednesday the 25th, the Russians attacked the redoubts which we had been ordered to construct along our front, and which were armed with two guns each, and filled with Turks. C. never liked these redoubts. The Turkish gentlemen were beaten out as soon as the enemy's

skirmishers came at the works, in which we understood they would fight till they all perished ; in running away they lost a good many men from the enemy's guns, which played upon them across the valley.
As soon as the redoubts were taken, a large body of
cavalry (4000 or 5000 strong) came on, some of them
facing towards our cavalry, and some against our
small body of infantry — six companies of the 93d,
and Turks in line with them. Two boys of the Guards,
Hamilton and Verschoyle by name, who were quartered in Balaklava with thirty or forty of their men,
came of their own accord, without any order, and formed
up with the 93d, showing themselves thorough-bred,
and the right men in the right place. The English
heavy brigade charged their opponents, five times
their number, and beat them in splendid style. The
lot advancing against us was also driven back by our
fire ; but the Turks in line with us ran away. A good
deal of cannonading was going on the while ; but some
regiments from the plateau opposite Sebastopol came
down, and showed sufficient front to deter the Russian
infantry from coming on. The British cavalry, having
been successful, should have been let alone ; but some
unlucky man had the unlucky idea of making the
light-cavalry brigade charge a battery of eight guns
which was firing at them. Lord Lucan, who commands the cavalry, objected ; Lord Cardigan, who
commands the Light Brigade, objected : but the staff-

officer who brought the order, which I hear was a
written one, was positive, and, they say, insolent.
Lord Lucan, instead of putting him in arrest, sent on
the poor Lights.  They galloped right into the battery, and killed the gunners, but they could not take
the guns away ; and they found themselves under a
cross fire of artillery, and surrounded by a very superior number of cavalry, through which they had to
cut their way back.  Their loss was frightful, I know
not what, probably half their number.  Here the affair
ceased for the day.  We are now left to keep this
position with Turks who are worse than useless, 1200
Marines, the three Highland regiments, and the assistance on our left of a body of French, about 4000.  C.
and his staff remain in the centre battery, No. 4, with
the 93d ; and if it be decided to maintain Balaklava,
here we shall stand and die.  We have put the Turks
in the rear, feeling sure that if we did not so place
them, their natural modesty would soon take them
there.  The abandonment of Balaklava is mooted.
Against the force of Russians now before us, who have
possession of the redoubts where the Turks were, and
who number at least 20,000 infantry, with more very
likely coming up, I doubt the possibility (always supposing said Russians attack with vigour) of our holding on.  If they force our centre, we shall kill many
of them, and we shall be all killed on the spot where
we stand.  C. told the 93d they must die there ; and

he looked as if he meant it. Should that happen, the Marines, 42d, and 79th, would be cut off, they being on our right, with Balaklava harbour behind them. You may believe this is an anxious moment for all of us who care for the credit of England. We may, indeed, abandon the harbour, and occupy the heights on its west side, nearer the besieging armies, but that would be a great triumph to Russia ; or we may leave a few men to guard the trenches before Sebastopol, and turn upon the enemy and beat him, which we should certainly do. Once Sebastopol taken, our difficulties would be over, for our whole army would be free ; but the siege is drawing out, the defence is obstinate, and nobody knows how soon we may be able to storm. Meanwhile the Odessa force is coming. Our numbers are too small for the enterprise ; there are no more expected at present, I believe. I post this letter now because I know not if it will be possible to write up to the moment of post, as we may be attacked in an hour for what I know.

## LETTER XXXIV.

### SIR COLIN CAMPBELL'S DESPATCH OF THE BATTLE OF BALAKLAVA.

*To Major-General Estcourt, Adjutant-General.*

Camp, Battery No. 4, Balaklava,
27th October 1854.

SIR,—I have the honour to inform you that in the morning of the 25th inst., about seven o'clock, the Russian force, which has been, as I already reported, for some time among the hills on our right front, debouched into the open ground in front of the redoubts, Nos. 1, 2, and 3, which were occupied by Turkish infantry and artillery, and armed with some twelve-pounders (iron). The enemy's force consisted of eighteen or nineteen battalions of infantry, from thirty to forty guns, and a large body of cavalry. The attack was made against No. 1 redoubt by a cloud of skirmishers, supported by eight battalions of infantry and sixteen guns. The Turkish troops in No. 1 resisted as long as they could, and then retired ; and they suffered considerable loss in their retreat. This attack was followed by the successive abandonment of Nos. 2, 3, and 4 redoubts by the Turks, as well as of the other posts held by them in our front. The guns, however, in Nos. 2, 3, and 4 were spiked. The garrison of these redoubts retired, and some of them formed on the right and some on the left flank of the 93d Highlanders, which was posted in front of No. 4 battery, in the village of Kadikoi. When the enemy had taken possession of these redoubts, their artillery advanced with a large mass of cavalry, and their guns ranged to the 93d Highlanders, which, with 100 invalids, under Lieutenant-Colonel Daveney, in support, occupied very insufficiently, from the smallness of their numbers, the slightly rising ground in front of No. 4 battery. As I found that round shot and shell began to cause some casualties* among the 93d Highlanders and the Turkish battalions, in their right and left flank, I made them retire a few paces behind the crest of the hill. During this period our batteries on the heights, manned by the Royal Marine Artillery and the Royal Marines, made excellent practice on the enemy's cavalry, which came over the hill in our front. One body of them, amounting to about 400, turned to their left, separating themselves from those who attacked Lord Lucan's division, and charged the 93d Highlanders, who immediately advanced to the crest of the hill, on which they stood and opened their fire, which forced the Russian cavalry to give

---

* The author has heard this doubted, because there were no casualties returned; but he saw the men himself struck down by cannon-shot, both Turks and Highlanders, about a quarter of an hour before the cavalry charge.

way, and turn to their left; after which they made
an attempt to turn the right flank of the 93d, having
observed the flight of the Turks, who were placed
there. Upon which the Grenadiers of the 93d, under
Captain Ross, were wheeled up to their right, and
fired on the enemy, which manœuvre completely dis-
comfited them.

(Signed)   C. CAMPBELL,
*Major-General.*

---

## LETTER XXXV.

Camp, Battery No. 4,* in front of Balaklava,
2d November 1854.

I FIND you often get two of my letters together. It
seems that Lord Raglan keeps the mail-boat to the last
minute, so that sometimes there is only time to put
his own bag on board the steamer for Constantinople;
and the common people's letters are left for the next
occasion, which is a great shame. I enclose the Orders
on the action of the 25th, from which you see our
Highlanders got some credit.

---

* The 93d remained in the position they held until dark on
the 25th October, and then retired into Battery No. 4, just five
hundred yards in their rear. The 42d and 79th were posted on
the heights, to the right of the 93d.

"Head-Quarters, before Sebastopol,
28th October 1854.

No. 1. The Commander of the Forces feels deeply indebted to Major-General Sir Colin Campbell for his able and persevering exertions in the action in front of Balaklava on the 25th inst.; and he has great pleasure in publishing to the army the brilliant manner in which the 93d Highlanders, under his able directions, repulsed the enemy's cavalry. The Major-General had such confidence in this distinguished regiment that he was satisfied that it should receive the charge in line, and the result proved that his confidence was not misplaced."

After the redoubts in front were taken from the Turks, who ran away across the plain, the Russians pushed on their cavalry and guns, hoping to cut them up. One portion of the cavalry left the main body, and charged us, *i.e.* the 93d Highlanders, a weak battalion, which was formed in line, with a Turkish battalion on each flank. We had previously lost* a few men by round shot, and the line had been moved back a few paces to get shelter under the crest of the slight

---

* This has been disputed, because, from some mistake, there was no return made of casualties. Private Charles M'Kay lost his leg by a round shot ; private Kenneth Mackenzie was wounded above the knee by a splinter of a shell. Test. Dr. Monro, surgeon of the regiment, whose letter I have.

hill. As soon as the cavalry began to charge, C. advanced his men to the crest again, and opened fire. The Turks ran away to the rear, into the village of Balaklava, crying, " Ship, ship !" However, the commandant, an old officer of the Royals (Lieutenant-Colonel Daveney), put a sentry to stop the vagabonds. One of my native servants (all trembling) went off with two of my horses, and was not found for hours afterwards.

The little 93d stood fast, and fired away. The cavalry could not bear the fire, and swept off to their left, trying to get round our right flank, and cut in on the Turks. But C. wheeled up the Grenadier company to its right, and peppered them again, and sent them back with a flea in their ears. You see what Lord Raglan says. After this the main body of Russian cavalry advanced against ours, and was completely routed by the Heavy Brigade. The poor Light Brigade made their charge afterwards on the other side of the redoubts, so I could not see them ; but they suffered dreadfully : ———— must have had a wonderful escape. I have not seen him, as I cannot stir from here. We are making trenches, forts, and batteries all round us, to try and render the position secure against a large Russian force which is camped about two miles from us.

The defence of the lines of Balaklava bids fair to form a large feature in the history of the siege.

The French have got very near the wall on the Russian right of the town, and intend, as we hear, to assault to-night. That attempt, however, is put off. We expect, whenever they do so, to be ourselves attacked here, and we are continually under arms and looking out,—a perpetual picquet; very wearing; and now it freezes at night, which makes the tent pretty cool. I continue in good health. If we take the place, I opine we shall immediately turn on our friends in front and drub them, which will give me much satisfaction, as they are always tormenting, especially at night, and should be made to know that their place is as far as they can get from the Highland Brigade. All this war-stuff is very sad, and you must make the best of it. The life is hard for the poor men, who have perhaps not the same feeling that I have about the necessity, for the sake of our country, of beating these Tartars into reason. I must now stop, for I hear a shot.

THE author has seen no English account of the battle of Inkermann which gives a clear description of the state of affairs before and during that battle. He has therefore thought it might not be unacceptable to introduce here the plan taken, but corrected, from Captain Anitschkoff's work, and a compilation, with some corrections added, from that and some other sources. Captain Anitschkoff seems generally to

be pretty accurate, with the exception that he charges
Lord Raglan with falsehood as to the numbers of his
men who were engaged, and with a misstatement as
to the number of Russians killed. When an officer
brings such charges, he should not be surprised at
being suspected of understating his own numbers.
As it is to us quite certain that Lord Raglan was
incapable of setting his name to a falsehood, it may
be taken for granted that his Lordship's statement of
the numbers engaged was perfectly accurate. This
he puts at 8000 English and 6000 French. It may
be well here to mention how the allied troops were
posted. And to begin from the left : from Cape
Chersonesus, the ground to the most western or left-
hand ravine, leading down to the harbour, was occupied by the French. This ravine was called by the
Russians Sardanakina ground. This post near the
walls of Sebastopol was held by two French divisions,
viz. the 3d, under Prince Napoleon, and the 4th, or
Forey's, both under command of General Forey. On
their right was the camp of the English divisions:
the 3d, England's ; the 4th, Cathcart's ; the Light
Division, Brown ; the 1st Brigade (Guards) of the 1st
Division, under the Duke of Cambridge ; and on the
right of the whole the 2d Division, under De Lacy
Evans, or rather of General Pennefather, as General
Evans was sick on board ship. The 1st and 2d
French Divisions, under Bosquet, composed a corps

of observation, and were posted on the edge of the plateau, called by the Russians Mount Sapoune, looking towards Chorguna. The Turks and the 2d Brigade of the 1st Division (Highlanders), under command of Colin Campbell, as well as all the English cavalry, under Lord Lucan, were in position in front of Balaklava, and on their extreme right two battalions of Marines held the heights to the east of Balaklava harbour. D'Allonville's cavalry was in reserve behind the besieging army. Bosquet had covered his front with intrenchments; but the English, who held the northeast corner of the plateau of Mount Sapoune, looking towards the ruins of Inkermann, had not found time to spare from the labours of the siege to make any sufficient defences. They had, in fact, much fewer men than the French, as the latter had received a reinforcement of about 10,000 men on the 30th of October. The Russians had also received very large reinforcements in the beginning of November. In fact, by the Russian accounts, the allied army at the period of the battle of Inkermann consisted of 35,000 French, 23,000 English, and 12,000 Turks—total, 69,000 to 70,000; while the Russians acknowledge to 82,000 men, and they had the advantage of being all of one nation and under one general-in-chief. Prince Menschikoff lost no time in making an offensive movement, although the allies were in possession of all the heights. Properly speaking, the allied position was

impregnable. The position towards the town of Sebastopol was defended by numerous batteries, armed
with ship and siege guns. That part of Mount Sapoune held by Bosquet was scarcely attackable, on
account of the French works thrown up there; and
since the combat of Balaklava extensive lines had
been thrown up, which were defended by strong detachments; so that an attack there was likely to be
attended with great risk of failure, and could only
succeed by making enormous sacrifices of life. Thus
there only remained one point that was really practicable, namely, the narrow *défilé* from the Inkermann
bridge, where the old post-road climbed the heights,
and which the English had protected by a few slight
field-works. A success on this English right wing
would have given the Russians an immense advantage. If they could occupy the heights on both sides
of the Kilen ground, or ravine of the careening creek,
they would have brought their offensive army into
immediate contact with the garrison of Sebastopol.
They could, if once fairly established there, have employed their cavalry against the allies, in which arm
the Russians were far superior; and the allies would
have been forced to abandon the siege of the eastern
part of the town, that is, of the Malakoff and Redan,
the docks, and the Karabelnaya suburb. Prince Menschikoff, seeing all this, determined to make the attack
with two columns, one to issue from bastion No. 2, or

K

the Little Redan, and the other to cross the Chernaya
by the Inkermann bridge. In order to divert the
attention of the allies, Prince Gortschakoff was ordered
to advance at the same time against Bosquet ; and a
sortie of the garrison was ordered from bastion No. 6,
or the Quarantine Bastion, against the French left.
With these views, the right column, which was to
issue from the Little Redan, was placed under command of General Soimonoff, and was composed of 29
battalions and 38 guns ; total, 17,500 men. The
left column, under command of Lieutenant-General
Pawloff, was to attack over the Inkermann bridge,
and amounted to 20½ battalions and 96 guns ; total,
13,500 men. These two columns, therefore, according to the Russian statements, amounted to 31,000
men and 134 guns. The troops from Chorguna, under
General Prince Gortschakoff, numbered 30½ battalions
and 16 guns ; total, 20,000 men. At Mackenzie's
Farm 6 more battalions and 36 guns were posted.
The columns under Soimonoff received orders to take
up the ground on the left bank of the ravine of the
careening creek (*ravin du carénage*), for the purpose
of attacking the centre and left wing of the English.
Instead of doing which, this column advanced along
the right bank of the ravine, and attacked the English
right, for which purpose Pawloff's column had been
destined. It is hard to explain how such a mistake
was made : it may be said, that the order of march

was not clearly explained; yet a ravine is usually treated like a river. At any rate, if General Soimonoff had a doubt, he ought to have asked for explanation on the evening before the attack. The direction of Soimonoff's column was distinctly shown in an instruction (No. 1521) which General Dannenberg sent to Soimonoff on the evening of the 4th November. This instruction stated, " I desire that your main reserve should march behind your right wing, as your left is perfectly secured by the ravine of the Kilen ground." Whereas General Soimonoff brought his right wing to rest on this ravine. General Schabokritski commanded the reserve in question. It was a most fortunate mistake for the English, as the Guards would have been attacked in their own front by Soimonoff, and could not have gone off to the right to assist the 2d Division ; besides which, the troops of the two columns, commanded respectively by Soimonoff and Pawloff, came into action behind one another ; and the ground was so narrow that they could make no use of their superior numbers, as they could not deploy, but were forced to attack in columns of companies, which the English Minié balls penetrated from front to rear. The English battalions, formed in line two deep, had thus, with inferior numbers, the superiority of fire. The morning broke with rain and fog; and the gray coats of the Russians enabled them to come very near before they were seen. The English at first thought it was only a strong sortie; but hearing cannon and musketry on every side, knew not which way to turn : on their left the town-batteries thundered, and were assisted by Soimonoff's artillery ; from Inkermann, the regiments of Borodino and Tarutin, of Pawloff's column, were ascending the heights, and Gortschakoff was threatening the rear of the position; while the lines of Balaklava had a large force opposite to them. Nothing could be done but to resist to the uttermost wherever they were attacked. Soimonoff's column, at 5 A.M., was formed outside the Little Redan, or bastion No. 2. It marched at six. Major-General Wilboa, with four battalions of the Koliwanski Regiment, and four battalions of the Tomski Regiment, and two field-batteries, was in advance, with the Uglitz, Butirsk, Susdal, and Wladimir Regiments on his right. These troops formed on their own left of the Careening-Creek Ravine, with two light batteries in reserve. They made the first attack, and Pawloff's column did not reach the scene till they had been forced to retreat. The left column, under Pawloff, began their movement from the Inkermann bridge at 5 A.M.; but the bridge had been partially destroyed by the English, and had to be repaired. First came the regiment of Ochotz, then the Borodino and Tarutin Regiments, with a light battery ; then the regiment of Jakutzsch, a field-battery, the regiment of Selensk, and the artillery reserve. After crossing the Chernaya, the regiment

of Ochotz turned to the right, and moved along the
Sappers' Road ; the Borodino Regiment, with two
companies of riflemen in front, ascended the heights
through the ravines opposite to the bridge, and the
Tarutin Regiment marched to their left along the old
post-road.  When the two columns, Soimonoff and
Pawloff, had ascended the heights, they both fell
under command of General Dannenberg, and acted
according to circumstances.  General Timofjef commanded the regiments of Minsk and Tobolsk, which
were to make the attack on the French trenches from
the Quarantine Bastion.  The corps from Chorguna
was to move at 6 A.M. along the Woronzow Road, to
occupy Bosquet's troops.  Brigadier-General Codrington visited his outposts at 5 A.M.  As he was returning, some shots were suddenly fired at the left of the
outposts of the Light Division, and immediately afterwards a heavy fire was heard towards Inkermann.
On the one side the heads of Soimonoff's column were
approaching, on the other Pawloff's skirmishers began
to open on the English.  General Pennefather, who
had command of the 2d Division, in consequence of
the sickness of Sir De Lacy Evans, placed Adams's
Brigade, consisting of the 41st, 47th, and 49th Regiments, near the unfinished redoubt No. 1, which is
situated just where the old post-road arrives on the
top of the plateau.  In its rear, but in front of the
camp of the 2d Division, there was the insignificant

redoubt No. 2, not armed with any guns, although
Captain Anitschkoff says there were two Lancasters
there ; and on its right, or east of it, redoubt No. 3 ;
which three redoubts were intended to protect the
right of the English position, against which the main
attack was directed.  On the left of Adams, Pennefather placed his 2d Brigade, composed of the 30th,
55th, and 95th, on the ground along which Soimonoff's
troops were advancing.  Behind these two brigades,
which received the first onset of the Russians, the
rest of the English army took up in all haste the following position: Cathcart's 1st Brigade, under Goldie,
between Pennefather and Buller; his 2d Brigade, under
Torrens, in rear of his 1st Brigade ; the Brigade of
Guards, under the Duke of Cambridge and Bentinck,
behind Adams's right wing ; the other Brigade of the
1st Division (Highlanders) was with Colin Campbell
at Balaklava ; the 1st Brigade, 3d Division, under
John Campbell, in reserve behind Brown's Light Division; the 2d Brigade, 3d Division, was in the trenches.
In this manner, all the British army, except the Brigades of Colin Campbell and Eyre, were very shortly on
the battle-ground ; and leaving out these two brigades,
the remainder, according to English statements, only
amounted to 13,000 men;—so says Captain Anitschkoff, with a remark that their numbers far exceeded
that amount.  The English camp was at the head of
the Kilen ground, or ravine of the careening creek,

on both sides of which they could manœuvre; while
the Russians were confined to the ground east of that
ravine. The first attack of the Russians was very
successful; not so much on account of their superior
numbers, which, in that confined space, could not be
made use of, but from the surprise and the violence
of their attack. In this first fight only three regiments of Soimonoff's, viz. the Tomsk, the Kolivansk,
and the Katharinenburg, and two regiments of Pawloff's, viz. the Borodino and Tarutin, took part. These,
according to Captain Anitschkoff, made twenty battalions, or 13,000 men; and he pretends that the
whole 13,000 English were engaged with them, which,
if true, would be curious, considering the surprise.
The Borodino and Tarutin Regiments drove in the
English outposts, and ascended the heights with great
rapidity; the first by the hollow way, the second by
the old post-road. The brigades of Adams and Pennefather were forced back, and the Russians passed the
redoubt No. 1. At the same time the regiments Tomsk
and Kolivansk, supported by the Katharinenburg, despite the withering fire from Codrington, Buller, and
Goldie, attacked Adams and Pennefather with the bayonet, and a bloody hand-to-hand encounter ensued.
The 2d battalion Tomsk, and 1st and 2d battalions
Kolivansk, succeeded in storming No. 2 redoubt, and
spiked, it is asserted, two Lancaster guns, and they
even got so far as the camp of the 2d Division. As to

the spiking of two Lancaster guns, Captain Anitschkoff is mistaken : there were no guns in position on
the Inkermann heights. The five-gun battery, in
front of what became the Victoria Redoubt, had one
Lancaster gun and four others ; but they were never
spiked, though the Russians at one time came very
near this battery, and by going along the ravine had
got actually into its rear ; but there were no guns in
No. 2 redoubt. The 2d and 4th battalions Katharinenburg went round the upper end of the Kilen ground,
got on its left bank, and spiked four field-guns in the
English camp. Not being supported, they could not
hold their ground, and were driven back. The English right, however, were gradually obliged to give
way ; but they defended themselves step by step with
the greatest obstinacy, and their Miniés told with
fearful effect. The Russian officers, the gunners, and
the draft-horses, served as targets. In a short time
there were either killed or wounded Soimonoff, Wilboa,
the commanding officer of the artillery of the right
column, Colonel Saghos, and nearly all the officers
of the three foremost regiments. Having lost their
valiant leaders, and having suffered most fearfully
from the English fire, the Russians were at last forced
to retire into the hollow way, where the stone-quarries
exist, as shown in the Plan ; and here they formed
again, under the protection of their batteries, which
had been posted in a judicious manner by General

Schabokritski. Immediately behind the batteries the Uglitz and Butirsk Regiments were drawn up, with the Susdal and Wladimir Regiments in reserve. Thus at ten o'clock the battle seemed to have turned into a cannonade. At the same time, the Borodino and Tarutin Regiments, which had thrown themselves on the 2d Division, were driven back by the sudden appearance of the English Guards, and two and a half battalions of French, sent by Bosquet to support the hard-pressed 2d Division. Their attack had, however, materially assisted Soimonoff.

So ended the first act of this bloody contest, which a second one soon followed of a far more desperate nature. At seven o'clock Lord Raglan and his staff had appeared on the field. In order the better to observe the course of the action, he rode into the front line, where General Strangways, the commanding officer of Artillery, was killed at his side. General Dannenberg, who commanded the Russian troops engaged, stood on the height behind the batteries of his first line, and directed the march of his columns. Death reaped a rich harvest around him; staff-officers, aides-de-camp, and orderlies, fell close to him, and he had two horses shot under him. At the beginning of the fight, General Bosquet came into the English camp with four companies of rifles, two battalions of the line, and two batteries of horse artillery, and offered assistance to Cathcart and Brown; but the proud

Englishmen declined his aid, saying they had still troops in reserve, and would only ask for it in case that the redoubt No. 1 should be taken by the enemy. Without further parley, Bosquet sent off his men in this direction; and the assistance they gave to Pennefather and Adams has been mentioned. Bosquet himself returned to his camp, to see with his own eyes the nature of the attack which was threatening him from Chorguna. He soon satisfied himself that it was only a feint; in consequence of which he immediately made every preparation to have the greatest part of his force ready for the first request for support, knowing that a strong reserve would very probably decide the battle. He soon received from English officers the information that their right was sore pressed. The Brigades Bourbaki and d'Autemarre of the 2d Division were quickly despatched to the threatened point ; only one brigade remained on that part of Mount Sapoune to oppose Gortschakoff. The French Commander-in-Chief, Canrobert, had also betaken himself to the English camp ; and he remained close to Lord Raglan during the whole battle, although wounded in the hand. By this time the bloody struggle on the Inkermann heights had recommenced. The three rear regiments of Pawloff's column, which had marched along the Sappers' Road, arrived at eight o'clock on the battle-field, just as the foremost of Soimonoff's troops had retired into the stone-quarries. First came the

Ochotzk Regiment, and after it those of Jakutsk and Selensk. General Dannenberg immediately pushed on these gallant troops against the English. The regiment of Ochotzk threw itself on the flank of redoubt No. 1, which was defended by the Coldstream Guards. Surrounded by the enemy, these valiant Englishmen fought with the greatest gallantry, paying no attention to the shots which the Russian batteries beyond the hollow way were showering into the redoubt, causing infinite loss. Several times the Russians got into the embrasures; but their efforts to enter the redoubt itself were in vain. At last, after the Guards had lost 200 men, they gave up hope of being able to hold the redoubt, and, with a frightful loss, they cut their way through the surrounding Russians. But the Ochotzk Regiment bought their success very dearly; their commandant, Bibikoff, fell mortally wounded, and nearly all the staff and superior officers lay on the field of battle. The regiments Jakutsk and Selensk, under General Octerlone, now crossed the hollow way, through which the post-road rises to the heights, and attacked with fresh strength; while the English had been reinforced by Cathcart's division. The Coldstream Guards, with the two other battalions of the Guards, advanced again, and drove the Ochotzk Regiment out of the redoubt; but only for a time, for the Jakutsk Regiment retook it. Bentinck was wounded, and twelve other officers of the

Guards were killed. The 4th Division suffered no less, being attacked in flank by the Selensk Regiment. Here Cathcart fell dead in his vain attempt to cut off the retreat of the Selensk and Jakutsk Regiments ; for while retiring before the Selensk Regiment, that of Jakutsk poured in a hail of bullets, killing Cathcart, and wounding Goldie and Torrens, his two Brigadiers. The thick smoke of the musketry concealed the ground. The Guards, the 2d Division, the 4th Division, and the French battalions which had first arrived, began to give way before Pawloff's troops. After an obstinate defence, redoubt No. 2 was taken by the Russians, who for the second time got into Pennefather's camp, in the front of which there had been placed an English battery of six guns. The Russian riflemen concealed in the copses killed nearly all the gunners and horses, and took two of the guns.

Upon both sides, up to this moment, the fight had been continued with the extremest fury. The scale was now beginning to turn in favour of the Russians, who had still four regiments which had not been engaged, while nearly all the English reserves had been brought up : there were still three battalions behind the slight rising ground on which the Victoria Redoubt was afterwards constructed. In every battle there is always a moment when the physical force of the contending troops is materially reduced by their prolonged and extreme efforts; while the moral force

has reached its minimum from the continual strain on
the nerves; at such a moment the arrival of a fresh reserve often turns the fate of the day. It was now 11
o'clock A.M. The third and last act of this murderous
conflict approaches. Bosquet arrives; amidst the roar
of the guns, the trumpets of the Zouaves are heard,
with the Chasseurs de Vincennes and the Indigènes
advancing at a run. The English shouted for joy;
inevitable necessity had compelled them to ask for
assistance. Close behind their skirmishers came all
three French brigades, and, passing to the right of the
English, attacked the Russian left, who had now to
fight for their artillery; and Pawloff's three regiments
did this with surpassing bravery, and with perfect
success. The retreat of the Russians was covered by
the regiments Susdal and Wladimir, which regiments
defended themselves against the French with the
greatest obstinacy. When the artillery had gained
the Inkermann bridge, the Russian infantry made
their retreat, pursued by the allies, till the latter got
under the fire of the steamers Wladimir and Chersonesus. The loss of the English was 2622 men;
that of the French 1726, in which it is probable there
was included the loss incurred by Timofjef's sortie on
the left. Captain Anitschkoff makes that of the Russians 8769; but it is known that the English buried
5000 Russians, and it is probable their loss may be
reckoned at full 12,000 men. The remarks of this
Russian staff-officer about Lord Raglan's returns and

statements are very offensive. It is evident that Captain Anitschkoff has no knowledge of English gentlemen's habits, nor of the way in which the returns of the British army are made out.

Although all the officers of our army are perfectly aware that these returns were sent correct to the Adjutant-General of the army, countersigned by Lord Raglan, and that no person belonging to the English army would believe for one moment that his Lordship would put his name to a falsehood, still, as foreigners have made such a statement,—for I remember hearing the same thing confidently asserted at Berlin,—I have thought it well to consult with some of the Brigade-Majors; and I now present our estimate of the forces actually engaged, and the numbers which we believe to have been killed, wounded, and missing, in each regiment; from which it appears that, according to the estimate of three intelligent Brigade-Majors who were engaged, the actual number of English infantry under fire was 7938, and the killed, wounded, and missing, 2443; the additional number to make up the 2622, given by Lord Raglan, were artillerymen and a few cavalry.

*Divisions and Brigades engaged at Inkermann, 5th Nov. 1854.*

FIRST DIVISION.

| | | Strength. |
|---|---|---|
| 3d Batt. Gren. Gds. ⎫ | | |
| 1st Batt. Coldstr.  ⎬ 1st Brig.   .   .   .   .   .   .   . | | 1300 |
| 1st Batt. S. F. Gds. ⎭ | | |
| Highland or 2d Brigade absent at Balaklava. | | |
| | Carry forward   .   .   .   .   . | 1300 |

*Divisions and Brigades engaged at Inkermann, 5th Nov.* 1854 (continued).

Strength.

Brought forward . . . . . . . . . . . . 1300

## SECOND DIVISION.

30th, 41st, 47th, 1st Brigade.  
49th, 55th, 95th, 2d Brigade.

All these regiments were under 500, and the 95th very weak, probably 300, say total . . . . . . } 2500

## THIRD DIVISION.

Only one wing of the 50th was engaged. The 1st and 38th Regiments were behind the rising ground on which the Victoria Redoubt was afterwards constructed, and never fired a shot. ⟵ — — — } say . . . . . . . 250

— ⟶ *Fourth Division.*

20th, 21st, 57th, 1st Brigade.  
63d, 68th, 1st Battalion Rifles, 2d Brigade.  
Two companies 46th Regiment.

Two companies 68th Regiment were at head-quarters. All the regiments were under 500, and there were of this division about 900 men in the trenches. } 2000

## LIGHT DIVISION.

7th, 23d, 33d, 2d Batt. Rifles, 1st Brigade.  
19th, 77th, 88th, 2d Brigade.

The 1st Brigade had in the battle . . . . 1219  
The 2d Brigade ditto . 1119 }

2338  
Deduct 19th Reg. . . 450

1888

It is to be remembered that our regiments mean only one battalion; from each of these a certain number of men were taken away to form the provisional battalion at Balaklava. The Russian regiments had four battalions.

Four companies of the Rifles were detached at Balaklava. The 19th Regiment was in reserve behind the rising ground on which the Victoria Redoubt was afterwards constructed. This regiment never fired a shot. } 1888

The division gave 900 men to the trenches.

Total strength engaged 7938

*Returns of Killed and Wounded at Inkermann.*

| | Officers. | Sergeants. | Drummers. | Rank and file. | | Killed. | Wounded and missing. | Total. |
|---|---|---|---|---|---|---|---|---|
| **FIRST DIVISION.** | | | | | | | | |
| 3d Batt. Gren. Gds. | 3 | 4 | 1 | 71 | K | 79 | .. | } 232 |
| | 6 | 6 | 1 | 140 | W | .. | 153 | |
| 1st Batt. Coldstr. | 8 | 3 | .. | 59 | K | 70 | .. | } 191 |
| | 5 | 6 | 2 | 108 | W | .. | 121 | |
| 1st Batt. S. F. Gds.. | 1 | 2 | .. | 47 | K | 50 | .. | } 173 |
| | 8 | 8 | 2 | 105 | W | .. | 123 | |
| **SECOND DIVISION.** | | | | | | | | |
| 30th, | 2 | .. | .. | 25 | K | 27 | .. | } 127 |
| | 5 | 5 | 1 | 89 | W | .. | 100 | |
| 41st, 1st Brigade. | 5 | 2 | .. | 32 | K | 39 | .. | } 137 |
| | 6 | 4 | 2 | 86 | W | .. | 98 | |
| 47th, | .. | .. | .. | 20 | K | 20 | .. | } 70 |
| | 2 | 3 | .. | 45 | W | .. | 50 | |
| 49th, | 2 | 3 | 1 | 37 | K | 43 | .. | } 150 |
| | .. | 8 | 1 | 98 | W | .. | 107 | |
| 55th, 2d Brigade. | .. | .. | .. | 14 | K | 14 | .. | } 91 |
| | 5 | 5 | .. | 67 | W | .. | 77 | |
| 95th, | .. | 2 | .. | 25 | K | 27 | .. | } 142 |
| | 4 | 2 | .. | 109 | W | .. | 115 | |
| **THIRD DIVISION.** | | | | | | | | |
| One wing of the 50th only engaged. | 1 | .. | .. | 12 | K | 13 | .. | } 31 |
| | 1 | .. | 1 | 16 | W | .. | 18 | |
| **FOURTH DIVISION.** | | | | | | | | |
| 20th, | 1 | 2 | 1 | 27 | K | 31 | .. | } 174 |
| | 8 | 9 | 1 | 125 | W | .. | 143 | |
| 21st, 1st Brigade. | 1 | .. | .. | 14 | K | 15 | .. | } 118 |
| | 6 | 12 | .. | 85 | W | .. | 103 | |
| 57th, | 1 | 3 | 1 | 12 | K | 17 | .. | } 91 |
| | 3 | 6 | 1 | 64 | W | .. | 74 | |
| 2 companies 46th, | .. | .. | .. | 11 | K | 11 | .. | } 40 |
| | .. | .. | .. | 29 | W | .. | 29 | |
| 63d, | 3 | .. | .. | 13 | K | 16 | .. | } 112 |
| | 7 | 9 | 2 | 78 | W | .. | 96 | |
| 68th, 2d Brigade. | 2 | .. | .. | 11 | K | 13 | .. | } 56 |
| | 2 | 3 | 1 | 37 | W | .. | 43 | |
| 1st Battalion Rifles, | 1 | 6 | .. | 16 | K | 23 | .. | } 112 |
| | 3 | 6 | 1 | 79 | W | .. | 89 | |
| Carry forward . . | .. | .. | .. | .. | .. | .. | .. | 2047 |

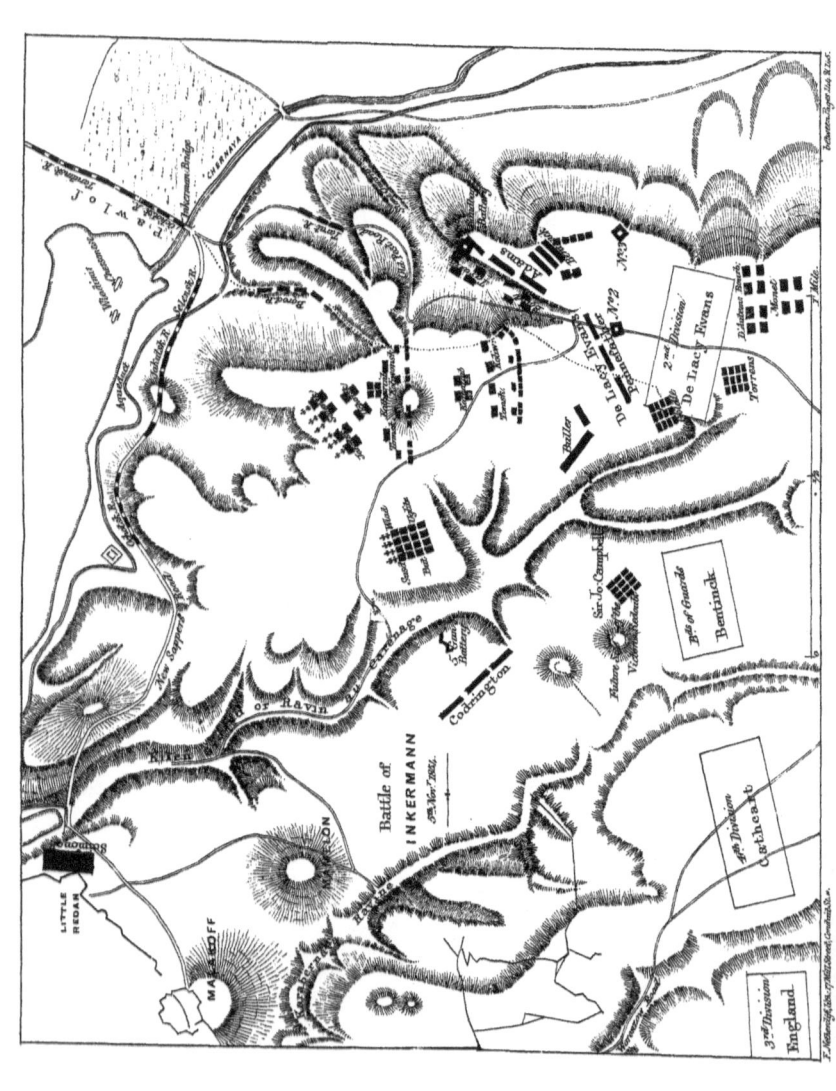

Battle of
INKERMANN
8th Nov. 1854.

*Returns of Killed and Wounded at Inkermann* (continued).

| | Officers. | Sergeants. | Drummers. | Rank and file. | | Killed. | Wounded and missing. | Total. |
|---|---|---|---|---|---|---|---|---|
| Brought forward . | .. | .. | .. | .. | .. | .. | .. | 2047 |
| **LIGHT DIVISION.** | | | | | | | | |
| 7th, | .. | .. | .. | 8 | K | 8 | .. | 68 |
| | 5 | 2 | 1 | 52 | W | .. | 60 | |
| 23d, 1st Bri- | .. | .. | .. | 7 | K | 7 | .. | 43 |
| gade. | 2 | 3 | .. | 31 | W | .. | 36 | |
| 33d, | 1 | 1 | .. | 9 | K | 11 | .. | 67 |
| | 2 | 2 | .. | 52 | W | .. | 56 | |
| 2d Battalion | 1 | .. | .. | 8 | K | 9 | .. | 36 |
| Rifles, | 1 | .. | .. | 26 | W | .. | 27 | |
| 19th, | | In reserve | | | | | | |
| 77th, 2d Brigade. | 1 | 2 | .. | 18 | K | 21 | .. | 61 |
| | .. | 2 | 1 | 37 | W | .. | 40 | |
| 88th, | .. | 4 | .. | 34 | K | 38 | .. | 121 |
| | 3 | 9 | 1 | 70 | W | .. | 83 | |
| Total . . . . . | .. | .. | .. | .. | .. | .. | .. | 2443 |

Besides the Artillery loss, Lord Raglan
   says his loss was . . . . 2622
Deduct . . . . . . 2443
                                      ─────
                                         179

## LETTER XXXVI.

Camp, Battery No. 4, Balaklava,
7th November 1854.

ANOTHER terrible battle on the 5th. Our Balaklava party were not in it. They say that the two
Grand-Dukes have arrived with large reinforcements ;
at any rate, on the morning of the 5th they came on,

some 40,000* Russians, against Sir De Lacy Evans's Division, with seventy guns. Although our numbers were very small, they never gained much ground, and were finally beaten back into Sebastopol, after many hours of fighting. Their loss has been tremendous as well as ours; and we cannot afford it. Our Government must send us some men, and they must do it without stint. It is even now a question in my mind whether we can hold our own here till succour arrives. We are besieging an enemy equal to our own in numbers, with another superior one outside and threatening us continually. They will have to offer a large bounty to the militia, and give us 20,000 or 30,000 men, besides lots of French. Nicholas will bring every soldier he has to drive us into the sea. In every battle we shall lose a large number of men, without taking into account disease, which still continues to thin us. The matter looks graver every day : a *duel à mort* with despotism requires numbers as well as bravery, for which quality the French give us most flattering certificates. In Canrobert's Order yesterday he speaks of our *inébranlable solidité*. The Coldstream Guards buried nine officers yesterday. All the Guards behaved magnificently. But they were not brought up in order ; they rushed to the fire in companies, urged on by the natural valour of officers

---

* By the Russian account 34,000 and 134 guns.

and men. My friend Bentinck has got a shot in the arm ; Sir G. Cathcart, Goldie, Torrens, Strangways, killed,—Torrens not dead yet, but shot through the lungs ; Brown wounded, and a host of others whose names I have not got yet ; Lord St. Germans' son is one. Our loss altogether, 1700 wounded, 444 killed ; 38 officers killed, more than 90 wounded. How many such battles can we fight ? Ah me, I am very tired; we are on the watch constantly night and day. Half of the men constantly behind the parapets, all sleeping with loaded muskets under their blankets, to be ready in a moment. The strain is tremendous—not on the men (for they do not think), but on the officers, who are responsible. Before next spring there will be an army (French and English) in the Crimea of 200,000 men ; they cannot do it properly with less. Let us only hope we shall be able to hold on here till they come. I have little more to say. My health is good, and I feel equal to any exertion. You may expect to hear any day that Balaklava has been attacked. We have fortified it as much as we can. I will give you a characteristic trait of the 42d and 79th Highlanders. They are posted on some hills a mile to our right, and were ordered to dig breastworks in their front, to cover the men from the enemy's fire, so as to fight with the advantage of showing less of their persons. On being reproached with not making the ditch deep enough, nor the parapet high enough, the excuse was, " If we made it so, we could not get over it to attack the Russians !"

---

THE Plan annexed to Letter XXX., showing the attack on the lines of Balaklava, is here repeated, *mutatis mutandis*, together with a sketch to show the position held by the allied forces in the lines of Balaklava, and also that held by the Russians in and behind the Turkish redoubts, and at Kamara, from the 26th October till the 6th December; when Liprandi's troops retired over the Chernaya, keeping their outposts at Chorguna and Karlovka. During the six weeks of very bad weather, the troops under Sir Colin Campbell were in continual expectation of being attacked, and had as hard trench-duty to perform as any others in the army. Half of the men spent every night in the trenches, and the rest lay in their tents fully accoutred, with their loaded muskets by their sides. A continual watch was kept with good spy-glasses from battery No. 4, from the camp of the 42d, and from the Marine heights, which latter position afforded a better view from its height. Every movement of the enemy was observed and noted down, and a daily report sent up to head-quarters. After the 6th Dec. 1854 nothing remained of the Russians on the left bank of the

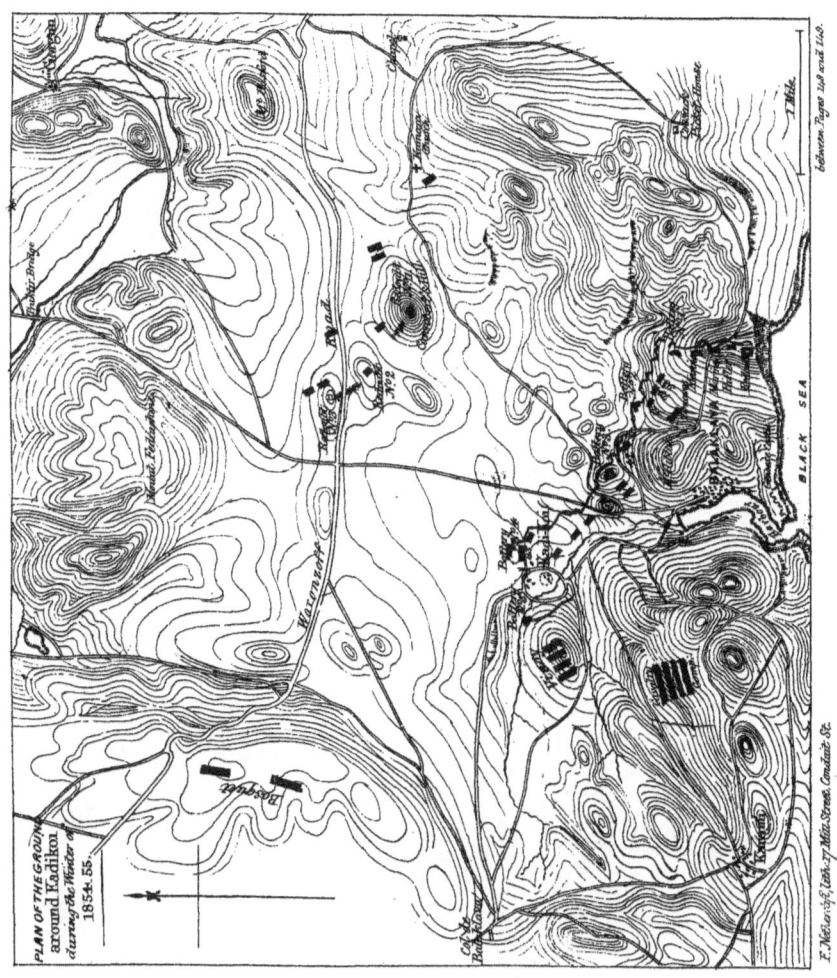

PLAN OF THE GROUND
around Kadikoi
during the Winter of
1854-55.

BLACK SEA

E. Weller, Lith. 77 Mill Street, Conduit St.

1 Mile

between Tyvos 195 and 196

a. *Marine Heights*
b.b.b *Lines of Balaklava*
c. *Battery Nº 3.*
d. *Loopholed house in Church of St. Elias*
e. *Battery Nº 4.*
f. *Abittis*
g. *Genoese Tower*
h. *Balaklava Harbour*

Chernaya except a few Cossacks in Kamara, which furnished videttes on the redoubts along the Woronzow Road. This state of things continued till the 25th May 1855, when the French and Sardinians were moved out, as described in Letter XC., and relieved the Highlanders from outpost duty. Sir Colin's troops, however, were not moved up to the siege till the 18th June, from which period they assisted in the trench-work till the 18th August, when they were sent to Kamara to support the Piedmontese, and only returned to the siege for the assault on the 8th September.

## LETTER XXXVII.

Camp, Battery No. 4, Balaklava,
12th November 1854.

My last word was, "I hear a shot ;"* we are always hearing something which makes us get under arms, and prepare for an attack upon us. It has not been made ; perhaps they are waiting for reinforcements, perhaps they do not like the look of us. We are promised more soldiers to defend our position, the importance of which is acknowledged by all. The war has now come to a state out of which I cannot

---

* This was in Letter XXXV.; the Author has skipped a Letter.

see my way. The weather will soon be so bad that
active operations must be impracticable. During the
whole winter, unless Austria should move, Nicholas
will be pouring down his troops from the north and
east. He will have collected an immense army; and
as the Russians are very good soldiers, they cannot be
beaten without having something like their own numbers to meet them. Will England and France send
200,000 men to take Sebastopol? I know that the
decision come to by the allied generals was, that the
siege must stop in its present state until we shall have
men enough thoroughly to invest both sides of the
harbour, and to beat the enemy in the field. We
could, I dare say, do that now by raising the siege;
but what is to become of us afterwards? Meantime
the officers are all tired of it; many want to sell out,
losing ever so much on their commissions; and these
men are the more to be pitied, because, after they have
acknowledged their want of endurance, of patriotism,
&c., they cannot go. The soldiers must have officers,
and the officers must just stay and do their duty, eating
their leek. By all accounts the Russians have suffered
most awfully on the 5th; and they will suffer still
more in health from the bad weather which has now
set in. The roads will break up, and their supplies
will be impeded in moving, while ours will come by
sea. So long as we can hold Balaklava, all is well:
only I do not know what transport the commissary

has to carry things up to the camp before Sebastopol. The roughest, rudest side of war is now presented to us ; all pretensions to finery, or even decency, are gone. We eat dirt, sleep in dirt, and live dirty ; but our hearts are high, and it will take a deal of Ruskis to chaw us up. Nevertheless, send us 30,000 Englishmen ; for if the enemy were of my mind, we should be hard enough pressed now, and we may be so any day.

---

## LETTER XXXVIII.

Camp, Battery No. 4, in front of Balaklava,
17th November 1854.

HERE we are in winter, and I still in a tent. There has been a frightful hurricane on the 14th. The weather had been rainy and windy for two or three days previously, so that the ground where we encamped was quite a swamp, *i. e.* deep mud. We had just got our morning dose of cocoa, and the soldiers their rum, when, about seven o'clock, the squall came down on us. I was dressed in waterproof clothes and a sou'-wester; and was standing outside ; most of the others were in the tents. All the tents fell in about three minutes ; in some the poles broke, in others the pegs drew. As to mine, the wind rushed in at the door, and split it right up; so my servant and I spent an hour lying on the wet canvas, to keep it compactly down, and prevent the household goods from being blown away. Just at the first destruction of the tents, the air was loaded with all sorts of articles— Highland bonnets, shoes, chairs, bits of wood, and all the papers, news or official, in the camp. My box or trunk, which I pillaged, or rather bought from a pillager, to hold my documents, was blown open for a moment, and the wind had just time enough to whip off one document, and pour in a shower of water. The paper was found afterwards, some 300 yards off, in a vineyard. The army before Sebastopol, I hear, suffered more than we did, because it is colder up there; they have also less wood, and the rocky ground objects to holding tent-pegs. While this wind was pulling us to pieces, the poor shipping outside the harbour was undergoing a harder fate. They had not been able to get into harbour for some days, on account of the wind that blew right in, and they were anchored in deep water, with terrible cliffs close to them. Many are lost, and they say 400 seamen, besides stores to an immense amount. It is to be hoped that such storms are not common here. I observe that the houses are all roofed with loose tiles, and that no precautions seem to have been taken to load the roofs to keep the tiles on, which makes me hope that the Crimea is not generally very windy. It is wonderful how the men bear it; and there are not a great many sick. We are still digging our de-

fences, and we are now going to begin building huts ;
looking out anxiously at the same time towards the
enemy's position on the one hand, and on the other
towards England and France, wishing for men and warlike appliances. You have thought fit to invade Russia,
and must send armies of Russian dimensions to cope
with the Czar's troops. These Ruskis are capital
soldiers as to knowledge of war as a profession; but,
in the longrun, they will not stand before English and
French. Our national misfortune is, the want of
an army of reserve. Supposing the men obtained,
how can we train them in time ? Had the Government been alive to the difficulty of their undertaking,
they would, so soon as they decided on war, have
called out every militiaman in England, which should
have been done last April. These men would all now
be trained soldiers ; and a handsome bounty of 10*l.*
or 20*l.* a man would have given us as many as we
could wish for. The same principle applies to the
artillery, in which force the Russians are very strong,
and first-rate as to quality. Infantry,—I mean English infantry,—can take guns, and guns cannot take
infantry ; but the loss they inflict is very great. The
French have plenty of trained soldiers ; but even the
trained soldier is not complete till he has had the
fire-baptism. We do not much expect the Russians
to attack us again till their next reinforcements come
up. The troops who were beaten on the 5th at the

battle of Inkermann suffered so much that their
*morale* must have been shaken. The calculation is
15,000 killed and wounded. This loss was inflicted
on them by less than half the number of English and
French, that is, 14,000 beat off 40,000, and killed
and wounded 15,000 of them. On this occasion we
were in position, and the Russians made the attack
with the advantage of a surprise. At the Alma the
Russians were in position, and prepared. From that
you may judge the difference between the two nations.
We now hear that 8000 English and 20,000 French
are actually on their way. When they arrive, if the
weather be tolerable, I judge we shall attack the
enemy, and drive them further off, which will relieve
such of us as survive from this perpetual picquet
duty. At any moment the Russians might come
down on the Balaklava position in half an hour from
our first perceiving their movement, and they might
before daylight come so near without being noticed
that our musketry would reach them. Our principal
want now is firewood; for the present we have
enough, but very soon it will be consumed; and unless the Government has already taken active steps,
our situation will be deplorable. With fire and food,
I think our men will keep up well enough. All this
may interest some of your friends, if not yourself. I
never go 100 yards away from my tent, unless I am
sent on duty to some other part of the line; so that

I know nothing of what goes on elsewhere. I am sorry to say a great many of the officers are quite disgusted with the hardships we suffer, and want to go, selling their commissions for the regulation ; but they cannot be spared. I wonder they are not ashamed. I would not be any where but here, where I hope I am of some use. To glory and all that stuff I am rather indifferent : glory, when looked at close, and while it is being earned, is rather an ugly thing. No military glory can be acquired without causing the misery, mind and body, of thousands. However, my head works unceasingly to drive this machine, and keep it ready for action.

## LETTER XXXIX.

Camp, Battery No. 4, Balaklava,
22d November 1854.

WE have papers to the 3d. No change here ; cold, and wet, and discomfort reign over us and around us. Sickness among the men from exposure is increasing ; but some more troops have arrived, which will give us near 19,000 infantry. We are promised a good many French. The siege does not progress. The Russians watch us, but seem afraid to attack ; and we cannot do so either, for want of men. No doubt, as soon as they arrive in sufficient numbers, we

shall have another battle, and then the siege again ;
a pleasant prospect for the winter. The papers talk
of a winter campaign preparing between Austria
and Russia. In these gloomy dark nights, up to our
ankles in mud, we rise and go round the sentries, for
fear of a surprise, and watch the enemy's fires. It
is really a very hard life, yet I never was in better
health. We eat enormously of coarse food, having the
worst cook in the world—a very dirty Glasgow soldier. The Turks are a despair ; they are very lazy,
too, at their work, unless the Pasha stands over them.
Our Highlanders, under direction of the engineer-
officer, or rather of a sapper, are digging a deep exca-
vation, over which they mean to put a roof to cover
themselves, if possible, before the snow comes. I shall
probably weather it out in a tent. As soon as the
defences of this place are completed and tolerably
secure, I hope C. and the Highlanders may get clear
of the Turks. They ought to make him a Lieutenant-
General, considering his great services, which would
double his pay ; but he has no interest. The French
rewards to officers and men for the battle of the Alma
have arrived, and have been distributed. None of us
have got any thing as yet, which I think a mistake ;
nothing acts on the young and ambitious so well as
prompt recognition. To get, after all, what ? Perhaps a step in rank, or the right to receive letters with
" C.B." after one's name. Probably the rewards will

cost the country 5000*l*. ; possibly they will wait till
the campaign is over, so that some more may be
killed without receiving the rewards, such as they are.
The ladies seem to be upon a new scheme, bless their
hearts ! I do not wish to see, nor do I approve of,
ladies doing the drudgery of nursing. Perhaps they
may be of some use to keep the poor soldiers' wives
and the nurses in order. I hear that already the hospital at Scutari is much improved. All we want is,
to give the military surgeons leave to spend money,
without the risk of being blamed for it afterwards.
A more devoted set of men than the regimental surgeons I never saw ; but they have been brought up
all their lives under the tyranny of the Inspector-
General, whose object it is to please the Government
by keeping down the estimates.

I have written a very stupid letter; but my fingers
are cold, and my heart is sad. Stupid as it is, I will
add, that when a soldier goes into hospital, the Government stops 10*d*. a day out of his pay, to pay
for his physic and food ; the difference between that
expense and 10*d*. goes to the Government. So that
the doctors are encouraged to keep the men on a low
diet, in order to gain credit for economy, *i. e.* expend-
ing men instead of pennies.

## LETTER XL.

Camp, Battery No. 4, Balaklava,
27th November 1854.

Yours of the 8th came to me two days ago. A very short time after it was written, you must, by the papers, have received full particulars of our battle of Balaklava; and now, at this time of writing, you must have heard the accounts of the battle of Inkermann, when so many Russians were killed and wounded. I suppose they are waiting for reinforcements like ourselves, for they seem quite quiet. ———'s regiment is quartered miles away from me ; and, as I am tied here, I can give you no account of him. Our cavalry is now quite inside the fortified lines, and in perfect safety; and no doubt the officers take off their clothes at night, and are pretty comfortable, which is a great element towards being in health. It is doubtless very sad to have one's friends in peril; but remember, that we are now fighting for our country, to which we all owe a life. Should we fail in this contest with Russia, the power of England will be broken; and freedom will receive a blow from which it may not recover for centuries. But we will not fail; with our good swords in our hands, and our women in our hearts, we are not to be conquered. Send us men and munitions ; we are longing to attack the enemy, whose outposts are before us. Meanwhile the works

are progressing, and gradually surrounding more and
more of Sebastopol. But the roads are so bad, and
our arrangements of transport so behindhand, that
we cannot get the guns up to the new batteries,
which are intended to clear the Inkermann valley. I
hope you have a plan of the place, which is more
than I have. I made a small map of this position;
but I have never had time to copy it, or, indeed, a
place to do it in. Soon I expect to be in a house
close to this; and as our defences are improved, I
shall also have a little more time and rest. We hear
of the arrival yesterday of fourteen large mortars, with
which, when we can get them up to the front, we
may perhaps destroy the Russian line-of-battle ships
in the harbour, whose guns have been a great annoy-
ance. For some days past there has been incessant
rain and storms of wind. The soil we are on is mud
and marl, and we are all muddied over, and most
wonderful figures; but the men are cheerful, and our
Highlanders tolerably healthy. They are very thought-
less. We are driving them to complete their huts,
which will be quite necessary to enable them to bear
the winter. You have made no reflection on the
Nightingale movement, which to me is a very amusing experiment. It is useless to exhort you good people not to be in a fright about all of us here, nor to
be troubled about our death, if death is to be our lot.
At least we hope to give you the consolation that we

shall not die in vain.  "Gang through" is my motto ;
let us not look to the right hand nor to the left, but
straight on to our great object.  The survivors who
return to their country will be hailed with national
acclamation, and those who perish will have their
tear and silent memory where their living affection
was placed.  We have a new Pasha just landed,
Osman Pasha ; he is of higher rank than Rustem
Pasha ; but I have not yet seen him.  He has brought
1400 more Turks with him.  I hope they will not
run away like the others ; it is a miserable thing to
see a rabble of men with arms in their hands run-
ing away from an enemy, who is pounding them with
round shot and shells : they say it is for want of discipline.  I know not ; but think our men would fight
any how ; and the Russians must think so, for we at
Balaklava are at bay; yet they do not venture on us.
One more great battle won will perhaps enable us to
invest Sebastopol on both sides, and then the place
must fall.  The war may last many a day afterwards.
I look forward to nothing else.  The Russians are
obstinate soldiers, and are defending their own soil.
Ignorance and bravery make them formidable foes.

## LETTER XLI.

Camp, Battery No. 4, Balaklava,
2d December 1854.

THERE is a rumour that from some blunder of the postmaster all the army letters which should have gone by the last post were left behind ; that was a fast mail, this a slow one; Lord Raglan's bag went all right. You will perhaps find in this accident some dark design on the part of Government. I shall reserve my judgment, professing at the same time more faith in blunder than in any thing else. All life is a blunder, as we may see and feel. All matters, weather included, look sad and murky. French and English reinforcements are come in. The change in my lot has been that yesterday we took possession of a house with a large figure **8** on it,—a mere hovel, which has hitherto been the 42d hospital. By way of a joke, I undressed and went to bed with sheets, &c., and found it very uncomfortable. I cannot do so regularly ; but I risked it ; I mean the chance of not being on my horse within five minutes, as soon as needful, in case of an attack. I shall sleep as usual to-night, and am inclined to think that bed is a foolish invention. Asiatics never do go to bed in our sense ; they loosen their strings, which is not necessary, as I can testify. —— has applied for a medical board ; in other words, he is going home. The

M

discomfort is what the comfortable fellows cannot stand. We who do stand it will get no credit; not that I want any; but you see the privates cannot go home, so why should the officers? To be sure, the privates *never* do go home except when really sick, or when their regiment goes, while officers who choose to pay their passage do usually get leave; still it seems to me that on this peculiar occasion the officers should stick in the mud and weather it out with their men, as they would physical danger, which may also be nearer than people suppose. Our cavalry disaster was all a mistake — temper, impertinence, want of judgment, and want of a proper disregard for the opinion of an imprudent staff-officer, who was killed, led our Light Dragoons into the sad catastrophe. We are all making huts for ourselves, or for our horses, which animals will be wanting by and by, and must be looked to. The four horses I brought from England are all well, and stand the work like their master. Our occupation—I mean staff-officers—is looking out for the enemy, thinking of eating and drinking and sleep,—tame cats, with a touch of the wolf and other savage creatures. Writing official letters, by the way, is that an occupation? I have just written eight, more or less important, which will be sent off at daylight. Sometimes a humaner moment arrives, and we write to our friends, and become men again. I have looked in a looking-glass to-day for the first time since landing in the Crimea ; my beard is getting long and grizzled, my face brown and healthy, my body thin, and my expression reckless and cynical. That is only a mask : it is always off in these Letters, and the poor devil is seen as he is. So far as I can learn, the French and English are going to begin the siege again ; they are getting up more guns, and, I suppose, will take the place when-ever they choose to slip the invincibles at it. But the invincibles are not immortal, and cost a good deal of money—not, however, beyond their worth. If ever men did a fair turn of work, these soldiers have done one. The real wonder is, that any of them are alive. The Government at home are giving them a new suit of clothing and many extras gratis. This is wise ; a small unexpected gratification acts powerfully on these poor fellows. We hear the French soldiers are begin-ning to murmur at the length of inaction under which they suffer. Canrobert shoots out an order every now and then to console them.

By the by, talking of orders, I did not expect that our despatch of the battle of Balaklava would be pub-lished. I suppose Lord Raglan found he must pub-lish Lord Lucan's, and so put C.'s in with it. When I was writing it, C. said, you had better say some-thing about the staff; but I suggested that we were sure of plenty of fighting, and should have a better opportunity. In Lord Raglan's own despatch he says very little about C. The truth is, that by his judicious management of the 93d he saved the whole batch of Turks from being cut to pieces. I am his Adjutant-General; and if I only had a bit of interest, or was Lord Tom Trumpeter, the opportunity would have been seized to promote such a promising and gallant young fellow. The next news we expect will be the despatch of the battle of Inkermann, and the consequent arrangements for reinforcing this army. Occasionally I have to go out from the redoubt to receive flags of truce. It is a very odd sort of feeling. You see three or four horsemen about a mile off; one carrying a lance with a white flag, and another trumpeting. You mount and ride out to meet them, and find a gentleman-like young officer, speaking good French or English; a few words of extreme politeness pass, and each party returns to his own place. The last time they gave me a purse with fifty gold pieces, a bundle of clothes, and letters, for prisoners of war whom we have got at Scutari.

I am afraid you will find this a dull letter; but I am dullness personified; a leaden mantle hangs over us all at present; besides which I think I am getting up a cold, brought on probably by too much comfort, or perhaps by the hole in the wall just by my head.

## LETTER XLII.

Camp, Battery No. 4, Balaklava,
7th December 1854.

WE now hear that our letters for the last three or four posts have been late from some stupidity of arrangement on the part of the directing powers. The brigade of Light Cavalry has been removed down from Sebastopol to our neighbourhood. We have been going on strengthening our position ; but yesterday were surprised to find that during the previous night the Russians in our front had decamped with all their guns, infantry, &c., leaving only a few Cossack picquets to burn their huts. What the next scheme may be, who can tell ? It seems likely that they found our position too strong and too well defended to be attacked ; perhaps they may be concentrating their force for a general attack on the front ; perhaps preparing to resist a new French army, which some people think will be landed on the north side of Sebastopol. We shall for a while not be so much on the stretch here ; the weather has also cleared, and to-day is as fine a sunshiny day as one could wish to see. I am busy making stables for our horses and mules, and preparing to be snug for the winter. Now that the Russians have retired, I should not be surprised if C. were to be moved off to some division near Sebastopol ; and all our

labours in the defences and in making huts and
stables will have been for other people's use.   It will
be a great change, after having got into a house, to
be called upon to turn out in the dead of the winter
and go to the front; but I expect it.   I think they
will hardly try the assault without C., who has more
experience in his little finger than the whole set up
there.    But there is all the artillery to get up first,
and then to batter.   The first siege-guns are quite
worn out with firing; and, in fact, the second siege
is about to commence, as soon as we are ready.   I
see by the tone of the English papers that they have
taken the alarm at home, and that we shall have all
the available soldiers and plenty of French.   If we
could have some of the departments a little better
organised, the affairs of this army would soon come
to rights.   An army of this size in India would have
with it 30,000 camels for transport; I believe we
have here in this place about 150 mules.   The consequence is, that there is the most shameful difficulty
in giving the soldiers their rations.   We shall not be
able to take the field till we are provided with this
transport; and we might have had it long before this,
if the Government, or some one whose duty it is, had
chosen to spend money in Turkey in the purchase of
horses.    The easiest way now would be to send carts
and horses, with their forage, out from England.    In
France the transport for the army is an organised

permanent body ; but Parliament never would allow this expense during peace, and we now suffer for their parsimony. The French have a regular baking establishment, and eat bread almost always; we never. They have fresh meat much oftener than ourselves; and their situation in every respect has been improving, while we have retrograded.

## LETTER XLIII.

Camp, Battery No. 4, Balaklava,
11th December 1854.

I DO not want to make any particular secret of my opinions, although any man who dares to think, and still more to speak, risks injuring his prospects. Even if he cannot be punished directly, there is a mark set against him. My view of the state of matters here is open to any one. The mistake that has been made has been a very common one in our country, viz. not keeping up certain military establishments in peace, because people took it into their heads that war could never come. In France there is a permanent wagon-train always organised, a permanent commissariat, and also a permanent ambulance; these three departments hang very much upon one another, and the defects of one cause a mischievous drain upon the others. For instance, the few

mules our commissariat possess to carry provisions
for the troops eight miles off on the Plateau will be
borrowed to assist in forwarding ammunition; the
regimental *bât* horses are taken from the regiments
to assist the commissariat; and so it goes on in a
vicious circle.  The English people having destroyed
these above-named departments, which existed during the Spanish war, or which rather were then
formed, its Government, on deciding upon war, should
have instantly begun to organise them again.  This
is a matter of time as well as money; there has
now been time enough allowed to slip away; but
nothing is really organised yet.  The few mules still
alive are without shoes, which ought to have been
brought by the commissariat.  A ship sent by the
authorities here to Constantinople for mules is put
into dock there for some trifling defect; the want of
the mules prevents the troops sometimes from getting the whole of their rations up, although the stores
here are abundant.

Who appointed the Quartermaster-General,—a
man in feeble health and totally without experience?
He fell sick and went home, and just when we were
going to embark.  Airey is appointed in his place.
Airey is a clever man; but if they had appointed
Sir George Murray, Wellington's quartermaster-
general, he could not have rectified in a month the
mistakes and omissions of the whole previous eight

months. Airey, when I knew him, commanded the 34th Regiment, which was in very good order; and he had served as military secretary to Lord Aylmer in Canada, and in one or two departments afterwards at the Horse Guards; but he had no experience in the field. If he had been made Quartermaster-General last February, he would have learned much, and matters, I have no doubt, would now have been better. Our army was shot on shore in the Crimea without baggage or transport. This might have been tolerated if our sojourn here was intended to be for a week; but as soon as it was palpable the affair would be a long one, the first necessity to be provided for ought to have been transport. Lord Raglan should have forced the commissary to have it ready. Thousands of public and private animals were left behind at Varna, many of them to die from neglect. This was under the pretence of conveying more soldiers; but soldiers unprovided with the requisites to keep them efficient are sacrificed in a very foolish, not to say reckless, manner. The French,* with very inferior shipping to ours, came, as I believe, all complete. They have been daily improving their organi-

---

* The French used their men-of-war for transports; ours were kept in fighting condition to be ready to meet the Russians had they offered battle. When the Russians sunk their ships, the English men of war might have carried any thing which was wanted.

sation ever since ; and, in fact, the French soldier has never been so well off as at this moment here in the Crimea, where we are suffering so much. We have now before Sebastopol 3,300 sick, who will have to be brought down to Balaklava to embark on French ambulance mules ! And this when our army belongs not only to the richest country in the world, but to the country richest in horses and ships. Many of the staff and general officers were appointed from interest. It seemed either that Lord Raglan did not expect war, and so gave places to any one who had influence, or, if he did expect war, he intended to do all the work himself. The Adjutant-General served in the 43d ; I doubt if he ever commanded it ; he was appointed Judge-Advocate. And when the Government decided on that office being held by a civilian, Estcourt was pitch-forked into the important office of Adjutant-General, with high pay and powers ; but his business is discipline, which he endeavours to combine with amiability ; a most charming man in private life, but quite out of his place here. I know not who was the planner of the Turkish redoubts, standing on ground which we never ought to have occupied at all, because we were too far from it to support the troops placed there. As soon as I came down, while working at these redoubts, C. told me he did not like them. Some one from head-quarters insisted on guns being put there : these the Turks

abandoned to the Russians. Had the 400 Highlanders been Turks, or even had they not been commanded by such an officer as C., Balaklava would
have been entered by the Russian cavalry; and the
success of their attack would have given the infantry
columns (30,000 men, remember) so much confidence,
that no one can say what the result might have been.
Reinforcements of troops are comparatively useless
unless they reform and reorganise the departments
I have spoken of; that is my last word, "Radical
Reform."

12th December 1854.

Yours of the 23d has just reached me. What
you say about Lord Hardinge having stopped the reinforcements is very possible; he nearly lost British
India by stopping the troops who were moving up
before the battle of Feroseshah. There is a grand
row getting up between Lords Raglan and Lucan.
The words "misconception of orders" have roused
Lord Lucan's ire. Long before the catastrophe, C.
foretold that the cavalry would have disaster from
the way he heard them taunted by young gentlemen
who were called staff-officers.

We hear of plenty of troops coming for the French;
and I suppose an assault will be tried as soon as the
guns have battered a bit. Murderous it will be, and
frightful to think of. They say that when troops
storm, they become like demons, and kill their officers

if they try to stop their barbarity. It is very likely, I may say certain, that C. will get a division; but unless he is promoted to Lieutenant-General, the pay is not increased. What will become of me I cannot guess. If I am not killed, I suppose I shall be employed somehow; there will be so few who have stuck to it all through.

## LETTER XLIV.

Camp, Battery No. 4, Balaklava,
17th December 1854.

WE have nothing new here for you. They continue getting the great guns up slowly towards the front to begin the second siege; and we have a strong rumour that Austria has at last been forced to move and attack the Pruth, which, if true, will prevent Russia from sending any more troops here. We have just been building up a stable for our poor horses and mules; but last night we had an alarm, and found the wall had given way; it was only of loose stones, and the roof had fallen in. However, neither man, horse, nor mule was hurt. The French soldiers are becoming very impatient. The other day, as Canrobert was going along the trenches, he was followed by cries, "*L'assaut!*" Our poor men are more composed, and remain very quiet; but they will assault quite as vigorously as the French. The French su-

perior officers appear to think it necessary to let their
men hear a great deal more of their plans than is the
custom with us ; and I have little doubt that every
French soldier has been discussing the report of the
Austrian alliance, with a full understanding of its
importance. Our men never hear of such things in
orders, which probably in this case the French will.

Christmas is near, and no frost yet ; a little snow
and sleet yesterday, but no cold to speak of, although
one would find a fire agreeable. We cannot afford
wood for that, as we have had to collect this material
comfort with much labour and time, and we reserve it
for cooking. Now we are in hopes that there will be
rations of coal given to us. Every thing is said to be
coming except peace, of which I hear no rumour, and
shall be sorry to hear of one, if it is to be a peace
dictated by Austria as the price of her assistance.
Nothing will satisfy me except the complete humi-
liation of Russia ; and I would rather march to Moscow than not succeed in bringing down Nick's high
stomach. What is to be made of his discomfiture at
Silistria ? That is a puzzle. Our interpreter, a Polish
gentleman and a very sensible man, who was with the
Turkish army on the Danube, gives two reasons for .
the place not having been taken : one was, because
the garrison could not run away ; the other, that the
Russians were not in earnest in wishing. to take it.
Sure I am that the Turks here have not the smallest

chance, if left to themselves, against the Russians. We cannot trust the Turkish officers with the working-pay for their fatigue-men; so I have a mighty bag of shillings, and pay them myself when they return from work,—1s. among four Turks.* They all drink rum when they can get it; but although the doctors wish they should receive it as a ration, their Government is afraid of shocking public opinion by ordering it.

## LETTER XLV.

Camp, Battery No. 4, Balaklava,
21st December 1854.

THE shortest day! A balmy feeling, warm easterly breeze, dry ground, and bright sunshine. Such is this climate—even more variable than our own! Yesterday was equally fine; and we took the occasion to make a little *promenade militaire;* the French cavalry along the plain, and the 42d, a wing of the Rifles, and the Zouaves along the mountains on our right. We saw no soul or ~~Cossack~~; but came to the deserted picquet-house of the ~~latter gentry~~, where we captured two cooking-pots and a lance. The cavalry in the plain had a slight skirmish with the Russians; and this over, we all retired within our entrenchments.

* When the Turkish officers reported this, the Pasha forbid his soldiers having any working-pay at all.

We hear that Austria has positively made a triple
alliance, offensive and defensive, with France and
England, which will more equalise the forces. The
arrangements in the army will, I dare say, soon be
made. 'Arrangement' is a delicate word. The Duke
does not return. Major-General Bentinck, commanding the brigade of Guards, got a wound in his arm ;—
he is rewarded with the command at Portsmouth !*
C. will have the 1st Division ; and I suppose it will
happen somehow or other that I shall go with him.
The weather has become so much finer that our men's
health is improved ; and gradually they will receive
additional comforts and treats and fuel. But Sebastopol will be a long job, depend upon it. Certain,
however, as the greatness and power of England is the
ultimate fall of the place, and the complete humilia-
tion of Nicholas. We have just got papers to the 1st,
which is not so late as we expected to receive them.
Kossuth's long speech is great bosh ; I dare say very
eloquent, especially where he informs the nation that
we shall be beaten. In reply, I say, he lies in his
throat ; we shall not be beaten. You saw in the
beginning of this Letter the account of the lovely
weather. It is now some unknown hour in the night
of the 21st or morning of the 22d, and rain has been
coming down at a great rate. My watch is broken,
and gone to Constantinople ; while another one is

---

* He did not, however, hold it for some reason, but returned
to the army.

supposed to be on its way from England by post ;
meantime I, who am the most punctual man in the
world, never know what o'clock it is.   Our Admiral
is gone ; which seems to please the sailors very
much ; they think Lyons is likely to do better without him.    It is at least certain that ————————
did not approve of this expedition ; and experience
has shown that he was right, — that we were not
prepared nor organised for such an undertaking.
However, he will not get much credit for his clair-
voyance.  I think I wrote to you before we left Varna
to send us 30,000 more men.   Of course I had not
the means of knowing how very deficient we were
in organisation.   A small bit of the great machine, I
revolve on my own pivot, and cannot see very far
from it.   The people about head-quarters alone have
unlimited powers of inspecting.  I cannot go to see
what is doing in the front, nor where the French are ;
all is hearsay.  The guns, however, go on booming
occasionally, telling me that the roar will begin again
some day.   Our life is one of perfect peace.   The
lonely Cossack vidette looks like a bird ; and we cannot
see the Russians, who are casting up entrenchments*
in our front, without a glass ; with that aid, they are

---

* These entrenchments were very extensive.  Opposite the
Tractir Bridge, that is, on the right bank of the river, about
three-quarters of a mile from the bridge, they made a redoubt
and zig-zags and lines, which were all taken by the French on
the 25th of May 1855, with scarcely any resistance.

plainly visible, working like bees to hem us in. A detachment of 200 Turks has been ordered from here to make stables for the cavalry ; so it is evident that arm is going to be kept quiet. There is great talk here of raising second battalions to the regiments. This would promote many officers. We are now laying up a stock for debating. War will come to an end. The Peace Society will urge that an army should not be kept up where there is no appearance of its being wanted. The half-pay list will be loaded ; the dead-weight grumbled at ; and we shall begin the next war as bravely and as badly prepared as when we began this one.

---

## LETTER XLVI.

Camp, Battery No. 4, Balaklava,
22d December 1854.

Now that my letter is gone, and that I have got off a load of official business, it seems as if I had a thousand things to say. Here is rain ; rain coming down without mercy ! Oh, dear, the poor men ! How wretched those before Sebastopol ! a portion of them remain in their turn day and night in the trenches, where they cannot move ; for if they show themselves, the enemy fire on them immediately. Here our people have rather a better time ; we are

N

out of shot, and we do not keep so many in the
trenches.    And then their life is very monotonous;
there is nothing to amuse them.    Poor fellows, they
behave themselves wonderfully.    As for me, I sometimes repine; at my age, and with my small rank,
doing the duty which is fit for a man of thirty.

27th December.

I am edified at your rescinding your fixed idea
about us officers, always excepting Captain ———.    I
really do not see why he is not to run off with women,
provided they like him well enough to go ; but it
seems strange they should choose such a *compagnon
de voyage.*    We hear that X. and Y., two unknown
quantities, were so ill received, that they will have to
return to the army here.    They are both men of
interest ; but it is very wrong to screen them, and
very hopeless, moreover.

C. has got a regiment, which means more pay.
He cannot have too much for his merit: there is no
one here who can hold a candle to him.    I am made
a substantive Major, which gives me 2s. a day more
half-pay.    I do not see why I should not have been
promoted in rank like other people.    We also hear of
the Crimean medal for men and officers, with clasps
for the battles.    The list of promotions I have not
yet seen.    Here, opposite our lines, the Russian force
has diminished.    From our highest point of view we

can see very few men, but immense works, which they may occupy at any moment. Possibly the Turks at Eupatoria may be drawing them away. If we find they are really gone, we shall most likely be sent up to the siege. The French have got their guns and ammunition into the batteries before Sebastopol, and they are now assisting in getting up ours ; so that very soon fire will be again opened. This time, I believe, we shall assault, and, I suppose, get in, paying dearly for the entry. I know that Gladstone does not build much on the Austrian alliance. The people about Lord Raglan have strange rumours of peace, which I cannot believe. " Can the Ethiop change his skin, or the leopard his spots ?" Nicholas cannot make peace on any terms France and England would agree to ; and so our poor Government will be compelled to threaten Austria with revolution unless she fights, and fights in earnest. We hear of huts, flannels, navvies, and potted meats, in yachts, all coming. But Christmas is come and gone, and our men are nearly all without cover, except the tents. Our artillery horses are dying of cold and hunger. We have had two sharp frosts, with fine sunshiny days. In fact, the climate would not be bad if we all lived in houses and slept in our beds a-night. Mr. Peto's man is come to make a railway. I wish Mr. Peto would contract to do the siege, and send away all the people whom he did not think worth preserving ; I mean not worth their salt. The fighting men would be delighted, and would know who should bear the blame of deficiencies. Our Commissary-General was a commissary in the Peninsular War, and refers every thing to that period. The principal want of our army is a regularly - organised wagon - train, which would have enabled Mr. Somebody to convey forage and food to every part of our army in any weather. Our little infantry is full of courage and cheerfulness, and you may be proud of speaking their tongue. The archers of England are like their sires 500 years back ; and in my perambulation among them I am constantly reminded of private Williams and Fluellen, Harry the king, &c. ; all which is so true to the life, that it makes one wonder more and more at the universal knowledge of Shakespeare.

## LETTER XLVII.

Camp, Battery No. 4, Balaklava,
31st December 1854.

HERE is the end of the year. On the 2d January I shall be fifty, and still a boy in some things. The papers have not yet reached me, so that I do not know what Ministers are doing. They will be pushed, doubtless, to do all they can by public opinion. Yesterday we went out with the French to make a re-

connaissance towards Baidar. The French exchanged
a few cannon-shot and took a few Cossacks, besides
burning the barracks and the forage of some Russian
Hussars at a village called Varnutka. The enemy in
our front is in small numbers ; our real enemy is the
want of transport to carry up houses and food to the
front, that is, to the soldiers before Sebastopol. It
is no use sending soldiers till we have the means
of protecting them from the weather; they will die
faster than you can send them. Snow is over all
now,—not very deep; but the sky looks as if more
were coming: a sad prospect for our poor men still in
tents. I am expecting a watch, which will not come.
I hope it will go. Perhaps it has been addressed
" Constantinople." Nothing with that address which
is worth having ever reaches the army. Without a
watch, the dreary night seems drearier and longer
than ever. I go out and ask the sentry, who is often
an hour or more wrong. C. is to have the 1st Division, unless the Duke returns. What I shall do
is unknown. My holding the situation of Assistant
Adjutant-General ought to give me my promotion ;
but I have no interest. Peace may be made. The
war, however, is still very unfinished, and a peace now
would be fatal for our country. Nicholas never will
give up Sebastopol except upon compulsion ; and we
shall not, in my opinion, be able to take it without
an assault, unless by a long operation of sapping and

starving them out, for which a large army, well found, will be requisite.

New-year's morning

The snow is gone again, and the papers are lost; so I shall not see the debate.

---

## LETTER XLVIII.

Camp, Battery No. 4, Balaklava,<br>4th January 1855.

THERMOMETER at freezing-point; snow eighteen inches deep; no wooden houses, and great difficulty in getting up provisions to the troops before Sebastopol. The men of our command are to carry bags of biscuits, weighing 112 lbs., on sticks between two, with a relief of two more men, for a distance of four miles, in snow and mud. This is for the purpose of forming, if possible, a depôt of fourteen days' food for the troops in front, lest the snow should entirely stop the communication, and expose our poor men to starvation. This measure ought to have been adopted much sooner. Now the weather is so bad that we cannot send the biscuit, because it gets wet and spoiled. All arises from want of transport, on which subject I have written at large to ——. Our own men are still most of them in tents; they began making huts, and are still striving to continue that work. Why the wooden houses, which have arrived, are not at once distributed, I cannot tell. It is very hard to be part of a machine, to see it working ill, and not to be able to move a hand to set it right. Inexorable officialities forbid. When the people in England find that their efforts and expenditure have been in vain, and that the men are not in wooden houses, but in tents at this time, there will be a storm of indignation. Sidney Herbert is told this and that and the other, and asserts it in the House. It is not true that the men have fresh meat regularly. Here I know that our men have salt meat, and scarcely ever any vegetables. He states that the regiments which have come out lately are armed with Minié rifles.* That is not the fact. If the departments had been up to their work, we should by this time have been provided with transport, and a proper train of men to work it, instead of miserable Bulgarians and Maltese. We are in the thick of the winter. If it should freeze hard after this snow, as it very likely may, the carts and horses we have will not be able to go without being roughed, which it will take a considerable time to effect. I believe we shall not have a cavalry-horse alive in a month. Meantime we hear

---

* The rifles were distributed to them after arrival at Bala-klava.

from deserters that the Russians are becoming short
of ammunition, and that water is scarce with them.
They have been digging fresh wells, in which the
water turned out to be salt. So the siege is telling
on them. The guns are fought by Finland seamen,
who at first were numerous enough to afford a relief.
Now they only stand to their guns by day, and retire
to rest at night, which amounts to half the Russian
gunners *hors de combat*. We shall take the place, I
have no doubt, unless all our men are destroyed by
the severity of the winter before we have our batteries
armed and ready to open. The number of sick from
the Guards in the trenches is very great; the men
never have dry feet; the tents are become very thin,
and let the rain drip through them; and our prospects
in this respect are terrible. But the men are heroes,
and the survivors cannot be too highly rewarded.
The families of those who sink should be all pensioned
by the nation; those who go through should be
formed into a Legion of Immortals. One who has
not seen this place cannot conceive the sufferings of
men and officers; and they are so cheerful under it
all, poor fellows! These ought to be the Queen's
Guards. There are officers in the regiments of Guards
here, who, in consequence of the war, and the privileges of their corps, are obtaining their promotion to
the rank of lieutenant-colonel in about six years' service. It is no answer to say they are brave. All the

army is brave. The Government is promoting sergeants in their own corps,—those of the Guards into the Line; their own regiment is too good for them. This is not very flattering to the Line. The wooden houses weigh two and a half tons; how shall we move them?

*5th January.*

There is such confusion at Balaklava that no one ever reckons on getting any thing that is his. I am quite in distress for a watch, and calculated on having it per post, instead of which it is to come by long sea in a parcel. *Telle est la vie !* You ask about starvation. There has not been that ; but some of the divisions have been occasionally on quarter-rations for want of transport to take it up to them. We individually are so near the ships that we can carry it up on our backs. As to Austria, I only speak in a military point of view. If she advances on the Russian armies, they must lose the Crimea, and very likely would have to make peace. If you could see war, you would enter into the views of the Peace Society ; the sufferings are so terrible, even of the poor horses. Omar Pasha arrived at Balaklava last night ; he is come to arrange about the feeding his army, which is on its way to Eupatoria ; where, I suppose, he will form a strong entrenched camp, and where any number of French and English soldiers may be landed afterwards to take the north side of Sebastopol.

## LETTER XLIX.

Camp, Battery No. 4, Balaklava,
7th January 1855.

FREEZING hard for the last three days, with a
good deal of snow on the ground.  The poor men !
Ours are comparatively well off ; for, being near Balaklava, they can get fuel ; but in front ! there is no
carrying charcoal in any quantity there ; the brushwood is all exhausted ; and I fear they seldom get a
warm meal.  Biscuit and rum, that they do get.  A
private soldier of the Light Division, to whom I spoke
yesterday in Balaklava, told me very quietly that on
the previous night (thermometer 20°) he had been
twelve hours in the trenches.  He started for Balaklava at daylight without breakfast—a good seven
miles—leading horses to load with rations for his company, and had to return with them, and would reach
his company about dark, to go into a cold tent, and
a turn in the trenches in the morning.  The man did
not look ill ; in fact, none but people of the hardiest
constitution can stand it ; all the others are dead
or dying.  There have been accidents, too, with the
charcoal—suffocation.  This is terrible work ; and
the winter may, and sometimes does, last till May.
Thirteen Turks frozen to death in the trenches here
three nights ago.  We (our lot I mean) are waiting
for the result of the Duke's medical board ; if he is

put into orders to go home sick, C. will be appointed to command the 1st Division ; if there is no vacancy of either Assistant Adjutant or Quartermaster-General in that Division, I shall resign my staff appointment, which would place me in the 4th Division, and become Aide-de-camp to C. This will be a great descent in the scale of staff-officers. We shall have a beautiful division; and the Highlanders are very strong, about eighteen hundred bayonets. They will, of course, bring us up for the assault ; and if we carry the place, we shall have plenty of laurels or tears ; both, I dare say. It must be taken ; and I hear that our women are showing their minds very plainly on the point of gentlemen going home who are not sick. The people at White's cut ——— ; and ——— found also he could not stand it. They are coming out ; but they are both damaged. You know we all expected the Russians would come on again, as we could not tell at first how hard we had hit them.

I have been writing answers since four o'clock this morning to letters of people of all ranks, who have sent presents for the men of warm clothing. C. has been promised three fur coats already; they are not here, however. Some of the letters are very good, and most of them national. I am sure we shall get plenty of English recruits, far better than a Foreign Legion.

## LETTER L.

Camp, Battery No. 4, Balaklava,
10th January 1855.

I AM too sure that my poor watch has gone the way the thousands of parcels which are despatched from England have the habit of going, viz. the wrong way. I have sent a friend of mine another cheque, and begged him to send me out a watch by post. Should the first one make its appearance by mistake, I shall easily sell it. You cannot imagine the inconvenience it is to me to be without a watch. I have to regulate every one else's time about duties ; and it is pitiful to see me hunting about for some one whose watch is still going, to find out an approximation to the time. Yesterday I was obliged to go on duty to the Light Division, which is before Sebastopol. The ground was covered with melting snow, regular slush, with hard frozen ground underneath ; so that riding was a ticklish matter. I found sad misery among the men ; they have next to no fuel, almost all the roots even of the brushwood being exhausted. They are entitled to rations of charcoal ; but they have no means of drawing it, and their numbers are so reduced, that they cannot spare men enough to bring it six or seven miles from Balaklava. The consequence is, they cannot dry their stockings or shoes ; they come in from the trenches with frost-bitten toes,

swelled feet, chilblains, &c.; their shoes freeze, and
they cannot put them on. Those who still, in spite
of this misery, continue to do their duty, often go into
the trenches without shoes by preference, or they cut
away the heels to get them on. None of the fine warm
clothes have reached them yet. I heard of one company going into the trenches fourteen men strong ;
all the rest dead, sick, broken. One night lately
forty-five men went into the trenches, of whom nineteen were sent out during the night; nine died. If
this goes on, the trenches must be abandoned, or occupied by the French, lest we should be annihilated.
I heard of men on their knees crying with pain. Of
course there are men, and plenty of them, who will
never give in, but rather die on the spot for England
and duty ; but these cases of weakness are evil, and
contagious symptoms of the *morale* being shaken.
Transport ! *voilà tout*. Every thing should be carried
to the men's tents for them ; but I see no signs yet of
an organisation of transport. There is a rumour of
some such attempt in England. I expect every day
that, from sheer want of numbers, we shall have to
take our Highlanders to the siege, and try if that
splendid brigade is made of tougher materials. But
then how is Balaklava to be guarded ? The officers,
of course, are not suffering actually quite so much as
the men, though quite as much in proportion to their
previous habits. They manage to get larger boots,

and their feet usually are smaller. The ammunition-boots sent from England are capital, but too small; the largest size sent ought to have been the smallest. It is now quite mild, every thing thawing, and threatening rain. I do not know which weather is worst for the poor fellows; and I can do nothing to help. Alas! it makes me very sad to see such men lost in such a way. Our numbers for duty at this moment are just about what they were before the reinforcements came. I have heard of a whole regiment not being able to turn out seven men for duty. Many of the frost-bitten men will lose their feet; many will recover; but the army, meantime, is cruelly weakened. The French suffer little of all this; for they have plenty of organised transport. There is some one wanting to lick matters into shape at Balaklava. They have sent down Major Mackenzie and Captain Ross, both excellent officers, recently appointed to the Quartermaster General's department; but they are under the Commandant, who is their senior officer. Lord Raglan rode into the village yesterday to investigate into the state of affairs, and the admired disorder which rules. Major Mackenzie told his Lordship every thing he saw wrong, without the slightest disguise. ———— was present. When Lord Raglan was gone, he said to Mackenzie, "Why, you told him the truth." "Just what the man wants to hear," was Mackenzie's reply.

This is quite Indian ; this was the dragon which Sir Charles Napier grappled with, and the contest cost him his place and his life. India is a rotten job from bottom to top. The boasted Sepoy army are known, to all who have seen them tried, to be very timid ; yet they are praised by Lord Hardinge, Lord Gough, and Lord Ellenborough, which is incomprehensible to me, as they ought to know better ; while the Company and its officers are afraid of their army.

11th January.

It rained gently all day yesterday, but the temperature was mild. The French are carrying up shells for our use, and I cannot but think that the fresh bombardment must take place soon. It will continue for several days, and then the assault, which the soldier longs for, in the hope of getting rid of the terrible trench-duty. It is now—I have just looked out—freezing slightly. I cannot tell whether it be two, four, or five o'clock in the morning. The sentry says it's half-past one; and the cocks are crowing, who, I should think, ought to know best,—and no rational cock would crow at one in the morning in January. At any rate, time and the hour will bring our morning misery. By the last mail all our papers miscarried ; but accident brought me one with the debate on the vote of thanks. I am inclined to think, that one reason which might be fairly adduced on

the Foreign Enlistment Bill for adopting it, is, the
probability of our obtaining trained soldiers in this
way more quickly than by training Englishmen; but
I dare say the patronage is also taken into account.
We must have soldiers; there are here now of the
infantry, rank and file, not more than 16,000.   Deduct 350 a week *hors de combat* by sickness; 5000
killed and wounded in the assault; where is the
army, after that, in the spring to drive the Russians
out of the Crimea?   They are losing forty a day at
the hospital at Scutari; many who do not die will
never be fit to join again; and of those who do re-
join, many relapse as soon as the causes which made
them sick begin to act again.

12th January.

Very early in the morning.   A hard frost, and
snow just opening on us, with strong north wind.
Last night I heard, on pretty good authority, that
Canrobert wants to open fire within ten days; that
Lord Raglan wishes first to get up fifty more guns;
that there has been a discussion on the subject, and
a compromise has been arranged; that there is to be
a feint of making this attack of fifty guns on our
right; from which I deduce we shall bombard and
assault the place before the end of the month.   The
French are very impatient at the delay, and Canrobert
wants to be a Maréchal de France.   Meantime Lord
Stratford tells all the people at Constantinople that

peace will be made, which I do not believe. That has been the cry of the Ministry all along, and has prevented them from being ready for war. I really believe that some of them thought the sending 3000 Guards to Malta would be considered a formidable move by Nicholas. I got my papers last night, which ought to have reached me many days back ; they come up to the 22d, but most of their news has transpired orally. Lord Ellenborough looks more cut out for a War-Minister than any one else, and a great War-Minister we must have if this war is to go on, or at least to go on successfully.

4·45 A.M. I have just found out the hour. A corporal of marines has come from the heights with two French prisoners whom he captured outside the lines ; they had made a fire, which had alarmed all the picquets. They spoke an Italian patois ; and had sbaglioed the strada to cut boschi, and so were making themselves comfortable for the night. This kind of rovers are always suspected of meaning to desert. I see Layard is in an ugly scrape. Perhaps Sir E. Lyons may not find himself able to do much more than Dundas.

## LETTER LI.

Camp, Battery No. 4, Balaklava,
15th January 1855.

You talk of Christmas Day being so merry to
some people. I never can remember any merriment
in it ; for I had not a happy childhood, although I
had the best of mothers. Now, every day passes to me
like the last, Sunday and Monday, Christmas alike,
without joy; yet I make a grim jest occasionally, and
perhaps pass for a facetious fellow enough. We got
the *Times* of last Christmas, which is any thing but
a jest to the head-quarter people. Whether it be the
forerunner of some change, I cannot augur. I have
heard a rumour from England that C. is to be appointed second in command ; raised over the heads
of all the well-protected men, to be next to Lord
Raglan. I believe it would be a very wise step, so
far as it would go ; but it would give him no power of
displacing ineffective staff-officers. We still have no
apparent attempt at organising transport. The mail
of the 29th has come, but our papers and letters are
not delivered. The snow has fallen fast and furious
for the last two days, and is two feet deep. Yesterday, for the first time, there appeared a general order
to the commissary to carry fuel to the soldiers in the
front. It remains to be seen whether he has the
means of doing so. Fancy all these men without

fuel ! How can they grub for roots of trees under the snow ? Sure I am that in this deep snow and hard frost, without fuel, many must perish ; and that this morning, when daylight comes, thousands of them will have nothing to cook with. Raw meat, biscuit, and rum is all they can get. Why was not this order given a month ago ? Why ? Because there was still a little brushwood to be obtained by hard work on the part of the men, already overtaxed by their labour in the trenches. Exquisite reason! The Turks are dying frightfully; and they are even deserting—a thing usually unknown among them. We are going to begin a battery, as I told you, on the right. I hope you have a plan. In this weather work is impossible. Canrobert, who, while not responsible, was always the first and most dashing of soldiers, is now obliged to reflect and go slow, which his men cannot understand. We may have a month or six weeks of this weather. How many will survive it ? The mass of the Russian army is in the rear, where they doubtless most of them are housed in villages. I confess I do not see my way through it. The climate cannot be controlled. The wooden houses should have been here six weeks ago. I have seen one up, with a stove in it ; it will be very comfortable. Before winter is over, most of these houses will be up, I dare say ; but it will be too late. Yesterday the 18th regiment, which has been at Balaklava for some time, was sent to exchange places with the 63d regiment, the latter having only 50 men left. By the by, remember that C. is not responsible for the state of Balaklava ; he does not command there. He thought he did, and began knocking the staff-officers about, and the new commandant, for various misdeeds, when an order came out to place the troops under command of the commandant. Private interest with some one. Should the rumour I have alluded to prove true, there will be a rare commotion, as C. will stand no nonsense when he has the power to stop it. We are here in comparative comfort, as this hovel has a Russian stove, and being near Balaklava, we can procure charcoal ; so that we do not suffer from cold ; but we may be moved at any moment to the front, to pitch our tents in the snow, and bear what the others are bearing. Luckily we have got all our horses and mules in good health ; and if we are moved, we shall by these means continue to obtain our supplies, by sending six miles ; but it will be hard work for the servants and orderlies, who, however, will get their own at the same time. We shall have to use all our own animals and the other officers' horses to get up things for our men ; for we shall put small faith in commissaries. " Who would be fed, themselves must find the mules." My unhappy watch ! I am not even told what ship it is to come by, which would give me a chance. I calculated on receiving it on

Christmas Day or thereabouts. The post goes by
Marseilles, and the parcels by long sea. There is
no person at Balaklava to take charge, no consignee ;
and packages are pillaged in the most shameless manner. One came yesterday to Shadwell, containing
furs ; it was brought in the "Alma" by an officer of
the Guards ; they actually pillaged that, while in his
charge, and stole two fur caps and sundry other
articles. Hayter and Howell ought to have a correspondent and a warehouse here ; and they will, I suppose, have both, when the outcry becomes loud enough.
You ask, in a jeering manner, how I digest ———
getting into the House. It is part of our constitution,
that people of the lower classes should be able to rise
to any position in the country; and I admire the constitution, and wish to stick by it. He is, I suspect,
however, a great quack, and much overrated. The
democrats have more reason to boast of De Lacy
Evans, for he is a right good soldier. Peace continues
to be talked about. Without peace, we, here in the
Crimea, have no option but to conquer or perish. We
cannot embark while the Russian army is within a
hundred miles of us. I mean it is absolutely impossible, even if we abandon guns and stores and every
thing ; and that the people of England ought to know.
Nothing will do, except an army of French and English strong enough, after we get into Sebastopol, to
march out and drive the Russians out of the Crimea ;

and to do that, will require a movable army of
150,000 men. This absolute necessity for men ex-
plains in a great degree the foreign enlistment bill.
Of course we can stay where we are and defy Russia ;
but England cannot mean that her whole army
should be shut up in this corner for an indefinite
period. They must, in case of continuing the war,
gird up their loins and find a new Minister awake
to the grandeur of the crisis. You want in England
an army of reserve of 100,000 men, complete in artillery and complete in transport, and you want 50,000
men here equally complete; with them, and 100,000
French, I believe we can do any thing in the Crimea.
But we dare not go into the heart of Russia. The
mightiest genius that has appeared for ages, and the
greatest of all generals, tried that and failed. Our
General Raglan is 67, Brown is older, C. is 62, but
he is an exception to all rules, for he is as active as a
boy, and, I think, will, sometime or other, unless he
is killed, command this army. As to the cavalry, it
is gone ; I do not believe there will be a horse left
by spring. The troopers themselves are not suffering
from sickness ; they have no trench- or night-duty,
and being near Balaklava, they can, if they know how,
make themselves pretty comfortable.

## LETTER LII.

Camp, Battery No. 4, Balaklava,
18th January 1855.

NEWSPAPERS to the 1st. I see in one of them a bit of ——'s letter. Lord Raglan is beginning to move about and show himself. It does seem rather hard for him to be attacked without the power of defence. Look to my case ; my watch case. I required a watch for my duty. I sent the disabled one by the master of a man-of-war to Constantinople for repair, and to be returned to me. It has never come back. At the same time I sent the money for a new one to a friend of mine in London, who had served in navy and army, had knocked about in the Colonies, and was in business in London. I described the watch I wanted, I told where it was to be procured, and how sent to me, viz. in Lord Raglan's bag. I felt quite sure of receiving it by return of post. Not at all ! My friend thought fit to send it by long sea. The newspapers may say it was want of organisation, or not going about, or some obtuseness of mine which prevented my having a watch. I cannot see that I neglected any precaution ; and yet my want of this very watch might make my column late for the attack. A thaw has come on to-day. I have just heard from General Vinoy that he saw yesterday a Turkish officer who spoke French, and who had just returned from

Eupatoria. There are 33,000 Turkish and Egyptian troops there, and Omar Pasha is coming with the rest of his army, and cavalry and artillery. If two French divisions of 8000 men each join him, they will make a fine diversion for us. They talk, however, of the French landing at Kaffa to cut off the Russian retreat to Kertsch. If they are blocked that way, and the road to Perekop threatened by Omar Pasha, while the main French and English army attack them on the other side of Sebastopol, they will be taken to a man. From signs I see, I really do believe that we shall soon open fire.

## LETTER LIII.

Camp, Battery No. 4, Balaklava,
22d January 1855.

THE papers are making fearful attacks on Lord Raglan, which I am very sorry for. We cannot really know if the attacks be just ; and we are sure that now is not the moment to publish them, when probably most of the mistakes are in process of being mended. How can an army go on with every soldier reading such assaults against its general ? The French army would mutiny in a similar position ; but Napoleon is too wise to allow such things to be published. Will it ever be clearly shown who was to blame ? The Duke of Newcastle will evidently go first. Your best man to fill his place is Lord Ellenborough beyond all doubt, and he is a Conservative. The next best man I could name is Dalhousie; and I do not know what to say about Lord Grey. I hope they will leave Lord Raglan where he is. I do not see any one able to take his place; not exactly for military skill, but as a grand seigneur, and an admirable diplomatist. The art of commanding an army is not like reading and writing—it does not come by nature. Practice is every thing. Lord Raglan has now had some of that. De Lacy Evans has fallen into bad health, or he might have done. Whoever gets it, if they do recall Lord Raglan, will have to mend the broken threads which his Lordship has doubtless been spinning with a view to make his army efficient, and there will be a loss of most valuable time. The new right battery, of twenty-two guns, is to be made. From my own notion of our siege, I am not for hurrying; I would make every disposition of guns possible before beginning. We must make the assault as little murderous as we can, for we want our men to fight in the field afterwards. I believe even Canrobert has come round to agree that it is better to make our works as perfect as may be before beginning. But the soldiery, who suffer, poor fellows! are impatient. The weather has now become fine, and the snow and frost are gone.

## LETTER LIV.

I SENT you a very short letter by the last post, for I was hurried by business and had no time. We continue in these parts to be a good deal put out by the attacks made on our Chief in the papers. I see also a letter from an Anglo-Parisian, making an assertion about the staff, which is not true, at least in my case, for I did get a first-class certificate at Sandhurst in the year 1832. Now let me tell you what that is. The course of examination in my day was common mathematics, algebra, trigonometry, map-making, and fortification. Those who went any deeper into mathematics, and chose to stand an examination in the higher branches, such as the differential calculus, got this extra certificate, or at least do get it now; for it is so long ago that I forget whether there was a document added to the certificate; but I remember that I did pass in such things. Now, a man may know all these lessons, and yet be a very bad staff-officer. They are useful, no doubt, but they cannot supply what nothing but experience will give. Will the differential calculus help a man to organise a transport train? The knowledge I acquired at Sandhurst did, however, cause me to be promoted (by purchase) to be a captain. For when I went to the siege of Antwerp, my letters were always conveyed to the Duke of Wellington, and they turned out to be by far the best information he got on the subject of that siege ; and he consequently desired the folks at the Horse Guards to promote me, and employ me on the staff. I was then a lieutenant of Heavy Dragoons ; but I was never off the staff afterwards, until I retired as a captain of my own accord, finding I could not get any promotion either regimentally or unattached, after eighteen years' service. I held appointments both in Quartermaster-Generals' and Adjutant-Generals' departments ; and once, for three months, I did the duty of Adjutant-General to the army in Ireland, so much to old Blakeney's satisfaction, that he applied to the Horse Guards to have me promoted to Major (by purchase) ; which, if I had been a Lord, would, I dare say, have been done. I therefore maintain that I had very considerable experience in the duties of a staff-officer ; and I may say, without any risk of its being contradicted, that there was not any one of them who had been so long employed on the staff as myself. I do not count aides-de-camp. I was made Brigade-Major, not by the Horse Guards, but by C. ; those who had interest were made assistant-adjutant, or assistant quartermaster-generals ; the brigade-major is only a large adjutant, over the three regimental adjutants ; the assistant adjutant-general is over

the two brigade-majors, to issue orders from the
general of the division. C. and I have both had
much experience; but his has been always in war,
and mine, till now, never. We, however, possess no
power to remedy any radical error existing in the two
departments, viz. those of the Adjutant-General and
Quartermaster-General at head-quarters. We can
only represent and lament. The Quartermaster-
General of this army, when the expedition to the
Crimea was planned, might have objected to start
unless transport was provided; and if he agreed to
go without it, he might at least have insisted on its
following immediately; and he, for his own sake,
should have put his opinions on record. Perhaps he
has done so. The Commissary-General should have
been put under the screw, and Lord Raglan, urged by
his Quartermaster-General, should have been made
to demand from Government a regular wagon-train,
which they would not have dared to refuse him. He
ought to have had it in Bulgaria. I am told that
they are preparing one in England now. Meantime
we have rumours of peace here; a fatal step for England, and for Europe, if it be true. I have just read
this over; it has been lying by for a day or two; it
is very full of I's. They are sending out such a quantity of things for the men, that I believe many will be
thrown away; they cannot be carried. The furs will
become matted with mud and filled with vermin, and

a perfect nuisance. From England there should be
sent a hundred furriers to clean and store them up
for next year ; for after March these furs will be quite
useless to any one who has to move about. The shopkeepers in Balaklava have received orders to move
out of the village, and to erect huts for themselves
near Kadikoi. This will clear the streets in Balaklava.
No one will go there any longer to drink, and the
houses given up by the shopkeepers will become available for stores or for hospitals : the folly was ever
letting any shopkeeper in. War cannot be made upon
amiable principles ; it is a stern reality. I believe
they thought that all the inhabitants were to remain
peaceably in their houses, that no grapes were to be
pulled, no fowls seized ; in fact, placing 50,000 men
between starvation and stealing, and fondly imagining
they would prefer the first. Now the valley is entirely
stripped ; there is not a tree, nor a bush, nor an inha-
bitant remaining. Almost all the cottages are down,
which looked so white and smiling among the vineyards ; even the vine-roots are many of them extracted,
it having been discovered that they make excellent
firewood—*des souches superbes*, as the French say.
In the spring, the mass of dead horses and men, and
all the various débris, will make this place very unhealthy, I should fear. We have buried 2300 Turks
already. I do not know how many English, but too
many. They are constantly sending both English

and French sick away. Our army is dwindling down
to a mere handful. When it is too late, Lord Raglan
has been obliged to say to Canrobert, that he cannot
hold his trenches for want of men.* He should have
said so two months ago ; not having done so, he went
on working his men to death, with barely one night
out of the trenches, while the French had always two
nights or three, for what I can tell. The consequence
was, they had plenty of men to spare for their own
comforts, besides being provided with transport. Now
the French army has sent a force to the right attack,
which has taken a portion of the trenches off our
hands, and thus relieved our poor soldiers materially.
But I am afraid the seeds of disease must have been
planted in many of them who still keep up. I find
that many of our own 93d, close by, who have been
suffering from fever, are going to die, and, on examination, ulceration of the intestines has been discovered.
The men here get scarcely any thing but salt meat,
and they do not eat it now. The French have always
had fresh meat for the officers, and every other day
for the soldiers. I do not approve of the distinction ;
but that is the fashion of their army. Why or how
they have had fresh meat every other day, and fresh
bread baked every other day, for their whole army,

---

* It is stated that his Lordship did apply for this relief, but
that the French put it off from day to day.

which is probably four times as numerous as ours,
while we have been left on salt meat and biscuit, is a
question that forms a part of the great investigation
and retribution that I hope will fall sooner or later on
the guilty person, whoever he may be.   England will
cry for her men.   Fame will point out their graves in
the bleak Tauris.   Let us hope that a noble revenge
will be taken, by pardoning, where possible, the faults
which are not to be attributed so much to the indi-
viduals, as to a system which we must abandon, or
we perish as a military nation.   I saw yesterday 200
sick carried on board on French mules ; I saw the
gaunt faces ; not one ever likely to do a day's duty
again.   It is useless making a victim of the Duke of
Newcastle, or of Lord Raglan.   The worst defects
will be remedied now, whoever is put to manage.
They are hard at it now in the House.   That House !
Give me Cromwell to do this job.   One and indivisi-
ble must be the power to act really with vigour.   The
weather has become very agreeable.   Sharpish frosts
at night, and beautiful sunshiny days, so that our
poor fellows will be able to dry their socks and boots.
But the mud is unutterable.   In the morning it is
hard on top, and a good stamp lets you through into
slush ; by 10 o'clock it is melted, and wading lasts
all day.   Stilts have not yet been adopted.   If I
was only young, I think I should appear very shortly
flamingo fashion.   Railway not begun.   Crimean-

fund people not come; that is to say, two gents are come, I believe; but no goods yet manifest. The best good thing that could be sent for the soldiers would be tablets of the French dried preserved vegetables. Even that is now supplied to the French troops. You might, out of curiosity, buy one and cook it yourself. It is in hard small cakes. Soak it in warm water, and the leaves imbibe the liquid at all their pores, and swell, and become themselves again, and are afterwards cooked like any other vegetables. It may be called a perfect invention. I believe the original inventor was Masson or Chollet; but the Germans are imitating. They are made of all sorts; and some of the coarser kinds, ticketed *provisionnement d'équipage*—I suppose intended for ships' crews—would be of the greatest benefit. You could not find out they were not fresh vegetables. A surgeon, a friend of mine here, tells me he would not wish to give our men, who appear still healthy, meat every day. He would prefer only to do so every other day, and to give them vegetable diet on the blank days; for he says their stomachs would not stand their usual feeding; and that if they got into garrison at Malta without this precaution, they would all be ill.

25th January.

The astounding intelligence reached camp last night, by the *Times* of the 8th, that the four points are accepted without reserve. My papers have missed this time ; but I see they will patch up a peace, without half punishing Russia ; and now our army, which a year or two of war would have placed upon a proper footing, will go back to its old condition of a number of regiments, and no army at all. It is a sad misfortune that we did not take Sebastopol, because I think the terms we should in that case have been forced to demand would have been much harder. Fighting any more now would be brutal, for there is no argument of war ; the enemy having accepted our terms without reserve. I therefore expect very shortly to hear of an armistice. It will be many months before we can get all our material away from this country; and I conclude it will be probable that a joint force of French and English will remain in Turkey, to put, if possible, that country into some sort of order. C. will, perhaps, be left in command of the English part ; so that I may see a good deal of Turkey yet, before my thread is cut. The moment peace is made, there will be a terrible lot of men fall sick, who are only kept going now by the spirit that is in them.

26th January.

We hear, by letter from Vienna, dated 14th, that peace is still far off. Nicholas only trying to gain time. The rogue !

P

## LETTER LV.

Camp, Battery No. 4, Balaklava,
29th January 1855.

THIS day, twenty-nine years ago, I got my first commission. I have been one of a board to receive the statements of the head railway man about a proposed Balaklava railway. The first thing he said was, that he should want labour and horses—500 men, and I know not how many horses! Really, now, is it not provoking? If we had had labour, we could have made a good road without him; and if we had horses, we could even now send up our stores without a railway. They do not bring any locomotives with them; only wagons,—weight, one and a half tons,—to be drawn along a tram-road by our miserable ponies. The navvies not come. If they had sent the latter with spades and sledge-hammers, to make a good macadamised road, that would have been far more sensible, in my opinion. The labour and expense of making a railway would have made a grand road indeed, upon which every sort of cart, pony-chaise, or truck, could have been drawn. However, we are in the hands of the Philistines. I saw another French general (Mayran), besides our friend and neighbour Vinoy. They all screamed at the idea of going away without taking the place. It is, I believe, quite decided to attack the Round Tower,* by the new French battery on the extreme right, as well as by our own batteries opposite to it, so as to bring a cross-fire in some degree. They propose firing night and day, to prevent the Russians repairing their works, and then to launch the infantry, who, after all, must pay. Nothing but infantry can get in; when the assault there succeeds, I suppose a lodgment will be made in the White Tower, or rather in its ruins, wherein to place new batteries. Our loss, if the Russians make a respectable resistance, which I have no doubt of, cannot be calculated at less than 5000 men, killed and wounded. Should our assault fail, which is possible, from the obstacles being greater than we can now discover, the loss will be still more; and remember, in these attacks, it is the best and most dauntless soldiers in both armies who fall, for they will be the foremost. In the field of battle, drawn up in line, the chance is equal; but when the storm begins, the bravest rush first, and have often made a bridge of their bodies for the succeeding columns. Possibly we may be kept here to protect Balaklava; but what I think most likely is, that a detachment from the Highlanders will be ordered, not to deprive them of the honour of being present. All these arrangements are *in petto* of Milordo Raglan. I see by the last Army-List, that our Bala-

---

* The Malakoff.

klava division is put down as a separate command;
however, in the town we do not command, and are not
responsible.  The newspapers have got the account
of my Cossack lance.  I have sent it in the "Sanspareil" to —— to stick up in his halls.  We have
some sort of an idea that there will be formed a Highland division for C.  The 71st is here, and the 72d
and 92d are coming.  That would clear us from the
Guards, with whom we wish to have nothing to do :
their privileges and pretensions are very inconvenient.
At present, our men are occupied putting up the
wooden huts.  As soon as they are housed, we shall
have to proceed to repair our fortifications, which are
a little damaged by the frost.  For if we are to remain here, no doubt, as soon as the valley of the
Chernaya is dry again, and the ground hard, we shall
have a large force of Russians hemming us in, and
hanging over us like a thunder-cloud, and we shall be
again constantly on the *qui vive*, not taking off our
clothes ; all the work of the beginning of winter over
again.  You will, if I live, have a continued history
of war's alarms, from a very poor Froissart.  The Crimean fund, whatever that is, has arrived yesterday in
the " Fairy" yacht.  I came on her quite by surprise,
looking so nice and clean and Cowish, with the white
ensign and burgee displayed.  All this is very kind ;
but great stuff.  If they would only send plenty of
horses and carts, and fat beeves for the soldiers' din-

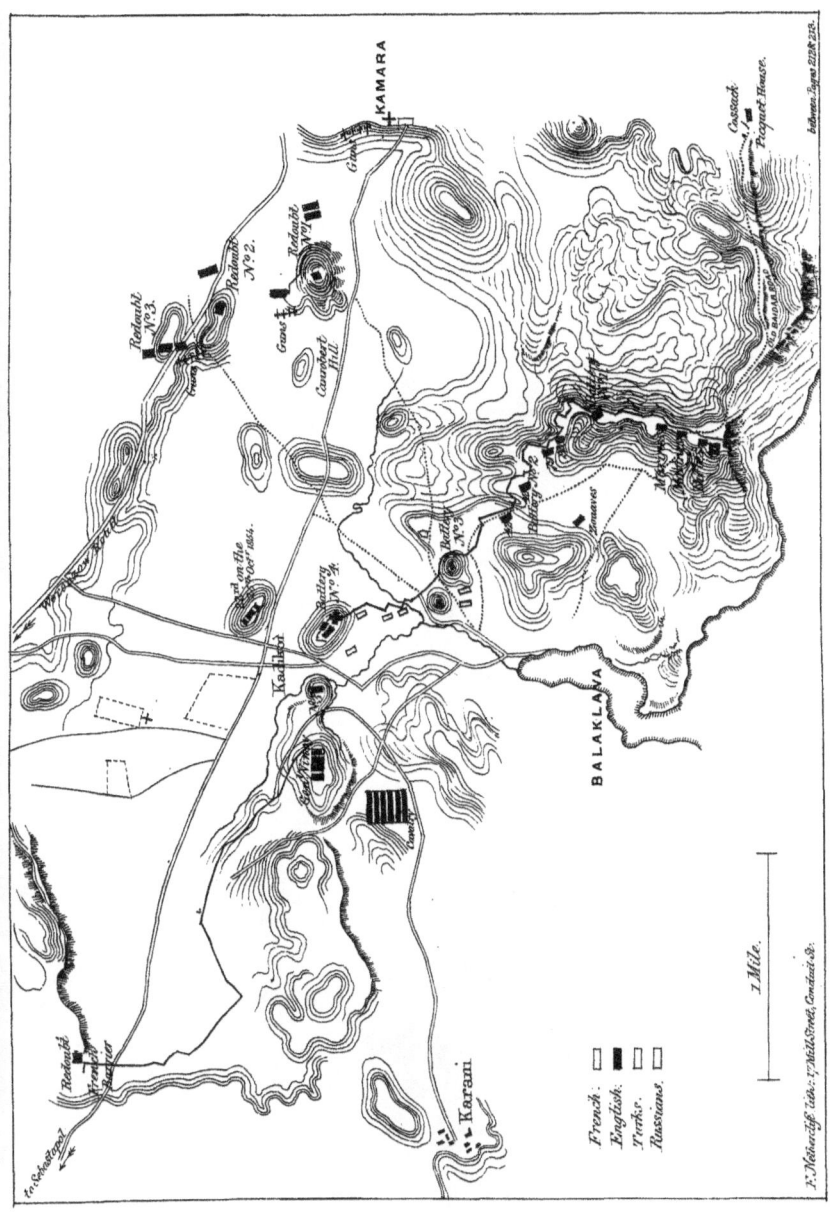

French.
English.
Turks.
Russians.

1 Mile.

F. Netherclift lith: 7 Whitehall Street, Comhill St.

ners, it would be more use than a forest of hashed venison. I hope, before I write again, to send you a tracing of our position here on a good large scale, as I have got a drawing-board made by the Sappers. Take care who sees it, and do not let it be copied.

## LETTER LVI.

Camp, Battery No. 4, Balaklava,
1st February 1855.

I now send you a sketch, which will give you a good idea of our position. Do not let it be copied, or it will get into the *Illustrated London News.* You had better preserve the letters I write to you. I have no journal or record of any sort, except copies of some official letters, during all these months left behind ; but my letters to my various friends must make a rather voluminous collection. Keppel has come in the "St. Jean d'Acre." When he got to our camp, he seemed much surprised that we did not look miserable or desponding. The heroes who went home must have told wonderful tales, to account for their presence in England. You speak of De Lacy Evans's letter, throwing blame upon Lord Raglan. Of course it does ; but Lord Raglan could not make the required fortifications without men, and all his men were

guarding and making trenches before Sebastopol and
in front of Balaklava.    When your army is too small
for your enterprise, what is to be done ?    Yet soldiers
must be enterprising.    Lord Raglan's fault has been
the not refusing to act at all till his army was fit to
move, and complete in every respect.    You talk of
Napier's indiscretion, letting destructive cats out of
the bag.    Surely we have destruction enough going
on around us, without longing to indulge a taste
for destroying the constitution of the country.    With
respect to the sketch of position I send, the Russian
cavalry came over the hills where the green troops are
painted, and the charge against them by our heavy
cavalry was made about where an X is drawn, near
a vineyard.    The Russian cavalry ran away over the
hills again ; the charge of the Light Cavalry took
place behind those hills, and out of our sight.    The
Turks in redoubts Nos. 1, 2, and 3, as well as in two
others, which are not laid down on the Plan, but
which were occupied by Turks, along the Woronzow
Road, ran away, mostly towards the 93d ; the said
93d remained on the little eminence till dark on the
25th October, and then quietly moved into the battery No. 4, where six companies have remained ever
since ; and we spent our time in watching continually,
for weeks, the Russian guns and infantry in the redoubts, and between them.    Their force was about
20,000 infantry, which were encamped in the re-

doubts, and further back. The Chernaya, or Black River, is about a mile from No. 3 redoubt. We hear that the two Grand-Dukes are returned to Sebastopol, and we, therefore, have every reason to expect an attack. We are arming our batteries. The French have driven mines right under the Russian works on our left. The mines ought to be a profound secret; but I hear they are mentioned in the English papers! If the Russians know where the mines are, they will make a counter-mine, and spoil them. O freedom of the press, what an implement of war art thou! Meantime I hear from the commissary that they are getting a few animals, and that they are doing better with their transport. They have ordered Admiral Boxer here; it is said he is very rude. I hope he will not be so to the merchant-captains, who have now been for some time accustomed to the gentle and sensible Captain Heath, of the "Sanspareil." Violence and bad language is not the way to make people work willingly; and our merchant-captains of these great steamers must not be so treated. They have one and all of them been most obliging and even kind in their behaviour to men and officers; and we shall be shocked if they are insulted. Some navvies are come, and the foundation for the railway is begun; but it will be a long job, I fear. In the mean time we have had ten days of beautiful weather. Many of our Highland huts are up. The days are becoming longer;

and I hope some recovered sick will return. The
state of the English army is 14,000 duty-men, 10,000
sick absent, 5000 sick present, and, in fact, there are
only 11,000 men (English) besieging Sebastopol !
The Russians, of course, have also suffered from sickness in a degree which we cannot estimate. Perhaps
the diplomatists by this time have come to an armistice; who knows ? That would be a poor conclusion ;
but Russia may be more pressed than we know of.
My sphere of activity here is very circumscribed. I
have neither rank nor power ; but I do my best, with
a despairing heart, to make things go right. No
watch come yet ; it is a terrible want. I hear, however, of parcels addressed to me in " Foyle," " Clyde,"
and " East Anglian," none of which ships are come yet.
Possibly I may rescue some of these parcels from the
chaos of Balaklava, perhaps even the watch itself ;
but I depend more on the second one by Lord Raglan's
bag. The other letters and papers are sorted at Constantinople. The post-office people in London supposed they would find sorters there to be hired, which
turned out to be a mistake ; but I understand they
have sent home for a number of practised English
sorters : meanwhile our papers are continually going
wrong. Now I must turn away to do some letters
on military business, for the day is breaking, and my
duty begins. I must frame an order about the soldiers' wellbeing ; driving the lazy, and poking up the

indifferent, to attend to vegetables, and rum, and lime-juice, and many an etcetera, which may conduce to keep our remaining men in health for the coming struggle. A parcel has come for me. A present from ——, with food, and a plaid, and books. How good-natured! I thought at first it was the watch. Frost has set in again, nearly as cold as before; but not much snow. So long as it is dry, our men, having warm clothing, will not suffer. The Russians near us are not moving, although for prudence' sake we are all on the *qui vive*, as at first. I believe that Lord Raglan has had a letter from the Duke of Newcastle, laying all the blame of every thing upon him; he has been much affected by it, and that in so composed a person is very remarkable—I mean his showing it. It is not quite right, for they ordered him to come to the Crimea. I hope he can prove that he represented that his army was not properly provided with transport. That is the main fault; and if he was ordered to come without that necessary provision, he is no longer the culprit. But I should not be surprised if he were to resign, which I shall regret, for I know no one so fit for this command. We hear that the 10th Hussars, with 700 horses, are near. I do not imagine that they will come beyond Scutari at present. Two new generals are come. One went up to join his brigade, but he found the ground damp where his tent was pitched, and so returned immediately to Bala-

klava, until the commissariat could carry up a house
for him ; the first duty of a general being to make
himself comfortable.   The other has been lamenting,
and even crying, at the state of affairs.   What does
any one come here for except to die, when it becomes
a man to die?   These sort of generals are enough to
cow any men except ours.   They ought to be sent
straight back to England, ticketed, " With care, and
to be kept dry."

---

## LETTER LVII.

Camp, Battery No. 4, Balaklava,
8th February 1855.

THE watch has come !   The second one, now on
its way by post, will readily find a purchaser.   We
are all on the look-out now, having had a report last
night of 35,000 Ruskis coming to attack us by the
old Baidar road.   Now that you have a plan, you will
see how they may be expected to arrive from the small
Cossack picquet-house.   If they could force through
by the Cut Road, which you will find laid down, they
would stream right into Balaklava ; and though they
would probably be all cut off by General Vinoy's
Frenchmen, they would be able to do us an infinity
of mischief by destroying stores.   But I think that
we are too well posted, and that they will be beaten

back with ignominy. As they find our preparations
for bombarding every day getting nearer completion,
the probability of their attacking increases. The attack at Inkermann stopped the siege, and they may
hope for a similar result by another onslaught ; but
the French are now very numerous here—they say,
80,000 men—and if attacked in front, would give a
good account of their enemy. We and the French
are both pushing on our trenches and batteries. A
division of French has moved to our right, before
Sebastopol, and thus relieved some of our men from
the trench-duty, which was wearing them down. The
French are very impatient for the assault, and talk of
making it in spite of their general. The Guards are
ordered away from the siege to Balaklava to recover
themselves. They are not coming to our lines, but
to the village in our rear, and they will have to take
all the fatigue-duties on the wharfs. We have good
reason to think C. will be made a Lieutenant-general,
which will materially increase his pay, besides ena-
bling him to hold a higher command. I am told there
is another tremendous article against poor Lord Raglan, and that the officers of the Guards are sending
letters abusing him, which are handed about among
their female connections at Court and elsewhere. In
fact, this is very unkind of them, for the Guards have
always been favoured so far as possible consistently
with their pretensions of taking all duties that other

soldiers perform. They broke down in Bulgaria long
before any of the others, and are not a sort of troops
adapted for foreign service. I have been up all night
expecting this attack, and it amuses me to write.
This letter will not go till to-morrow, so I may have
some event to put in, though I do not think so few
hours can make much difference. My last papers
were only to the 19th instant; some have come to
the 22d, and we may soon hear what the Ministry
will do. I hope they will not be so base as to make
peace.

                              In the middle of the night.

A tremendous firing going on at Sebastopol. A
sortie, I suppose. I have been reading the beginning
of the *Autobiography of a Working Man*, which has
touched me extremely; the poor man's utter poverty
is hard to conceive by those who have never felt it.
His love for his mother, too, comes home to every
manly heart. When I was a little child, I can remember the poverty of our household, and my darling
mother slaving herself for her little ones, looking with
dismay at the diminishing loaf, and thinking of its
high price. There had been some lawsuit which tied
up my father's small property, and money was scarce.
She was not at all clever; only good, better, and
best to me. While I am writing, the cannons are
roaring, and here I feel the tremor of the explo-
sions; but it is so constant a noise that, unless in

the night, when all else is quiet, small notice is taken. This evening I heard a telegraphic message had arrived with the news of a vote of want of confidence in our Ministry. We shall not know, of course, for a long time what will turn up, or whether we shall mend our condition. We have every reason to believe that a large force of Russians is collecting against our Balaklava position. They are publishing too much in the papers. The officers' friends are much to blame; it discourages our men, and makes the enemy think we are worse off than the truth will warrant. In war there must be suffering. *Eau de rose* has no place in that stern scene. A little more suffering perhaps than might have been necessary—inexperience—and now they change the government to give a new set of mistakes. Happily for us soldiers we have a plain line of duty—to endure and persevere; there must be no retreating. I consider it would be better that we should all perish to a man, than that the country should give in for us, and make a shameful and useless peace; the same battle to be fought over again by another generation. I am now going to lie down. I was up all last night, and must be on horseback before daylight; so a nap in my clothes will be prudent.

## LETTER LVIII.

Camp, Battery No. 4, Balaklava,
12th February 1855.

I HAVE been reading some of Ruskin's book.
His admiration of Gothic architecture I can appreciate. It has always been my favourite style; yet
you see when I built the White Cottage I did not
adopt it. How can I excuse myself in the eyes of
Ruskin? Not that I want to excuse any thing. I
was bound to build something which should not be a
landlord's fixture, and my material was therefore necessarily iron. The only fault I acknowledge is in the
pitch of the roof, which is quite wrong; the flat curve
was, however, drawn by an architect. It is now within
a few days of a year since my departure from England.
I did not come here entirely on the patriotic principle,
partly for friendship. When I was young, I might have
done so; but I did not know till I tried that I should
still find myself so strong and hardy as it has been
proved I am, nor so fit for war. We have now, I trust,
passed over the worst of the winter; but there is still
occasional snow, varied by rain. The army before
Sebastopol has but few huts up yet; so that it is to be
dreaded that our sick-list will not diminish for some
time to come. I have private reasons for thinking it
likely there will be a Highland division made up for C.
The Highland Brigade has answered so well that I

think the step will be a wise one. I could have wished
to see the Ministry of War given over to Lord Ellenborough ; he knows more about the organisation of
an army than any other public man in England. Roebuck was suspected of trying to make a cross by his
motion. I am glad to see he has turned out honest.
Of all those going out, I only regret Molesworth and
Gladstone. There has not often been a greater opportunity lost than this one by the Duke of Newcastle.
He had absolute power, as I believe, and boundless
wealth to work with ; yet made a total mess. What
a chance it is for an Englishman to be born a duke,
and what dukes some would have made ; only the
education would have been so different ! In a day or
two I will send you a sketch I have got of our position. It will illustrate the plan I have already sent
you ; together, they will give you a capital idea of our
position ; the first being the ground-plan, and the
other the elevation, looking at us from the enemy's
side. Do you take any interest in it ? Perhaps I
am sending things you care not for; yet it is my
time I am giving, hardly won, from the midst of in-
terruption by the calls of duty which continually
press upon me. When I succeed in getting my letter
written, for the moment I feel satisfied ; but when I
look it over, it seems so meagre compared with what
it ought to be, that I am often inclined to throw
it away. I don't, though ; for I hope there is still

some basis of truth, and some faithful record of fact, which may be not entirely worthless. I am now going to Balaklava to sit on a Court of Inquiry as to the way in which a wounded man was carried on board ship. I was one of the court which sat to examine into the state of affairs on board the "Avon," and our report gave the doctors such a dressing that they now tremble at the idea of a Court of Inquiry. I am frequently employed in this way. I was one of a board to receive the statements of the railway people ; and I made a protest alone against employing the labour in this way, because the making a railway entailed the necessity of also making a macadamised road between the rails, which, when made, would only be available for the railway wagons and horses, whereas a good ordinary macadamised road would have been available for all sorts of carts, mules, &c.; and such a road must be made in addition to the railway road,* requiring immense extra labour. I do not think the railway will be ready for months ; long before which I trust the allied armies will be in Sebastopol, and their navies in its port. I am sure we must open fire very soon, for most of our batteries are armed, after which it is usual to begin firing as soon as possible, for fear of the enemy getting into the batteries and spiking the guns. When you hear of the fire opening, pre-

---

* Such a road was made afterwards.

pare yourself by the next mail to hear of the assault, when the highest hearts of both armies will throw themselves into the Russian works with a full determination of staying there alive or dead. Shall we ever have a Homer to tell of this siege? I have seen nothing in verse at all worthy, except a scrap about the cavalry charge. Yet, when England can produce such soldiers, she must surely have some Homer to record their deeds. I am afraid this letter is very badly written; but I am writing against time, and penmanship as well as grammar must suffer. You will supply the defects of the latter, if you can get over the former difficulty; at any rate, you will excuse.

## LETTER LIX.

Camp, Battery No. 4, Balaklava,
14th February 1855.

My watch came by post yesterday, just a week after I received the other by long sea. Shadwell was delighted to buy it. I wound it up, set it, and gave it over to him; and in the afternoon he wound it up again, and broke the mainspring! so it will go back by post to his brother for repair; and when he recovers it again, it will be a travelled watch. I send the tracing I promised.* The Battery No. 4 is that behind

---

* This sketch is introduced at Letter XXXVII., p. 148.

which we live. The tents are not so numerous as they appeared on the heights when the sketch was taken, as our men are now all hutted. Last night we were startled by the entry into our mansion of Lord Lucan, in a flurry, just recalled home on account of his row with Lord Raglan about the famous cavalry charge. It has become a point of discipline, and the junior goes to the wall; but on this occasion the junior has got a seat in the House of Lords. It is a terrible blow to him; but it shows that the Government that was intends to defend Lord Raglan. My papers, as it too often happens on interesting occasions, have missed. Had they come, I surmise they could not have told us who is to be the Prime Minister and who the Secretary of War. Palmerston and Grey, I hope, as Lord Ellenborough cannot come in with Whigs. We know from close observation that Ruski has made the defences of Sebastopol wonderfully strong, and I think the engineers do not much like the job before them. We have strange reports about the possibility of C. being made commander-in-chief. I hope not; I think Lord Raglan very competent; and it would please C. much better to command a Highland division under him. In that situation he would be perfectly comfortable, and would manage his division as easily as one regiment. That some very great change will be made in the constitution of the army, I have no doubt. I hope they will copy the French organisation exactly; it was invented by the genius of the great Napoleon. ———, who is coming out at the head of the Army Transport, is a man, as I hear, full of zeal and energy, and very brave, not with any particular talents. All signs portend a great war before us, which is a great evil, but inevitable. Nicholas cannot give in, and at present he need not, for his Sebastopol is still his, and of course he flatters himself that he may keep us out for an indefinite period. However, I think we shall close up round it and invest it, and stop the supplies, if we do not attack it by force. Colonel Niel, the French engineer sent here by the Emperor to report, I believe looks grave. We are going to make an attempt upon Miss Nightingale. She keeps all our men when they are discharged from hospital, and makes nurses of them, not considering that the other men are doing their duty in the trenches. I believe she has about 300 men of the Highland Brigade thus employed. There ought to be men enlisted as nurses, and the soldiers should be left to fight. The chief medical officer out here ought to have been intrusted with Nightingale powers. Depend upon it that it is the interest and the glory of a medical officer to take care of his sick; nothing but want of power has been the cause of deficiencies. Every department has a pluck at us : clerks, orderlies, officers' servants, all prime soldiers. The Commissary of the Highland Brigade alone has seven ; all the

officers one each, the mounted officers and the staff
two.    I think between these servants, and regimental
hospital orderlies, and various others employed by the
quartermasters, that the absentees may be reckoned
at least at sixty per battalion, besides Miss Nightingale's 300, in fact, nearly one battalion out of three.
There is, besides, the band and pioneers non-combatants—some thirty more.    The nominal strength is
over 800, and it is doing well in these times to bring
500 into the field.

15th February.

We finished yesterday a Court of Inquiry which
sat to investigate a report made by a staff-officer that
a wounded man, who had been sent down from Sebastopol on a French mule, was not provided with the
necessary conveniences for being transported from the
mule to the boat.    We found, however, on examination, that a surgeon and four men were employed in
carrying this one man, and, in fact, that the arrangements were very complete.    I have read the first night's
debate.    Lord John comes out of it very badly, for,
on his own showing, he ought to have retired a long
time ago.    If he had done so, our reformation would
have begun much sooner.    I object to the phrases
he uses about the army, " heart-rending," &c.    The
army, with all this persuasion, will think itself worse
off than it is.    You, who have had a constant stream
of information from one present, have also read the

papers. Now I feel convinced that although my facts may have corresponded with some recorded by them, still the tone has been very different. As a general fact, I maintain that there has been no whimpering among us; a few exceptions do not alter this truth; the soldiers have been wonderfully cheery all along, and I think our misfortunes have brought out into strong light the heroical part of the English character. Probably the worst of the bad weather is now over. If we can recover our convalescents out of the Nightingale's claws, with transport under ———— well arranged, our increased numbers, added to the Sardinian contingent, will enable us to sally forth and drive away Ruski, so as to surround the place and make its capture sure. We were able yesterday to recognise one of the young Grand-Dukes on No. 3 Redoubt, observing our position. He was known to Leicester Curzon, who had travelled with him. We described him to Curzon as an excessively tall thin young man, to whom great respect was paid, and who was playing in a kittenish manner with the staff around him. Perhaps they were planning some way of attacking us; but I think not, the ground is too soft for them to get their guns away, after we have beaten them back. C. is made a Lieutenant-general. That gives him an increase of pay, and is a compliment. Sir G. Brown is returned; he is a fine old fellow, but he is excessively short-sighted, and I never saw him with spectacles.

It seems to require nerve to wear them; for I can imagine nothing but vanity to prevent blind people from using such means for seeing. Codrington also is short-sighted, but I believe he does wear spectacles on important occasions. Eyre wears them always. It is a terrible defect for a soldier not to have a long sight. I am amused at your account of ——'s anxiety to come out here. What on earth would he do? become a franc-tireur in a hole in the ground close to the Russian batteries? I understand we shall soon have some better arrangements, thanks to Mackenzie and Ross, about the reception of parcels, and that they will come as safely, though not so quickly, as letters by the post. We shall never, I think, be very far from the sea: our line, when we advance, will be towards Bakchi-serai, with perhaps part of our army watching the road to Kertsch along the south side where Theodosia or Kaffa is situated. There is no marching across the steppes in summer for want of water, or in winter for the mud; so that a transport-train will have a fair chance, as it will never have any long journeys to perform. The railway will doubtless be pushed forward as we advance, and very likely will branch out at right angles along the whole rear of the allied armies. When our numbers get up again, we shall be able to afford the navvies assistance. Once Sebastopol taken, the fatigues of the trenches will be forgotten, and the soldiers will only look forward with pleasure to meeting the Russians in the field, where we all feel confident of beating them easily.    I am afraid this is a dull letter ; but what can you expect from hence, where monotony reigns ?

## LETTER LX.

Camp, Battery No. 4, Balaklava,
19th February 1855.

THE mail, with letters up to the 2d instant, came in the day before yesterday, which were very interesting to us ; and I am glad to see that the Duke of N., who has been an unfortunate man, really comes out very well in his defence against his late colleague, Lord John.    The papers could not tell us who was to be every thing in all the offices ; but we hear by telegraph, Pam premier, and Lord Panmure war—warming-pan for Lord Dalhousie.*    I believe the latter is a good appointment ; but he had better come soon. We have news of our own, too; no less than 40,000 Russians, with sixty guns, having attacked the Turks at Eupatoria, and of their having been beaten back, leaving 150 dead.    Their artillery totally destroyed one Turkish field battery, killing the horses, and dismounting the guns.    They attacked a part of the works which was not quite finished.    The allied commanders have received telegraphic advice that we are

* This seems to have been an incorrect report.

to be attacked along our whole line, which is indeed very likely, as Nicholas must be much affronted at our planting ourselves so coolly on his soil. His military chiefs must try to dispose of us; and as there has now been a good long spell of beautiful dry weather, it is likely they are preparing, although I scarcely think they can have men enough to attack the Turks at Eupatoria at the same time as Balaklava. Our railway is making progress, and by tomorrow night will have reached Kadikoi. We are making an inundation in front of our fortifications here, in the flat part of the right of No. 4 Battery, where a brook runs through the parapet. It will be very shallow, but will conceal ditches; a formidable obstacle is an under-water ditch, into which you suddenly flop, when you think you are only wetting your feet. The object of such obstacles, as well as of *trous de loup* and abattis, is not so much to make the ground impassable, as to break the order of formation of an advancing column; order once broken, the attack is almost sure to fail. Quantities of boxes, full of clothing and all sorts of odds and ends, have come to us for ourselves and for the Highland Brigade; and such capitally made things as the men have never been used to. They send oat-cakes and currant-buns, and bottles of whisky. I have no means of knowing if the different county regiments of England receive things in the same proportion; but I do know that between private gifts and those of the Government our men are over-loaded with warm articles, and our main difficulty will be what to do with them when we move, for to carry them is out of the question. I have warned the Quartermaster-General's people that they should build a large store, and send to Constantinople for a hundred furriers, to clean and put by the things against next winter, which I think we shall spend in Sebastopol, Bakchi-serai, and Simpheropol. I believe this climate to be remarkably healthy, with the exception of some particular localities. Balaklava itself is probably very unhealthy; and now, from the quantity of dead bodies buried near it, and the abominations thrown into its tideless port, I am prepared to expect pestilence there and in all this valley, as soon as the sun becomes hot. We have been burying dead horses round us for the last few days to a large amount; poor animals which perished in trying to get up to the camp before Sebastopol. I was walking among the vineyards in front of our defences yesterday, and I saw that the vines were beginning to move. We have protected them, as they make a very good defence. In this country they scoop out a hole round each vine, which makes a sort of *trou de loup,* and the long branches hanging about in the summer will make a thicket; in rear of the works, they have been extracted root and branch for fuel. I suppose very soon we shall have crocuses and snowdrops, and the war and the flowers will awaken together.

----

## LETTER LXI.

Camp, Battery No. 4, Balaklava,
21st February 1855.

It was decided on the 18th that a considerable French force, say 18,000 men, and our few, perhaps 1800, should issue forth from our lines, and make a reconnoissance, with the hope of surprising the Russian troops at Chorguna, a small village, towards which we had made frequent advances. It is on a line with our battery No. 4, and Canrobert's Hill (the old redoubt No. 1), only three miles further off. However, on the night of the 18th, this intention was modified to the amount of putting it off till the next day. On the 19th Lord Raglan, and plenty of staff-officers, French and English, came to our quarter—I mean to that of C.—and it was decided on going out that night. The hour first proposed was one o'clock in the morning, which was changed to half-past two. We made all our arrangements during the evening. There is no moon now. At eleven it began to rain; at midnight the wind changed to the north, and it blew hard, with a drifting snow. It was im-

possible to see ten yards ; in this weather, which
lasted all the rest of the night, and until the middle
of the day of the 20th, we had to make our way, so
as to be in position above Chorguna at half-past five
in the morning.  The 42d, 71st, 79th, and 93d, with
twelve guns, and about 300 ·cavalry, composed our
force.  The three first-named regiments were to march,
so as to join the 93d, the guns, and the cavalry, under
Canrobert's Hill; and then all to pass on, leaving that
hill on our left.  C., Shadwell, and I, being nearest
the 93d, started with them.  No sooner did I get
outside the work, through a small sally-port next to
our old house, which forms part of the battery No. 4,
than I found that I was totally blind ; for besides
the night being pitch dark, the snow drifted on my
spectacles.  Well, the 93d came out and started.  I
was desired to go and look for the artillery, and tell
it to move on.  I thought I knew where it was, and
tried to go there ; but soon found I had lost my way,
and was reduced to the condition of a blind man.
I ·wandered about with my horse through vineyards
and ditches, and could make nothing of it.  At last
I came to a broken cart, and a small heap of stones,
and concluded to stand there till daylight, as I knew
not where I was going.  The snow fell all the time.
My horse shivered under me with cold.  At last
I dismounted, and jumped about to avoid sleeping,
which would have finished my campaign in a very in-

glorious manner. When day began to dawn, I found that I was not far from the fort, having wandered about in a circle. I could see nothing of our troops, and their track was obliterated by the snow; while going towards Kamara, I saw a man at a distance, who looked like a Cossack, but who turned out afterwards to be a staff-officer; so I went back into the battery to make our Dragoon orderlies come along with me. While they were getting ready, an Aide-de-camp of Lord Raglan's reached our quarter, having wandered about all night with an order for us not to go out, as the weather was so bad that General Bosquet would not start with his French force. Here was a pretty job; our small force out alone, and supposing they were supported by 18,000 French. I thought it best to go immediately to General Vinoy, who commands a French brigade on the heights to the left of our position, and above battery No. 5, just beyond Kadikoi. He is placed there to give us support in case of an attack, and was to have joined General Bosquet on this occasion. He received the counter-order, and of course did not go out; but from the top of his hill, when light came, being provided with a good glass by us, he had been able to perceive a movement of troops on the top of the hills beyond Canrobert's Hill, and he immediately concluded that C. had not received the counter-order. Vinoy at once got his men out, and was just going to mount when I arrived. The danger was, that the Russian force should be larger than we expected, and able to overpower our people ; in which case Vinoy would have arrived very opportunely. However, when we reached the ground, we got sight of a very few Russians, and nothing was done. Every one was very cold, and very glad to get back ; with the satisfaction at the same time of having obeyed orders, and made a very severe and difficult march in such weather, without any casualties. I took a good sleep in the afternoon, and after dinner took a very long one indeed for me, for I was dead tired. I know nothing worse than finding yourself lost in the snow, and being reduced to standing still till daylight, like a ship lying to. I heard from those who got off with the party, and reached the ground at the time proposed, that the Russians were quite taken by surprise. When it was over, every one was pleased with this little variety. To-day has been fine, and a good deal of the snow has melted, but it promises to freeze hard at night. I fully expect we shall, when we get another spell of dry weather, make an onslaught on these people : far we cannot go, for we have no transport ; but we might go out for two or three days, as the men could carry so much provisions. We have no news of how the siege is getting along, but the railway has reached Kadikoi, and I dare say will soon begin to be useful. We are all anxiety to get positive news about the Ministry, and the probable changes

in the army. Poor Lord Aberdeen must be rather
unhappy at such universal desertion. How far better
it would have been for him to have resigned, when
he found war was to be. Now he is turned out finally
and for ever; which shelving is, I suppose, a dreadful
thing to a public man like him. Yesterday, I saw
the first snowdrop,—graceful foreboder of spring and
the horrors of war. It seems likely that there will
be a large force sent to Eupatoria, sufficient not only
to hold the place, but to advance towards Bakchi-Serai.
Then we shall see if we have, among French or English, got a real General, one who can handle 100,000
men; quite a different and a much more uncommon
faculty than that of manœuvring 20,000. Now I
have an idea that Lord Ellenborough has this power
of being a general on a great scale, and that is one
reason why I should like to see him War Minister.
Lord Dalhousie I shall be sorry to see in that office,
not because I do not believe him to be a very capable
man, but because I know he did not behave well to
C. in India, and very likely bears him a grudge for
resisting him and for resigning his command. My
chief is *au mieux* with Lord Raglan. It is very pleasant for him, for he can get small matters done by a
direct application without minding the staff-officers
about the F.M., which saves time and helps the service.
We have had so many things sent out now, besides
our original baggage, that I am looking forward to a

horrible packing up and sending into store of all that
cannot be carried.

## LETTER LXII.

Camp, Battery No. 4, Balaklava,
25th February 1855.

On the night of the 23d the French made an attack on a Russian advanced work near the Tower of
Malakoff, or the White Tower, as we called it at first.
The plan was apparently known to the Russians, from
some person's indiscretion, for they were ready prepared.
The Zouaves, under Colonel Cler, advanced silently to
the work; when they came within fifty yards, the Russians began firing; the Zouaves ran on without firing
a shot, and got possession of the work, bayonetting
a good many. But the Russian fire of musketry and
cannon was too much for them. Their support of the
*Infanterie de la Marine* gave way, and the Zouaves
were driven back, losing 17 officers, killed and wounded,
8 and 9 respectively, and 500 or 600 men; a disastrous affair, and the first military—that is, fighting
—check the Allies have received. The success of an
attack by the very best troops even on inferior ones
posted behind trenches is always problematical. Our
neighbour and friend Vinoy, who long commanded the
Zouaves, is very much distressed at the killing and

wounding so many of his brother officers, besides his own nephew, who is wounded in two places. I do not know now whether in the plan I sent you battery No. 5 is introduced, or the hill behind it, on which Vinoy's brigade is posted for our assistance. We are very intimate with General Vinoy, and like him much. I am constantly called upon to write him notes in C.'s name, which I dare say amuse him, as probably the French is a little peculiar. The Guards have come down here, and are camped in our rear, where they will have nothing to do. Their coming here places them under C., as they form part of the 1st Division ; so that if he permanently commands that division, I shall drop into being Assistant Adjutant-General to the 1st Division, as I suppose they will hardly separate us now. But we are in great hopes of having a Highland Division. Between the Guards and the Line there is a difference of just two inches and a penny, besides the privileges of the officers. I send you a Crimean snowdrop. Do you remember the autumnal crocus, gathered when the Russian shot was falling ? that grew on a bare desolate spot enough, but these wild flowers of our Kadikoi are springing where nothing but themselves remain to put us in mind of the blooming valley which we entered last September. Such a desolation is hard to conceive. The only plant here besides a lonely snowdrop is the railway plant and the soldier and his sword. You have heard, I dare say, of the Provost-Marshal.   He is the policeman of the rear of a camp, and has the power of flogging troublesome people without judge or jury.   One of the navvies has passed through his hands, and the rest of that fraternity appear to be much amused at it.   He roared like a bull; and I hear afterwards had the philosophy to remark, that he had been flogged for the honour of his country. They grumble considerably at salt provisions, so different from the beefsteaks and porter they were used to at home.

## LETTER LXIII.

Camp, Battery No. 4, Balaklava,
1st March 1855.

WE cannot expect much news from England till Parliament meets.   I see in your letter you had a great opinion of ——.   We, who thought he was appointed, debated the question of his merits, and we were inclined to think the goodness of the selection was doubtful.   He always spoke so acrimoniously of every one, and might perhaps be called an impracticable man.   —— is truly a small one, but he may have wit enough to close with the offer of feeding the soldiers by contract.   It is done so now virtually, for the Commissary contracts with all sorts of people, and pretends to be very economical in his

R

money bargains. I was informed yesterday that great
efforts are to be made to open fire in ten days. As
it was the officer commanding the siege-train artillery who said so, and as it was spoken openly, I
conclude that Lord Raglan has ordered it; but I cannot think it wise to let it be known in Balaklava for
the use of the Russians; they hear every thing by
their spies, and probably much that is not true, for
that village is the fertile mother of lies. I never go
there without hearing of some wonderful battery, or
movement of troops, under our very noses, and where
we are continually watching, and generally at present
seeing no alteration. Our Highlanders are ordered
to carry up shot to the siege; but I am glad to say
the railroad will help them a little, that is, as far as
Kadikoi. The line runs right into the Ordnance
Wharf at Balaklava, and the thirty-two pound shot
will be placed in empty sandbags, and then in a
wagon, and drawn by the railway horses to Kadikoi;
where the men will parade, and shoulder their load
of cold iron. We did hope that this shot-carrying
was over. It is the proper business of the artillery,
and is imposed upon the infantry in consequence of
the non-competence of the artillery to do their own
work. They take the labour of the infantry in the
most thankless manner. These *corps d'élite* will be
much improved by a thorough reform ; all the good
things at Woolwich are monopolised by a family

clique, who look upon the establishments there as belonging to their sons and nephews, so that it seems almost more provoking than the Guards' arrangements, whereby the aristocracy have such a pull over the rest of the nation. That is a part of the constitution. In the army here there are thirty-nine battalions, each commanded by a Lieutenant-Colonel. There are here likewise three battalions of Guards, all the captains of which are Lieutenant-Colonels, and which battalions, including their Commanding-Officers and Majors, produce about thirty-three Lieutenant-Colonels, all of whom have a right to compete, and do compete successfully, with the thirty-nine Line men for employments in the highest staff situations. As the Guards gain by their privileges a more rapid promotion to the rank of Lieutenant-Colonel than usually falls to the lot of us poor working-soldiers, the inequality is the more felt. I hope you understand it, and are prepared with me to grumble. But nothing will be done. It requires to be a military man to comprehend the nature and the reasonableness of our complaints. No one of that profession, that I have yet seen in the House of Commons, appears to be able to grapple with the question. F. D., a most good-natured Irishman, tried to bring forward something in the House ; but his motion was lost, and the Guardsmen and the Navy combined together to black-ball him for the Senior Club. There was not an officer of the Guards at the ballot. Bernal Osborne, one of the Ministry, said the system was rotten. Why does he not do something? The Duke of Wellington protected the Guards. If there is to be a privileged corps, it should be composed of officers and men picked out; the first, not for being of good families, but for distinguished service, and the latter not merely for being six feet high. There was a remark made somewhere about Lieutenant Lord —— Cecil being promoted to be Lieutenant and Captain in the Guards. That promotion ought to have gone to some Lieutenant out here, who had been taking his turn in the trenches for the last five months. We hear of General Simpson coming out. They say he is a most gentlemanly person; but I do not think that he has much war-experience. Lord John's journey to Vienna is a pregnant circumstance, but he will make nothing of it till we have completely beaten the Russians in the field, and out of Sebastopol, which fortress they are daily making stronger and stronger. Osten Sacken wrote a very handsome letter to Canrobert, on the conduct of the Zouaves the other day, and had their bodies buried with military honours, the ceremony superintended by their Adjutant-Major, the only officer left alive in the hands of the Russians.

## LETTER LXIV.

Camp, Battery No. 4, Balaklava,
5th March 1855.

I MUST fob you off with a very short letter, for I am very busy. The whole of the troops in Balaklava, and the brigade of Guards, are placed under the command of C., which at first will give me considerable work. I hear of more batteries being begun, which only puts off the longer the time for opening fire. I believe Lord Raglan is very anxious to begin. From something which dropped from a French General, I think the French are no longer so confident as they were in the success of an assault. They say, "We will try; if we fail, we must mask the place, and attack the enemy in the field." Every one who has the opportunity of seeing the improvements of the Russian defences seems to agree that they have made themselves wonderfully strong. We here (Balaklava) meantime are doing the same thing, and with this increased force we shall doubtless keep them out. The railway is beginning to be very useful as far as Kadikoi. It saves the fatigue-men a good deal of time as well as labour. But the men at the siege are worked very hard. Every other night in the trenches. Luckily the weather has become fine, and no rain or extreme cold. I have put up a hut, a wooden one from England, and have got room to walk about in it, though it is but a poor White Cottage.*   I must finish, for I am obliged to mount my horse.   I have been up since half-past three, and was on the heights soon after four.   Bright moonlight and a brilliant sunrise.

---

## LETTER LXV.

Camp, Battery No. 4, Balaklava,
8th March 1855.

ON the evening of the 6th, a despatch reached C. from Lord Raglan.   The original just come from Bukarest signed by Colquhoun, the Consul-General, announcing the death of the Czar on the 2d ; merely a telegraphic message, with directions to send it by special steamer from Varna. We went off immediately to give our news to Vinoy, by which he was much surprised.   His Aide-de-camp, Abbatucci, exclaimed, " Ah, ils nous ont tué notre Nicholas."   To the allies his death is a certain gain, as it is impossible to believe that his son will have his abilities or, at least, his experience.   Meanwhile I do not expect immediate peace, as some of the people around me do, nor do I wish for it.   Our army, they pretend, is on the point of being remodeled, to which plan peace will be fatal.

---

* This White Cottage is a large room built in the author's garden, where his literary friends met once a week.

With peace, the army drops into its ancient mismanagement. That, indeed, would be no reason for not
making peace, although it would be itself regrettable.
The objection to peace is the difficulty of getting any
security that Russia's wings are clipped. I see no
signs of that being the case. The 20,000 Turks to
be raised by the English will be a very different kind
of troops from any now possessed by the Turkish Government. They ought to be backed by a large army
and an allied contingent, and hold the Crimea for the
Porte. That is the only solution I see which will
guarantee us a return for our expenditure of men and
treasure. You mention —— as a dying woman. I
was once slightly acquainted with her; she seemed
not to be a woman at all, and only a poor sort of
man. However, she is clever, and writes amusing
books, though I never read any of them except ——.
Her confession of faith is only vanity. How does she
know any thing about it? and it is curious that she
was credulous to a high degree in other matters, and
her credulity was sometimes so great, that I know of
her inventing things which she asserted to be facts.
Lord ——'s disgrace puts me in mind of some French
doings before the Revolution. Praslin? but he always
was a black sheep; a sharp fellow too in general. This
time he has sold his reputation with the British public
for 20,000l.—a losing bargain; but he went for the
whole estate. Why does Lord R. praise ——? because

it is the custom to praise men of rank. Being praised
and being praiseworthy do not always go together.
I am sorry to see the papers continue to abuse Lord
Raglan, and you put in a bit. You quote a sentence
of mine, " Lord R.'s fault was not refusing to act at
all before his army was complete." Fault is a con-
ventional word. I suppose he told the Government
all his deficiencies, and still they ordered him to go ;
he could not very well refuse, being a soldier. I believe he did all he possibly could do in way of remonstrance, and was overruled. His has been a very hard
fate, not to have been killed at the Alma. The new
Bill for enlisting older men for a short time is an old
Bill which was resorted to during the Peninsular War.
I wish you would get me into the War Minister's confidence. They are not doing any good yet with the
army, and nobody seems to look the question fairly in
the face.

The question is, do you choose to have your army
officered as at present by the aristocracy, and the men
enlisted as volunteers ? If you do, the making sergeants into officers is a mere absurdity, and a base
submission to the press. If the present plan is bad,
do not make it worse by patching. Destroy it altogether ; and let us force all Englishmen to serve, as
the French do, in the ranks. You then have a fair
sample of the nation to make officers out of. I can
tell you a curious fact about the French system. Their

officers will not submit to receive among them as an officer any one who has entered the army as a *remplaçant* (viz. for money) ; in which, with their system, I think them quite right. There have been a great many sergeants made officers lately in our army— men of thirty or forty, junior ensigns. In the French army there are many deserving soldiers, who have no chance of ever rising to be officers, because they have not the education required. They get "la croix," and a pension, and perhaps a place. I do not pretend to say which plan is the best, ours or the French, in theory ; but the French army, in practice, is better than ours. Not the men ; our men are the best, the most willing, the most enduring in the world. We want officers who shall be officers as well as gentlemen ; and if this war goes on, we shall make them. If peace comes now, adieu to hope. Every thing will be starved back to the lowest point, and we shall have nothing left to us but a heavy half-pay list, and the memory of the Crimean War. Since the arrival of the Guards here, C. has been placed in command of all the troops in and around Balaklava, except the cavalry, which I am sorry for, as he will come in for some of the abuse about Balaklava, unless he can put it to rights in a week, which is no easy job. We are walking rapidly into spring, and we shall have a new set of diseases. This valley, I apprehend, will be very unhealthy, as will be likewise the Valley of the Chernaya. The mass of dead bodies of men and horses, not very deeply buried, must give out pestilential vapours as soon as the sun becomes powerful, which it probably will next month. There was an idea of employing quick-lime in the Turkish graves; but that would, they said, shock their prejudices, and so it was abandoned. Just at the head of the harbour there are 2300 Turks buried.

## LETTER LXVI.

Camp, Battery No. 4, Balaklava,
9th March 1855.

THE papers are come with news of the Peelites going out. I cannot agree with you about an investigation just now. Our business is to push the war; every publicity concerning the army does nothing but pure mischief, so far as success against the enemy is concerned. I will tell you how they manage in India. One white Queen's regiment is brigaded with two black ones; when the line advances against the enemy, the white regiment keeps its pace and goes into fire as Englishmen always do; the black regiments on the flank hang back, and wait the result. As soon as they see that the English have broken the enemy, the Sepoys advance, and get all the credit; the custom of the Government in India for

patronage purposes being to puff the Sepoy army.
If, however, the enemy should be too strong, and
their fire should overpower the white troops, and
compel them to retire, the blacks all run away, and
throw the whole blame on the British soldiers, without whose countenance they would not have advanced
one step. The Indian officers engross all the loaves
and fishes ; and it is said they are now coming here
to take possession of places which our officers, who
have weathered out such a campaign, ought to have
in fee simple. *Sic vos non vobis*. As to the assault,
do you fondly believe that the French will attempt
that without us ? Depend upon it, there are no men
so impressed with the surpassing valour of Englishmen as these very French, and they will make no
assault without us. I am quite opposed to these
commissioners they talk of sending out. No good
will come of it. All we want is transport and food.
It really seems as if you, who have had more regular
and accurate information than any one in England,
are much more inclined to believe the camp-gossip
collected by the papers than my statements. I see
a long story about a threatened attack on Balaklava.
The facts were these : at the period spoken of, spies
came in from Baidar, and some officer who could talk
a few words of Turkish, got out of them that there
were 35,000 Russians in the valley of Baidar coming
to attack us. C. never heard of it, while it was all

over Balaklava. I was quite surprised on going there
during the day to have all sorts of questions asked.
Meantime the spies went to headquarters; and at 10
o'clock at night we received official information of
the probability of an attack upon our right up on
the hills. We had our own reasons for doubting;
but of course gave notice to our troops to be on the
alert, and also directed the commandant to send up
two battalions in support, one on the right of No. 3
battery, the other in rear of the 42d Highlanders,
before daylight, particularly desiring that he would
not make a row, but send them up in silence. Instead of doing that, at one in the morning he woke
Admiral Boxer, who immediately began to land seamen, and alarmed all the merchant-ships, whose seamen commenced loading pistols, and doing all sorts
of absurdities. There was no enemy there. But
nothing will persuade the commissaries and parsons
who stick about Balaklava that something dreadful
is not impending; likewise they have an idea that
the Russians have been making batteries and bringing guns to Canrobert's Hill: this story has been
current for weeks. Nothing can be more absurd.
We spend our lives in watching the Russians. They
cannot move without our seeing them from the heights,
where the Marines are. Nevertheless there it stands
in the *Times*.

## LETTER LXVII.

Camp, Battery No. 4, Balaklava,
12th March 1855.

I AM sorry that I cannot send you a good plan of
the lines before Sebastopol.   As I never can go there
myself, I am obliged to be contented with patching
up what I can from hearsay.   Yesterday I went with
C. as far as Lord Raglan's, and there I found they
were rather in a bustle—the Russians having pushed
on their outwarks in such a manner from the Tower
of Malakoff as would force us to open fire.   It seems,
however, that the French batteries on the right of us
are not ready, and I doubt if we have ammunition
enough up.   The Russians, having done every thing
they could to complete the defences of the place, are
now making outworks, the taking of which will necessarily increase the duration of the siege, the loss of
life, and the consumption of ammunition.   I understood that our batteries were ordered to open last
night, that is, yesterday afternoon.   They have not
done so ; it is now half-past two in the morning, and
at daylight I expect to hear a roar of guns.   We
must drive the enemy from this new work, because it
is much nearer to us than any of their other works ;
and if they can hold it, they will put mortars there
and shell our camps.   In fact, they are besieging us ;
and I should not be at all surprised if we were to

take the field, to enable us to invest the place, and stop the supplies entering it, of which we hear that enormous convoys have lately been introduced. I thought Lord Raglan was looking worried and old, which is not surprising, considering the badgering he has undergone. I hear whisperings against Canrobert from the French. He has been pushed on to the supreme command with great rapidity, and has officers under him who are his seniors, and distinguished men too ; Pelissier for instance.

The notion is that he is too amiable to treat these men as he would others with whom he had not been associated as their junior in Algeria. Altogether I am afraid we want a great general, and these commissioners will, I suppose, come and displace one after another till they find the man. You remember how the French commissioners used to torment their generals in the first revolution. But they not only displaced the unsuccessful general, they also displaced his head ; a degree of vigour not to be expected in these milk-and-water times. We shall soon have been a year out ; some of our troops reached Scutari this month in last year, and we have made no impression upon Russia yet. John Bull, who has been amusing himself all the winter with sympathies and warm clothing, having naturally a practical turn, will begin soon, I opine, to get angry, get his tail up, and shutting his eyes, he will pitch into somebody. It

<br>

certainly would be a curious thing if the second, or as he calls himself the third, Napoleon were to crown all his doings by becoming a great conqueror. I think it very likely he may be the best general among us. He has energy and obstinacy and courage, *à toute outrance.*

There is no calamity of a national kind we can suffer so great as a disgraceful peace. It would be better to have a ten years' siege. The weather continues fine; and I mean very shortly to pack up a lot of winter things which have accumulated, and which cannot be carried. I shall then be ready for the campaign. Something must be done; that is clear, and it is not a new chief of the staff that will do much good. Simpson has no war-experience at all. He commanded a brigade in India, which was never engaged. They say, however, he is very amiable, as if that was any use for this job. So is Lord Raglan, so is Estcourt. The disciplinarian of the army's distinguishing quality—very amiable! He ought to be the Devil, as they called old Cameron of the 9th in the Peninsular War.

The new command, or rather additional number of troops, besides Balaklava, placed under our orders, gives a good deal of extra trouble. The powers here are trembling at the impending investigation. They ingeniously, as they thought, contrived that C. should have none of the responsibility of Balaklava. When we first arrived here, he set upon some innocent staff-officers stationed in that village; they complained, I conclude, that C. had knocked their hats over their eyes, and so out came an order that he was to have nothing to do with Balaklava. Nobody in their senses would have wished to rule in such a place. It is, however, improving. I had to report upon it yesterday, and have proposed terrible things, such as turning all the commissaries and their hangers-on out of it, and making it into stores and offices, with no nightly occupants except a guard. I doubt the chief having nerve to take the thing by the throat in this manner; but C. is now on velvet, having officially stated what should be done. It would have been done long ago, had he been allowed any power. I find on measuring, that it would be possible for the enemy to drop shells into the harbour from guns placed on the old Baidar Road, opposite our extreme right. Nobody knows it; but one shell would produce a wonderful result among the people squatted in Balaklava.

## LETTER LXVIII.

Camp, Battery No. 4, Balaklava,
15th March 1855.

WE hear that Lord Raglan's bag is come, and that we have some alterations in the army. General

Simpson, Chief of the Staff, is here, and we find he is
made a Lieutenant-General, and antedated to August
last, so as to make him senior to Sir R. England,—
Dick Britain, as they call him,—and of course to C.
Sir G. Brown is appointed second in command,*
which takes him away from his division, and gives
him power to interfere any where in the army. This
looks like Lord Raglan staying, which I am glad of.
How that man has been deserted and run down by
the aristocracy he belongs to, and whom he has
favoured all his life ! Sir John M'Neill and Colonel
Tulloch, who are to overhaul the commissary, are
also here ; so every one is preparing to receive con-
dign punishment, as if we were all arrived 'in the
kingdom of heaven. It will be many a year before
the facts, I mean *all* the facts, about this joint siege
by the French and English will become known.
Meantime the Russians are pushing on their outworks, and we apparently cannot stop them. We
now hear that Liprandi, who is said to be one of the
best of the Russian generals, wanted the Inkermann
attack to have been made upon Balaklava instead of
at Inkermann. But Menchikoff would not agree ;
the latter is gone away, and Osten Sacken commands, which I think accounts for an increased

---

* It is questionable whether this appointment ever took
place.

S

vigour and audacity in the enemy's measures. I heard General Rose, who is British Commissioner at the French head-quarters, call the occupation by the Russians of a certain hillock,* which we had proposed to take, a "reverse." Doubtless he had heard it so called by the French engineers. The weather is now most agreeable ; but unfortunately the warmth and dryness of the season is at least as favourable for the Russians as for us. Our letters and papers by this mail have not yet been delivered; but we know that papers to the 22d have arrived, and that the Whig Government is established. They are treating us very cruelly ; most of the appointments in the new transport train have been given to officers of the Company's service. These, I think, had been fairly earned by the subalterns of the regiments here, who have gone through this horrible winter work. In India, the Queen's officers stationed there never get a share in any thing except the hard fighting. Of that they get the whole. But the Company gives a good pension to retired Governor-Generals. I have just heard why we have not got our letters : Lord Raglan's bag from the Foreign Office is the only one arrived. There was just time to put it on board the "Telegraph" steamer at Constantinople before she started. I sup-

---

* On this hillock the Russians constructed the Kamschatka Lunette; we called it the Mamelon vert.

pose we shall have ours to-day. It is impossible to exaggerate the improvement which the fine weather, and the transport of their rations by the commissariat, has made in our men's appearance. Yesterday Colnaghi's limner was here; he is to publish a print of the position of the Highland Brigade, with portraits of C. and staff,—such figures as he will make us! I hope soon to send you a plan of some of the lines before Sebastopol; you will then understand the accounts you read in the papers of attacks on different batteries. From my constant occupation here, I can never get up there to see what they are doing; and there is no one whose duty it is to report to me, although we have an electric telegraph from Lord Raglan's to here. We have a rumour that the new Emperor has proposed an armistice. I do not think it would do us much harm, if we are allowed, during its continuance, to go on completing the railway and drilling our men; but peace would be fatal. The army would sink back into its old condition, and the hope of improvement would be dished.

We are employed now daily, in company with the French, in cutting coppice-wood to make gabions outside our lines, with a French covering party. Yesterday General Vinoy had occasion to find fault with two of his men, who had not cut their fagots so soon as the rest. "*Mon Général, que voulez-vous?* I am a watchmaker, and my comrade a jeweller."

16th March.

No mail yet. It appears that we have succeeded in joining the French and English trenches before Sebastopol; so that the Russians will be prevented coming beyond our trenches. The two parties are now so near that there must be a collision, I should think, immediately. The weather continues quite beautiful; and the commissioners must be astonished at the roseate hue thrown over every thing, and I dare say ask themselves what they were sent here for. They have taken up their quarters in a steamer which, as I am told, costs Government 2500*l.* per month: a pretty expensive palace. We are now—I mean C.—trying to clear the Augean Balaklava by sending as many people as possible into tents outside, and endeavouring as far as he can to leave nothing there but stores and offices.

---

## LETTER LXIX.

Camp, Battery No. 4, Balaklava,
17th March 1855.

I HAVE no faith in Palmerston's Government. I believe we must have a new set altogether, if we are to do any good. The Peel people had no right to take office after the House had decided on the in-

vestigation, unless they intended to hold office while
the investigation was going on. I think I foretold
to you months ago that an investigation would take
place. As it is to be secret, I do not think it will do
any harm. Being a most ardent hater of shams, I
hope sincerely that the exploration may be complete.
Meantime *we* have *our* commissioners here.

Sir J. M'Neill is to overhaul the commissariat.
He seems to be provided with powers to do any thing
he likes, and is now about to institute bakeries. That
might have been done before; but how could we
have carried the bread to the front when we had so
much difficulty in getting biscuit there? The new
chief of the staff, Lieutenant-General Simpson, is
come with his rank antedated, making him senior to
Sir R. England and to C. Now I think this is very
unjust. These officers have gone through all this
terrible campaign; and I have heard no complaints
against the first, and high praise of the second.
Simpson would have been quite as effectual a chief
of the staff, had he come as a Major-General. He
served one year as an Ensign in the Peninsular War,
and as a Lieutenant in the Guards at Waterloo. A
perfect man of the world, I should say. Probably
Thackeray did not consider the proposition of the
*London News* very long. Albert Smith would have
made much business out of Sebastopol.

You say you preserve my letters, and speak of

them as literary productions. If any man writes at all, he must write his best when he writes nothing but truth, or what he thinks to be truth. The charm can only lie in that, which is perhaps a rare literary merit. The full true tone strikes its respondent chord in every heart.

Lord Lucan on reaching England went straight to the Horse Guards, as I hear, and demanded a court-martial. He will make no explanation in the House of Lords till that is granted; but it may be refused. I read his letter; it is clever; but a man in his position had no need to take into account the impertinence of an aide-de-camp. An officer who had had more practice in war would have put him under arrest, and would have refused to charge without a second order. At least I think so. I am glad you have received the sketch of our heights, which I doubt not makes the ground-plan much more understandable. In the latter you may introduce the 71st Highlanders camped on the ground between the Battery No. 3 and the head of Balaklava Harbour, on a sort of spur which runs out in that direction from the Battery Hill. The Brigade of Guards is camped on the left of the harbour, on the hills between the harbour and the cavalry camp; a line from the latter to the bridge where the rivulet runs into the harbour would pass through them; they are very weak. With respect to the lady nurses, I have been inquiring. I find Miss

Nightingale queens it with absolute power; all the authorities being afraid of the newspapers. I asked, "Are these ladies any use?" Answer: "As nurses, no; but very useful." "How?" "When I want any thing which the Purveyor dares not give me on my requisition, I go to the lady nurse, and obtain at once what I want." You see the ladies would appeal to public opinion, which would back them, right or wrong.

It is only a question of expense. The Medical Departmental chiefs used to favour the surgeons who expended the least in physic and food, and the doctors cannot shake off this idea—keeping down the estimates at the expense of the soldier. Physic, they tell me, is quite useless now; lemonade and milk is the best diet.

As to the army-promotion business, I do not see what purchase has to do with it. Suppose a great cargo of sovereigns were sent here, and that every officer received in hand the regulation-price of his commission, with the information that he might do what he liked with it, and that purchase was done away with, we should then be in the same state in which the Artillery and Marines have always been; and I never heard that their promotion was more rapid than that of the Line, neither are they poorer or richer, so far as I know. I am quite ready to take my money back, and see no objection if J. B. chooses

to make me a *cadeau*.   But sergeants of Artillery and
Marines are never promoted in their corps, and very
rarely any where else.   When purchase is abolished,
I do not see that we gain by that abolition any better
chance of fairness in promotion.   The privileges and
extra rank of the Guards will remain untouched ; and
the man who has votes in Parliament will still go to
the Horse Guards and have his son promoted or
placed upon the staff as heretofore, only without
purchase.   The effect of the system of purchase seems
to have escaped observation.   It is supposed to increase the rapidity of promotion ; if so, the man who
cannot purchase will rise to the head of his rank
sooner than where there is no purchase, and consequently will have all the chances of death vacancies,
which always go by seniority, unless the senior officer
is very young indeed.   The only thing I do object to
is taking officers out of the ranks, so long as the
ranks are filled, as at present, by the scourings of the
worst parts of London, Dublin, Glasgow, Liverpool, &c.
Give us the conscription, and I shall be quite satisfied ;
then gentlemen will enter as privates, whether they
like it or not, and will inevitably be made officers.   I
have, however, to add, what will, I hope, comfort you
a little, that in my opinion the mass of our officers
are very incompetent from the want of having received
proper military instruction after joining.   I think them
extremely negligent in the manner of performing their

duty; and when they are compelled, as they occasionally are, by a commanding-officer, to perform their duty strictly, they think him a beast, and call him so too; but they have to work all the same. Do you know whether Socrates was only a full private, or an officer; and if the latter, was it by purchase?

## LETTER LXX.

Camp, Battery No. 4, Balaklava,
19th March 1855.

On Saturday night (17th) a terrible fusilade took place between the French and the Russians. It lasted for two hours, and we listened to it with painful anxiety, but had no means of knowing what was taking place. Yesterday (Sunday) C. determined to give our men a day's rest, the first since we have been here (five months); and as that left all our men within the lines, instead of outside cutting wood for gabions, we decided to pay a formal visit to General Bosquet, who had sent us a large canister of snuff from Algiers. Bosquet commands the troops on the Inkermann side of the attack, on the right of the British force before Sebastopol. He looks about forty-five. Began in the Artillery; left the Polytechnic School No. 1 of his year. Head like Napoleon's, and is evidently a man of very great ability, and totally without fanfaronnade. He spoke a good deal about the situation of affairs. " This is not a siege," he said, " neither is Sebastopol a fortress ; the enemy's position from their right at the mouth of Sebastopol Harbour, to their left stretching away towards Bala-klava, is one entrenched camp. Behind them is a large, powerful military nation, with all its supplies, which they can pour into Sebastopol at pleasure. With our engineers' plans, I do not see how we are to succeed. I command thirty-four battalions ; of these, sixteen are in the trenches every night. A fort-night more of this work will give me a terrible sick-list. The remainder of my thirty-four battalions are under arms continually. We sleep neither by night nor by day. Last night we had a lieutenant-colo-nel killed, eight officers wounded, and a hundred men *hors de combat.* This will go on constantly, and is a serious drain. *La partie est bien dure.*" This is about what he said, and a good deal for a French-man. The Russians have riflemen in pits, who keep up such a fire, that advancing with our works is stopped, — I mean both English and French ; and until we can drive these riflemen away, and hold the ground on which they are, we cannot get on. The French troops ought to do this, but I suspect they are becoming discouraged ; they find themselves as much besieged as besieging. When the situation is fully understood by the Emperor Napoleon, I anticipate that he will employ all the ships, French and English, which it is possible to obtain, and land 50,000 or 60,000 men at Eupatoria, to attack the reverse of the Russian position. The Russian engineers have earned great honour by their defence, and the soldiers are evidently not the least afraid of the French. Meantime the enemy may suddenly throw 100,000 men on Eupatoria while held only by Turks, and take the place, which would prevent us from landing there ; and depend upon it, without that *pied à terre* we never shall make a descent again in the Crimea without being vigorously opposed. As we left Bosquet's tent, Canrobert arrived, and he expressed his anxiety about the Balaklava end of the line, hoping C. kept a sharp look out on his right. It is evident that the chiefs are nervous, and probably have information of some massing of Russian troops against us. At present we can see nothing suspicious ourselves, and I for my own part am more inclined to think they will try Eupatoria. I shall make an attempt before next week to send a plan of the attack towards Inkermann, where all this nightly fighting goes on ; provided with that, you will understand all this better. The majority of people here think that peace is likely, and that we shall not wind up with a great battle. The feeble sort of Ministry we have at home makes this possible, but I think not probable ; and in my opinion it would be very unfortunate should this peace be made before

we have given the Russians another grand overthrow.
I predict a Derby Ministry before a Radical one.
When it becomes apparent, as it seems to me probable,
that the Palmerston Whig combination cannot stand,
all the aristocratic soul of England will shake with
terror at the notion of Bright and Cobden ; and the
great rogues of both parties, and of all parties who
have any connection with the Lord knows who, will
support Lord Derby.   During these ministerial shuffl-
ings what a vexed man must ———— be !   Not able
to meddle, and deprived, I should suppose, of his
usual pretty pickings of patronage.   When the Bright
and Cobden people do come in, I expect to be amused
at the usual action of office on them ; my theory
being, that office makes rogues of those who were indifferent honest before.   If it does not make them
rogues, it makes them act like rogues ; for they hold
on, yet find they cannot do any one of all the
things which they have spent years in declaiming
about.   You have your Daffy's elixir of universal
suffrage ; if it lands us in a democratic despotism,
after a good deal of fighting and misery, I shall think
the survivors fortunate.   I can tell you a story which
is curious if true.

Lately at Constantinople it was decided that
some building should be purchased and fitted for
another hospital.   When the plan was all arranged,
the engineers applied to Lord Stratford for the money.

His Lordship found the amount so considerable that he paused, and said to the officer, "You can go on preparing your timber and getting all ready, so that no time will be lost, and I will immediately write home for an authority, which I have no doubt will be granted." Miss Nightingale, not informed of this conversation, and seeing no work going on, sends for the engineer, and asks why and wherefore; when she is informed, she inquires, "What is the sum?" and coolly draws a cheque for it upon ————. Is this the way to manage the finances of a great nation? *Vox populi?* A divine afflatus. Priestess, Miss N. Muffetetic impetus drawing cash out of my pocket! However, ———— is gone; and I hope there is not to be found another Minister who will allow these absurdities.

It is now three o'clock in the morning. All night the people in the bazaar go on knocking up sheds. They are coining money. Here, where there are no messes, I find the officers live as dearly as in England, unless they are satisfied to live on salt pork and biscuit, at the risk of their health; for they do not get the fresh meat and vegetables now supplied by Government to the men. Our party never have any of it, at least, and we have had no cook till within the last two days; but now General Vinoy has sent us a French soldier who cooks very well, and who no doubt will keep down the extravagance of the establishment, which has been as remarkable as the badness of our dinners. We have, however, all of us been well; and if bad cooking could kill, we should have been dead men. I can assure you that I am now so accustomed to sleeping in my clothes, that I imagine I shall find it difficult to go back to the ordinary habits of Englishmen. It is so very convenient to be able to jump up at any moment and shake oneself; a dog's life it may be called. So I am going to lie down for a couple of hours, then a cup of coffee, and resume the business of my office, which is pretty considerable. I have now a pile of documents to be worked upon lying beside me six inches high, which will all be disposed of before nine o'clock to make way for their successors.

---

## LETTER LXXI.

Camp, Battery No. 4, Balaklava,
23d March 1855.

I HAVE the pleasure of sending you a sketch of some of the trenches before Sebastopol, which you may depend upon as correct. Take care who sees it. Originally the English held all the ground on which those trenches, both blue and red, are placed; but that amount of trench has been created since the French took the right. We English are now in the centre between two French armies. The

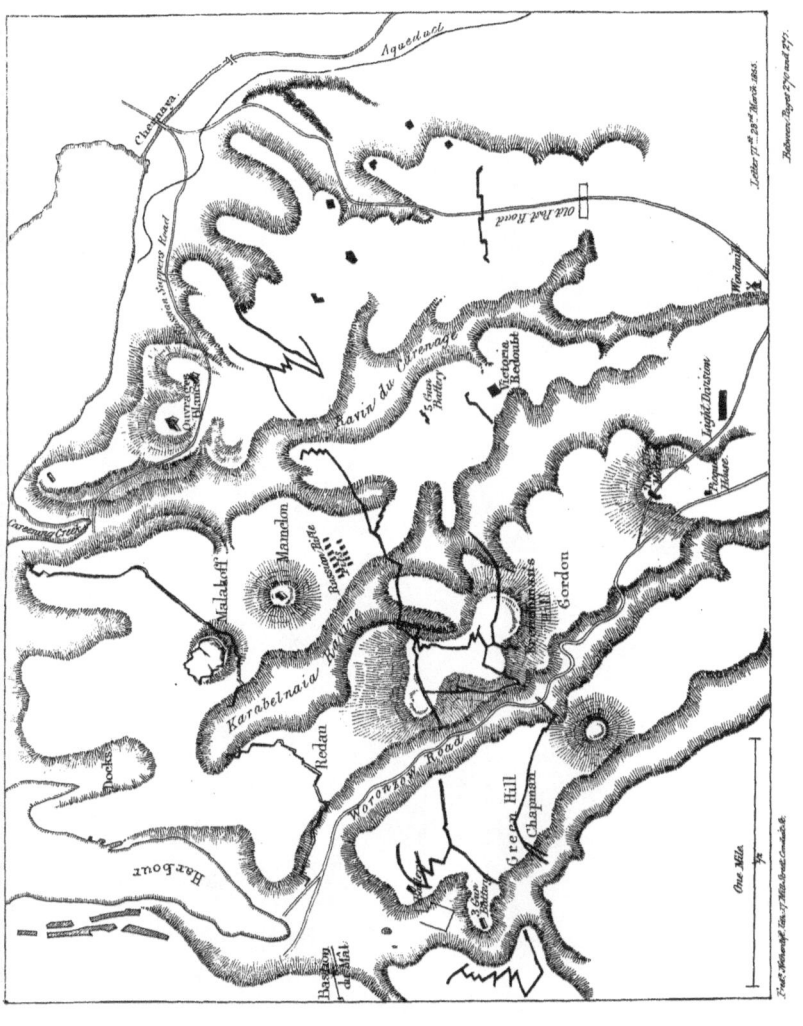

Aqueduct

Tchernaya

Old Fort Road

Ravin du Carenage

S. from Battery

Victoria Redoubt

Woronzow Road

Light Division

Inkermann

Quarry Ravine

Inkermann Hill

Gordon

Ouvrage Blanc

Mamelon

Malakoff

Bastion du Mât

Dock

Karabelnaia Faubourg

Redan

Green Hill

Chapman

Harbour

Railway

One Mile

Letter 17th 28th March 1855.

Reference Paper 270 and 271.

Pub.d. Witham & Co. 7 Pall Mall, London.S.

French left attack is not represented in the present
sketch; and as it will not be the serious attack, the
omission is of less moment. At this time of writing,
the French are driving a sap from their part of the
second parallel towards the Mamelon, in front of
which are the Russian rifle-pits. When this sap is
sufficiently advanced, these riflemen must retire, and
then the sap will reach the redoubt on the Mamelon,
which must be stormed; it is the outwork to the
Malakoff Tower. Our railway is advancing rapidly,
and will become a formidable attacking weapon by
carrying guns and ammunition. Meantime the
French have made small assaults on the rifle-pits,
from which in the dark they have usually driven
the Russian soldiers, who returned at daylight. The
provoking young English officers make their remarks
on the French not holding the ground,—a ground
which is untenable; and I am sorry to say I have
heard of English soldiers passing French ones and
saying, " No bono Frances." A bad feeling of this
kind springing up would be most lamentable; for
the French are excessively sensitive. They have seen
English soldiers fight, and the sight of that majesty has revealed many things to them. But our
men are not what they were. Depend upon it the
French would value our appreciation of their bravery
more than any thing we could do for them; and we
risk offending them by allowing the gabble of the

young officers, who know nothing of war. War!
those who have seen most of war know how to make
the most allowances. You speak of the investigation
in the House, and ask what awkwardness might come
out of it. Suppose it comes out that 60,000 Frenchmen have died out here. Do you think the French
Emperor will see much sense in publishing that dis-
covery? He has had the power, and his officers the
good sense, to stifle their complaints; but I assure
you they have suffered severely during the winter.
Poor Lord Lucan! poor Lord Raglan! Which is
the poorest? It is clear which has the best of the
argument; and you naturally take part with the
weaker. I have been long a soldier, and I never
knew a case of a man defying his commanding-officer
who did not come off second best. In this case,
before I saw the letter of Lord Raglan, I did not
consider Lord Lucan's a clear case. Quite the contrary; and now he has no case at all.

All the people sent out to work the Commissary
and the Staff are hard at it; but the weather is
better. The weak are dead; and the strong who
live ridicule these people who come with power which
no one had before, and ask for men, exactly what
we could not give.

With regard to the plan, you will see a windmill
put down. We Highlanders were originally camped
a little to the left of it,—that is, it was on our right

hand as we looked towards the enemy. The shells
then sometimes came among us : now our advanced
works divert the fire, and the place is quiet enough.
I never have time to go up there ; but I dare say in
the end I shall be able to send you plans of the
whole position back to Balaklava. I have been very
hard-worked in the letter-writing line lately. Yesterday I wrote twenty-seven, some rather long. From
a perusal of some of them you would learn more of
war than many officers know. Our important family
news is our French cook : M. Pascal Poupon, a soldier of the 20$^{me}$ de ligne, cuisinier de profession, lent
to us by General Vinoy. Before his advent, our dinner was always a piece of mutton, when we could get
it, stewed with French vegetable tablets. Now we have
six dishes at least instead of this one, which after a
year began to be a little *fade.* The Emperor Napoleon
is confidently expected here. I dare say he will turn
out to be a capital soldier—will have plenty of power,
and no fear of an investigation. But he cannot make
the place surrender ; and I believe every day adds to
its strength. There is, however, an end to all things.
Our means of bringing up ammunition from England,
and by rail up here, will shortly be easier and quicker
than those of the Russians. We shall gradually ac-
quire a superiority of fire, and our sap will advance.
Only keep up the supply of cash, we are sure to succeed at last ; but do not go about to say the soldiers

T

were tired. Depend upon it, the tax-payers will be tired first. I am amused at the evidence given before that absurd Committee. Evans surmises that people expected to make war without wounds. I have heard that Miss Nightingale has shaved her head to keep out vermin. I wish she would let our orderlies alone. There are twenty-four ordered this morning to go on board ship, and half will catch the hospital fever; it is really provoking. However, there is rebellion among some of the nurses. Miss —— has added herself to the hospital of the 42d; and will not acknowledge the voice of the Nightingale, who has written an official letter to Lord Raglan on the subject. I suppose he will order a court-martial composed of nurses, who will administer queer justice.

## LETTER LXXII.

Camp, Battery No. 4, Balaklava,
25th March 1855.

I AM particularly glad that you have the Plan, because with its assistance you will understand what is going on. When I sent my last letter of the 23d to post, I did not know what had occurred in the night of the 22d. The Russians made a strong sortie, which I dare say has been mentioned in the papers. Yesterday I had occasion to go to the front,

and I went into the advanced trench on Frenchman's Hill, which is also sometimes called Gordon's
Battery or Attack, from the name of the Engineer
officer. I went down the right-hand zigzag, and
into the new mortar battery, and along the English
trench to where it joins the French lines in the ravine. The attack on the night of the 22d was made
by the Russians, who advanced against the English
front on Frenchman's Hill, and also against the
French lines and the right of the English. The
English trenches were very imperfectly lined with soldiers, and the enemy got through them; and therefore of necessity got into the rear as well as on the
left flank of the French, who had to change front
to meet them and drive them back, in doing which
the French lost about 300 men. They are naturally
rather sore at the English for not manning their lines
better. The worst part of it is, that the young English officers, who knew nothing about it, talk with
a chuckle of "the French being licked last night."
While I was in the trenches yesterday, a flag of truce
was hoisted by both parties for the purpose of carrying away the dead bodies, which lay pretty thick in
front of the French lines and around the Russian
rifle-pits, which are short trenches with parapets,
from whence they annoy the allies considerably.
The Mamelon is a much more considerable eminence than I was aware of, and has a strong for-

midable redoubt upon it. There is nothing to be done by us except to sap beyond the rifle-pits on each side of them if possible, and turn a regular trench along the line where they are. We shall have then to continue sapping till we reach the ditch of the work on the Mamelon, which we shall have to fill with fascines, or bags of hay, in order to cross it and storm the work. After which we shall have to make a lodgment there, and sap again up to the ditch of a much more formidable earth-work, which has been thrown up round the remains of the Malakoff Tower, all the while exposed to a heavy fire and losing men every night. The ground we shall have to sap in is all rocky and very unfavourable. From these facts you will perceive that we have a long job before us, and that we shall require much patience and endurance. When the flag of truce was hoisted, about 700 or 800 Russians came out of the work on the Mamelon with stretchers to receive their dead, which our men and the French collected and carried to them. I was among the Russian soldiers, who were all mixed up with ours. Among the dead there were two bodies of Albanians, with white linen petticoats, called in Italian "fustanelle." I believe the Russians have a Greco-Slave legion. The hostile soldiers were perfectly civil to one another, and were all unarmed. Two hours afterwards they were firing at each other.

Such is war. Whenever I get any further information, I will send a small tracing, which you can copy on your plan, to keep yourself *au courant;* but I fear the additional trenches will be made very slowly. There is no objection to your showing the Plan; but it must not be copied, or it would be in the newspapers directly. In fact, I would rather newspaper people should not see it. Private gentlemen not in that line will do no harm. I have read the account in the *Times* of our attempted reconnoissance on that frosty snowy night. Since a short time (3d inst.), C. has been put in command of Balaklava, and we have had a great deal of extra work. His plan has been adopted, viz. to get all the people out of that village, and to leave nothing there but stores and offices. Of course driving people out is no easy job—in the face of Lord Raglan's good-nature and the intrigues of the sufferers. The Commandant obliges folks with lodgings for themselves, their horses and servants, leaving the unfortunate soldiers to clear up their dirt. It has required quite a literary campaign to defeat him and them, and to put the powers at head-quarters in such a logical position that nothing remained for them but to give plenary powers to C. This amounts to a death-blow to all the skulkers and humbugs who hang about Balaklava. I hope you understand these plans ; the more people live in Balaklava, the more does dirt accumulate, which it falls to the soldiers to clear away. The Commandant has been showing with pride how much Balaklava is improved, and points it out to the commissioners. A sharp fellow Sir John, and knows mankind, or he would not have risen from being an Assistant-Surgeon in the Company's service to the post of Ambassador to the court of Persia. His brother Sir Duncan has also risen to the highest dignity of the law in Scotland. The quantity of letters I have to compose is very considerable indeed. Luckily for me, I have had pretty good practice, having been so much employed on the staff in my younger days. The weather continues generally quite charming; very warm at midday. When windy, the dust is unpleasant, that is the only drawback. The insects have not yet come out of their winter-quarters; long may they stay there! although they do not bite me. I seem to defy every thing that hurts other people.

## LETTER LXXIII.

Camp, Battery No. 4, Balaklava,
26th March 1855.

I BELIEVE the French intended sapping into the rifle-pits and making an advanced trench there, instead of which the Russians have done so. In fact they are besieging us. Their next step, in all proba-

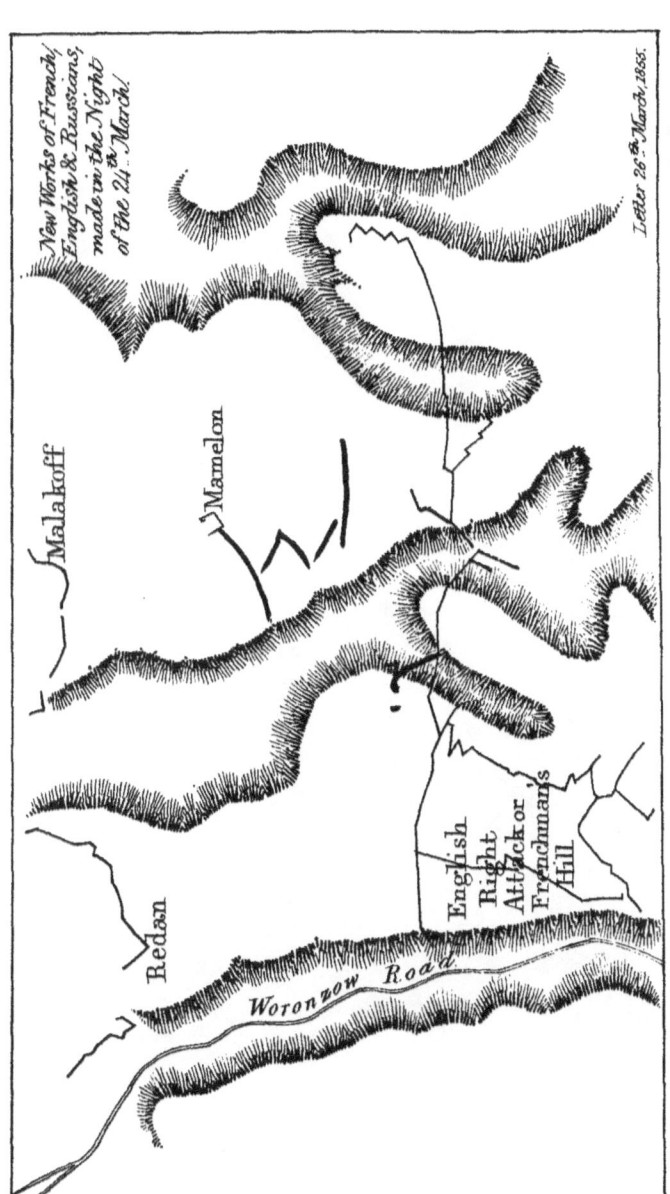

New Works of French,
English & Russians,
made in the Night
of the 24.ᵗʰ March.

Malakoff

Mamelon

Redan

English
Right
Attack or
Frenchman's
Hill

Woronzow Road

Letter 26.ᵗʰ March. 1855.

To face Page 376.

F.G. Netherclift, lith.

bility, will be to work back to the Malakoff Tower, making the redoubt on the Mamelon into a regular outwork of the place, compelling us to storm it before we can go on. The English advanced trench cannot, I fear, be pushed on, as it will be exposed to the fire of the Redan.

We are in a fix; and how the engineers will unfix us remains to be seen. We hear from spies, that last Friday week (this is Monday) the Russian troops at Bakchi-serai were assembled, and a proclamation read to them to the effect that a general attack was to be made on all our lines, both of attack and defence. I think it very likely, as they must know we are going to be reinforced. I do not believe there is any danger of their getting through us, but we shall lose men, which we cannot afford; and I dare say the Russians will think themselves gainers if they can compound by losing three for one.

30th March 1855.

I am amused at the story you poor people in England have swallowed about ——'s treachery. I saw him three days ago riding at the head of his staff. No news that I can see or hear of. I cannot say that I think this war is now about to terminate in a peace. If it does, so much the worse for England and for the world. These investigations are not at all interesting to me. They can tell me nothing

which I do not know, and probably will tell many
things which should not be publicly known at all.
——, I perceive, ascribes the fact of the health of the
Highland Brigade being superior to that of the Guards
to the Guards having been overworked in the trenches,
while the Highland Brigade was doing nothing at Balaklava. The Guards, in the first place, completely
broke down in Bulgaria, so much so that they could
not carry their packs, and we were also not allowed
to carry ours. To this piece of folly I ascribe much
of the inconvenience suffered afterwards in the Crimea.
It is probable that, if the question of allowing the men
to go without packs on their march to Varna had
never been raised, no one would have thought of landing them in the Crimea packless. With regard to work
here, the Highlanders as a body had quite as hard
work as any of the men at the siege, during the worst
part of the bad weather. They had to dig three and
a half miles of trenches, to sleep all of them on their
arms, and half of them in the trenches every night,
during frightful weather, besides carrying shot, shell,
bread, charcoal, &c. to the depôt at Lord Raglan's
head-quarters, for the rest of the army, and their
own rations for themselves.

Lord Lucan, as you remark, had better have held
his tongue. I think it very likely that when Lord
Raglan is put into a corner by other people besides
Lord Lucan, he will defend himself quite as trium-

phantly. Moreover I do not see that it follows as a necessary consequence that any officer making a mistake such as Lord Lucan's shall therefore be dismissed from his command. You probably know the maxim, that he who has made few mistakes in war has not made much war. I am now on the point of going to put a Commissary under arrest. The Sanitary Commissioners are poking about. The burden of their song is : Give us some men, and we will do such and such things. Now if we had been able to afford the men, we could, if we thought them wise things, have done them ourselves. It was just men that we wanted and do want. They ask for servants and huts and fatigue-parties to put them up, and swagger about with great impertinence. They put me in mind of the old times with the French armies in the Revolution. They have not, however, the power of getting our heads cut off. I have not obtained any further information as to the progress of the opposing saps—the battle of spades and pickaxes. The real thing to admire is the patience of the soldiers, watching the slow, slow advance, and going day after day and night after night to protect the trenches; while none of them seem for a moment to doubt our ultimate success, or would dream of giving it up. Some officers, perhaps, who find the life irksome, long for peace, and possibly on almost any terms. This, however, is by no means general. I hope I have settled the Commissary with-

out putting him under arrest ; no small piece of diplomacy.    They say some one attributes the breaking
down of the Guards to the want of porter, limiting
the bounds of their sphere of action to ten miles
from Barclay and Perkins'.    While the newspapers
were abusing Lord Raglan for not riding about the
Camp, I understand the poor man was suffering from
the stump of his arm.    How he must be tormented
by all these civilians sent out to investigate, and who
do not all of them do their spiriting gently !    I believe some of them were excessively rude to him, who
is the mildest and blandest of men in his manners.

## LETTER LXXIV.

Camp, Battery No. 4, Balaklava,
2d April 1855.

To-day I went to the trenches with General Vinoy,
who is sent from Kadikoi to take his turn there.    I
had a good look, and send you a trace ; but they have
done so little that it is scarce worth while.    Every one
speaks now very positively of our opening fire in a day
or two.    It has been asserted so often that I do not
know what to say.    I think the engineers are very
sombre about it, but they must do something.    We
are plagued with these Commissioners, who are inclined
to be very impertinent.    How J. B. can expect Lord

Malakoff

Mamelon

Redan

To face Page 353.

F. G. Netherclift, lith.

Raglan to carry on this war, and at the same time attend to all the absurdities of those people, is beyond me. They say they have unlimited powers as to money, and all ask for soldiers, to clean here and build there. If I was Lord Raglan, I should embark them, and sail them back again, and ask for their powers to be used by any of the officers here. What good is likely to come from the inquiry in the House I do not see. All the real witnesses are here; I mean all those who would be disposed to do common justice to Lord Raglan. There has been a photographer too, who took a few camp-views and suddenly went off. I scarcely know how to explain his difficulty. Too much truth. What is called decency, and the natural wants of the animal man, exist here in an antagonistic position, and all his pictures presented such peculiar and unusual details, that he concluded to abandon the enterprise of communicating the naked truth to the British public. When I was in the trenches, they were stopped at X X by the round shot from the Mamelon, but I suppose will push on at night.

## LETTER LXXV.

Camp, Battery No. 4, Balaklava,
4th April 1855.

I HAVE heard, and I believe, that the affair will begin on the 8th; by which time the Piedmontese will probably have arrived, and they are so strong at Eupatoria that 10,000 Turks are expected from thence, which looks like relieving us and sending us up to the assault. Having gone through all the rest, it would be hard on the Highland Brigade to be out of that; moreover, they are about the best troops, that is, the most confident in their leader. I understand the ships will hover about at the mouth of the harbour as if they meant to go in, which will have the effect of keeping 3000 or 4000 artillerymen on the northern side. Our newspapers do not look very peaceful, and I have no faith in peace till somebody is considerably reduced in strength. Meantime I have no doubt our own poor are beginning to suffer, as the prices of the necessaries of life must have risen, and the private charities must be cut down to a certain extent by the expansion of flannel and plum-pudding towards the Crimea. I have just had an interview with two old ladies who were before this war the happy possessors of three houses in Kadikoi. When we arrived, they ran away, and two of the houses are down, the other dismantled and inhabited by some military creature. Poor things! they showed their last spoon, which they were going to sell for food; they had a young child with them, whom I fed with sweetmeats and cakes. Horrible war! However, if these unfortunates had stayed quietly in their houses, they would not have been molested. Drink, or a storm, are the only things which would tempt our men to injure women, and they would not have been all drunk at once. This storm, if we get in, will be a sad business. I only hope the Russians will have humanity enough to send away all the women. The soldiers will be driven into the sea or bayoneted, every man. Our officers will not be able to save them. The Russians will fight valiantly for their fatherland and for their conquests; nothing but utter exhaustion will bring peace, unless our Ministry consents to a disgraceful one. Peace made, there comes our domestic storm. The miserable way in which the aristocracy have managed matters shows that they have no particular right to govern; but they will fight for it nevertheless.

5th April.

This day twelvemonth I sailed from Woolwich. I see so much folly around me that I forget my own folly, which is the greatest of all. All remains as I have said, and I believe it will come off. I am very busy packing up a quantity of things to put into store, in case of a sudden move, which I anticipate.

## LETTER LXXVI.

Camp, Battery No. 4, Balaklava,
9th April 1855.

I TOLD you I thought fire would open this morning;
and now I hear them pounding away. Since the 20th
February we have had the most charming weather
imaginable ; but, alas, yesterday it turned to rain, and
blew and rained hard all night, and continues doing
so now.   This is much against us, as it will make the
ground so slippery when we try the assault, which
must come very soon.   As long as it is possible to
get the artillery to continue firing, we shall always be
doing good and making the storm easier ; the artillery will fire what they think reasonable, and then
propose to let the poor little infantry loose.   The
gunners are divided into three reliefs; and a continual fire is very fatiguing work, besides the casualties.
Their only real excuse for not battering much more
than is usual will be the want of gunners ; for by aid
of the railway we can get up as much ammunition as
we choose.   I hear no rumours as to who will be selected for leading the assaulting columns.   I scarcely
think it will be us, as there are many people who believe we are sure to be attacked here.   If the Sardinians arrive in time, I should then calculate on our
going to the siege.   What are you going to do with
the army when it is sufficiently condemned by the

inquiry? If we are all killed here, I should advise
having no army at all. In place of it, make contracts
with Cubitt or Peto or some other great undertakers
to fight our national battles. But if we survive, we
shall be very troublesome; for some of us are disposed
to think that as a body we have deserved better of
our country than to be hung up for the ridicule of
Europe; and we shall defend ourselves. The firing
is going on fast and furious in the middle of the tem-
pest. We dare not move from here to find out what is
doing, but I suppose you will find it all in the papers.
My notion is, that, when the fire is pretty well silenced, the two Russian batteries (*ouvrages blancs*)
on their left of the Malakoff, beyond the Careening
Creek, will be attacked, as well as the redoubt on the
Mamelon, continuing at the same time our fire on the
rest of the place. We shall make lodgments therein
and batteries, and go on thence by sap to the crest of
the glacis of the Malakoff, the ditch of which is twelve
feet deep, very broad, and both scarp and counter-
scarp revetted and perpendicular, or very nearly so.
The passage is made either by sapping to the said
crest, blowing in the counter-scarp with a mine, and
sapping across the bottom of the ditch, or by rushing
suddenly up with a quantity of fagots, which are thrown
into the ditch to fill it up, and make thus a causeway
across. The soldiers then dash on, and scramble up
the exterior slope of the parapet, and jump in among

the enemy. If the latter give way, they are all bayoneted ;—no mercy. If they stand fast, there is a desperate combat with bayonets and the butts of the muskets, frightful to think of; yet without it we cannot take Sebastopol. When Bergen-op-Zoom was stormed, it was by surprise. The English, under Lord Lynedock, got in, and got entire possession of the fortifications ; but when daylight came, the garrison, superior in numbers to the stormers, formed in the streets, being of course well acquainted with the town, while the English did not know where to go ; and at last they had to agree to march out again. It was a daring and desperate deed as ever was performed. In this business there will be no lack of valour on any side.* If nothing prevents the assault, successful or not, it will be the military feat of our new half-century, and will be a sort of Waterloo ; French and English emulating with one another, and the gallant Russians, fighting also for their country, will not be behind in the giant struggle. They are such capital soldiers, all of the three, that it is quite a pity to kill such men ; and yet I see nothing else before us. The three armies, in case of our success, will lose 20,000 men, killed and wounded ; and I sit coolly writing to you within three days of such a probability.

---

\* An unlucky prophecy. Just that was lacking.

## LETTER LXXVII.

Camp, Battery No. 4, Balaklava,
13th April 1855.

THE firing still goes on, and, I am told, with small
results. If they do not make a hole somewhere, the
infantry will have a job to get in ; and, as the firing
cannot last for ever, the moment must be close at
hand when we shall storm or not storm. If it is
thought impossible to do the first, our siege cannot
go on. We must take the field, and invest the
place ; for which object, be so kind, O asses of England, to send us men, and not scavengers—commissioners, I mean. Omar Pasha has been here. He
ate bread and cheese and drank sherry, talking bad
French all the time. He has brought 25,000 Turks
with him ; and we get four battalions for our position.
I think I told you I was one of the members of the
Court of Inquiry which condemned Dr. ——. The
proceedings of that Court must have gone to England.
Well, they found there some capable men—Cameron
and Romaine. Why did not they give them an order
to put things to rights ? They would have been very
good scavengers—commissioners, I mean. All I should
have asked would have been power. Neither Cameron
nor I would have gone to Scutari, because we should
not choose to leave the field with the enemy there.
In Balaklava they have made an Aide-de-Camp Com-

U

mandant, and he is supported by Estcourt against C.
Dragons a many have we encountered. The Sanitary
Commissioners, it now turns out, have no powers.
Their orders are to point out to us what is required,
and to ask Lord Raglan to do it ; as if we did not
know perfectly well what is required without these
creatures. It is truly worthy of England to send a
doctor from London, with a tail, to teach C., who has
lived about forty years in a camp, how to keep it
clean and his men in health. They only produce
confusion, and take up Lord Raglan's time. If I
were he, I should put the whole brotherhood on board
ship, and send them back ; and if the Government
thought fit to recall me, let them. No man has a
fair chance of governing an army with these inquisitors
over him. I live in the hope of seeing Louis Napoleon take the supreme command of the allied armies.
He is a man with a will. The admirable donkeys in
England, who are now occupied in holding up the best
and bravest soldiers in the world to ridicule, have sent
out a pack of young Indian officers, with local rank,
putting them over the heads of the captains and
subalterns of this army, who have spent six months,
without a murmur, in the trenches. It is enough
to cause and to justify, if any thing can do so, a
mutiny. Take care ! Lieutenant-Colonel M'Murdo,
who is not an India Company's officer, served a campaign or two in India with Sir Charles Napier. He

got from being a Captain to the rank of Lieutenant-
Colonel, and a good staff-appointment in Ireland.
They form a Land-Transport Train, and out he comes
with the rank of full Colonel, before he has done
any thing. Why did not they wait till he had done
his work? I believe him to be a good and zealous
officer; but there are plenty just as good, who have
gone through all this winter campaign and got nothing. The case is still harder when an East India
Lieutenant gets rank as a Captain here, because a
Lieutenant cannot have brevet rank, and a local Captain can. So these Indian Lieutenants not only get
the rank of Captain to begin with, but they will also
be made brevet-majors when any fight takes place.
Meantime there is a scream about purchase, as if
purchase had any thing to do with it. I am sick of
your cries and sympathies. I would ask for some
small instalment of common sense and justice. Abo-
lish purchase to-morrow, still the richer officers will
bribe their superiors to retire. They do it in the
Artillery; they do it in the India Company's army.
You must change human nature. Perhaps a Commissioner can do that. I do believe there is more
foolish babble at this moment going on under all
your noses, and buzzing into and out of your ears,
than would stock the universal menagerie of fools for
a century. I have not yet read Drummond's speech
against ——; but I fell upon the article of the *Times*

ridiculing Drummond. —— is not to blame ; it is
the people, whose diseased appetites call for his wares.
He necessarily must think their taste excellent, admire
their appetites, and minister to them.    But he sees, I
suppose, their long ears.

## LETTER LXXVIII.

Camp, Battery No. 4, Balaklava,
15th April 1855.

WE hear that the French have ammunition for
ten days, and that our people have been ordered to
stretch out theirs.    The effect is not much, and I am
almost tempted to fancy that the fire is kept up to
help the negotiations.    There has been a great deal
of very foolish talk going on in all the newspapers
about this war.    A wondrous condolence, a flood of
sympathy, and muffetees for the sufferings of men
and officers.    Hard work and suffering is only another name for war ; and a siege carried on in winter
inevitably brings with it as a concomitant an unusual
share of exposure and sickness : enough and to spare
has been said about it.    The various inquisitions now
at work will table all that is tabular, and preserve a
memorandum of misery which will soon be forgotten
by the masses.    But who alludes to the glaring injustice which Government is now inflicting on the officers

of this Crimean army; men who have remained here
with their soldiers all through the winter, night after
night, in mud and snow, under fire, in the trenches?
It was sufficiently galling to have the Guards, with
all their juvenile captains holding the rank of lieutenant-colonels; that old sore which will never be
healed. But now the Government have sent a bevy
of officers from the East India Company's service,
dropped down from the clouds. One lieutenant-
colonel to have the rank of colonel in Turkey; nine
majors to have the rank of lieutenant-colonel; seventeen captains to have the rank of major; thirty-seven
lieutenants to have the rank of captain; four second
lieutenants and one ensign to have the rank of lieutenant. These men receive all the time the pay of
the regiments they belong to in India, so that, strictly
speaking, the places they hold in the Turkish contingent are staff-appointments. What has this lieutenant-colonel done that he is to command all the lieutenant-colonels out here; or the nine majors, to pass
over the heads of the majors now in the trenches?
Why are seventeen captains, not in our service, to take
rank over our own regimental captains; and why are
thirty-seven lieutenants to have higher rank than the
subalterns of the Line? The officers who have lasted
out through this winter have a right to these appointments and promotions. If it suited the Government
to oblige the India Company by making a job for

their officers, why not pay in money, instead of giving them rank ? If the cruelty of this scheme was understood by poor gaping J. B., it could never have been perpetrated. In case of the Turkish contingent and any of the British forces being employed together against the enemy, and that the Indian lieutenants, with the local rank of captain, distinguish themselves, they will be made brevet-majors ; while the Queen's lieutenants, doing equally well, cannot have brevet rank, not even that of captain. It is a rank job ; and none of you seem to complain.

16th.

Last night the fire was very heavy on both sides. The French succeeded in advancing their sap in their left attack, towards what they call the Bastion du Mât, part of the Russian works near the head of the inner harbour. They exploded a mine which had been made in the direction of the proposed sap, which loosened all the earth ; and they ran down with gabions and completed a lodgment within sixty metres from the wall of the said bastion, where they are now making a battery. They lost about 100 men. It remains to be seen whether they will do more good with their guns at this short range. I believe they have a mine with 50,000 lbs. of gunpowder under the Bastion du Mât. If the Russians have not found it out and cut the *saucisson*, or even taken possession of the mine, it will explode, and open a way into the town. The Russian reinforcements are coming up by driblets; but we hear of three divisions being on their way, which will not be much under 40,000 men. All the troops from Bessarabia have cleared out, and are arriving, except the garrisons left in Ismail and Reni; so the sooner you send more men, the better. It is tedious work, this new method of taking places, or rather, this old method of taking new places.

## LETTER LXXIX.

Camp, Battery No. 4, Balaklava,
20th April 1855.

THE mail of the 2d came yesterday, with no letters for me; so I judge you have been working pretty hard at your book. Our siege is given up apparently for the time; at least the fire slackened, and no assault. I believe they found that the third cannonade had not produced any result sufficient to justify an assault; and, as I make out, they are going to work nearer and nearer with their batteries, hoping to succeed at last in that way. Woolwich and Chatham Schools, if they only knew it, have eaten much dirt on the occasion. At least we bystanders, who have always heard them praising themselves, are of

that opinion. At midnight, C. received a note from
Vinoy, forwarding the news from Bosquet that the
sound of wheels had been heard coming from Inkermann towards our position, as well as hurrahing ;—
so it behoved us to be up all night, and look out for
an attack. Accordingly we scurried about to get all
the troops ready ; but when we looked out for them
at daylight—no enemy ! Yesterday, Omar Pasha
made a reconnaissance with fourteen Turkish battalions, and some mountain-guns carried on mules. He
went out by the extreme right at daylight, and by
the cut road. I went with him. We placed two
battalions and a half in position, to defend the pass
from Baidar, just where the Cossack picquet-house is.
The other eleven battalions came slowly winding out
through the palisades, and formed in columns on the
east slope of the range of heights which run down to
Kamara. After they had assembled there, we pushed
on along the tops of the hills and down the valley,
still bringing up our right shoulders, till we reached
to the northern extremity of the same range, and
could look down on Kamara ; then down went two
battalions, and occupied the church and churchyard
of that village. The rest halted, while Omar and Co.
took some luncheon. From our position we could
see right down the Valley of the Chernaya, and that
there was a good deal of water and marshy ground
there still. We also looked directly towards the bare

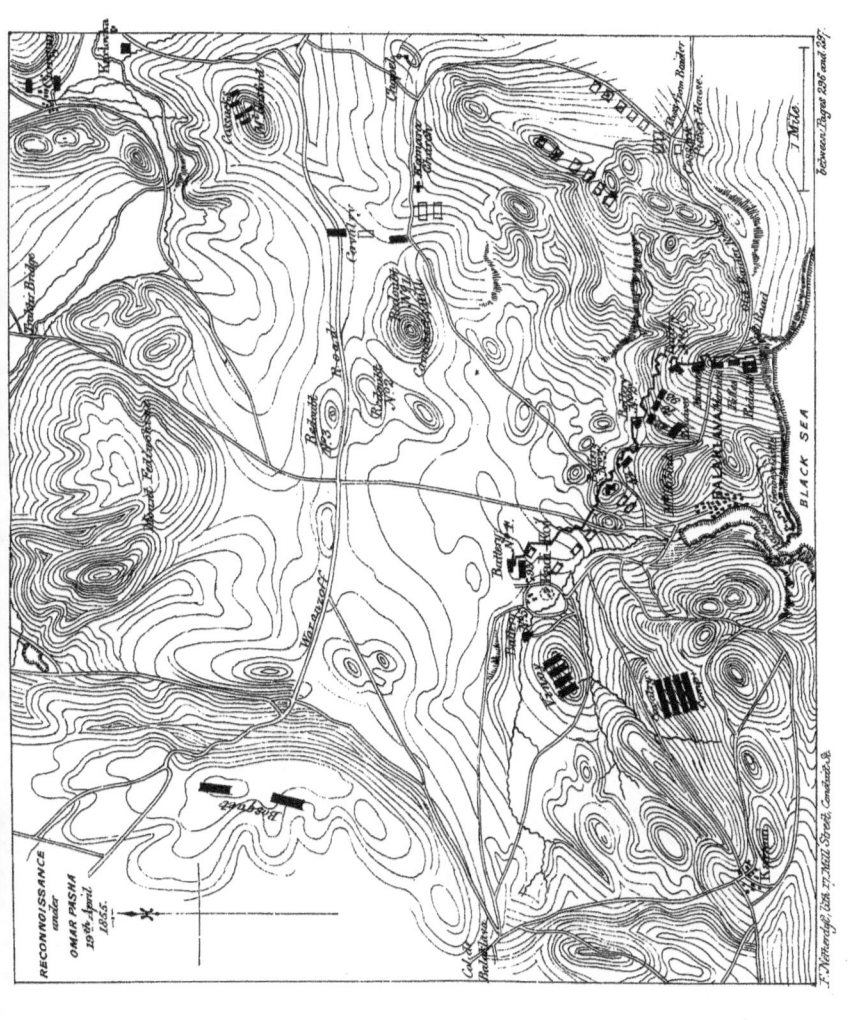

RECONNOISSANCE
under
OMAR PASHA
19th April
1855.

BLACK SEA

1 Mile

Between Pages 296 and 297

F. Wetherall, Lith. 77 Mill Street, Conduit St.

brown hill which the Highlanders occupied on the 20th February—the snowy morning of which I have spoken. It was covered with Cossacks admiring us. This hill lies about a mile to the north-east of Canrobert's Hill, and its eastern extremity hangs over the village of Chorguna, while the Chernaya winds under it in graceful bendings. At the same time some French, English, and Turkish cavalry, with guns, had made a combined movement with us through the plain in front of the lines of Balaklava, and were drawn up with their skirmishers in front, facing towards the east, their right being in Kamara. We saw that the Russians in Chorguna, and behind their intrenchments on the right bank of the Chernaya, were in small numbers, with only four guns in position, and plenty of impediments in all the gorges between them and the river. After resting the infantry for an hour in the position I have described, we all descended into the valley, and pushed on a couple of battalions in skirmishing order, while some rockets were fired by the Turks who were with the cavalry on the plain, which drove the Cossacks off the bare hill already spoken of. We then made an advance, and occupied the said hill, and could look very closely into Chorguna and another small village called Karlŏvka, about a quarter of a mile south of Chorguna, on a bend of the Chernaya. Very pretty villages, not much dilapidated, with poplar-trees growing about, and the Russian troops on the hills above, scarcely out of cannon-shot. Here was the extreme point of our reconnaissance. Down below us there were huts, which had been made by the enemy when they were in force here in the autumn ; these huts were planted pretty thickly even on the left bank of the river. Our skirmishers spread themselves a little down the hill, and the two opposing forces stood at gaze. Meantime some green and inquiring young plungers (vernacularly, heavy dragoons), and some other officers, thought it clever to ride in front of the skirmishers and try for spoils in the Russian huts. They found, I believe, some lances, a water-jug, and some very dirty combs and brushes; in appropriating which they no doubt exercised the rights of war, but they forgot that the Russians were very near them, and might think it a liberty. In fact, a few gray-coated men crept quietly down among the poplars, and opened fire upon them ; the result of which was, one of them tumbled off his horse, and all the others galloped back as fast as they could, with their tails between their legs. The dismounted man on foot brought up the rear, but with his back to the enemy. The plungers, having thus shown their ignorance of war and their prudence under fire, came back to us amid considerable jeering ; for, as was remarked to one of them, the first time he was under fire, he ran away. Now you have the facts of this reconnaissance.

The Turks will be pleased with the promenade. The new troops looked very well, and were manœuvred respectably. I am sorry to say fevers are now very prevalent among our people.

---

## LETTER LXXX.

Camp, Battery No. 4, Balaklava,
23d April 1855.

WE know that two more Russian divisions have come up, making probably 30,000 men, and, I suppose, they are preparing another attack on the Turks at Eupatoria. Our bombardment is over; we are pushing on the sap on the left of our attack in front of the Redan. Poor Colonel Egerton of the 77th paid with his life for the possession of some rifle-pits there, which have been added to our trenches, and we have pushed on the sap into the Woronzow road, making an advanced parallel. There is a quarry which has to be stormed, and then, I suppose, they will get up a new battery within 400 yards of the Redan. The French are also getting on with the sap on the right of their left attack, near the Bastion du Mât, which is at the head of the inner harbour. It seems likely the Allies will get possession of some of the works there by dint of sapping. The bombardment, I fear, has been nearly useless; still every one is confident of getting in, whenever it is thought proper to try. The place nevertheless, in my opinion, will not fall till we can send out a force from Eupatoria of 70,000 or 80,000 men, to attack the Russians and drive them away towards Bakchi-serai and Simpheropol. I confess I shall be very sorry if the negotiators make peace till we do this, for the sake of England. Meantime Roebuck's Commission is doing its revolutionary work as fast as you could wish, and helping to destroy the reputation of representative governments; going as straight as an arrow to despotism : such is my view. One of your inquisitors here, Dr. Gavin, has been killed by his brother, who accidentally let off his pistol. What on earth had he to do with a pistol? I see the *Times* is now going to torment Lord Raglan about taking the field; but I should hope his Lordship has had enough of his first campaign, and that he will not budge an inch till he has every thing complete in the way of transport, provisions, &c. The baggage-animals will have to carry, besides ammunition, rum and biscuit, sufficient forage for themselves and for the cavalry, for at least a fortnight's consumption. I suppose in that time the army from Eupatoria, and from hence, would have time to beat the Russians and to make their junction complete at Inkermann; after which the fall of the place will be secured. But I see nothing before us, except the entire capture of the Crimea, likely to produce any good effect in the negotiations. Let Austria advance, and I think we shall be able to expel the whole Russian army ; we feel perfectly confident of beating them in the field, and that feeling alone is worth many battalions.

## LETTER LXXXI.

Camp, Battery No. 4, Balaklava,
26th April 1855.

You will, no doubt, have in the papers an account of Colonel Egerton's death. During the last two days there have been two councils of war, and we think that they will get more batteries made, and nearer the enemy. The quarries in front of the spot where Egerton was killed are still occupied by the Russians ; the English soldiers are anxious to take them, but Lord Raglan forbids, as there will be such a tremendous fire on them if they try to hold on there. The feeling among the English that the French are not up to the assault is, I am sorry to say, prevalent. I understand that Lord Raglan believed there were more English guns in position when fire was opened than he found to be the case. I consider that the last ten days' battering has been nearly useless. Your militia is all to pieces; and where is the bold Government to propose the ballot to the bold John Bull, who would go to war, and finds he has to pay both in purse and person? We (army) are now placed in such a position in the Crimea, that we cannot move out without a great loss of men; and where are they to come from? Depend upon it, volunteers are not enough; we have got the whole power of Russia moving upon us. The whole nation oné conscript, driven on by religion and the necessity of clearing their territory of strangers. Our wretched Government is useless; they are not up to the emergency. I believe they feel it to be so. There has been a longer and more decided step towards revolution made in England during the last year than in all my time. Why all the lords in the creation are to govern, when they do it so badly, is the question. We have telegraphic news from Vienna in eight hours. It can be done in five, but occasionally the Austrian Government is using the wires. We heard that Lady —— had been meddling in the negotiations, and was inclined towards Russian friendships. It is whispered that Drouyn de Lhuys was gone to counteract her doings, and to keep up the negotiators to sufficiently stringent terms against Russia. There will be, I suppose, a change of government in England; whether they will try the Tories before the Radicals come in, is to be seen. Lord Ellenborough is the best, and, indeed, the only man I know of really quite fit to be War-Minister. Should he come in, there will be a great change in

Malakoff

Mamelon

Redan

Harbour

Bastion du Mât

Quarry

Woronzow Road

Green Hill
or
Chapman's Left Attack

Cemetery

3 Gun Battery.

French man's Hill

Right Attack of Gordon.

E.

Egan's Battery.

E. At this spot
Col. Egerton was
killed 20th April, 55.

Letter 20th April.

Scale 4 Inches to 1 Mile.

Fred.k Whrmeffs 12a–13 Mill Street Conduit St.

the army here; I would not even answer for his not displacing Lord Raglan himself. If I had to settle the army, I should make C. chief of the staff. He would soon make the staff-officers look up. The man they have sent is a very amiable person, quite a man of the world and of the *laissez-faire* sort. War and amiability are incompatible. You must come down like Thor's hammer on carelessness, or idleness, or incapacity. It is very provoking to see how things go; the official letters, which much of my time is spent in writing, many left unnoticed, and all watered down till there is no brandy left in the mixture: very little water was put in originally, you may suppose. Our letter-book, if ever it is seen, will show up plenty of people. Want of power, when one feels able to wield it, is a very sad want indeed. What can be more ridiculous or sadder than the appointment of ———— to teach our soldiers war? There is not a commanding-officer of a regiment or a general of brigade out here who, having gone through the winter, would not be fitter for the command. Judicial blindness has smitten the ruling classes in my country. We know who are the two who settle our military appointments: a hopeless combination; while the expense of the whole affair is something appalling. All our poor soldiers out here are, however, in the highest spirits, and ready to knock their heads against any wall behind which they can find Russians. They are the

true England; stars whose brilliance will be historical
when aristocratical names are forgotten or covered with
immortal shame. I believe they would fight and die
to the last man in this wild Tauris, rather than give
in or give up. Beaten they can never be. Remember
they are not chosen; a great majority entered from
poverty or misconduct. What an army would the
conscription give us! I beg your pardon for laughing
at the Nightingale and other birds of her feather. I
believe that she has been of use. When will she go
home? As Christophero Sly says, "Would it were
done!" They expect her here, and also Lord Stratford. Will she wear a wig or a helmet? You see I
cannot help laughing at her, as I have a keen sense
of the ridiculous.

27th April.

Lord Stratford came yesterday with his wife and
two daughters. They landed, and rode up to our camp,
at which funzione C. and S. were present. The ladies
flew at the hospitals as if they were professionals. It
really seems a morbid taste for horrors which has been
gotten up among them. They talked with considerable appearance of wisdom to a Miss ——, whose peculiar amusement in her livelier hours is scrubbing floors.
But we have also here in another hospital a certain
Miss ——, who has rebelled on geographical principles.
She avers that she signed articles to obey the Nightingale as her lieutenant in Turkey in Asia, but not in

Russia in Europe; there, she says, lies the error i' the bill. She drinks her bottle of claret, and has her own private reasons, besides her benevolence-bump, for coming here; but her geography seems to be out in this matter,—her object being to strew flowers on the grave of an officer who died in Bulgaria.

> " With the slight difference of the Euxine Sea,
>     Crim or Bulgaria are the same to she."
>
> *Byron.*

These women carry on a quick and *bien nourri* fire of notes, fending and proving and tormenting general officers, including Lord Raglan. The great ladies live on board ship. Lord Stratford goes to head-quarters. Lady —— has also arrived, and I suppose will incontinently take command of her brigade.

Miss Nightingale is daily expected; I do not know whether she has present a sufficient number of nurses to try the geographical question before a court-martial. I suppose I shall keep the roster, and make them pay toll for an overslaugh. Amid this grim war female *tracasseries* are quite out of place; but most people have agreed not to be provoked, and only to laugh at them.

To tell me that the service of the hospitals could not be as well or better performed by women who have been brought up to labour, is merely ridiculous. But it is the fashion; and they have powers quite

x

fabulous given to them. I wish I had a little trusted to me.

---

## LETTER LXXXII.

Camp, Battery No. 4, Balaklava,
29th April 1855.

SINCE writing last, we know by telegraph that the Conference is broken up. We hear that the points were all agreed to ; but that Russia insisted on having an island in the Greek Archipelago. We are getting more batteries up nearer to the enemy, and with heavier guns ; but since the two signal failures of the Artillery I am not sanguine. We must take the field to do any good. The line which Austria will adopt has not been alluded to. The article from the *Moniteur*, published in the *Times*, is very interesting. If Louis Napoleon is not killed in England, I expect to see him out here commanding the whole. He is brave and clever, and is more likely to be a good general than any one I can hear of. We have no outlet from hence, except into the valley of Baidar, which is not strongly fortified against us. Chorguna and Karlovka are only outposts of the Russian army ; the main body stretches from behind Sebastopol, by Inkermann, Cherkes Kerman, and Khorales, to the mountains, which make the north side of the valley of Baidar, up which mountains there are only goat-paths. The Belbek is strongly fortified; so is the Alma. Wherever we attack, we shall have trenches to storm; but it must be done. The most likely plan would be to land at the Katcha, and mount up that stream till we should threaten Bakchi-serai, where the Russian dépôts are; that would force them to fight on more equal ground : but the allied force should not be less than 70,000 men, and we must hold this position in the mean while, and indeed till our victorious army shall appear above the Inkermann heights; say 45,000 French, 15,000 Sardinians, and 20,000 Turks, with all the English field-batteries and cavalry. I think that might do; but I doubt the French liking to fight without some English infantry; and I do not know where they are to come from, unless we could trust Balaklava to Turks. I hear they have gazetted Bentinck a Lieutenant-General in Turkey, antedated one day senior to C. It is really too bad. Court influence: "Quem Deus vult perdere, prius dementat." We have had some cases of cholera already; no doubt the summer will have its victims as well as the winter. War is a great consumer of man; we all know that, and yet we wonder and scream. Fevers, too, are prevalent, and the heats are not yet begun. Certainly it was not without reason that I translated that appendix to Moltke, just before I left England; but they would not be warned. The wise borrow, the fools purchase, their experience. In either way it is a very sad possession, like the most of our memories. To-morrow, they say, another mail is due, with, I suppose, Napoleon's reception ; the next ought to bring the overtures of the government. Poor England, purse-proud and boastful, how low art thou fallen !

---

## LETTER LXXXIII.

Camp, Battery No. 4, Balaklava,
4th May 1855.

YESTERDAY we shipped off the 42d, 71st, 93d, and a wing of the Rifles, for the expedition to Kertsch. Fancy our indignation ; they have taken our beautiful troops, and lent them to Brown, leaving C. and Colonel S. behind. I never saw C. so much vexed. There is no general here who has been truer to Lord Raglan than C. He has uniformly defended him, not only because he thought him usually in the right, but also from a feeling that the proper soldier has of defending his general ; and this is the way he treats him. C. asked to go and serve under Brown, who is his senior officer ; but Lord Raglan made an excuse about this position, which he would not risk in charge of an inexperienced officer.

We are very low about it. The plan is to land at Kamish, nine or ten miles south of Kertsch, to

take all their batteries in reverse, and push on to
Yenikale ; the fleet trying to take some war-steam-
ers at the same time ; these, however, will, I fear,
escape into the Sea of Azov. There are 3000 British troops and 7000 French, with some artillery and
cavalry. Brown commands the whole, and is a very
fortunate fellow to have such a chance. Papers to
the 20th have come. I see the reception of Louis
Napoleon has gone on *à ravir*. I hope soon to see
him here, and a good army in the field. We must
now capture the Crimea, which has always been my
plan; but we must have a really large army, 200,000
men will do. Our small expedition just gone is expected back in a fortnight. The French have made
another successful advance towards the Bastion du
Mât. I believe they are only thirty metres from
the wall; and the English praise their behaviour on
this occasion. Pelissier is there. Vinoy said to me,
" S'il n'entre pas, personne n'entrera." The Légion
Etrangère lost more than twenty officers. We also
cannot get on without losing men and officers too. I
fancy Omar Pasha came here to relieve us, *i. e.* the
Highlanders, and to let us go to the assault. But
when that was deferred, he went away again. We
continue getting up more guns, and placing our batteries nearer. Poor —— is dead ; his warring done,
his arms folded. People of my temperament, who
may chance to be Quakers, must have a hard struggle

to keep so. It seems impossible for me to look at things from their point of view,—non-resistance, and all that sort of stuff,—while they are resisting in their own way as obstinately as any existing bipeds. However, I must snatch a little time and write to his sister. I can safely tell her that war is a very ugly thing, with very little lace and feather belonging to it. What we have a right to admire in war is the display of very admirable qualities called out by it in poor uneducated brave men, who have nothing to gain except perhaps the approbation of the company they belong to, and of their own conviction or conscience, or that thing we cannot shake off, which is so variable in its quality that the same might belong to an angel or a demon at different moments. You know how I have praised these poor peasants all along ; yet they have wonderful vices—drunkenness, lying, thieving. Still there they are—humanity; enduring and daring all things for a principle, many of them I verily do believe. Rest is for ever denied to me ;—and how I long for it ! I cannot be sure of five minutes. The wants of some thousands to be ministered to by my pen and personal activity. If I was one of four, viz. either the French or English admiral, or the French or English general, I could send you these letters in sixteen hours and a half. Such was the pace of our last message from England, and such the slowest rate at which news from hence will reach the government. Any good news you will therefore have before my letter starts from the Crimea : any bad news it is left to me to communicate ; for that they will keep quiet till the mail arrives. We shall have a change of ministry, I think. If you cannot find a man, give us a woman, who is a woman, and not a donothing. I think we should at least fight under a woman, like our German ancestors of old. I am ready to fight under Louis Napoleon. He is a clever fellow, and I wish him better luck than befell his uncle the prophet. Are we not fighting under his Shibboleth now? Cossack or Republican ! The Cossacks are before me ; I see them every day. Are the Republicans here? the French? myself? No, truly ; I hate a Republic : yet cannot feel contented under the rule of foolish lords. The devil is unloosed. We must fight for the name of England ; for auld lang syne ; for the love of our women, who should not have the shame of submitting themselves to any but brave and true men. This is rather an incoherent letter; but I have been interrupted fifty times.

## LETTER LXXXIV.

Camp, Battery No. 4, Balaklava,
7th May 1855.

In my last I mentioned our shipping-off our regiments for an expedition to Kertsch. Well, to our astonishment, yesterday, back the whole concern came, recalled by telegraphic message from Paris and London. They were just preparing to land. My reading of it is, that the Emperor of the French is coming here to command the whole, and that he will not let the army be frittered away in petty enterprises. I had as great an objection as you have to Louis Napoleon ; but I think that, since his *coup d'état*, we have reason to think there were attenuating circumstances, as it appears certain that the generals whom he put in prison would have put him there if he had not taken the initiative. It certainly would have been more manlike to go there, if the French people chose to allow of it. I suppose he thought, like Cromwell, that he would govern so well that the people would forget his treachery to them. What are our own people doing? Are there any more rational plans in progress for carrying on the war? Are any of the army-appointments which turned out bad ones cancelled? Not one ; confusion over all. We are in a mess; and I see no attempt at getting out of it. I am thoroughly disgusted with the state of things, and as radical as you are, which is a strong phrase; but I see my country in danger of being sacrificed by incapables, and I have no power to do any thing.

C. has applied to be relieved from the charge of Balaklava, in consequence of the support given against him to the Commandant by Estcourt and by the Chief of the Staff, to whom he was Aide-de-camp in India. Is it any wonder that this army is going to the devil?

## LETTER LXXXV.

Camp, Battery No. 4, Balaklava,
11th May 1855.

SINCE the return of our expedition to Kertsch, nothing has been heard save lamentations, and very strong language against Canrobert for recalling it. It is said that Napoleon could not have known the expedition was already gone when he sent his orders to keep the army together. We know that the Russians have received very large reinforcements, and that last week they had 42,000 men in Sebastopol itself. The first body of the Piedmontese is arrived, 5000 strong, with General Della Marmora. They have not yet landed, on account of the weather,

which has suddenly changed to rain, heavy and con-
tinuous, rendering the ground one mud.

Miss Nightingale is here ; but she has not yet
paid me a visit.   One result of her arrival I perceive,
however, very plainly, in the increased number of
orderlies they are taking out of the ranks, to employ
them in the hospitals.   It is really too bad.   Why
do they not form a corps expressly for this duty ?
We are now obliged to take our finest men, just as if
they were going on guard, and we are forbidden to
relieve them.   The same men are compelled to remain until they become sick ; then we are ordered to
send others to replace the men so expended.   The
result of this arrangement is, that the duty of the
soldiers not employed in hospitals remaining the
same, an additional share of night-duties falls on those
who stay with their colours.   But our chiefs are so
pusillanimous that they submit, for fear of being attacked in the papers.   If I had been required to
make a plan for supplying hospital-attendants, I
should have proposed to select a certain number of
medical officers, and some military officers who were
not in very strong health, and I would then have
surveyed the army, to find out the men in every
regiment who would be least able to bear the fatigue
of marching and carrying weight, or the exposure to
cold and wet ; these men, to the number required by
estimate of the doctors, should have been incorpo-

rated into a regiment of nurses under the above-mentioned officers, whose sole duty it would be to attend to their discipline and conduct. I think the formation of such a corps* would not have materially weakened the fighting army, and that the men would have soon become very efficient for their own special duties. Out of every batch of recruits I should have continued to pick the most weakly, so as to keep up the numbers of the nurse-corps. This body would, with a little instruction, have produced cooks and every sort of skilled labour requisite for the comfort of the sick; and Miss Nightingale might have had her wicked will of them without the interference of any officers except those belonging to the sick department. I would give them promotion from the ranks, so that any one who showed particular dispositions for this sort of work might rise to a situation which would enable him to carry out his views. I see no reason why there should not be a corps of women attached to them, to perform women's work; I mean, women from the working-classes, to wash and sew, and a regular dépôt in England, and a complete military organisation. The way we are acting now is absurd, and makes me sick. But I have no power; I can only groan. In the last twenty-four hours I have sent nine fresh orderlies from the Brigade of

---

* Some such a corps has been formed.

Guards, to be permanent nurses—great big grenadiers ! There are six steamers always going between
this place and Scutari, with soldier-nurses on board
permanently. Of these, there are always some who
catch the fever ; and, on the ship's return, they have
to be replaced. This is besides the soldiers employed
in the hospitals at Balaklava, Scutari, Abydos,
Smyrna, and the attendants on the regimental hospitals. No wonder our nominal army is small in
effective strength. Conceive a party of 100 reapers
used on this principle. How many would remain,
after six weeks' work, in a feverish neighbourhood ?
Philanthropy is a plaything to these ladies, and they
make ducks-and-drakes of our splendid soldiers. By
their assistance, the doctors have completely swamped
the military officers. However, at the rate we are
now furnishing men, the matter seems to me to have
become so serious that it will cure itself. As a mere
money calculation, it is a fearful waste, considering
what each soldier costs, and that all his military
training does not, in the smallest degree, render him
fitter for nurse-tending. The ludicrous part of it is,
that this duty should, by accident, have fallen on the
Guards,—the biggest men in the army,—from the
chance of their being stationed here, and not in our
front line. The most serious matter has its ridiculous : " *du sublime au ridicule*," &c. The siege is
not advancing. General Pelissier says he is kept

back! He is the man who smoked the Kabyles; which, I believe, was thought cruel at the time. War has little to recommend it, even to me, who am not a philanthropist.

## LETTER LXXXVI.

Camp, Battery No. 4, Balaklava,
14th May 1855.

WE have had three days' heavy rain; and now the summer has begun again hotter than ever. The Piedmontese are landing *Bersaglieri*, as they call them (*bersaglio* is a target, I think, in Italian; *cible* in French). They have long green cocks' feathers in their hats. The idea is, that they will occupy the old redoubts which the Turks were driven out of last autumn on the day of Balaklava. News we have none. The *Gazette* has reached us, with some recent promotions, of which the Guards have got a very large proportion; I think ten brevet majorities out of thirty-three. There are only three battalions of Guards here. By all accounts I can collect, we are making ready for another bombardment and for Louis Napoleon. The officers have been ordered to provide themselves with baggage-animals, which looks like taking the field. Something must be done.

There are yachts dropping in : "Stella" came yesterday, with Frankland on board ; and the "Ione"
to-day, with Sir Henry Oglander.  As I could do
nothing else for them, I sent them some horses, to
ride about and see the humours of our great *spectacle*.
The life here must be intolerably monotonous to the
officers.  Books very few ; I have just got hold of
two numbers of the *Westminster*,—old ones ; which
is quite a catch.  Suddenly, however, we shall be
ordered to move and to fight ; and a grand battle it
will be, you may depend upon it.  The numbers will,
I suppose, be swelled up to the dimensions of the
great battles at the beginning of the century, and
Alma will be forgotten.  I never expect to see again
so beautiful a sight as that attack at the Alma.  The
English moved as if they had been at a field-day.
I do not think I said much about that battle in the
picturesque point of view.  All the horrors of the
dead, dying, and wounded put it out of my head at
the time.

The *Times* is beginning to call for the electric
telegraph.  If they give up that engine for gossip, it
would have been better, as far as any military advantage we may expect from it, that it should not
have been laid down, as all news by it which is published in England will be sent to St. Petersburg
instanter.  You are mad !  We expect the Duke of
Newcastle here directly.  His evidence seemed very

honest. But in England they have not more nerve
than here, when it comes to displacing people.

## LETTER LXXXVII.

Camp, Battery No. 4, Balaklava,
16th May 1855.

THE post comes to me, an immense sack of letters
and papers, which I and my clerk sort and distribute.
You ask why I dislike Roebuck's Committee? It is
not because I wish any one spared, but our army is
held up in such a ridiculous light to the world. If it
is to be granted that abuses will be cured by the publicity, and that they can only be cured in that way,
then I should approve ; but I doubt both statements.
What fun it would be if they were to call for all letters from C. and Colonel S. to the Chief of the Staff,
to the Adjutant-General, and to the Commandant,
which relate to the state of affairs at Balaklava! What
a haul they would have! C. has got rid of Balaklava
at last, to his and my great joy. The place will be
put to rights, and the embarkations and disembarka-
tions, and every thing else there that requires brains
to be used, will be managed by Mackenzie and Ross,
who are two capital fellows. Layard has made a great
mess. He pitched upon Lord Burghersh and Arthur
Hardinge, without being aware that both of them had

been in India. Young Hardinge entered the army in
1844, and was Aide-de-camp to his father in the great
battles in India. Had he been a Captain at that time,
he would have got a Brevet Majority for the first
action, and a Brevet Lieutenant-Colonelcy for the second. But he was then a subaltern. As it is, he
has become a substantive Lieutenant-Colonel and Captain in the Guards in eleven years. Wilson had nothing to complain of. He would have had his promotion without purchase if he had withdrawn his name
for purchase, and allowed Hardinge to purchase over
his head. Layard has done us a great deal of mischief
from not being up in his facts ; and mischief to himself by his obstinacy, when he was clearly in the
wrong. There is such a splendid case against the
extra rank which the Guard officers enjoy, that it is
quite provoking to see it spoiled. Recently there
has been a slight alteration made, and from its operation people hope that the captains and lieutenant-
colonels in the Guards will not become full colonels so
soon as hitherto ; but there is one thing quite clear,
viz. that they will become lieutenant-colonels much
sooner than the Line ; and as to staff-appointments,
all the best of them must be held by field-officers.
Regimental field-officers of the Line cannot be put on
the Staff without going on half-pay, while the captains
of the Guards can go on in their own regiment while
so employed ; consequently the Guards have a sort of

monopoly of staff situations. I dare say you do not understand a word of all this. No civilian can make it out, with all the law possible in his head. I have never been able to get at the pay of a captain and lieutenant-colonel in the Guards. The regulation-price of the commission is about 260*l.* more than that of a lieutenant-colonel of the Line; but I believe their pay is made up to near 500*l.* a year; whereas the lieutenant-colonel of the Line only receives a guinea a day, and not even that when he is on leave. What I understand is, that the difference between the hospital stoppages from sick soldiers and the actual expenses incurred for them goes into a stock purse, and is divided amongst the captains and lieutenant-colonels of the Guards; whereas the surplus, if there is any, in the Line goes to Government. This surplus thus going to Government was formerly at the bottom of much that was condemnable in our hospitals; for it was the interest of each regimental or other medical officer to feed the patients badly, and to economise physic, as the inspector-general was thus enabled to keep down his estimates, and oblige the War-Office. Wheels within wheels. I see Colonel Cameron and myself have been named as officers on the staff who had received first-class certificates at Sandhurst; we passed on the same day. Cameron never was on the staff at all till quite lately; but he was fortunate in rising up in the 42d, of which he got the command

Y

by purchase in seventeen years, which made him full
colonel by the brevet of last year.   He would have
been a first-rate Quartermaster-general to this army.
There is no better regimental officer, and he is besides
very highly instructed in every way.   His father was
Colonel of the famous old 9th Regiment, in which C.
saw his early service.   Cameron was the senior officer
of the three commanding-officers of the Highland
Brigade ; and C. represented his qualifications to
Lord Raglan, and got him named to succeed himself
in command of it.   So much for his being selected on
account of his first-class certificate !   I resigned my
staff appointment, and went on half-pay in December
1843, I think, as a captain, after serving eighteen
years, and trying in vain to purchase an unattached
majority.   They pretended there was no half-pay
major to sell.   In May 1844, Captain Blucher Wood,
Lord Hardinge's nephew, being a captain of 1841,
got an unattached majority as soon as he found
he was going out to India, on Lord Hardinge's
staff.   He was then put into a regiment out there
as a major, and in the same year, 1844, he became
a lieutenant-colonel, and of course a full colonel by
the last brevet.   I was a captain about eight years
before him, and had served on the staff in the Medi-
terranean and in Canada.   So much for want of interest.   I was not selected for the staff here on account
of my first-class certificate, or on account of my

known capacity as a staff-officer, but from my being
a friend of C.'s, who asked for me. Neither was I
appointed to the branch which requires mapping, and
such knowledge as is acquired at Sandhurst. After
our campaign here, when the cocked-hat promotion
came out, I was not promoted; my rank was already
that of lieutenant-colonel, so they made me a substantive major, raising my half-pay from 8s. per diem to
9s. 6d. Major Pakenham was made on the same occasion at once a substantive lieutenant-colonel. So I
remain in this position, that if there is more fighting,
and my name is mentioned, I shall be made a substantive lieutenant-colonel at 11s. per diem, but no
promotion. Whereas Pakenham, having now jumped
at once from major to substantive lieutenant-colonel,
will be made in the brevet a full colonel clean over
my head. It's a do; but I have no interest, and fare
accordingly. Of course, with all this present in my
mind, and at my age, I have not any ambitious prospects; but one does not like to be put upon. I send
you all these details, because I feel inclined to write
a few facts to-day. The dates I got out of Hart's
Army-List, which is generally pretty correct. The
Nightingale is on board ship in Balaklava harbour;
and C. has been to visit her. I shan't go; I object to
the whole concern, and will not help in the foolery.
We are all very sorry to find Louis Napoleon is not
coming. I believe they are planning now how to go

out and fight the Russians, so as to invest the place;
but I fear our numbers are too small to do much
good. Pray turn out the Government, and put Lord
Ellenborough in. He is the only man who has a notion of what we want.

18th.

I see the newspapers are very unfavourable, or
rather very damaging, to our staff-officers here; and
I suppose there will be a great change,—I hope it
may be for the better. The cry for Indian officers is
cruelly unjust to our regimental officers, who beyond
all question know much more of their business than
the Indians. In fact, the Indian officers command
native troops, who are managed by the native officers;
and those Englishmen who are not able to get upon
the staff do next to nothing; besides which, any one
who shows talent is certain of being employed somehow away from his regiment. C. and S. gave an
entertainment yesterday to General Della Marmora
and his staff, which went off very well. The Sardinian General looks under forty. He was an ar-
tillery-officer, and seems very intelligent. He speaks
English tolerably, and French very well. They all
seem very much inclined to fraternise with the English; and no doubt if we fight and win a battle
together, that disposition will be increased. I understand that as soon as the whole Sarde force is
collected, we shall move out towards Kamara, and

occupy in force the position which the poor Turks were driven out of. Our friend little Rustem Pasha is gone away. He was a civilised amiable little man, and showed himself to be a brave one on the 25th October 1854, as we had the satisfaction of telling some of the Indian officers employed in the Turkish army, who wanted to run him down.

## LETTER LXXXVIII.

Camp, Battery No. 4, Balaklava,
21st May 1855.

AT last we have an event, viz. the dismissal of General Canrobert, and the appointment of General Pelissier in his place. Will that be ominous of an English dismissal? General Pelissier has been till now in charge of the siege, but always complained that he was kept back. We shall now see when he is head if he can go any faster. It is my impression that, in spite of the arrival of a great many more French troops and of the Piedmontese, we shall not push on our right wing till some sort of lodgment is made in Sebastopol. We made a promenade yesterday morning from our heights with a battalion of Turkish riflemen, three companies of marines, and the 42d. We only found a few Greek troops and some Cossacks; but the excursion was an amusement for the men. The country looked beautiful. The question of Indian officers, I see, continues its march. They are now to take rank with us out of India. This being decided, and so many of them stuck in here, the next step will be to open the good things in India to the Queen's officers. I think Lord Ellenborough's scheme is, to take all the patronage of the Indian army out of the hands of the Board of Directors, and all that of the Queen's army from the Horse Guards, and give the whole to the War-Minister. The officers will be allowed to exchange freely from one service to the other; and the aristocracy will get hold of the loaves and fishes there, as they do at home. This will be a death-blow to the Leadenhall-Street potentates, and a fine *contre-coup* to their dismissal of Lord Ellenborough. The papers speak of the presence in London of the officer who collected the troops for the great battles of Lord Gough. If those who write about it know the facts, they insinuate a monstrous misrepresentation; and if they do not know the facts, they are very ignorant. In India all the transport of an army is managed by the civil *employés*. The military staff-officer merely writes, " I am coming ;" and he finds the whole resources of the country assembled for the convenience of his troops. The Government sweeps up all in the most reckless manner, just as in Russia; and the military officer gets the credit for a great deal of

arrangement. However, we shall have these gentlemen sent out here to rule over us ; taking away our
earnings, and teaching us how to fight. God help
them ! their only knowledge of fighting is seeing a
few Queen's regiments turning the fate of battles lost
by the hopeless timidity of the black troops. Always,
as I am told by an eye-witness, when an advance is
made against the enemy, the Sepoys hang back till
the British have succeeded ; they then rush up, and
say, " How well we have done !" But if, on the contrary, the British fail, the military quality of the
natives is shown by the wonderfully active manner in
which they run away, and the unanimous accusation
that it was the fault of the whites. The honours of
the Indian officers are won by the valour and conduct
of the Queen's troops and the Company's artillery ;
now the newspapers by their cry are going to bring
these Indian officers to show us how to fight ! The
Indian officers will find the Russians a very different
foe from the Asiatics they have been accustomed to
skirmish against. Their irregular horse will do but
little against the Cossacks, who are of the same description of troops, but who are highly national. No
Cossack ever deserts or is surprised ; their vigilance
is quite wonderful ; but they do not fight—that is not
their business. We hear that our new batteries are
nearly armed ; so you may expect daily a report of
the third bombardment ; after which, let us hope, we

shall get hold of some part of the body of the place. To-day the English mail is due. Will it bring us any news? None good, I fear. The governing clique will hang together, and shuffle the few cards they have. Cholera is here; very shortly we shall have the papers full of it, at the risk of a panic. Fevers also are prevalent; and we are under the full dominion of the doctors and the ladies, none of whom, by the by, do I ever see. I know of their presence by their works—absorbing soldiers in the most reckless style, and no doubt telling their own tale at home. The inquisitors now present cause a most amusing uneasiness. You see we are by no means thankful to the people who send us such ambassadors. Their blue-books will be large and heavy. I suppose they will be all going back very soon, with wonderful stories. They will have nothing to say against the British infantry, officers or men,—that is a comfort. Long ago I remember trying to excuse the follies of young officers, when you covered them with sarcasms. Your mind must be rather changed with regard to them, I hope. Much of the good conduct of the men has been due to the support and encouragement given to them by their officers; officers who will never be heard of out of their own regiments, but who have deserved well of their country.

P.S. The old Kertsch expedition embarks again to-morrow.

## LETTER LXXXIX.

Camp, Battery No. 4, Balaklava,
24th May 1855.

THE new French General is pushing on, I believe. After a bloody combat, on the night before last, he got possession of the cemetery,* which has advanced him very materially ; meantime two or three divisions of the French army, Omar Pasha with 25,000 men, Gen. Della Marmora with what Sardinians are landed, move out to-morrow morning. The French right will rest on the bridge over the Chernaya (Traktir), opposite to which there is a Russian redoubt. The Turks will come next to them ; Della Marmora at Kamara ; and we, I believe, with a small force are to go out and defend the turn of the road towards the Baidar Valley, feeling at the same time towards La Marmora. I am, as you may suppose, terribly busy ; have, however, found time to make a sketch of the country into which we are going. We shall, I suppose, be said to be holding the line of the Chernaya, with a hope of drawing off some of the garrison after us out of Sebastopol. We are sadly put out at the Highland Brigade being lent to Brown for the Kertsch expedition. C. said to him quietly, " I am giving you good troops." " I would as soon have my own," was

* This is quite on the French left, away towards the Quarantine.

the answer; the rude soldier not entering into the feelings of C. at parting with men whom he had trained for a twelvemonth, thus to make the reputation of any one who had the good fortune to command them. However, we must make the best of it. The Russians are intrenched all along their position.

## LETTER XC.

Camp, Battery No. 4, Balaklava,
28th May 1855.

You will get a pinch of our news so regularly now by telegraph when the news is good, that, strictly speaking, one ought not to write at all about the events here. However, I intend to continue doing so for a while longer, till I see how it works. I sent a little *croquis* of the country, telling you also that the French were going out, or rather the allied armies. It was on the 25th this took place. I, who had nothing to do with it, mounted our heights to Battery No. 1, and I saw the French advance; they crossed the Chernaya by the bridge, attacked and took the redoubt on the opposite side with little opposition, and spread themselves away to Chorguna and Karlovka. The Russians were quite surprised, and made a rapid retreat; an officer was shot in his shirt. In the huts at the redoubt and at Chorguna they found

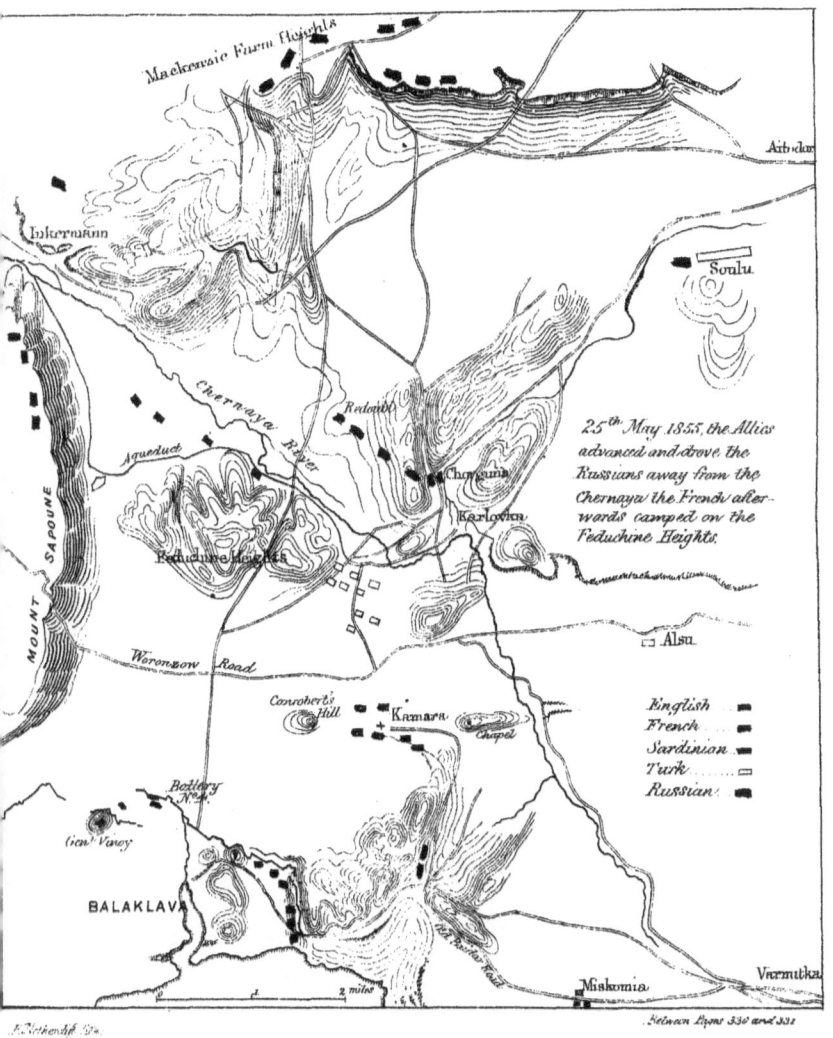

Mackensie Farm Heights

Aitodar

Inkermann

Soulu

Chernaya River

Redoubt

Aqueduct

Chorgoun

Karlovka

MOUNT SAPOUNE

Feduchine Heights

25th May 1855, the Allies
advanced and drove the
Russians away from the
Chernaya the French after-
wards camped on the
Feduchine Heights.

Woronzow Road

Alsu

Conrobert's
Hill

Kamara

Chapel

English
French
Sardinion
Turk
Russian

Battery
Nº 4.

Gen! Vincy

BALAKLAVA

2 miles

Miskomia

Varnutka

E.Weller lith.

Between Pages 330 and 331

books, letters, and articles from the *Times*, besides
money. The enemy retired towards Sulu. The
French destroyed the redoubts, and then returned
and took up the position I indicated in the sketch ;
the Turks rather behind them on their right : the
Piedmontese at Kamara and a few English covered
their right towards Baidar, or rather towards Miskomia. Yesterday morning I went with Gen. Della
Marmora along the old Baidar road. We had our
troops outside in position. I could go much further
than I ever went before, and we got so far as to look
down over Varnutka, a village deserted and partially
destroyed, situated in a small plain, the whole of
which is meadow-land ; a very sweet-looking spot,
but there was not a soul to be seen, not even a Cossack. We then went, accompanied by a few soldiers,
to our left, so as to look down on Karlovka. The
country is all deserted. I then returned to my hut
here, and C. went off to breakfast with Gen. Vinoy,
who is encamped just opposite the bridge (Traktir)
over the Chernaya. When I got home, I found the
news of the fall of Kertsch, without any loss to us,
and immediately galloped off with it to Gen. Vinoy's
camp, and being there, rode down to the bridge, beyond which the French are now constructing a bridge-
head. This is the bridge over which we marched on
the 24th September last. Our bivouack on that
night was very near General Vinoy's present camp.

It was dark when I was there before. I remember
riding my horse under the bridge to make him drink.
The river is quite shallow, a nice rippling rapid trout-
stream. Just eight months ago I was there before,
with many a fine fellow now under the sod, or invalided for life. This Kertsch business may be of immense importance, giving us the Sea of Azov. The
men-of-war steamers, I understand, went straight for
Taganrog, at the mouth of the Don, and we are sending twenty heavy guns to place in battery at Yenikale,
so as to keep the Straits of Kertsch open. I suppose
very soon we shall get up on the plateau to our right
of Inkermann, and attack the Russian army there.
Meantime Pelissier will press the siege. We are
still in some doubt as to whether C. will have the
permanent command of the 1st Division, or whether
there will be a Highland division formed for him.
General Bentinck is expected every day ; and he will,
I dare say, make pretensions to the division in which
the Guards are. He has the Court interest, and understands how to manage. The two last mails have
gone astray. I believe my letters have followed the
Highlanders to Kertsch. The Russians, I now feel
inclined to think, will burn every thing, and retire before us, without offering a very vigorous defence in
the field. They burned every thing at Kertsch, I am
told. If this be their plan, we shall probably, before
the summer is over, have possession of the Crimea,

except the steppes, which I should suppose must be untenable by any army, for want of water. Our point is Bakchi-serai and Simpheropol; once there, with Eupatoria on the left, and Kertsch on the right, the enemy must go off to Perekop. Our present advance and success will encourage the Austrians. If they move in earnest, our task ought to be easy enough, and we shall have the towns of the Crimea to winter our troops in. I never saw any thing more beautiful than the country here; the whole plain is a mass of flowers—campanulas, larkspurs, and a many that I do not know. I came to one place that was all roses, the low dog-rose, which I never saw before: they are generally long-legged, sprawling bushes; but these were tidy compact little fellows, which looked as if they were just turned out of a flower-pot. The India Company, I perceive, will not have any thing to do with the amalgamation of the two armies. In that case they should not come here and take our earnings. Reciprocity all a one side! Miss Nightingale still here—sick, they say. Your inquisition, or committee, seems never ending, and you have not caught any body yet. The only one killed is poor Captain Christie, who died before his trial, at which he was sure of acquittal. The *Times'* Correspondent has an article in one of the last copies stating that the position carried so easily the other day was impregnable. I confess we are all rather scandalised at the weakness of the defence. As the Russians retire, they will become stronger ; as we advance, we shall become weaker, for we shall have to establish posts on our lines of communication. I suppose the French will continue sending troops ; but I do not see how, in this country, we shall be able to make the natives feed the army, as was the custom in their German wars. Perhaps, before peace is made, we shall find ourselves on the Rhine : that would be a better investment for the French than Crimean acquisitions ; and I should much prefer campaigning in a country where I could speak the language.

<hr>

## LETTER XCI.

Camp, Battery No. 4, Balaklava,
30th May 1855.

The position occupied by the allied armies in front of the lines of Balaklava is very nearly that indicated in the little tracing I sent. We expect every day to open fire again, and attack and make a lodgment somewhere in the place. From letters found at Kertsch, we hear that during the winter the Russians buried 50,000 men out of 80,000 ; but they were not such fools as to put it in the papers. Our troops are now gone from Kertsch to try and take Anapa and Soujouk Kaleh ; so we may be some time

without the Highland Brigade. I think it is a mistake to scatter the army so much. It is stated that
the enemy has brought twenty battalions to reinforce
the troops at Mackenzie's Farm ; I conclude they
think we shall try to get up there. *Pas si bête.* It
is also stated that the French and Turks plundered
frightfully, and that they have had a fight, and fired
on one another. All these are mere reports ; we
have no details. Where there is no resistance, it is
quite contrary to the custom of war that any plundering shall be allowed ; and I hope the English have
not been guilty of it, nor of ill-using the women, which
is one of the blackest chapters of war : it is bad
enough without that horror. We hear that Lord
Ellenborough has been beaten by a large majority;
which I am sorry for. He is the man who ought
to be War-Minister. Meantime there has been a
mighty job swept away by the overthrow of the
Board of Ordnance. You predict a very radical
overturn of every thing, but not yet. I confess I
want to see a good deal of alteration ; the miserable
working of our Government when matters are so
critical has much disgusted me; and there must be
many others who feel the same, but do not see
exactly how to mend the ship. Since the allied
force has taken up a position on the Chernaya, I
go to bed regularly ; but I had got so used to sleep
in my clothes, that I scarcely appreciate the change.

Yesterday I took a ride to the siege, and had a good look at the French left, or rather the right of the French left (the Bastion du Mât). They have got their works quite close to the Russian bastion, —about thirty yards off, I should say,—and all our advanced batteries look fearfully near; they will of course open very soon, and I suspect a simultaneous attack will be made on the whole line, including the Batteries Blanches on Mount Sapoune,* as well as on the Mamelon. The soldiers are in such spirits that I cannot doubt our getting in somewhere; after that there will be numerous internal defences to take, the Malakoff frowning at the French, and the Redan looking any thing but pleasant. We shall have to advance *pas à pas*. But I have no doubt at all of ultimate success, and never had. Give us time, and make the newspapers hold their tongues. I am not much alarmed at your revolutionary schemes, which, if they were to succeed, would perfectly dismay you. The overturn of such an oligarchy as ours, even if its destruction were a pure good, can only be brought to pass through infinite suffering, from which the Lord defend us! This is the 31st May, the summer is quite established, and a most agreeable climate it is. All

---

* The Russians appear to have called the whole plateau from opposite Inkermann to the Col de Balaklava by the name of Mount Sapoune.

that is necessary is a tolerably good house. The heat is much exaggerated,—in fact, it is Italy without the malaria and the charming amiable people, whom it is impossible not to like, despite their faults—for some of them, perhaps. I believe it is your hatred of aristocracy which makes you hate poor ——. Be not deceived! He is a most innocent and plebeian red tapist.

1st June 1855.

Newspapers came to the 18th. I am afraid the Government is going to live. We hear of our gunboats ravaging about in the Sea of Azov, taking flour-ships, and doing various damage to the enemy.

Yesterday 3000 more troops were embarked from hence to join the Kertsch expedition, whereof 1000 English. Anapa, I conclude. All which doings will have a lively effect on the British public, and perhaps make them like war. We have still to mount the plateau, and fight the main army of Russians at Mackenzie's Farm or elsewhere ; but I want the noble J. B. to understand, that when his valorous troops, by the assistance of the Indian officers, shall have taken the Crimea, the talked-of peace is not by any means so necessarily at hand. We shall have to keep an army here, and fleets all about the coasts, and taxes, and every thing comfortable,—I mean likely to bring about your blessed revolution. Russia will win in the long-run, I think.

z

Patience in tax-paying cannot endure for ever : you will all be tired of the war ; Russia will quietly slip back to Sebastopol, build new ships, scheme new schemes, and some fine morning, when we are all republicans, a sudden pounce will place her at Stamboul. I cannot believe that any amount of calamity will break up Russia. It is a great nationality—not to your taste no doubt, but such is the fact. No enemy will dare to invade her territory beyond such small nibbles as we are now making. I was talking to Lord Aberdeen's son yesterday ; he is a staff-officer here: he seemed quite satisfied that if Austria moved at all, it would be to assist Russia. Poor Austria is in a cleft stick. Nuts to your vagabonds. I hope in my letter on the India Company officers I have made you understand my views on the matter. You have given no opinion ; yet it is a subject on which opinions must be formed, not indeed absolutely by you, but by England. You are complaining of your weather, that truly British subject ; but, with a good house and fires, what is weather ? Here there are no such complaints ; nothing can be finer. To balance which, we have the cholera slowly increasing, and picking up its victims here and there. At present there is no panic, but the newspapers will soon make that. Has the *Times* received a stab by the new regulations ? *
I think it is a monster not easily quelled.

---

* The alteration of the stamps.

## LETTER XCII.

Camp, Battery No. 4, Balaklava,
5th June 1855.

I CONCLUDE the telegraph brings you a bit of news daily. More fish caught in the Sea of Azov. We, I mean C. and I, are disgusted at being kept here doing nothing; all our troops gone except the Guards, and a large force of the allies covering our front. C. has asked for leave to go and stay a while at the camp before Sebastopol, which request will, I suppose, be granted.

I must remain here to carry on detail duties. Every moment we expect to hear of the fresh opening of fire, and a new assault consequent upon it. Russia must be very much mortified at our success on her coasts, but the crowning slap will be her compelled retreat from Sebastopol, which I hope is nearer than any one could have anticipated. We hear that Russell, of the *Times*, got himself smuggled on board one of the ships of the Kertsch expedition, and that Sir G. Brown refused to let him land. The non-resistance of the Russians is supposed to arise from their not expecting that we could spare any troops from the siege for such an enterprise. I think it the more probable, because they could themselves spare none.

## LETTER XCIII.

Camp, Battery No. 4, Balaklava,
8th June 1855.

THE telegraph will have brought you tidings of our war. You have a plan of the trenches. I stood on the hill a little to the south and east of the three-gun battery, looking from thence right into the trenches in front of the Redan, where Colonel Egerton was killed. All our batteries fired fast and furious, when at 6 P.M. yesterday I saw the red soldiers filing into the trenches. As soon as these were all full, the men jumped over their own parapets, ran up to the Quarries, which lay between them and the Redan, and which the Russians had made into a work. They climbed the steep earth parapet, and vaulted over among the Russians, driving them away. Here they should have stopped and begun fortifying themselves ; instead of which, many of the men rushed on to the Redan, and some entered it ; but there had been no intention of taking the Redan on this occasion ; there were no supports ready; and they were driven back to the Quarry, where they stayed, and still remain, and it is now joined to our trenches. The loss during last night has been considerable, as the Russians attacked them five times, but were always driven back. The French took the two batteries on Mount Sapoune commonly called "les Batteries Blanches," after some

hard fighting, as these were closed works ; and, I believe, all the Russians inside were killed. A third
Batterie Blanche still existed close to the sea, which
the French carried, but could not hold, as the men-of-
war in the harbour fired grape into them. The French
took the work in the Mamelon at once, with scarcely
any loss ; but, contrary to their orders, they rushed on
against the Malakoff. Some of them got in and spiked
a gun, but they were driven back for want of support,
and were even driven out of the Mamelon, losing many
men ; but they attacked it again, and carried it, and
kept, and keep it. They say nearly 2000 men are
*hors de combat.* I suppose we shall very shortly
assault the whole place and carry it, killing all the
garrison. We shall then proceed to fight a great
battle, which gained will give us the Crimea. Of peace
I see no sign. I do not wish for it, although I hate
war, as every good soldier and humane person must.
The fine part of war is the British private: those who
have gone through this business should have ample
provision for life at the national cost,—a quart of
turtle and a bottle of champagne per man, with full
license to beget sons like themselves, legitimate or
otherwise. It will be a clear gain for the country.
They will really get 1*s.*, or thereabouts, per diem,
when incapacitated by age or wounds, and the Crimean medal. I know of officers who got Brevet majority and clasps for Alma, Inkermann, and Bala-

klava, who were on the beach at Old Fort, landing
stores when Alma was fought, and sitting at a desk
in Balaklava when the two other actions were fought.
All who wear uniforms are not heroes, and many a
Crimean medal will hang on an unworthy breast. Let
us deserve, at any rate ; that we can do, independent
of Lords, jobbing, or interest.

## LETTER XCIV.

Camp, Battery No. 4, Balaklava,
12th June 1855.

THE post is just going ; all my news is forestalled
by the telegraph. The third bombardment is over,
and I conclude the engineers and artillerymen are
busied in moving the guns from their rear batteries to
their front ones. We got to-day the news that Anapa
had been abandoned by the Russians, and was in the
hands of the Circassians. On the 9th, I went to see
the trenches ; and while there, a truce was agreed
upon to bury the dead. I went into the Mamelon ;
many corpses lay there with the most frightful
wounds. Some bodies in which shells had burst had
lost all form of humanity. Arms and legs were lying
about. I saw one half-body ; the trunk had disap-
peared ; only the legs and buttocks remained. The
Russians whom we saw had a sad and sombre aspect,

very different from the air they wore on the last similar occasion. The White Batteries on Mount Sapoune were wonderfully strong, and the Zouaves only got in from surprise: they found two planks left across the ditch, over which they rushed. The seamen at their guns fought, and were all killed. The infantry surrendered. Unluckily, the French ran on to the Batterie Blanche nearest the sea, and were there exposed to the fire from two troops of Horse Artillery, and a cross-fire from the Inkermann batteries, and lost fearfully. They went on contrary to orders. This battery has since been abandoned by the enemy. The French are now turning these batteries the contrary way. They lost many men for two or three days in the Mamelon, where they are also making batteries. We lost scarcely any one in taking the Quarries ; but the Russians during that night made five desperate attempts, all of which were beaten off. Our loss by nine o'clock the next morning was 650 men and officers killed and wounded, of whom 50 were officers, 12 killed.

The French lost 2500, or thereabouts. Our troops from Kertsch will all be back directly. Two regiments, the 72d and 63d, are now off Balaklava. All our various successes must have discouraged the enemy, and I hope we shall soon have the south side of the harbour. I think it probable, when the troops from Kertsch land, that we shall be sent up to the siege.

I can scarcely believe they will leave us here, where
there is no enemy.    I have had a letter from a friend
of mine dated Yenikale.    He seems to think that
with eyes, and a head, and a little dash, we should
have done a great deal more than we did there ; but
we have lost no one, only two Highlanders killed by
the accidental discharge of a French musket.    I cannot think many days will pass over before we shall
make some more important move.    It is now under
debate whether we shall advance from here against
Mackenzie's Farm, or wait till we have the town.    It
is almost a precipice up there, *i.e.* at Mackenzie's
Farm.    The enemy must be quite bewildered at our
sudden activity.    They were completely surprised on
the 7th, when we stormed their outworks.    Beyond
the Quarries, we have already made an advanced
trench, and we are evidently sapping up towards the
angle of the Redan.    It is only a question of days·
Their ships are well out in the roads, having warped
away from their various hiding-places in the creeks.
As soon as we can bring batteries to bear upon them,
I expect they will sink the ships.    Our long labour
and endurance are likely to close soon, unless some
stupid peace is made ; and the grand Battle of Bakchi-
serai will give us the Crimea, after which our road is
clear to Teflis and Georgia.    Having possession of the
Euxine, the Sea of Azov, and the northern slopes of
the Crimean mountains, no army of any amount can

march against us over the steppes, and we may hope
that the following summer's campaign will have for
the present effectually clipped the power of Russia.
For these successes in Circassia will be known all over
Asia, and will destroy the prestige of Russia. The
French and English are better friends than ever. The
great gallantry of the French in the last affair has
quite silenced those in our army who professed to
undervalue them ; and the English behaved as usual.
The difference in the Russian point of view of the
captures by the two armies is shown from their
having attacked the English five times during the
past night, and the French not at all ; but we are
there safe enough, and I can see my way into the
Redan with certainty : what internal defences they
have, remains for experiment. Between the Redan
and the Quarries they had many boxes of powder
with fulminating tubes to explode when trod upon.
During the truce, one of the Russian officers said
to Colonel Yea, " You had better stop your men
from running about here, for the fougasses will explode." They searched about, and found twenty. The
tubes contain glass tubes full of nitric acid. All this
is very sad for you, because we shall bring down the
pride of Russia without rousing the peoples to insurrection against Austria. I cannot help that. I
would rather that England and France in fair fight
should flutter these Cossacks. It will be a lesson for

a century, before the expiration of which, the mil-
lennium may be introduced. Then, as now, the art of
war will be no more learned; moreover, that study
will then be unnecessary.

---

## LETTER XCV.

Camp, Battery No. 4, Balaklava,
15th June 1855.

I AM in the bustle of giving orders and packing
up. The division, including the Highland Brigade,
marches to-morrow for the siege; so I have but little
time to write or say any thing. All our news reaches
you now so soon, that it is quite disheartening to
write at all about our doings here. I believe fire will
open again to-morrow, and doubtless very shortly
afterwards we shall storm, and, I think, most probably carry the south side of the town. Our division
will be in reserve, I conclude, and not employed, unless in case of a disaster.

I am surprised at your not having understood the
cause of the Kertsch recall. The French Emperor
recommended, as a general maxim, to Canrobert, not
to separate his forces. Canrobert thought that meant
to call back the expedition. As soon as his successor
was appointed, it started again, and had the success
you have seen. A letter was found on the table of

the governor of Kertsch from the authorities of Sebastopol, stating, in answer to one of his asking for assistance, that they could send none, as the Allied
Armies had crossed the Chernaya. We shall, no
doubt, if we take the place, advance immediately to
attack the Russian army in the field. It is estimated
they have 130,000 men, and 500 pieces of field-
artillery. I suppose, including all sorts, our army
may be 200,000, but less artillery than the enemy.
Yenikale has been fortified and garrisoned by Turks,
and some English and French, having besides steam-
boats to assist. I see that part of the correspondence
in the *Times* refers to C. and the Commandant, and
asserts that the authorities took part with the latter :
the fact being, that they were going to dismiss him,
till C. made their minds easy by saying that he did
not want to do him any harm,—he only wanted to
get rid of him from under his command ; whereupon
Balaklava was put under the Commandant independent of C.'s interference, who would thus be no longer
responsible. What a service ! I can only surmise
that Lord Raglan did not choose to offend the Napier
interest ; having before his eyes the flashing pen and
brilliant periods of William Napier, who would probably not have known the facts. His Lordship would
not have minded if he could have thrown the onus of
a dismissal on C. Thus do things fall out. As it
has been mentioned in the *Times*, I am in hopes

people will think that paragraph a good cause for a parliamentary interpellation. It is in the *Times* of the 31st May, and is by no means complimentary to C. You are quite right in thinking this is no place for ladies. Yet there are some here. Lady G. Paget; Mrs. Duberley, wife of a paymaster of Dragoons; and Mrs. Estcourt lately. These fair dames usually stop on board ship in Balaklava or Kamish Harbour, and seduce their husbands to run there after them, as many a weary staff-officer has found to his sorrow. Wilson's reason for leaving, I should think, was, that he must have given unpardonable offence to the Guards. In point of fact, I did not admire his behaviour; he had really nothing to complain of; and when that was shown to him, he did not frankly acknowledge himself to be in the wrong.

THE paragraph concerning C. and the Commandant runs as follows: "Sir Colin Campbell, the General commanding the troops in and around Balaklava, not having very much to do, and being possessed of an immense amount of animal energy, is obliged to find vent for his excitement now and then in a little official row with Colonel —— ; and one correspondence at least has taken place between the belligerents and head-quarters, which has not resulted disadvantageously to the Commandant of the town. No doubt the gallant officer will soon find some more active employment, and greater success, in the field; and an opportunity will be given to him and to the Highland Brigade of renewing the laurels of the Alma."

"Our Own Correspondent" only allows Sir Colin animal, not even physical, energy; as if he was discoursing of a lively pig. This shows how little he knew of the man he was running down. He also did not know the truth of the story he relates. The official documents are all lying before me now; and the case was so conclusively to the disadvantage of the Commandant, that the Commander-in-Chief was prepared to dismiss him, had not Sir Colin stated that all he wanted was to have him removed from under his command, or to be himself relieved from any charge in Balaklava. The latter was the course adopted. The Correspondent amusingly talks of the two belligerents, as if there could be any such a thing as belligerence between an old General Officer and a young Lieutenant-Colonel who was under his command. No, Mr. Correspondent; there was no belligerence, but a great display of exceeding good-nature and forbearance on the part of Sir Colin.

The next Letter, No. 96, is from before Sebastopol, and Battery No. 4 is abandoned for ever. This Letter was written on the day after the failure on the 18th of June. The First Division was moved up to be in reserve on the occasion, and then remained to assist in carrying on the siege. C. and his Highlanders were not sent to Kamara to support the Piedmontese till the 26th August.

————

## LETTER XCVI.

Camp before Sebastopol,
19th June 1855.

THIS morning's London papers will have given you the sad intelligence of yesterday's losses. The French failure involved our own. I suppose the Engineers will now begin sapping to get nearer. Our division was in reserve in rear of the 21-gun battery on Frenchman's Hill. We could see the French attack on the Malakoff Tower, or rather one of them, and the ground thickly sprinkled with corpses when they retired. Our own loss has not been any thing like that of the French, who count 6000 men and two generals *hors de combat;* but we have a great proportion of the officers engaged either killed or wounded, some of whom will be* very much missed. We shall know more of our loss from Lord Raglan's letter in the paper when it returns. There will be nothing published to the army. We, from our division, gave 2000 men to the trenches last night, to be there twenty-four hours: they were put in the Quarries. This is a strange change from Balaklava, where latterly we had nothing to do. I should imagine we

shall remain here now and see the siege out. The
telegraph is a great blessing in the respect that I
suppose the names of the killed will be given; and
thus people will be put out of pain. I saw all the
chaplains out gazing. I believe these men would go
to see gladiators. Their unbridled curiosity takes
them away from their work, which should be in the
hospitals, and not looking on coolly at brave men
killing one another. I am sorry I cannot inform you
of the precise day on which we shall take Sebastopol;
if it is to be taken by sapping, a good while off yet.
Whether Pelissier will try another storm, I cannot
guess. He changed the hour of the attack during the
night. It was to have been at six, and he attacked
at 3 A.M. Had he waited, we should have battered
and shelled the garrison for three hours, which might
have driven a good many of them away. It has frequently happened that a first assault has failed and
later ones succeeded; but in this particular case my
voice is for sapping, although my opinion will not be
asked. Some of the troops who attacked yesterday
got beyond the abattis on the glacis of the works
they assaulted. I know it is reported that two French
regiments got into the Malakoff; but I do not believe
it. How could they cross the ditch under such a fire
of grape and musketry? Such an attempt will only
succeed by accident. The White Batteries were just
as strong; but fortune favoured the French then, and

failed them yesterday. I dare say we shall have a truce to-day to bury our dead. Many officers' bodies are lying on the glacis, and we should like to put them decently under ground.

---

## LETTER XCVII.

Camp before Sebastopol,
22d June 1855.

We are fixed here now, to take our part in the siege, and our men are put in the trenches in and about the Quarries. I went all over them yesterday, and will send a small sketch. The position of our trenches, being on the northern slope of a gentle declivity, exposes them to the southern sun,—and fearfully hot they are.

S.                                                      N.

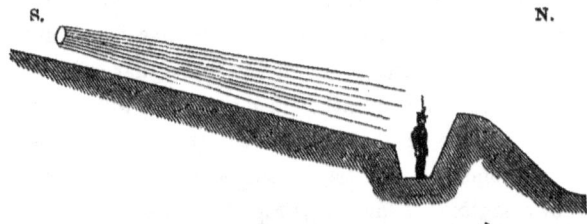

You observe the sun shooting his rays into the soldier's back. I hardly ever was more tired than after my examination of the trenches yesterday. The men who stay all day are regularly baked : they do not move about ; and if they pop up their heads over

the parapet to look at the Russians, pfing !—a rifle-
ball with its queer little note, melancholy but not
musical.

I hear the French are beginning a sap from the
Mamelon towards the Malakoff. We are strengthening our defences in the Quarries. The history of our
unfortunate assault is, I believe, something like this.
Such works as we had to attack, when there is no
breach and the guns inside intact, are usually considered safe from any assault excepting surprise; but the
French, who took the Batteries Blanches, which were
quite as strong as the place itself, were cockahoop.
It was generally understood that we should not be
able to hold the Redan, unless the Malakoff were
taken first. The French general (Mayran*) who commanded the storming party started twenty-five minutes too soon. He got two battalions inside, I am
told; but his supports were not near enough to follow
immediately, and the battalions were cut to pieces,
and the remnant driven back. Meantime, the French
having got in, the English thought themselves bound
to attack; but the Russian guns were ready for them,
loaded with grape, and not a man got farther than
the abattis. In the left attack, General Eyre got into
a cemetery, where he remained all day, under a tremendous fire. I believe we have made a lodgment

---

* He was killed.

A A

there, which is all we have gained by the loss of 1500
men, among which 92 officers ; and 3500 French—
number of officers unknown to me, but three generals.
We lost Colonel Yea and Sir John Campbell, both
doing the duty of brigadier-generals.

23d.

I have managed to make the sketch, which is on
the same scale as the old one, but is very correct : you
must take care no one copies it.   I am very sorry to
say that the ——— Regiment, which was in support of
the ——— Regiment in the assault, misbehaved : the
men would *not go out of* the trenches.   ——— commanded, and stood on the top of the parapet and
cheered them on ; not a man moved !   He beat them
with the flat of his sword.   To be sure, there was a
terrible fire of grape, to which it was scarcely fair to
expose men.   This regiment has always been in bad
order.   The strange part of that assertion is, that all
regiments are composed of the same sort of men ; so
that only bad management can be the reason for some
being worse than others.   You speak of water ; your
mentioning it led me to inquire : there have been very
great pains taken to secure every drop by making
many and large tanks.   I know the Engineer officer
who has the charge of the water-works, and I saw him
yesterday.   I am sorry to say that he does expect a
scarcity immediately unless we have rain.   They have
even gone the length of filtering the water used for

Batteries
Branches

Ravin du Carénage

Careening
Creek

Malakoff

Mamelon

Karabelnaia Ravine

Karabelnaia Ravine

Dockyard

Frenchmans Hill

21 Gun
Battery

Gordon

Redan

3rd Par.⁴

Quarries

Woronsoff Road

Green Hill

Chapman

Barrack
Battery

Quarries

Bastion du Mât

Garden
Battery

½   1   2   3   4   5   6   7   8   9   10   11   12   13   Yards   100   200   300   400   Mile.

Between Inkys and Sebas

F.G. Netherclift lith.

washing, in order that the horses may drink it. Now I expect every day that we shall have to send our horses to drink in the Chernaya or at Balaklava. I individually, who have plenty of horses and mules, may make one or two of them bring water enough for the rest and for myself; but I should be greatly alarmed should that become necessary, as the men would be certain to suffer, and a want of water in the trenches this hot weather would be really awful. With respect to the progress of the siege, I believe the French intend to make a large *place d'armes* (*i. e.* much trench) in front of the Mamelon or Kamptchatka Lunette, cutting into the abattis, wherein to collect their men for a new assault, so as to attack more in a body and more by surprise than the last time. We must just take patience, and proceed by rule. What can it signify how long we are capturing the Crimea ? Its capture will not bring peace on the terms we ought to have ; except when utterly exhausted, the Russians never will make peace. Are you prepared to go on until then ? If so, you may just as well be capturing this place in a gradual and scientific manner as by making other inroads. The real strain upon Russia is the expense and the stoppage of her commerce. During the truce the other day to bury the dead, I hear the Russian officers who came out were immensely got up—batiste shirts, with kid gloves, varnished boots, &c. They were very civil, but disposed to chuckle at our repulse : *rit bien qui rit le dernier.* I did not see them, as our division was under arms. It is a horrid sight, this burying the dead—such shocking wounds, and the corpses all putrefied by the sun. The Russians carry our dead halfway towards us, and we take them up and carry them to where the graves are dug.

Several of our general officers are sick. ——, who has an eye to the main chance, is off for good, and I dare say by the time this letter reaches you will be soliciting the governorship of Malta or Gibraltar. Codrington is gone on board ship. He will, however, come back to his work, and, I think, will have the command of the 2d Division, to the immense disgust of ——, who is senior to him, and only commands a brigade. He came out in January, I think. Codrington has shown himself to be a good officer, and has stuck to his tackle all through the winter trench-work, and has the best right ; and I think Lord Raglan will be quite justified by impartial men like myself. The principal objection to either one or the other commanding Line brigades or divisions is their education. They are disposed from long habit to let the Line officers have as easy a time of it as they have always seen allowed to the Guards officers, not taking into the account the admirable non-commissioned officers of the Guards. It makes the General very popular with the officers ; but is a great blunder notwithstanding.

## LETTER XCVIII.

Camp before Sebastopol,
26th June 1855.

I HAVE for the last few days, at my spare moments, been spelling over the speeches of our legislators. I cannot make them out. *Galimatias!* The plain sense of J. B. says we have got into a row, and we must fight it out. Splitting argumentative straws, where the prestige of England is at stake, seems very unworthy of the occasion. I should think your friend Gladstone has ruined himself in public opinion. You see cholera is doing its work. Pennefather gone, not to return ; Codrington on board ship ; ditto Sir G. Brown. Luckily it does not seem to prevail among the men, only isolated cases ; but the season is hardly come. Last year, in Bulgaria, it began on the 23d of July. We are making a new battery in the right attack, where our division takes duty. I suppose the assault will soon be made again. The French lay the blame on the mismanagement of the last assault, not on the scheme. The men had been up for five nights in the trenches ; they had had nothing to drink except water before attacking ; the whole character of the operation was feeble in consequence. The probability is, that the English and French will attack the Malakoff together, merely keeping down the Redan\* by fire of cannon. Nobody here doubts of success; but it will be a bloody business. I have been appointed Assistant Adjutant-General to the 1st Division, which I scarcely expected, as there are so many men with influence: but I have been here the whole time, and it would have been a strong measure to displace me. After the fall of Sebastopol, they will perhaps remodel the army, and form a Highland Division. Who can tell? there are so many chances and changes. I shall be curious to see the report of Roebuck's Committee. A furious onslaught is made by the *Times* on Colonel Gordon for his opposing the embarkation of Russell with the Kertsch expedition. He probably was only executing his orders. The people at head-quarters have acted very foolishly, that is, weakly. They should either have altogether forbidden Russell's landing or remaining in the Crimea, which they could have done, or they should have treated him frankly, and made use of him. A very small dose of civility from Lord Raglan would have tamed and made a friend of him; but they have, on the contrary, done all they could to insult him, and yet have left him here with full opportunity of punishing them. Of the two lines they chose neither; between two stools, they

---

\* I have been assured that it was not intended to assault the Redan at all; and that was the reason why the English approaches from the Quarries were not at this time pushed on, as the French did theirs from the Mamelon and the White Works.

have fallen to the ground. What does the public
know of Colonel Gordon, except that he has been
abused in the *Times?* He is one of the fortunately
born, and has got on accordingly ; but he works like
a horse at his duties, which are by no means light.
He has been present the whole time, and in all the
engagements. His manners are unpopular, and he is
rather disliked in the army ; but he is a very honest
man, and will speak his mind to the highest here,
although bred about Court. He will rise in spite of
the *Times;* as, indeed, will all the men out here who
survive through the whole affair, and who have held
any prominent situation. Gordon is the second officer
of the Quartermaster-General's department, holding
the rank of Assistant Quartermaster-General at head-
quarters. We expect that, when we take the place,
there will be a distribution of honours and promotions
to all hands who still have their heads on their shoulders ; but some of the best officers are getting killed
daily without any honours having been received by
them. I hope you will find much information in the
last plan I sent you : it is very accurate ; so take care
who sees it. When you read of the next assault, you
will have every part of the ground under your eye ;
and, although you are no soldier, you will certainly
make it out. The French are making zig-zags from
the White Batteries, and preparing a battery to play on
the shipping from the point of land to the east of the

Careening Creek, which it is to be hoped will destroy the ships, whose fire is very galling, especially that of some small steamers, which fired grape on the French assaulting columns while they were retreating. Poor Admiral Lyons is in sad grief : his son Jack of the " Miranda" received a splinter of a chance shell from the shore-batteries here the other night, which so lacerated the calf of his leg, that he is not expected to live.

----

## LETTER XCIX.

Camp before Sebastopol,
29th June 1855.

You will have read in this morning's paper of the death of Lord Raglan. The night before last we had the notification, and rode over to see his body. Poor old man, who has been so much abused, and who for so many years has had so much power ! A thoroughly amiable man, of the highest aristocratical tendencies. I have no doubt that he believed the world and its loaves and fishes was all expressly contrived for the scions of the Beaufort and other great houses. He was very clever and brave, and deserved a happier end. We are all naturally in great suspense, waiting to hear who will take his place. The loss of our Commander at this juncture is very embarrassing, as I doubt if he had any one in his complete confidence, and acquainted with all his plans, if he had any. The Chief of the Staff is now senior officer; a very gentle-man-like person, with not much experience, and by no means up to the crisis. He got his rank early by being in the Guards. Just see how that system ope-rates. We have five divisions, with a Chief of the Staff: he is a Guardsman, and three out of the five divisions are commanded by Guardsmen,—Bentinck, Barnard, and Codrington; while Lord Rokeby is very much discontented because he has not another divi-sion. Mark, none of these men had any claims at all till they came here, except the Chief of the Staff, who did command a brigade in India, which was not en-gaged. Is it any wonder we cry out? They have all risen to rank younger men than their neighbours, from the advantage of beginning in the Guards. Codring-ton has turned out to be a good hard-working officer. He got his brigade in Bulgaria, as soon as he was promoted out of the Guards by the brevet, and has no experience whatever in the field. Our chief offi-cers are going off rapidly. I went to Estcourt's sale yesterday, and bought a pony. He will not be missed except by his private friends, of whom so amiable a man must have had many. Sir G. Brown is gone away, very ill indeed. Some people hint at the possi-bility of C. being appointed to command. I cannot believe it; the position is so high, and the aristo-

cracy so strong. He is the only man here competent.
Public opinion may have, by mistake, found this out,
and may compel his appointment. He would be
miserable, I think, but capable of the job, having been
always engaged in fighting, and latterly in India having had the command of 50,000 or 60,000 men. His
contempt for jobbing and meanness and self-seeking
will make him a terrible reformer in those respects.
God help the Staff-officers who are not up to their
work, if he gets to the top! All the officers who are
senior to him—and they are not many—would resign,
I imagine; but speculation is vain. Probably twenty-
four hours more will bring us the information as to
Government's decision. The siege goes on just the
same. The French are making a strong battery at
the point of Mount Sapoune, on the east side of the
Careening Creek, down near the water. It is to be
made bomb-proof with materials taken out of the
Batteries Blanches in its rear, so as to protect the
gunners from the fierce fire which will be directed on
them when they open. The object is to destroy the
Russian men-of-war, whose guns materially interfere
with an attack on the Malakoff. We shall have a
battery to enfilade the Dockyard creek, or harbour,
and the French have another to do the same on the
left; so that we hope the ships will be finally disposed
of. They have still seven or eight line-of-battle ships,
whereof two are three-deckers, and sundry small armed

steamers. While these batteries are in progress, the trenches between the Mamelon and the Malakoff are growing daily, and those most advanced are within 150 metres of the ditch of Malakoff. In these trenches they will be able to put 20,000 men for the assault. We are hemming the enemy in, and obtaining a more concentric fire; and if we can succeed in sweeping the harbour and taking Malakoff, the garrison must surrender. Those who survive will have laurels to the extreme of J. B.'s powers, and centuries to come will tell of the great siege. I conclude the Government is only waiting for the termination to issue decorations to the officers who have gone through so much. The Crimean medal is not thought much of. None have come out here except those the Queen gave to some few officers who have come back since. Half-a-crown and a pennyworth of ugly ribbon from a grateful nation! They ought to extend the Bath, and assimilate it to the Legion of Honour. Those decorations which every one gets are of no value. The Waterloo medal was a similar blunder. The best soldiers of England who fought through the Peninsular War got nothing for it till thirty years afterwards. Every one would rather have the Legion of Honour than the Crimean medal.

## LETTER C.

Camp before Sebastopol,
3d July 1855.

WE are to convey Lord Raglan's body to the sea at Kamish to-day, but we remain without a notification of his successor. His death has happened during a lull in the performance of this siege; so that we can, I suppose, wait a few days without inconvenience. The French are sapping up from their trenches in front of the Mamelon, towards the ditch of the Malakoff. The batteries to pound the shipping will not be ready for a week, during which space of time it is not probable that any thing decisive will occur here. The appointment of the new Commander-in-chief is of moment to us all individually, besides the influence it may have on the fate of the war. He may be a friend to some of us, he may be indifferent, or he may be an enemy. Whichever of them he may be, in his hands will lie much power of selecting, of promoting, of rewarding, or of injuring all or any of us officers, more especially now that selection for merit is the rule of promotion. Never was there a greater fallacy than that. Selection means a job. Let the new Commander-in-chief be who he may, I feel convinced that circumstances will compel him to take men for other reasons than their merit. Personal staff, however, in our service has always been considered a way of giving

the general a private friend about him. They generally take their sons or nephews, when they have any,
qualified or not. Officers of the Adjutant-General's
and Quartermaster-General's department are on the
General Staff of the army; and those who appoint
them are responsible for their conduct, and that they
deserve the distinction. There seems to be a feeling
against the Staff, which is very unjust. They are
much harder worked than the rest of the army; for,
except the Aides-de-camp, the others are always on
duty; whereas the regimental officer, his turn of duty
past, is free to go where he pleases. To be sure, there
is additional pay for Staff-officers.

You speak of the heat here: we have had about
half a dozen hot days. It is now quite cool, and the
rain at this moment is falling in torrents. However,
some people feel heat much more than others.

They talk of C. being appointed to command this
army. I cannot believe it. I should be Military
Secretary, I suppose.

## LETTER CI.

Camp before Sebastopol,
6th July 1855.

WE have papers to the 23d. The Government
seems to have bottled up the bad news as long as they
dared. It must, I should think, have reached them
on the 19th; perhaps they were in hopes of another
immediate assault. Your letter finishes with what
you call a growl at the Parliament, and a picture of
the people standing by with folded hands. It also
begins with a growl at me. Why, I take you to be
simply the best-informed man in England as to what
is really doing here. Routine is the order of the day.
The command of the army has dropped into the hands
of the senior officer. One would think this would
have been a great and proper occasion to select a man
for some sort of merit, or at any rate for some experience in the command of an army. He has fits
of gout. While Chief of the Staff he never interfered
when he could help it, and I believe he would be
very glad not to have this charge laid upon him.

I think C. is delighted that the lot has not fallen
upon him. We now understand that, as soon as the
regiments can be collected, a Highland Division will
be formed, which he will command. It is not done
for his sake, though, but to give a separate command
to Lord Rokeby. Already the command of the army,

and that of three divisions, is held by Guardsmen,
and I quite think it possible that they may mono-
polise every division. Their superior rank tells tre-
mendously, and we now see how it works. We have
had some promotion vouchsafed to the army. Two
Guardsmen made Aides-de-camp to the Queen, with
the rank of full Colonel. There are here three battalions of Guards and forty-five battalions of the Line,
so that the rate ought to be thirty officers of the Line
made full Colonels. I think there were only two,
and one of them the Honourable Percy Herbert, M.P.,
who has already had wonderful promotion. Some
other officers have received what is called a reward
for distinguished service, that is, a pension of 100*l.* a
year : —— gets that ; I suppose to console him for
the reception he met with in England. I see another
disgrace fallen on British respectability—Strahan.
He was a neighbour of mine at Headley. He lived
in great style. His unfortunate wife is to be pitied,
fallen from her high estate. He will be transported,
I should suppose ; at least, he deserves it. I dare
say she has a settlement to keep her from starving.
Nothing can be more unjust than that the trader
should ruin hundreds of people, and then live on his
wife's jointure, as I have known to be done. Your
House of Commons seems determined to support the
Whigs, and nothing at all will come out of Roebuck's
Committee. Their not naming the culprits, makes

the whole thing a farce, but not thereby the less consonant with the views of the crew who govern. I do believe, if I survive and come back after five or six years, that I shall figure as a military reformer. No one can calculate on surviving. We have a desperate struggle to go through, and life must be cast away without scruple. The existence of England as a great power depends on our success here, and I tremble at the possibility of our Government making peace. There is no doubt of the fact, that a boat, with a flag of truce, carried back a carriage to Kertsch, and examined the locality under that pretence. I heard of it here, and it was mentioned in the papers. You may depend on its being true. I know those who saw the Engineer's despatch acknowledging it ! The new French battery to be made at the point of Mount Sapoune to fire on the Russian ships will be 3000 yards from them ; so that I do not put much faith in its effect. The French are sapping away up towards Malakoff; but that is a very slow operation. The ground is rocky towards the Malakoff. They will zig-zag along the ravine, a long leg, as they say in working to windward, in the soft ground, and a short one in the rock. We also are trying to get on from the Quarries. Lüders has joined the army with two divisions, say 30,000 infantry, which will probably about make up their losses. The French, I know, have only 70,000 infantry left ; we have 18,000 or 19,000; the Piedmontese, I suppose, 8000; total under 100,000 certainly; the Turk unknown. We want just exactly 100,000 more, to sally out into the country; but I see no prospect of this increase within any reasonable time. The Austrians are diminishing their force; so that the Russians may send more men here, where their force will in fact only be limited by their power of feeding them. Our position is therefore very serious, and we sadly want a real good General, who has been exercised in commanding a large force; I do not care if he be French or English, let him only be a good one. They say Lord Panmure's telegraph to General Simpson was, "Your appointment will be confirmed; make my nephew —— one of your aides-de-camp." This time there will be reciprocity on both sides. We have had some heavy rain, but the weather is most agreeable. We want trees to look at; I do, I should say; the whole plateau is bare to a degree; and books; I have only Shakespeare, which I read over and over again at any spare moments. There is no time here for regular study, even if the means were at hand. Some people are horrified at the prospect of a second winter, for which preparations are already begun. They are up a tree, and it makes me laugh. One of the Guards yesterday was inquiring if I did not want to go home. I said, "My profession is to be a soldier." But said he, "I paid 10,000*l.*" Poor devil, he has bought his gold too dear.

B B

## LETTER CII.

Camp before Sebastopol, 12th July 1855.

SINCE I wrote last, I have done a night's duty in the trenches, right attack, quarries, &c. C. decided on going in himself as general of the trenches, which duty is not usually done by the Generals of Division; and although, from the arrangements in this army, I was not called upon to do so, I went also, out of compliment to him. It is a curious place at night. I had been in repeatedly for a few hours at a time, just to walk about. The troops go down the middle ravine, where the English join the French trenches (see Plan). They are all told-off previously for their different posts in the various boyaux-de-tranchée, advanced trench, batteries, &c. They move along the trench which leads from the ravine to the Twenty-one Gun or Gordon's Battery on Frenchman's Hill, and then percolate along the trenches and saps. The front line of sentries is placed after dark outside the advanced trench, lying flat on the ground. This is to prevent a sortie. The enemy fire rifle-shots continually whenever they see a head. They also fire small mortars called cohorns, which are pointed nearly perpendicularly, and let their contents drop into those trenches which are too near for any other sort of fire to reach them: it is called, therefore, vertical fire. They also fire grape in the same manner; which comes down in

a shower of iron hail. Walking about in the trenches
is to me immensely fatiguing: the soil is now dry dust;
the sun beats in without any shade to keep it off.
The night is pleasanter; and it is very odd, lying down
in a corner, to gaze at the quiet bright stars, while all
sorts of discordant sounds are kept up with a ceaseless
assiduity. The whistling of shells, then the bursting of
them, followed by the whirring of the fragments, with
an uncertain notion of where they may alight. Ever
and anon a great mortar is discharged from one or
other of our batteries, which makes the ground shake.
Presently come wounded or dead men carried by their
comrades on stretchers to the rear. All this lasting
for months, with a prospect of its continuing for
months to come, makes me serious. Where are we to
get men? There is a regular drain of dead and
wounded nightly. C., who has now a good opportunity of judging, and who is a judge, said to me
quietly, that the more he saw of the place, the greater
did the difficulty of getting in appear to be. Yet it
must be done; though how they can hope that the
unfortunate soldiers will be able to hold all this extent of trench during the winter, is a wonder to me.
We keep still the confident hope that we shall be able
to take the place before winter; but we may fail.
Todleben, the Russian engineer, is wounded; but he
has done his engineering so effectually, that his death
would scarcely now alter the character of the defence;

and if he is only wounded, he has such a knowledge
of the ground, that he will be able to give his orders
effectually from his bed.    Our head-quarters interpreter is dead, and is a great loss.    Colonel Vico, the
French Staff-officer attached to head-quarters, is also
dead—much regretted ; both fallen by cholera.    The
army generally is very healthy, I am happy to say.
We have been much amused by Jacob Omnium's essay
on the *Upper Ten Thousand ;* it is too true, and I suppose is thought to be a great hit.    I wish he was doing
——'s work in Parliament.    To-day we ought to receive the papers acknowledging the despatches about
the unfortunate assault on the 18th of June.    Our
Division, I should think, will take part in the next
one ; for it is a maxim of war, that when troops have
been roughly handled, as the Light Division was at the
Alma, and ever since, besides failing in an assault,
they ought to be placed in reserve to recover themselves.\*    Let us hope we shall have better success.
We can see that the Russians are losing an immense
number of men ; their burial-ground is across the harbour, and is increasing daily very considerably.    The
French have nearly completed their forts at Kamish,
built evidently with the intention of protecting an embarkation in the face of an enemy.    That disgrace will,
I hope, not fall on us ; but it is well to be prepared.

\* The non-observance of this rule was one main cause of the
British failure at the Redan on the 8th September.

13th July.

The mail of the 28th just in, without much news. We hear that General Barnard, a Guardsman, now commanding a division out here, is appointed Chief of the Staff; so the Guards have both Commander-in-Chief and Chief of the Staff in their interest. Lieutenant-Colonel Pakenham, who has been Assistant-Adjutant-General under Estcourt, is to get, as we are told, his situation of Adjutant-General, which is an immense step for so junior an officer. He is of the late Duchess of Wellington's Pakenhams, a brother of Lord Longford, a good name both in army and navy, and he is a very good office-man. The people of England know not what they do. I have heard that people in power keep writing to know why we do not attack the enemy at Mackenzie's Farm, while our men have not quite two nights out of the trenches. A turn of the trenches means, being on parade at five o'clock this evening, marching down and being posted in the trenches, giving working-parties there under fire, continuing accoutred, and exposed to the various missiles I have mentioned, and not getting home to camp again until ten o'clock to-morrow evening. This every third day, with a prospect, as an easement, of being allowed to assault the place. This duty falls only on the infantry. The artillerymen have generally a far easier time of it in the batteries, and get all the credit; but their guns would be spiked in no time, if the infantry were not in

front of them to protect them from sorties. I hope
the powers in England are making preparations to
send out huts for all the soldiers before the winter sets
in. Last night I happened to be in Vinoy's camp ; he
is also come with his men to the siege. He has a
brigade in Canrobert's Division. Pelissier has sent
down the troops which failed in the assault, and
brought up these fresh ones. He knows war well,
and the effect of punishment on the morale of the
soldier. We went to see the 2d Zouaves play *Une
Chambre à deux Lits*, interspersed with the roar of
cannons.

## LETTER CIII.

Camp before Sebastopol,
17th July 1855.

THE situation continues what it was ; the soldiers
going daily down to the trenches, working there, and
being shot at. On our side, viz. the Right Attack, on
Frenchman's Hill, we are not advancing nearer to the
Redan, but we are completing our communications with
the French on our right, that is, in the Mamelon. I
was there yesterday for some time, looking about me.
The work performed both by the French and Russians
is enormous. The ground is very rocky and difficult to
excavate ; nevertheless, the French trenches extend
away to the Careening Creek, forming room for a very

large force. The battery, which they have made on the point close to the water under Mount Sapoune, will be ready, it is thought, in four days, and then we shall know whether we can destroy the men-of-war or no. Inside the Russian entrenchments, on the proper left of the Malakoff work, and towards their own front of the Careening Creek, there is a large sort of barracks, which they are now surrounding with a very high and strong gabionade, making in fact a formidable redoubt inside their front line. A gabion is a hamper with no bottom ; it is placed on the ground, and the earth behind it is dug out and thrown into the gabion ; they build them up in this manner, tier upon tier, with immense labour, and the work is not finished till it is so thick that a cannon-ball will not go through. At intervals embrasures are made with sandbags built like brickwork ; then steps are made inside, for riflemen to climb up to the crest, on which more sandbags are laid, thus,— leaving a small interstice, through which the rifle is projected. In  the Russian works they have pyramidical wooden boxes made so that the hole shall be as small as possible ; these boxes are built in with sandbags. Every one showing his head above the parapet is immediately saluted by a score of bullets. C., who is by no means of a desponding nature, shakes his head, and hopes we shall not have another 18th of June. He thinks we

ought to go on sapping till we get right into the ditch.
I doubt that being the plan intended, as it would
take so much time ; but it is the only sure way.   By
the bye, touching the sounding at Kertsch from the
flag of truce, the fact is, they did not want to sound,
and they did not do so.    The object was, to see behind
the batteries, in order to ascertain whether they were
closed at the rear ; and in that they succeeded.   I
hear of several promotions ; and I suppose it will come
to my turn sooner or later.    Lieutenant-Colonel the
Honourable W. Pakenham is positively to be made Adjutant-General at head-quarters, which will raise his
pay, besides other advantages, from 14s. 3d. to 1l. 17s.
per diem.    This Staff promotion is quite legitimate ;
but if he is made a full colonel, he will be put over
the heads of three assistant-adjutant-generals, all his
senior officers, of whom I am one ; and I think that is
not right, unless we are promoted at the same time.
We have all been working, according to our abilities,
in a similar position to his.    One of them threatens
to resign ; and if we were at peace, he would be quite
justified.    Filder is going away sick.    Our divorce
from the Guards is projected, but not yet passed into
a law.   I look on the appointment of —— as very
serious.    The people in England do not apparently
comprehend the situation, and the necessity we have
for an active, energetic, and experienced commander.

## LETTER CIV.

Camp before Sebastopol,
20th July 1855.

THE papers are come, and contain Lord John's confession, which ought to be followed by his execution. Rogues all. The nation is in a sad position. We want a nominal army of 500,000 men to do what we must do, if we are not to be stultified. The conscription is necessary ; if it cannot be carried, we shall not get men enough. Our Division goes into the trenches every third day, and loses there some twenty men out of 2800,—say, forty per week, besides sickness, which is a variable quantity. The French are proceeding by sap, and they approach nearer and nearer to the works of the enemy, from Malakoff to the proper left of that fort down to the Careening Creek (see the first Plan). They have the point of land on the east side of the creek, and are half-way down towards the sea on its west side. The Russian fortifications run along the crest to the western point. The sides of the hill containing the creek are excessively rocky and steep. The French have a small battery in the ravine looking right down the creek. A trace of their trenches would be extremely interesting ; but I cannot get it except by treachery, so I must do without it. I think they will now try to post themselves on this left or western point, and take

the enemy in reverse. But while we are working, the
enemy works likewise, and makes internal defences.
I see a long perspective of digging still before us, and
even ·the horrid possibility of another winter of open
trenches. I do not believe General —— will come
here ; he is very comfortable at home with his family.
His claims are null.

We have now got General Simpson to command
in chief ; General Barnard, Chief of the Staff ; and
three Divisions commanded by Guardsmen, who have
only become eligible for these important commands
on account of the early promotion which the miracu-
lous privileges of the Guards have given them. Simpson is the only one of the five who has ever been
abroad, with the exception of Lord Rokeby, who as
an ensign made the Waterloo campaign. General
Simpson rose in the Guards in fourteen years to be a
captain and lieutenant-colonel, and then exchanged,
I believe, to command the 29th Regiment. General
Codrington, when he came from England to join this
army, was, as I think, only a captain of a company in
his own regiment, with the rank of full colonel. The
brevet made him a major-general in June 1854 ; and
you might say that he jumped from the inexperience
of a captain, whose whole service was performed in St.
James's Street, to the command of a division—that is,
he only commanded a brigade for a very short time.
He, however, has been a very attentive and painstak-

ing officer, and is popular. But there are men here who have commanded a battalion for years, in every climate of the globe, some of whom are still commanding battalions, and some acting as brigadier-generals. Pakenham will do very well as Adjutant-General. It is a monstrous leap. His service here has been sitting all day in an office, every night in bed. He has been eighteen years in the army : just the length of service I performed when I went on half-pay in despair as a captain. My majority dates six years before his. You, being a civilian, cannot conceive the bitterness of men being walked clean over your head, leaving you only the resource of retiring, of which in war, with the enemy before him, a man of honour cannot avail himself.

## LETTER CV.

Camp before Sebastopol,
27th July 1855.

I HAVE just heard that I am made a Companion of the Bath. Twenty years ago what pleasure it would have given me ! The highest reward that we have for military service,—what a pity they do not open it to all ranks ! At present one must be a field-officer. I would give it to the private soldier, if I could ; instead of which, they talk of an Order of Merit. As

to ——, you call him a good man. What he is
good in, I know not ; but I call him bad, because he
upholds idle useless people, when their crimes are
exposed clearly before his eyes—perhaps out of good-
nature, perhaps out of laziness.   He is the worst man
of business in the world,—keeping papers lying before
him for weeks, not answering letters which are difficult to answer, screening and burking questions which
should have been faced boldly.   The last man in the
world to slay a dragon.   When he dies, he will nevertheless be a vessel of grace, for aught I know, as he
certainly believes in the Trinity, and is perfectly or-
thodox.   You are quite right in supposing that private letters were very worrying to Lord Raglan : they
used to be handed about.   I have even heard of their
coming to the Queen's self, through other ladies.   I
always thought he would be a great loss, although I
could not guess who would succeed him.   Our four
seniors now are, General Simpson, Sir Richard England, General Bentinck, and C., with General Barnard
as Chief of the Staff.   Under these our siege goes on
as well as could be expected.   When shall we make
the assault ?   Those who are so employed must go
with the determination not to come back, but to stay
in the place, dead or alive.   The papers have brought
us Lord John's dismissal, or resignation.   He is dis-
graced, but, I suppose, has a *clientèle* which will hold
on to his skirts till the English people cut them off.

The Duke of Newcastle is at Pera; and we understand Lord Stratford is coming here next week to bestow the Crosses of the Bath, which will be a very tiresome *funcion*, as they say in Spanish. You seem to think I do not estimate Roebuck justly. Perhaps so; but I do estimate him very highly, for I believe him to be a very honest man. He was once very nearly fighting a duel with my father; and it would have come off, only that C. was my father's second, and convinced Roebuck that he was labouring under a mistake. C. admired his behaviour very much, and always speaks very highly of him. These old stories are very amusing, after so many years. I wonder if the Administration reformers will do any good? ——'s reckless way of making accusations, and his general looseness about his facts, make me doubt his turning out to be a great leader in such a job. Supposing he carries his point and that of Higgins, and transfers the distribution of the loaves and fishes from the upper to the, or to a, lower ten thousand, do you think they will not favour their friends? Will they never push people into places they are unfit for? or will that simple transference of power from one lot to another alter human nature, and prevent its being influenced by the same sort of springs? I see no reason to think that if Captain —— had been in Pakenham's place, he would not have been promoted over my head by the Administrative reformers, if power lay in their hands to do so. The real injustice to officers which might be remedied, is the privilege of the Guards to have all their captains lieutenant-colonels in the army. With the nominal duty of captains, they have all the advantages reserved for lieutenant-colonels. Sir Arthur Torrens—present for one month with an army in the field!—never did man get rank so easily; and now, being wounded, he is selected for the pleasantest berth in the whole army, at Paris, while others are fagging away here. It is all in the day's work, however: some one must do it; some must be unlucky. The next mail will bring us news of the Government, and how Pam will manage. It matters little, for I see no hope of a really good government; only there are degrees in shame and in vacillation. Your wild Radicals seem to me quite as unfit as any one else. I hear that Lord Panmure does not consult Lord Hardinge in his promotions. Formerly, in the good old times, the head of the army at the Horse-Guards was very jealous of being interfered with, and many regulations existed to hedge him round, and to prevent people from breaking down his fortress. If it is intended to pick men out for advancement over the heads of their seniors, it will give cause for much complaint; ay, it will be more unjust than any thing that has yet existed in the army. The men of rank and connection will turn out to be the engrossers of

all the merit, and of course of all the promotion. God
knows they had their share before, under the old system. Pakenham, who is at this moment my junior,
and who is holding a similar Staff-appointment to
my own, by a wave of the pen becomes a full colonel,
and eligible at any moment to be selected as a major-
general. I shall send a letter of remonstrance, for
fear they should say I like to be passed over. I see
in *Galignani* that Bulwer has withdrawn his motion;
so I suppose the Government is to go on. *Quamdiù?*
I have just heard that we are meditating to push our
sap nearer to the Redan. The French are only thirty
yards from the ditch on the proper left of the Malakoff. The Russians are increasing daily their interior
defences. Sir R. England has just got his Grand
Cross of the Bath. He is going away. I wonder if he
has got the pains? Properly speaking, a soldier has
no right to his discharge, even after twenty years' service, if he be in good health. After that period, they
get the pains, and the surgeon gives a certificate to
that effect; so they take their discharge with a pension. Bentinck's ilia are harder. *Messorum ilia,* as
he is a shaver. The Duke of Newcastle is here encamped. I have not seen him. He will gain more
knowledge of war in a week through his eyes than by
reading reams of despatches. There is a monotony
here which makes it very hard to concoct a really
good letter. I fear mine must be full of repetitions.

Have you got any inkling of the intention of Government towards the French officers? They ought to distribute some Bath Crosses to them. The French always wear their decorations; we scarcely ever, as if we were ashamed of them: the genius of the nation forbids, unless when in uniform or going to Court.

---

## LETTER CVI.

Camp before Sebastopol,
3d August 1855.

You tell me that the Militia regiments at Aldershott put the Guards out of countenance. When the loss of non-commissioned officers becomes what it has been here, that *corps d'élite* must go to pieces; for their non-commissioned officers, which are the best in the world, discipline them. The officers are not brought up to do the dirty company work,—the interior economy, as we call it, on which so much depends; but they come to the army when there is war, and compete very successfully with the hard-worked Line officers, without having undergone the years of banishment, and the exposure to disease in every climate, which is the natural existence of our officers. Sir Richard England is off; and now we shall see whether Eyre will get a division. The 3d Division, vacated by Dick Britain, has been offered to Lord Rokeby. He

has refused, as he does not wish to separate from his
Guards. We simple fellows are living in the midst
of intrigues, which we cannot easily fathom, and in
which we would certainly not meddle, if we could
track out the ingenious thread. The great object is
to make up a Division for Lord Rokeby; and at head-
quarters they are as busy as bees, with the aid of the
telegraph to the Court, in attaining this object, which
amounts to leaving Eyre with only one brigade. Conceive the breaking-up of the 1st and 3d Divisions to
please this nobleman, who simply wants to send C., with
only four battalions, away from this attack, to replace
in the left attack half of England's Division, then at-
taching Eyre's brigade to the Highlanders; which, if
done, will have the effect of making C. the junior division general of the left attack, instead of being the
senior one in the right attack. I scarcely think they
will manage it, on account of technical difficulties of
detail. You are quite right in thinking C. does not
wish for the command of the army. But he is the only
person here fit for it; and people seem to forget that
the honour and safety of the army require the best man
to command. C. and Eyre are the only generals here,
since Lord Raglan's death, for whom the French have
the slightest respect—I mean, of course, professionally. If the arrangement I have been speaking of
should take place, it will give a third Division to a
Guardsman. Commander-in-Chief, Chief of the Staff,

and three divisions in their hands, what chances have common people? The *Gazette* of the 18th has brought Pakenham out a Colonel, in addition to his appointment of Adjutant-General. Wilbraham has made a remonstrance; so have I; and I dare say so has Brownrigg. It is just possible we may carry our point of being kept in our relative places. At any rate, I cannot be said to have submitted willingly to such an indignity. My letter will go home by this post, for Lord Panmure to digest. When Bentinck came out a second time, he was gazetted to be a local lieutenant-general one day senior to C. When Simpson came, he was made a local lieutenant-general senior to Sir Richard England, so as to keep them in their relative positions. Now I do not see why my junior officer is to go over my head, especially as I state my readiness to serve under him, *quoad* Adjutant-General. It is an act of great oppression, the promotion not having been gained by any wonderful deed of daring against the enemy. In fact, Pakenham has been so fortunate, partly from his connections, partly from the chance of his being in Estcourt's office, which brought him in contact with Lord Raglan, who hated new faces; and also, I must add, because he is quite competent. If the service requires him as Adjutant-General, that is no reason for punishing us. Justice requires that we should be made full colonels, which costs the country no extra pay, and that we

should be given the option of an appointment elsewhere, or of serving under a junior officer, which men
of spirit in the field will not object to. This is exactly a parallel case to that of Blucher Wood, who,
being a junior colonel to Colonel Brough, is appointed
Deputy Adjutant-General in Ireland, while Colonel
Brough remains Assistant Adjutant-General in a
district. To do the injustice there which has been
done here, they should have made Colonel Wood a
major-general over the head of Colonel Brough. I
have written this in the hope of making you understand the question, but I scarcely suppose I have done
so. Few people not brought up in the army can
make head or tail of such disquisitions. But, unless
seniority in rank is to be considered a disqualification,
our case is a strong one, as there is no pretence of
any glaring incompetence on our part, or of any wonderful merits on his. Our duties have been precisely
similar, except that he was a subordinate in the head-
quarter office, while we were the heads of our division office. We received the orders which he issued
in the name of the Commander-in-Chief, and distributed them to our brigade-majors; and the documents
which we had previously submitted to our Division
General were brought by us to the Adjutant-General's
office, to be submitted by Estcourt or Pakenham to
Lord Raglan, and now to the Chief of the Staff. There
was an advantage, however, in being about head-quar-

ters; for there were houses and offices, with plenty of
good clerks, and also subordinate officers.   Whether
England be in her decadence, I cannot tell: when
Rome was in that state, her armies still fought well;
the soldiers were the last to lose their hardihood.   I
am sorry to see that the Government is patched up,
although I believe Molesworth's is a good appointment; but he has still to show his administrative
faculty; that of pamphlet-writing has been sufficiently
proved.   General Canrobert is recalled to Paris; his
division found him in a false position.   While he was
Commander-in-Chief he would not promote the officers
of his former Division, for fear of being accused of
favouritism : and when he went back to it, he could
not, or would not, ask Pelissier to promote them, lest
he should reply, " If these officers are so meritorious,
why did not you promote them when you had the
power in your own hands?"

Canrobert and his brigadiers and all the officers
of every regiment always went into the trenches with
their men, *en bloque;* we put two officers to one hundred men, and name the general of the trenches by a
roster, or list; so that no regiment goes into the
trenches complete.   This plan, I dare say, saves the
officers from some trench-duty; but I think it quite
wrong ; the company and its officers should always go
together.   But this plan would not suit the Guards, as
it would compel their captains to go with their com-

panies, instead of taking their turn as field-officers.
In fact, they would be *de tranchée* every third day,
instead of once a fortnight; and now our Line lieutenant-colonels, who are in the same roster, are beginning to taste some of the sweets of the privileged
corps system. For, of course, where all the captains in
one brigade are lieutenant-colonels, it is rather a long
roster, so that the duty comes round seldomer. But
the proper military way of doing this trench-duty is,
to send in a whole brigade complete, just as it would
go to a field-day. But no; duty will never be so
performed here, for the interest of the Guards is too
strong at head-quarters; so two officers accompany
one hundred men into the trenches, where five officers
would be very useful. By the departure of Canrobert,
General Espinasse will get the Division, leaving our
friend Vinoy first for a Division, when one becomes
vacant. We hear they are going to give some Baths to
the French—an unprecedented honour. I hope Vinoy
will have K.C.B., as we promise ourselves the fun of
" Sir Joe"-ing him, and talking of " Miladi." I shall
have to compose a French complimentary note on the
occasion. Probably they will repay us with the Legion
of Honour. How wise the French are about their decorations! A private soldier can obtain La Croix
d'Honneur. It is saluted by the sentries, whoever
wears it. While our Bath can only be held by a
field-officer; and the aristocracy think the decoration

more important on account of this exclusiveness.    I
can tell you no news of the siege, which progresses
slowly.    I would fain hope Pelissier has some plan.

---

## LETTER CVII.

Camp before Sebastopol,
10th August 1855.

THE day before yesterday, there was a conference
of the Generals and Admirals, which, we hear, was a
final one; that is, they decided on some course of
action.    I am sure I hope they have a plan; any
plan, even a bad one, is better than none.    We are
losing our men daily in the trenches, and their lives
seem to go for nothing.    We hear of more mortars,
and more shells, and more of every thing coming, but
not of a General.    There has been great work here
about Lord Rokeby, who wants to have a Division;
after much fighting and squabbling, I believe he will
have to wait, for there are not troops enough here to
make a Sixth Division.    I wish I had the power of
getting ———— on the Staff, where he would have
something to do.    In the new *régime* of military
affairs, there is so much change and so much promotion, that no one can foresee what may happen.    I
may myself be one of the selected.    At present, my
appeal for the rank of Colonel is pending; after

reaching that rank, according to this warrant, all sorts of positions are open. But I have no interest beyond long and faithful service,—the universal and lightly-estimated claim. Lately, I have fallen in with *Consuelo*, a book which I had not seen for years. Sometimes a magazine or a number of the *Revue des Deux Mondes* falls in my way. Last night I got hold of Mrs. Inchbald's *Simple Story*. It is strange how different these old-fashioned novels are from the modern ones. Of literary pabulum we are sadly deficient; and I think I must order out some books, as soon as I find we are going into winter-quarters. We are now pushing up so very close to the Russian works, that nothing but a conviction on their part that they are impregnable can justify them in a military point of view in not attacking our position, as they did at Inkermann last autumn. It is said large bodies of their chosen troops are on the way from Poland; but I have no dread of the result. The French have the outposts, and they will not be surprised. By the way, I saw lately in one of the papers an article, in which Balaklava was spoken of as a surprise. Nothing can be more untrue. It may have surprised the Quartermaster-General, for aught I know; but the troops engaged were not surprised, and, in fact, expected the attack the night before. I wonder whether all those fellows who came down from the front after the Russian attack ever can have the face to wear a clasp for Balaklava. We might just as well wear one for Inkermann. There is a furious tirade about a Mr. Stone who died, and, as the *Times* asserted, with circumstances of neglect and cruelty on the part of the military doctors. The whole story is a tissue of falsehood. We have continual cases of cholera ; not very numerous, but enough to make us uneasy. At this season last year in Bulgaria we suffered much more. For myself, I am never ill. My duties take me much seldomer to the trenches than would be my lot were I a regimental officer. But even among them the casualties from fire are rare. We have had frequent storms lately; thunder, lightning, and rain — heavy and penetrating ; it always gets in at some corner of the tents. My boots this morning had a pint of water in each of them. They talk of more wooden huts coming out, but it must be very late in the autumn before we have enough for the whole army. In our Division the men are always made comfortable before the officers. The papers of the 24th have just come. I did not see the article you speak of by ——, but I am ready to take your word for its being well done. I am the only one of the party who takes the *Times*, and I never can get a quiet read of it. If it would not look ill-natured, I should order a second copy. Now I cannot refer; for C. has carried off my last batch to the hospitals.

You think me very foolish to come out here to

be passed over by junior officers, and jumbled up with the Guards, and endure the selection system. It is very true. I tell you, to be without power, and to see such a mess, is a sort of purgatory. Captain Osborne, R.N., has reached in his boat to the Russian bridge over the Putrid Sea, and found no soldiers, only carts innumerable, and such a sand that they could only get on at the rate of half a mile a day. I hope it may be possible to blow up the bridge, and so stop them altogether. I suppose we shall have no more critical moments for the Administration Bill till next session. How much may happen in the interval! how much room for vilifying the army, and for dilating on the sufferings of the men!—which must of course check the enlistments.

## LETTER CVIII.

Camp, before Sebastopol,
14th August 1855.

WE have, I am told, positive information of 40,000 fresh Russian Grenadiers, picked troops, some of the Imperial Russian Guard. This sounds like a large number; but as the losses of the Russian army here must have been very great, probably it will not run up the sum-total so much as people think. However, the deserters asserted we were to

be attacked on all points on the 12th, 13th,—the
Greek feast of Holy Waters; so the whole of our
Division went down to the trenches on Sunday, General and Staff included, and spent the night there in
the dust, waiting for an attack which never took
place. Last night we were, of course, not in the
trenches, but ordered to be on the alert; and I suppose we shall continue to remain under this alarm
till we assault again. The French are so near the
ditch of the Malakoff, and its contiguous works towards Careening Bay, that there is a moral certainty
of their getting in soon,—the only way to prevent
which, will be by a Russian attack on them, and us,
and every one. The enemy will hope that, as at
Inkermann, even though beaten back, they may make
such an impression as to stop the siege. We lost an
officer of the Guards yesterday morning, whom we
much regret,—Major Hugh Drummond, Adjutant of
the Fusileer Guards. He behaved very well indeed
at the Alma, when his regiment was broken and repulsed, killing several Russians with his pistol. At
Inkermann he was shot through the shoulder, and
might have gone home; instead of which, he stayed on
board the "Retribution" till his wound was well, and
then returned to his duty. He was very ill lately,
and might have been invalided; but he would not
stir: he merely went on board ship for a short time;
and had only returned two days ago to take his share

in the siege, when this unlucky shell came to terminate his short and brilliant career. Poor fellow! I was talking to him in the trenches a quarter of an hour before he was killed. His burial is to-night. These shells are thrown so as to burst over the trenches; no one can tell who will be hit. Sometimes they fall before they burst, quite close to people, who yet escape unhurt. Grape is fired in the same way, and falls "iron sleet in arrowy shower." It is very strange at night, with the peaceful stars looking down, to see these earthly meteors scattering destruction, and to hear their horrid noises, when but for them every thing would be so still and beautiful. Sometimes our own shells burst as they issue from the guns; and then the pieces do much mischief, as the men in the trenches are exposed towards the rear, though covered towards the enemy. All these dangers exist equally in a battle; but there, the excitement of advancing, and the confident feeling of overthrowing the enemy, prevents one thinking of the shot flying round. The passive and long-continued endurance in a siege, and in such a siege, is very trying. The new arrangement of the Division is, I believe, made. We shall have the Highland Division, and it will consist of, 1st brigade, 42d, 79th, 92d, 93d Kilts; 2d brigade, 1st and 2d battalion Royals, 71st and 72d Trews. The Royal is the 1st Regiment, or Royal Scotch; but they are not Highland. The

71st is to be sent back from Kertsch, when replaced by the 82d, hourly expected; the 92d is not yet arrived. I have not heard of the other Divisions yet, nor who will have the luck of being with the Guards. I have just hauled down the 1st Division flag, and sent it to Lord Rokeby, who will now command the 1st Division. I shall be Assistant-Adjutant General to the Highland Division; and we shall, I suppose, hoist St. Andrew's Cross.

---

## LETTER CIX.

Camp before Sebastopol,
17th August 1855.

I HAVE been reading Mazzini's letter. It is clear we should gain in the present war by revolutionising Poland; but not against the will of Napoleon, whose interest it is to stop revolutions. The letter is very clever, like all that Mazzini does; but it must not be forgotten that he is himself a party deeply interested. On the night of the 15th we got news that the Russians were going to attack something somewhere at Baidar, and on the Chernaya. So we dressed ourselves, and got ready; most of our men were in the trenches. At daylight the enemy came on, in number 50,000. They descended from Mackenzie's Farm, and some from Sulu, and they pushed on a

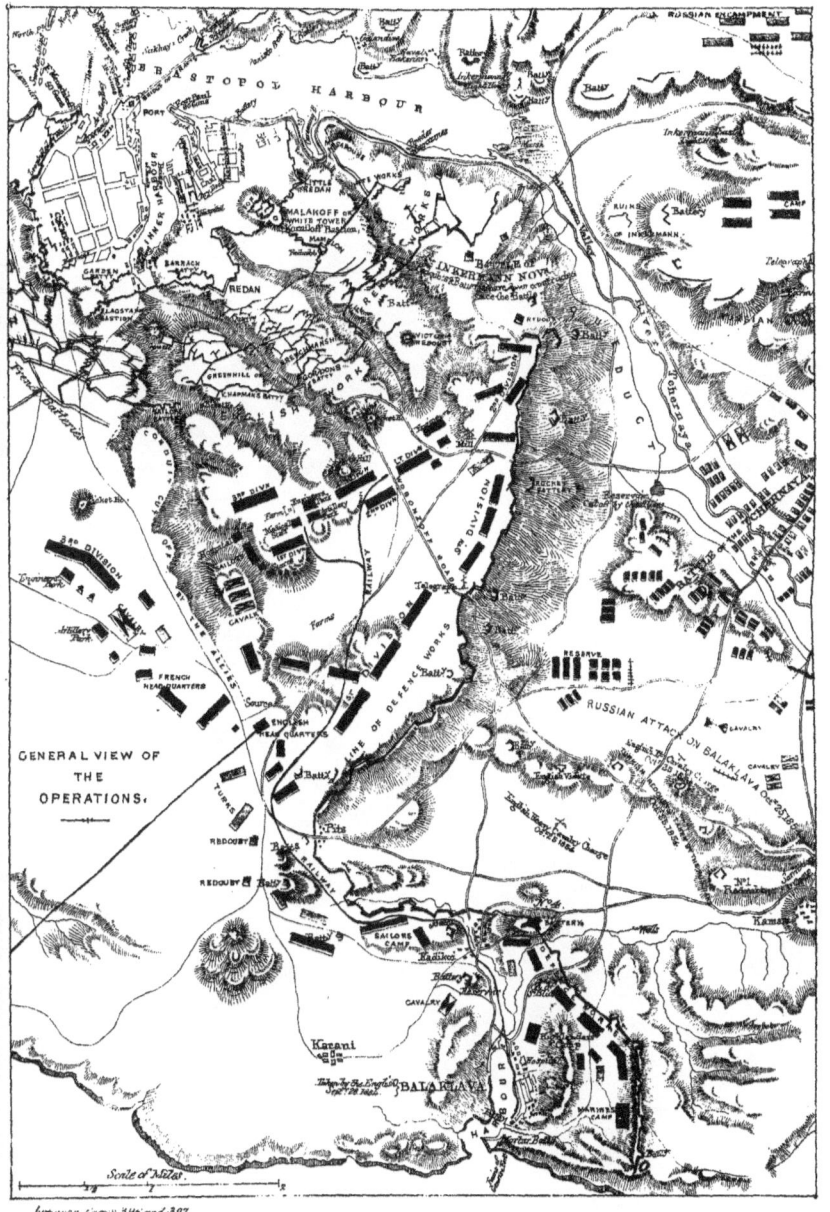

I went over the field of battle yesterday. You have a map which will give you a clear idea of the ground. The Turks were not engaged. The French hold the proper left of the position, with their own left towards the plateau on which we are encamped, and their right on the Feduchine Heights, above and to the southward of Traktir, extending a little to the right of the bridge. The Piedmontese joined them here, and their right went up to Chorguna. The ground, from the French position, down to the river, and for half a mile beyond it, was covered with bodies. I feel sure 2000 lay there. There are 1500 wounded brought in; and we shall never know how many got away, who were wounded in the arms and body. It is asserted, that the Emperor or Constantine gave the plan of the attack, with particular directions to drive us into the sea! A French officer who was taken two months ago has returned. He was kept a month at Simpheropol, and he saw a great deal of the Russian officers, who are all discouraged, and longing for the war to be over; the Russian police having to hunt them out of hiding, in order to send them to the siege of Sebastopol. The troops who made the attack at the Chernaya seem to have behaved with uncommon courage, advancing twice to the charge; it is supposed they expected nothing but Turks, whom they had beaten so easily before. The French fully expect ano-

ther attack in some other place—perhaps nearer the
Inkermann works, *i.e.* more to the Russian right.
We shall do nothing against the place till the new
mortars arrive, except keeping a steady fire of such
projectiles as we possess. There is a regular drain
in the trenches, which is very annoying. Every day
2,800 go in to the right attack, out of which twenty
are usually hurt. The enemy of course lose many
also ; it is said, near 300 a day. They have 30,000
sick and wounded at Simpheropol. Their surgeons are
execrable. All the inhabitants have been sent away,
and their houses are turned into hospitals ; so that
humanity is paying pretty dearly for the fancies of
Peter and Catherine.

## LETTER CX.

Camp before Sebastopol,
20th August 1855.

I AM so continually interrupted by business, that
it is very unsatisfactory to make an attempt at writing. Since the divorce of the Guards our military
matters have been a little in confusion ; and they
will continue to be so till all the arrangements consequent on the change shall have been carried out.
Meantime we have hoisted St. Andrew's Cross as
our Division-flag, on a splendid mast got from the

" Tribune," by way of a signal to the Guards that I think a deliverance has been wrought. The alteration has been made to please Lord Rokeby ; it will give him a larger plaything and a little more patronage. There are now three divisions (Bentinck, Rokeby, Codrington), and three brigades, (two brigades* of the 1st Division, and Windham's,) commanded by officers from the Guards ; which is pretty well, out of six divisions and twelve brigades, besides the Commander-in-Chief and the Chief of the Staff. This promotion of Pakenham over my head hurts my feelings ; and if I am not put in my proper place on the remonstrance which has been made, I shall have to take a line. It will be very repugnant to me to remain here after such an insult ; of course I must stay till this siege is over, at any rate : but it is a brutal way of getting rid of old officers, many of whom cannot afford to abandon their profession. I am not one of those. The generals, according to the new system, are selected from the full colonels ; and putting Pakenham (my junior) over my head on this occasion gives him almost a moral certainty, if the war lasts, of being made a Major-General, while I shall remain a Lieutenant-Colonel. Of course, if he had done any thing extraordinary, it might be put up

---

* Crawford, Ridley. *u'uf*
*see note at p. xvii of Preface.* D D

with; he has been just doing his office-work very well, but not a bit better than I did mine.

21st.

Last night, at midnight, we were roused by the news of an intended sortie on the part of the enemy; so we were all under arms an hour before daylight; but he would not come on. They have such a lot of men, that I feel sure they ought to make an attempt to stop our progress. The bombardment is incessant, and I should hope annoying to the Russians. What do you think of two wives of some of the *employés* at Balaklava riding about the field of battle on the Chernaya among the corpses; and two army-chaplains going all over the field plundering, that is, stripping the bodies of any thing they fancied,—arms, I suppose, as trophies? The French, whose property they were, complained, and a reprimand was issued in Orders. No person with humane feelings can go to see a field of battle, while the dead are lying about, without horror. Officers go professionally, to study how the battle was fought; but women and chaplains can be neither tender nor pious who go to such a scene. A dead body, composed and decent, is not to me a horrid sight; but on a battle-field—where the poor bodies are torn about by frightful wounds, legs and arms shot off, twisted into strange attitudes, exposed by the abstraction or derangement of their clothes, swelled up by the sun, blackened by the blood, while all the preparations are going on for burial in a great ditch—it is truly shocking. To-morrow, for what we know, our own bodies may be scattered about, a spectacle for these harpies.

---

## LETTER CXI.

Camp, Kamara,
27th August 1855.

I LOST the post on Saturday morning (25th). On Friday we got a sudden order to march that night down here to support the Piedmontese and Turks against an expected attack of the Russians; so I was up all night. We marched at 1 A.M. on Saturday morning, and took up a position about Kamara Church, with the 42d, 72d, 79th, and 93d, the only battalions of the Highland Division now present with the army. On our direct front north of us, the Pied-montese army was posted on the hills on the left bank of the Chernaya; on our right front and flank, along the Woronzow Road, with some posts beyond the river, were the Turks; towards Baidar more Turks, two regiments of French infantry and five of cavalry, under D'Allonville. On our left front two divisions of French, under Herbillon, covering the bridge at Traktir, with picquets beyond. We were informed that we should be attacked in the morning by from 60,000 to 80,000 men, including the Grenadiers just arrived from Poland. We got into position before daylight, and looked for the sun and the enemy; only one of those elements showed. After waiting some hours, it was concluded we should march back to our camp on the plateau, pack up our things and tents, and move down again to encamp here. We accordingly went back; but not in time for the post. We made our "*pacquets,*" and marched again at 2 A.M. yesterday. We are to be ready every morning for an attack, which the headquarter people say is certain to be made. The ground the various allied troops occupy was all held by the Russians last winter, while we watched them for many an anxious morning. In this fine weather it is beautiful. We are about a mile and a half from the Chorguna Bridge, about two miles from Traktir, and three hundred yards from Kamara Church. Our men are thus clear from the trenches, and during the day have nothing to do. We all sleep accoutred, in order to be ready for these boasted Grenadiers, whenever they choose to come on. Lord Stratford is arrived, and to-day holds the grand *funzione* of investing the Knights of the Bath. I shall not be present. C. is alone ordered up to receive his grand cross. From the usual dilatoriness of our Government, they have not arranged to give the French

their decorations.  Omar Pasha, however, has had
his at Constantinople ; and I conclude Canrobert
has had his from the Queen at Paris.  I am not so
sure as the headquarter people appear to be that we
shall be attacked here.  The position is very strong,
and the dressing the Russians got on the 16th will
not be very encouraging to their soldiers, if they try
it again.  However, an attack is quite *en règle*, and
ought to be made if they can screw themselves up to
it.  I should like to see our Highlanders make another Alma charge.  If we are beaten, we shall have
to occupy our old Balaklava lines, towards which our
retreat is open.  I do not for a moment anticipate
this being our lot.  Some sages suppose the Russians
are deceiving us, and are now on their march to
Kertsch, in the hope of recapturing that place.  There
is a great lack of accurate information, which is ill-
supplied by vague rumours as a substitute.  We are
nearly come round to our twelvemonth in the Crimea.
I have received the extract from Tennyson's new
poem.  One cannot judge from such bits ; bricks from
Babylon.  The metre you speak of does appear doubtful, and I am against such experiments, although
so much license is given to a lyric.  I look forward
to reading the thing as a whole, which is the only
way to measure a work of art.  He is our only poet,
and we must not be unfair to him.  His spirit is
mighty warlike.  Perhaps he will come here a new

minstrel boy. But the real thing would stifle his strain; the petty miseries and frightful horrors are equally unpoetical. Men like us waiting for the enemy might be depicted by Homer; but he would not enter into the shortcomings of my servant, my tattered clothes, and ill-managed breakfast, nor meddle with the wastefulness, carelessness, stupidity, and selfishness of many who are helping to do this great thing. What poet could draw the parson in a white choker, with beard and mustachios, pillaging the dead? That is only for *Punch;* his Reverence slung round with Russian muskets, and his servant turning over the corpses under his direction: also a party of ensigns on their ponies, stopped by the French sentry at the bridge over the aqueduct, forming line and charging the watercourse, and clearing it in triumph. Fine boys! The French begin to understand our eccentricities, and are only amused by them. Before this reaches you, the telegraph will have told you whether the Grenadiers have come to the scratch.

---

## LETTER CXII.

Camp, Kamara,
31st August 1855.

STILL expecting the enemy, who does not show; by which means he keeps so many soldiers away from

the siege, and increases the work for those who remain. I see by the *Gazette* that Wilbraham is made a
Colonel ; he is the senior of the three Assistant-Adjutant-Generals passed over by Pakenham, and has now
got back into his place. I much fear I shall not be
so well treated. The answer to my letter of remonstrance is not come ; if unfavourable, I shall have to
decide on something. When the siege is over, I think
the point of honour would permit me to resign ; but I
do not like to leave C., who probably finds me useful
to him. My want of books has set me to reading
tracts, which pious persons have sent out for the
soldiers. They are better written than I expected.
Yesterday, however, Sidney Smith's Life dropped
upon me accidentally, which will last me a few days.
With respect to the accident at Cremorne, it looks
like a judgment on the bad taste exhibited in making
a show of such an awful business.

As you say, it will be curious to see, when we
take the field, how Simpson and Barnard will manœuvre a large army against the Russian generals.
Lord Panmure appointed them ; and if they do not
turn out skilful, on him should rest the blame.

General Beatson has not been murdered by the
Bashi-Bazouks ; that is a mistake. I saw him once at
Scutari in very fine clothes. He was here also with
General Scarlet at the time of the battle at Balaklava.

The answer to my letter of remonstrance is just

come. "The principle of selection cannot be carried out if all officers, ~~junior~~ to the selected one, are also to be promoted." As if I did not know that. Remark, "*all.*"

I shall not be able to decide what to do without consideration.

---

## LETTER CXIII.

Camp, Kamara,
6th September 1855.

I AM so busy, that I have scarcely time to write. In this new position a plan was wanting, which I have been occupied in making. The French are strongly fortified opposite Traktir Bridge. The Sardinians opposite Chorguna and Karlovka; the Turks extended from the right of the Sardinians, with the Woronzow Road in their front; the right of the Turks bends away southwards to the old Cossack picquet-house on the old Baidar Road, leading to our old original Lines of Balaklava. We have here at Kamara four battalions of Highlanders, and thirty-two pieces of artillery, ready to support any one, and especially the Turks. Should the latter be forced, our position would be turned; and we should have to get back into the Balaklava Lines. Next Monday, the telegraph will have told the people in London of the assault. Scarcely any one here knows that it is to take place on

Saturday the 8th instant. At the same moment, if ever, we may confidently expect to be attacked here: the enemy is in force at Sulu, about five miles off; so the crisis is at hand. I told you in my last that I had been refused my promotion. Wilbraham has managed his; he was senior to me. Here is my final protest. " I have received a letter from Colonel Steele, Military Secretary, addressed by Major-General Yorke" (the Military Secretary in London) " to General Simpson, in reply to my remonstrance at the promotion of Colonel Pakenham over my head. General Yorke informs me that the ' principle of selection cannot be carried out if all the officers, senior to him who is selected for promotion, are likewise to be promoted :' a matter of fact which is pretty evident. I am nearly the solitary instance of a Staff-officer who has been present with the army the whole time without receiving a step of rank. So far as I know, there is no other. As it has been decided upon that I am not to be promoted, and that a junior officer is to be put over my head, I cannot help perceiving, what is clear to every one, that a punishment has been inflicted, and a stigma cast upon me, which I have not earned. Being at this moment in the presence of the enemy, I am precluded from requesting that I may be relieved from this Staff situation, in order to retire from a scene where I have been so treated. It is, however, very hard that a man of honour should be placed in

such a position as I now find myself in,—one which
no theory of selection can ever make tolerable to any
person with keen feelings. I beg you will be so kind
as to forward this letter through the proper channel,
in order to place my sentiments upon record, and to
convince my friends that I have made every effort
consistent with military discipline to avert and resist
my misfortune." This letter has been forwarded by
C., and may possibly affront some one. I cannot help
that; the fallacy of assuming that I proposed *all* the
seniors to be promoted will be palpable to you. No
warrant for selection could ever have contemplated
this kind of usage of officers in the field who have
done their duty well, as my chief will certify that I
have. I am driven out of my profession: at present,
with my notions of soldier-like propriety, it is impossible to go; neither can I ask any further favour. The
bombardment is going on, fast and furious. I saw a
great fire last night reflected in the sky, which I hope
may turn out to have been one of the Russian ships.
This bombardment will of course continue till we make
the assault. I have read Sidney Smith with utter disappointment. *Whom shall we hang?* has also fallen
into my hands; it is a bit of special pleading to defend
the Duke of N., who was by no means the real culprit.
The Duke is still here; and will, I suppose, go back
knowing something about it, especially if he waits till
November. It is now two o'clock A.M.; in two hours

we shall be under arms, expecting the threatened attack, for which we get ready every morning, sleeping in our clothes.

7th September.

We are ordered up to-morrow morning to form a reserve for the assaulting columns. I cannot find that Simpson has asked any advice from C. about this assault. It is a pity; for he has seen so much fighting, and understands the soldiers so well. The troops which assaulted on the 18th of June are very much pumped out; some of the regiments suffered frightfully at the Alma; they have been kept all this time in the trenches, losing men; they have made one assault, and failed. Of course, many of their best and bravest officers and men have been killed or disabled. There was an officer down here two days ago who told me he had been sent out with a hundred men of the —— Regiment to form a line of sentries after dark outside the advanced trench, and that they all ran away and left him, with the exception of six men. The heart is out of them. They ought to employ Eyre or C. for the assault, if they wish to make a sure job of it; but then Codrington would not get the credit, and he has friends about head-quarters, where C. and Eyre are not in good odour; I wonder why; they are the two best soldiers here, and, in fact, the only good ones that I see among the higher ranks. God help us!—we are in strange hands.

This begins the account of the greatest, and perhaps the only, disgrace of this sort which has ever befallen the British arms. Are we not to ask how, and why? Is the English army and nation to endure the discredit which has fallen upon them, solely from the appointment to supreme command of an incompetent person in himself, and the more incompetent because he had not moral energy enough to break through the trammels of a clique which hung about headquarters?

There has been published a small book, Selections from a Diary and Letters of the late Major Rankin of the Royal Engineers, who led the ladder-party at this disastrous assault. He could have told, and probably did write, much more than has been published. His brother, who edits the book, says in his preface, " Some passages, referring to the attack on the Redan, I have, for *obvious* reasons, purposely omitted; my brother not being alive to support the truth of his assertions."

The " *obvious* reasons," I suppose, are that this editor did not think the commanders and planners of this attack would like to hear what a gallant and intelligent officer had to say about their utter incompetence.

Major Rankin states : " I found the ladder-party, composed of men from the 3d Buffs and 90th and

97th Regiments, lining the sap in front of the Redan (called the Sixth Parallel), the trench which Cooke and myself commenced on my first night's duty in the trenches. The party consisted of 320 men, who were told-off to forty scaling-ladders, each twenty-four feet long. My instructions were, to advance with my sappers, armed with crowbars and axes for cutting through the abattis, and with the ladder-party immediately after the skirmishers had been thrown out. The (ladder) party was under command of Major Welsford, 97th Regiment, with whom I conferred for several minutes, and to whom I explained the point where the ladders were to be placed, in order to screen them as much as possible from the fire of the enemy. I then told my party of sappers what they were to do, and assembled the non-commissioned officers to point out the measures to be taken under their directions, in the event of my being either killed or wounded. These arrangements being made, I awaited the signal to advance; silently calling upon God to aid and assist me in doing my duty, and, if it were His will, to preserve my life. Suddenly there was a shout that the French were attacking the Malakoff. I looked over the parapet, and saw them rushing up the salient; they were apparently unresisted. The French flag in a minute was seen waving on the ramparts. All this happened so instantaneously that it took us all by surprise.

"We had anticipated a hard struggle, and we were ordered not to advance till a decided success had been achieved; but, as it were in a second, the dreaded Malakoff had fallen into the hands of the French. Our men could no longer be restrained; before there was time to get the ladders to the front, and before the sappers could advance to cut away the abattis, they rushed in a straggling line over the parapets, and dashed onwards towards the salient. I hurried up my sappers as fast as I could, shouting to them till I was nearly hoarse, and ran forwards with them and the ladder-party, with a drawn sword in my hand (my scabbard and belt I left behind). In the hurry and confusion many ladders were left behind. There was, however, little excuse for this, as the men had their places distinctly assigned to them, and should not have left the trench without their ladders. It was of course impossible to perceive that any thing of the kind had occurred, and still more impossible to have rectified it, had it been known. The only word was 'Forward!'—the only course to pursue, to advance as rapidly as possible. Nearly two hundred yards of rough broken ground and an abattis had to be crossed under the enemy's fire. The men advanced with the greatest spirit. I could see bodies, dead and wounded, lying along, and strewing the ground on each side of me as I pressed forward, shouting continually to the men to advance, and not to pause for an instant. When I came to the abattis, I found five men nearly exhausted carrying a ladder, and trying to get it over the opposing branches; the remaining three men, composing the party of eight, had probably been killed or wounded in the advance. I lent them my aid, and urged them on. The edge of the ditch was soon reached, and I was relieved to find the ditch not nearly so formidable as it had been represented, and as I had good reason, from the solidity and extent of the Russian defences, to suppose it was likely to prove. I was prepared for a broad deep ditch, flanked by caponnières, and for military pits, chevaux-de-frise, palisades, and all kinds of obstacles. The dreaded ditch of the Redan, however, proved nothing but a simple trench, perhaps fourteen or fifteen feet deep at the counter-scarp, and twenty, or rather more, at the escarp. I kept my ladders rather to the right of the salient angle, having been warned that the flanking fire would probably be severe up the proper left face. Half a dozen or so were lowered and reversed in a minute, and the men passed up them with eager haste. I set to work with every sapper I could get hold of, or to whom amid the din I could make myself audible, to tear down the rubble-stone work, with which the salient of the escarp was revetted, and form a ramp practicable for ascent without ladders.

"The long continuance of dry weather which preceded the assault must be regarded as a very favourable circumstance. The gabions staked to the ground with wooden stakes (with which the counter-scarp was revetted) were torn down, and used in forming, with rocks, stones, and débris, a small parapet across the ditch of the proper left face, and a similar counter-caponnière thrown up also on the other side. I had to work, however, with my own hands; it was difficult to get any one to do any thing; the men, as they struggled up to the assault in support of the advance, seemed stunned and paralysed. There was little of that dash and enthusiasm which might have been looked for from British soldiers in an assault; in fact, it required all the efforts and example of their officers to get the men on, and these were rendered almost ineffective from the manner in which the various regiments soon got confused and jumbled together. The men, after firing from behind the traverses, near the salient, for half an hour at the enemy, —also firing behind his parados and traverses,—began to waver. I rushed up the salient with the view of cheering them on, and the officers exerted themselves to sustain them; the men gave a cheer, and went at it afresh. The supports or reserves, ordered to follow, struggled up in inefficient disorder, but were unable to press into the work, as the men in advance, occupying the salient, *refused to go on*, notwithstanding

the devoted efforts of the officers to induce them to
do so. Whether it was that they dreaded some secret trap, or some mine which would destroy the
whole of them at once; whether it was that the long
and tedious siege-works had lowered their *morale;* or
whether it was owing to the dreadful manner in which
their Division (the Light, *most* injudiciously selected
to lead) had been cut up in previous actions,—it is a
melancholy truth that the majority of the assaulting
column did not display the spirit and dash of thorough
soldiers when assaulting the enemy. They refused,
however, to retreat, and seemed to look round for
aid; I trembled when I saw no one coming, and
looked continually anxiously round for the reserves
I considered, as a matter of course, would be advanced
immediately it was perceived that the leading columns
had failed to carry the position, and were commencing
to waver.*

"I had just given directions to the portion of the

---

* At this moment the whole of the trenches were crammed
with men : the first trench had Sir W. Codrington in command
of the remainder of his immense division ; behind him, General
Markham with his men ; and behind him, Sir Colin Campbell
with the Highlanders; but he had no orders to meddle with an
assault, the whole arrangements for which were put expressly
in charge of his junior officers, Codrington and Markham. So
long as their men remained in the trenches, no one else could
go on.

E E

working-party of one hundred men told off to me, which reached the ditch, what they were to do, and was returning towards the salient, when the sad repulse took place. What brought matters completely to a crisis I have never exactly ascertained; I heard, directly after I regained our trenches, that three officers of the 41st, after vainly striving to induce the men to advance, rushed forward together, and were all three shot down like one man by the cross-fire of the Russians behind their parados. This was the turning-point, according to this account, of the men's indecision; they wavered and fled. I was near the counter-scarp when I saw the whole living mass on the salient begin reeling and swaying to and fro; in a moment I found myself knocked down and lying on my face, with a number of men scrambling over me, their bayonets running through my clothes. I expected to have been stunned and bayoneted, and to have been left insensible in the ditch, or shot by the enemy before I could drag myself out of it. However, at last I saw an opening, and, holding on by my hands and knees, managed to force my way to it through the moving mass, and regain my legs. I ran then as fast as I could towards our advanced trenches, the grape whistling past me like hail, and the Russians standing on the top of their parapets, and firing volleys into the crowd of fugitives.

"In our trenches all was shame, rage, and fear;

the men were crowded together and disorganised. It was hopeless to attempt to renew the attack with the same troops."—

It was indeed truly hopeless ever to make an attack with such troops; a set of raw recruits,—undisciplined, unacquainted with one another and with their officers, and of different regiments mixed together. But the British Government chose the Commander-in-Chief, and he chose his own General, and his chosen General's own division, to make this attack, and to risk and lose the honour of England.

## LETTER CXIV.

Camp, Kamara,
10th September 1855.

In my last I told you that we were ordered up to the trenches. We marched on the morning of the 8th (Saturday). Our instructions were, to form the second reserve of the 2d and Light Divisions, which were destined to assault the Redan, under the management and arrangement of Generals Codrington and Markham. C. has never been consulted. We deposited our knapsacks and feather-bonnets in our old camp on the plateau, and filed into the first parallel just as the French began their attack on the Malakoff. We followed along the trenches the reserves of the assault-

ing troops, and finally took up the position assigned
to us in the third parallel, under a very heavy fire,
which caused us about seventy casualties. From
thence we could see the French rush succeed, and
the sad catastrophe of the English attack on the Redan, sad—not merely from our loss of life, but from
the palpable inexperience of the General, who did not
understand his métier, and from the actual misbe-
haviour of the reserves with him, who ought to have
followed the first assaulting columns. The French
have performed a marvellous feat of arms ; they were
lucky as well as brave. The Russians did not expect
them at noon ; if they had been prepared, no troops
could have got into the Malakoff, the strength of
which had never been estimated properly till it was
taken. The French assault on the Little Redan to
the proper left of the Malakoff was repulsed with immense loss, also that on the Bastion Centrale ; that
on the Bastion du Mât never took place. Our friend
Vinoy was the hero of the day ; he got in and maintained himself, and thus won Sebastopol, which became untenable when the Malakoff was gone. Our
column got into the salient of the Redan, but the support would not follow. The officers exerted themselves and sacrificed themselves in vain ; the men
stuck behind the parapet of the advanced trenches ;
they seemed paralyzed. The Light Division, mis-
managed at the Alma, were beaten there ; they have

been punished ever since, and so many of their best
men killed, that the heart was out of them.   The intrigue which kept them and Codrington in the front
will some time or other be exposed.   They ought to
have been sent to support the Piedmontese instead
of our Division ; but then C. would have taken the
Redan, or left his body there with those of his faithful Highlanders.   That appeared too great a risk to
be run by the clique at head-quarters.   The soldiers
of the Light Division had been so long exposed to fire
in the trenches, that they had got a habit of skulking
behind gabions ; "gabion dodging" is their own word.
Those who did go out, for the most part clung like a
swarm of bees on the exterior slope of the parapet of
the Redan, and finally they gave up and ran back
into their own trenches.   About four o'clock P.M. our
Division and part of another was ordered to occupy
the front trenches, and the beaten troops were sent
home.   We had just posted our sentries, and fully
occupied the trenches, when C. was summoned by
General Simpson, who gave him orders to assault the
Redan on the morning of the 9th.   Meantime, the
Russians, finding the Malakoff lost, began their evacu-
ation.   They exploded magazines in every direction,
making it impossible to move forward in the dark
and see what they were about.   The tremendous ex-
plosion, and the blazing of the town, which they set
on fire, made a very beautiful spectacle.   At one A.M.

we felt on cautiously, and discovered that the Redan was abandoned.    Before leaving, the Russians dressed our wounded, and they did not blow up the magazine in the Redan, which was very humane on their part. They made a magnificent retreat ; carrying off their whole garrison intact over the bridge, which they removed at daylight, leaving us in quiet possession of the ruins of the town, and about 500 guns in the batteries, besides a multitude of stores not yet ascertained.    They sunk their ships during the night, and have not fired on us from the batteries on the north side of the Harbour.    It is quite likely that they will now abandon the Crimea.    I was all over the Redan at daylight on the morning of the 9th ; it was very strong, but not enclosed at the gorge, as the Malakoff was.    The French surprised the Malakoff, as they did the Mamelon and the Batteries Blanches.    I do not believe we have any plan ; but I conclude, if the Russians quietly go away, we shall occupy both sides of the Harbour, clear it out, fill with our ships, and wait for spring.    We all feel intensely the disgrace of our failure, and also feel sure, if our Highlanders had assaulted instead of the others, that we should have taken the place.    General Vinoy lost fifty-five officers out of his six battalions.    We lost 154 officers altogether.    The French total is said to be 12,000 men *hors de combat*, ours 2000.    I have been over the Malakoff to-day, and into the town, which

is in ruins.  I only write now to say I am unhurt.
The crack young Generals Codrington and Markham
had the entire management of it; and a pretty mess
they made!  Codrington, who was with the front division, ought to have rushed up to the Redan when
he found his men wavering.

C. remarked to General Simpson, when he ordered
the Highlanders to assault, that they had marched
twelve miles, and gone straight into the trenches, and
would spend the night there, and that they had no
food.  "Oh, but the young people about me," meaning
his aides-de-camp, "are so anxious it should be
done!"  A nice general!  The devil help England!
No one else will help a nation which puts its reputation in such keeping.  The one capable man they
have, to be so commanded!  The cavalry is to winter
at Scutari.  That, I believe, is the only thing decided
upon; and now I suppose the diplomatists will begin
again.

---

## LETTER CXV.

Camp, Kamara,
14th September 1855.

TWELVE months ago we landed in this peninsula.
I send a woman's letter, taken from the body of an
officer in the Redan.  I cannot read it, but I dare
say you will find some one who can.  I have been all

over Sebastopol ; it is utterly ruined, but gives the
notion of its having been a pretty place. The enemy's
batteries on the opposite side of the harbour will reach
it, and make any troops quartered therein uneasy.
We are beginning to embark our siege-train out of
the batteries. No one knows what may be our ulterior movements. My own impression is, that the
Russians will leave the Crimea of their own accord
before winter ; at present they are very busy building
batteries, but that may be only to cover their retreat.
We have got the 92d Highlanders added to our Division ; the 71st is to spend the winter at Kertsch.
Your criticism on the "Simple Story" is very just.
It only requires a little practice to get over the old
fashion of the writing. There will now be so many
changes in this army, that it becomes impossible to
foresee who will stay. Bentinck, I heard, sent in his
resignation the day before yesterday; whether it will
be accepted, is another affair ; his going will make
C. second senior, *i.e.* next to Simpson. But I suspect
there is a scheme to make Codrington Commander-in-
Chief. I know there has been an offer of Malta to
C. He said the enemy was before him, and that his
place was here. O wise J. B. ! fat-headed calf of an
ineffectual cow ! what art thou about ? I do not believe they will let him arrive at the command of this
army. Luckily he is independent in his circumstances,
and so he can afford to decline the command at Malta,

which is, in fact, an insult at this moment to a man
of his antecedents. The best officer in this force to be
selected for shelving, by placing him in the charge of
the recruits at Malta ! The Government, having such
a man on the spot, is more silly than Governments
usually are, in not seizing the opportunity of putting
him into command, when, as it so rarely happens, that
post has fallen by seniority to his lot. Simpson is better; but he is going. The taking of the Malakoff was
a fortunate fluke for the French. The old guard had
marched out; the new guard had not marched in :
there was only a handful of men in the work ; the
General Officer commanding was eating his soup. The
Russians had a mine, which it only required two days'
work to complete, when they would have blown up
the whole of the French advanced trenches. The
French were driven back three times. Vinoy's strength
of character kept his men to their work. He planted
his sword in the ground, near the flag which was
hoisted at the gorge of Malakoff, and, with revolver
in hand, threatened to shoot any one who retired beyond the sword. If he had been killed, the place
would not have been taken. I understand the Russian
losses from our bombardment were excessive. Their
officers behaved admirably ; their men showed great
endurance ; but they want the intelligence of the
French. All that teaching can give, they have ; but
they are only serfs, after all, and cannot, in the long-

run, stand against free men. I think it will be a very great misfortune for the character of the English army, if we have not an opportunity of meeting the Russians, and beating them, before they go, in the open field. I do not doubt of our success, although so much depends upon the leading. However, we are not the army we were last year; so many old soldiers are gone, so many good officers. The Highland Regiments are fortunate; they never broke down at all, like so many others. I believe this army would be rendered more efficient than it is by the withdrawal of certain corps, whose *morale* has been shaken; but the chiefs know nothing about soldiers or human nature. The —— Regiment was dreadfully cut up in India; nearly all the officers, and an immense proportion of the men, were killed and wounded. It had been in admirable discipline, and was one of the finest regiments in India. The next time this regiment was engaged, although they were scarcely under fire and suffered nothing, yet they were quite nervous, and not to be depended upon. A wise general, therefore, will never employ troops in a ticklish operation.who have been much punished previously. Place them in reserve; their self-respect is preserved, and they gradually come to again. The greatest, and also the rarest, valour is shown by troops which can bear to be beaten day after day, and yet come again. To do this, you should have old soldiers, and not mere

boys. Some martinets, who have seen nothing but
parades in England, imagine that a boy put into a
red coat becomes wood or iron. There is as much
art in maintaining the courage of soldiers as in preserving their health: in both arts C——, from long
experience, as well as natural aptitude, is a master.
The bravest have always most compassion, and make
the most allowance for youthful nervousness. It was
well known in the army that this Division was
shaken. After the 18th of June they ought to have
been withdrawn in a great degree, or even before that.
They might have gone to the left attack, where we
were not pushing. A wise general has a head, and
uses it for thinking. At the late assault, our Commander-in-Chief allowed himself to be placed by the
Engineers in rear of the left attack, from whence he
could not communicate with the assaulting troops
without a great loss of time.

LETTER CXVI.

Camp, Kamara,
18th September 1855.

You ask about William Mansfield. He was formerly Colonel Mansfield of the 53d Regiment; a
very clever and accomplished man. He is now attached, with the rank of Brigadier-General, to the

embassy at Constantinople, as a military medium of communication with the Turkish Contingent. We have received notice that four of our Divisions are to be kept in readiness to move at a moment's notice, dependent, I conclude, on the decision come to by Pelissier or by the French Emperor. The unfortunate Light and Second Divisions are not to be employed. Codrington is universally reprobated. There he stood in the advanced trench, with all his Staff, about 250 yards from the angle of the Redan, with his men clustered on its rampart, neither advancing nor retiring for three-quarters of an hour. If ever there was a time when a General should have played the part of a grenadier,* that was the time. If he had rushed up, he might have failed in getting the men to move on; but he should have tried, and have died there. Could he have got fifty men to go over the parapet, the rest would have followed. England has suffered an indelible disgrace; and this young general, I should suppose, is extinguished. How the people could have had the idea of pushing him into supreme command, is beyond me; for he has literally no experience, and this war hitherto has been quite uninstructive in any sort of manœuvring. Markham I knew long ago; he is brave, but has nothing at all in him,—a rather dull man, I should

---

* Napoleon at Arcola.

say. This selection system, which is now proposed, will, if acted upon, place Military Officers in the same position as those of the Navy have always been in ; that is, young men of interest will be placed over the heads of older officers ; and the present old officers, not having been educated for such treatment, will not submit to the injustice, but will retire in disgust. Theoretically, a selection by merit is very good ; but with our Government, it must be a mere job. Of all who have been promoted, the two whom I know to have decided military talent are Brigadier-Generals Cameron and Rumley. Our Division Generals have been ordered to send a list of officers, non-commissioned officers, and men, who have served with zeal and distinction, during the siege of Sebastopol, since the 18th Nov. 1854. From these lists, Simpson is to make a selection of names for submission home. No accident can put me right now ; for they must antedate me above Pakenham, to do what seems to me common justice ; and that they will never do, even if they promote me, which I do not expect. We have not above six weeks now of weather in which an army could be moved. If nothing is done during that time, we shall go into winter-quarters, and I shall be adrift. I am sadly puzzled what to do. Possibly C—— may be sent on some command, to clear him out of the path of the crack young generals. If so, I may go on his personal staff. Lord Hardinge very likely will be displeased at my remonstrance, and his Lordship may suppose that a Committee of the House of Commons, having decided on giving him the power of selection, has also enabled him to change people's feelings and to reconcile men of intelligence and education like myself to any injustice;—in which idea, he and his House of Commons will find themselves mistaken.

---

## LETTER CXVII.

Camp, Kamara,
21st September 1855.

THE next mail will tell us how the universal J. B. has borne the news of the fall of Sebastopol. There has come a telegraphic message forbidding the destruction of the docks. Our people are reëmbarking the siege guns, &c. We hear that some 12,000 Russian guns have been found, some of them very beautiful. Their army is massed on the Belbek, and, we hear, very dispirited. No plan is yet decided upon, or, at least, no symptoms of moving. It is quite time we should begin making preparations for wintering; a few huts have arrived, which are ordered to Kertsch, for the 71st. The others will, I suppose, follow shortly. I hope our chiefs will not attempt any thing further this autumn. Our men are many

of them very young, and six months' quiet and
comfort will add greatly to their strength. It must
be decided very soon, as we cannot reckon on more
than six weeks of good weather. The last few days
have been very bad indeed, cold and rainy, quite
unlike last year. The expedition would have very
likely failed, if we had not been so fortunate in our
weather; it is now clearing up, and I suppose we
shall have the Indian summer. I am trying to persuade myself that, when we go into winter-quarters,
we shall still have the enemy before us. I would
fain not quit the army; yet know not how to stay.
There will most likely be a gazetteful of promotions
and honours; but I think Lord Hardinge will be too
much affronted at my protest to do any thing for me.
These great people, who have always had the world
at their feet, cannot understand an independent man,
who thinks nothing of them or their greatness. Your
administrative reform seems to have come to nothing;
it wants Cobden. They say the French are mending
the road up to Aitodor, which is at least a threat to
Gortschakoff. We cannot go up by Mackenzie's Farm,
but, once on the plateau now before us, we should
winter at Bakchi-Serai. You ought to get a good map
of these parts: if we move, you will know nothing
without a map; I do not mean a pretty sketch of the
scenery, but a faithful map, giving the roads, rivers,
and hills, which will be famous henceforward for ever-

more. The Allied Generals have agreed to let Omar Pasha take away the only three good battalions he left here ; the rest of the Turks might as well go with them. Before the assault these battalions were refused to him, to his immense disgust. This change will weaken our right towards Baidar ; but I do not think the Russians meditate any sort of an advance. How do the Italian Liberals bear the glory recently acquired by the Piedmontese ? The latter are in the seventh heaven. I cannot help hoping that this small country will some time or other get rid of Pope, Bomba, Austria, &c., out of Italy, and make a *regno d'Italia ;* for I do not put any faith in a United Italy, made up of little republican states; they would go to war with one another, and the devil would laugh at that.

## LETTER CXVIII.

Camp, Kamara,
24th September 1855.

WE are still in indecision here. A spy came back yesterday to Osman Pasha, whom I saw this morning : the statement is, that 10,000 Russians have gone back past Perekop; that the Russians are withdrawing guns and powder from the North Fort, or Sivernaya, to some place which is not known ; they have two divisions opposite Sebastopol, *i. e.* opposite to us, and three, or about 30,000 men, at Khorales; total force in the Crimea 70,000. The Russian soldiers are much dispirited; before the fall of Sebastopol, they were told to die in that place; now they are told not to attack us, but to resist to the last, should we attack them; but if we should cut off their retreat, they were to surrender,—which idea, entering into the soldiers' minds, is very ominous. Most likely the spy is a double one, and only tells part of what he knows; he promises that before eight days we shall hear something astonishing. The losses in the retreat are described as enormous, whole battalions slipping off the bridge into the sea: this is very likely, as it was a floating bridge, with no sides. I rode yesterday along the Woronzow Road to Baidar, which is a miserable Turkish village; the cottages wattle and mud; the people unmolested, and with some small shops, selling things at an exorbitant rate to the French. They have there four Divisions, perhaps 15,000 men, some miles to the north of Baidar, feeling the Russian outposts. I picked a tobacco-leaf out of a small garden at Baidar. They appear to cure their tobacco for home consumption themselves. The reply to Bentinck's resignation came yesterday by telegraph, after considerable delay; it was a refusal to accept it, and a direction to Simpson not to forward any similar applications. At the same time, I am convinced they are scheming something to put young generals

F F

in command. They surely will not try to compel the seniors to serve under the juniors, whether they like it or not; so that an old general will have to sham sick, or else resign his commission, in order to get away from such an intolerable position. —— has heard that they will take an opportunity of promoting him; I suppose he has friends. As Vinoy said to me last winter, when I was trying to arrange something for the convenience of landing his stores at Balaklava, "Je vois que chez vous tout se fait par politique." The feeling here is strong against Codrington for not going out of the trenches when he found his men hanging back. No one intends to allude to his personal courage, but to his ignorance of his *métier*. If Lord Panmure knows the truth, he will scarcely give him a high command : he ought to be recalled, if justice is to be done. I cannot comprehend the folly of the English nation in not giving the command of our army to C. ; he is not only the best, but the only competent man here. Markham never was a man of any ability; he was brave, and had extraordinary physical powers, but his constitution is a wreck ; and with that sort of man, the physique being gone, all is gone. Austria will be in a sad way at having taken part with the losing side. I trust they will pinch her well ; although, in truth, I do not see how to do it, unless by causing revolutions, which Louis Napoleon cannot very well do. The true reward for France will be the Prussian Rhenish Provinces ; and I have little doubt that is what they are looking forward to. We, I conclude, shall get nothing ; money cannot be expected from Russia, and territory she has none that would suit us. A French Division and some cavalry have been sent to Eupatoria, as a threat against the enemy's communication with Perekop. The fleet came off Balaklava and pretended to embark men ; they put all the marines on deck, and passed the Russian positions, on the north side of the harbour, cheering, to make believe we were sending English troops to Eupatoria ; but it is only a ruse. I do not think that any thing will be done. We are longing for the decision, in order that we may begin to hut our men, and make them comfortable before the bad weather ; but patience is our only motto.

## LETTER CXIX.

Camp, Kamara,
29th September 1855.

WE are all anxious to hear how you behave after the digestion of our failure and success. Here we are doing nothing. The enemy does not show the smallest sign of vacating the Crimea ; he is hutting and preparing for winter, on the one hand, and on the other, is firing red-hot shot into the ruins of Sebastopol, to annoy our fatigue-parties. Markham, the General, is gone home sick, quite broken up in constitution, I should say: his Division is to be kept for him, in case of his recovery, and of his being able to return in the spring. I believe that the Court had been planning to give Codrington the command of the army; but that Lord Panmure, the responsible man, has concluded that Markham shall have it, and that he positively would have been named in the spring: this design his illness will disturb; and should he not recover, Lord P. will have to look out for some one else. I cannot imagine what has given his Lordship so high an opinion of his capacity. In India, he was considered to be very brave, and the best ibex-shot in the country. Now, if this idea of mine be correct, as I do not doubt, what do you think of the wisdom or the consideration of a public minister who would leave senior officers here—nay, compel them to stay— during the winter in mud and snow, taking care of their men, entertaining all the while a fixed intention of placing a junior over their heads when the campaign shall be about to commence? Then their military honour would force them to remain in so false a position. Little more than two years ago, this very Markham was under the command of C. in India. I told you Bentinck's resignation had been refused, and that Simpson had been told not to forward any simi-

lar applications; knowing what I think I know, you
perceive that C., with his long and admirable service, is about to be situated as I have been since
Pakenham's promotion. Mind this goes no further
than yourself. The moment that we receive definite
orders to go into winter-quarters, which we expect
every day, C. intends to ask for six weeks' leave
of absence: he will go direct to London, and take
Lord Hardinge and Lord Panmure by the throat;
and, I think, will not come back to this army. I
shall wait till I hear from him, before doing any
thing. If they try to make me serve, after the injustice I have suffered, there will be nothing left for me
than to sham sick, which I disdain to do, or to sell
out. Strictly speaking, I ought to refuse any employment except on the personal staff, unless I am
promoted into my proper place, viz., a Colonel, with
date of 17th July; but in extremities my iron temper may have to yield a little, and I may have to
eat my leek. Nothing can possibly be more against
the grain. There is, indeed, the resource of writing
to the newspapers, with my name subscribed. This is
not legally a military offence, if done in proper language; but it is a course which I do not admire. I
have now put before you a little picture of the state
to which punctilios in the point of honour may bring
a man. Would that I were an M.P., or rather a
peer; had I been either, the wish would be unneces-

sary ; for I should not have been passed over.  Most
of the fleet is going away, as there are no Russian
men-of-war left ; I suppose one or two steamers off
the port to cruise will be enough.  The Admiral will
winter in Kasatch Bay.  He and the French one have
offered to carry 60,000 men in the line-of-battle
ships, now become useless.  I expect a horrible job
of arranging and selling off all my things and those
of C., about the end of October or the beginning of
November ; as I cannot believe they will find it possible to compel me to remain here.  You cannot help
me ; but you can understand how awkwardly I am
situated.

---

## LETTER CXX.

Camp, Kamara,
2d October 1855.

OUR position remains the same.  We have not
yet got the order to begin camping for the winter ;
but I believe it is decided that all the Turks here
under Omar Pasha are to go to Asia, and the Highland Division will have the outposts for another
winter.  I hope we may be able to get our men
hutted before the bad weather ; to do that in the
short time which remains will require all our energies.
We hear of successes of General D'Allonville at Eupa-

toria. Would that he had all our cavalry under his command! He would give them a fair chance.

There is news of a party of our 10th Hussars being surprised at Kertsch. Hussars should be all eyes, and those never closed. Personal bravery is only a small part of their requirements. Bentinck has, I understand, got leave to go home: he will never come back, and his departure will make C. second in seniority in the army; but I believe General Panmure has quite settled to improvise a young general after his own beau-ideal. They give us a clasp, in addition to the Crimean medal for Sebastopol: it seems to me this finish ought to have been a separate decoration. How would J. B. like the army in mural crowns? The enemy keeps firing very vigorously across the harbour into the town. The French are trying to repair many of the buildings; but unless the Russians are either driven away, or are so good as to go of their own accord, the place will be untenable. Napoleon, I suspect, thinks they will go, and has hindered Pelissier from attacking them. We have rumours here of an insurrection at St. Petersburg, and the flight of the Emperor to Moscow. The monotony of our state here is so great, that it is impossible to find any thing to make a letter out of. All our men are employed in cutting fascines for a road from Balaklava to the camp on the plateau. We are doing nothing for ourselves, and cannot even drill the young officers and the recruits.

---

## LETTER CXXI.

Camp, Kamara,
5th October 1855.

THE mail has brought in the despatches of General Simpson, relating how we did not take the Redan. I also received for perusal the answer of General Yorke to my last letter, a copy of which I sent you. The gist of it is, that such are the necessary results of selection; with a special serious advice to me to be moderate in my expressions when writing officially. It is indeed difficult so to write that a military complainant shall not become criminal; but I thank my good brains that I can say pretty near what I choose, and yet steer clear of the gripe of the law. The real object should be so to write that injustice may be impossible; there I fail. We shall soon have, I suppose, a fresh batch of promotions; and, perhaps, I may be made a substantive Lieutenant-Colonel, *i. e.* 1*s*. 6*d*. per diem more half-pay. I cannot answer Yorke's last letter, because I should be obliged to throw up my appointment, and I have settled to wait till C. reaches England. The 18,000 Turks under Osman Pasha are all going off to Souk-

houm Kale, and our seven battalions will take up
their ground; that is, cover the right of the Piedmontese, looking towards Sulu and Baidar. The
French, now at the latter place, will return when the
weather breaks up, and we shall have the outposts
as we had last winter, only further advanced. C.
will hut his men, and then go off some time in the
beginning of November. The Russians stop all the
spies from going up on the high ground where their
troops are posted; so that, I believe, we know absolutely nothing of their doings. The French made a
reconnoissance the other day about Aitodor, when
a Russian Division retired before them; that is, I
conclude, gained the strong part of the position.
The Russians, if they can keep the north side during
the winter, will help their diplomacy; that, I judge,
will be their only gain. In the spring they will
infallibly be dislodged, and we shall have the Crimea.
An expedition of, they say, 7000 French and English
is gone to Kinbourn, so as to block up the entrance
to Nicolaieff. The result of the extra 6d. a day
given to our soldiers, with back pay to the amount
of 45s. per man, has been frightful drunkenness.
They are quite incurable, poor fools. Danby Seymour is here sight-seeing; he is going to Asia, and
then to the Danube on his way home. Kinglake
stopped at Marseilles sick. I shall have a weary
time of it when C. goes, while waiting for orders to

pack up and sell off our things. I see by the papers
that Fenton, the photographist, has got his exhibition
up: you will be much interested by it, I should think;
probably he has taken some field of battle, and you
will see the horrid sight in all its gloom. There is no
mistaking a dead body killed in battle for any thing
else ; and a very mysterious and awe-striking object
it is, till habit dulls its terrors. Our weather this
October has turned out much more changeable than
it was last year ; but the men continue very healthy
in spite of their drinking. It is to be hoped that
next winter we shall not have so much maudlin sen-
timent and muffettees, as the goodies in England
favoured us with, under the influence of the newspaper spasmodic efforts to keep up the ball. We are
all hard-worked at road-making, and various preparations to meet the bad weather, which will surely
come in about three weeks. I beg to introduce to
your acquaintance M. Paul Ranguis, a French *libé-
rable*, or one who has served his seven years and
over in the 20<sup>me</sup> de Ligne. He has served fourteen
campaigns, and was present at the sieges of Rome and
of Sebastopol. Instead of embarking for France, he
has preferred becoming my valet ; and a very simple,
obliging, good creature he seems. Seven years, and
never punished ! for a young man and a Frenchman.
His *état* is that of ciergist, his country Gave, near
the Alps. He has enabled me to discharge the last of

my Constantinople Turks, who are an abomination; idle, lying, lazy, grasping thieves, by birth and education. When I leave this army, what shall I do? Curses on their selection system and their aristocracy, which drive me out of my profession for the second time! There is an amount of discontent in this army which must sooner or later bring a revolution in it. Clouds are gathering, only to be dispersed by a storm. We hear that there is to be an exchange of Crosses of the Legion of Honour, for ditto of the Bath: I suppose regulated by diplomacy, and the Legion of Honour issued according to the amount of people's connection with Dukes and Lords of high degree. The Commissariat here are furious; a young ——, who was Commissary to De Lacy Evans, has got promoted clean over the heads of a number of most deserving officers: two have already resigned; they are non-combatants, and can do as they please; but men with families dependent on them are compelled to submit to the indignity. I am much puzzled and perplexed.

## LETTER CXXII.

Camp, Kamara,
8th October 1855.

OUR division is now busy preparing the ground for their huts; but now to-day there has arrived an order stating how much, or rather how little, the soldiers are to carry in case of their being called upon to move in light marching order. The expedition to Kinbourn or elsewhere is embarked. I do not think it will come to any thing; the fort is on a tongue of land, and is frozen up in winter, so that the garrison could not be reached by us, and would be exposed to the attack of the Russians, who understand sledges, and who are fully equipped for winter campaigning. The next post which reaches you will, I suppose, bring you my account of the assault, and of our disgraceful failure. I have heard to-day, from good authority, that ———— has been refused his promotion, as well as myself; and that he means to go home as soon as it is certain nothing more can be done this autumn. You know my plans. I am now so situated, having held out a threat of resigning, that even if I repented of it, I could not well avoid taking the leap. It distresses me very much; but I am certain it is becoming to go. Perhaps it may prevent some one else from being unjustly treated. We know nothing of the Russians; but I see the French are disposed to press them from Baidar, in the Aitodor direction. As there cannot be more than about three weeks of tolerable weather, we shall soon know our fate. I do not expect C. will go till the middle of November. I shall not hear from him till the middle of December; so that I shall have plenty of bad weather to meet before I can go. I am very sad and put out at this affair.

---

## LETTER CXXIII.

Camp, Kamara,
12th October 1855.

THE mail has come, but it has not yet reached this excrescence of the British camp. The rumour has come, however, that Windham has been made a Major-General. He showed plenty of courage, and his want of knowledge of the profession cannot be considered glaring, with the example of his superior officers staring us in the face. His having begun in the Guards gave him early rank, and the chance of commanding a brigade on this occasion. Bentinck goes to-morrow. One of his brigades is gone in the expedition to Kinbourn; the other, which Windham commanded, being now vacant (Windham is commandant of Sebastopol), is given to Lord William Paulet, who has been all this time at Scutari. He

will have Bentinck's division.   We are exerting every
energy to get up huts for our division,—riding and
routing about from Kamara Church to Balaklava,—
one set of officers and men preparing the ground,
others sorting the huts, and others urging on the
Tartar carts, here called arabas.   We literally catch
Tartars, and keep them with a guard.  They are paid,
and get rations.   Besides sending our men to load
them at Balaklava, we have two relays of 1000 men
each, who carry pieces of the huts on their shoulders,
from Balaklava to the camp, about four miles.   The
moment the rain begins, all this will be stopped ; the
huts will have to go by the rail up to the front, and
come down the Woronzow Road, a tremendous round.
We have determined, if energetic exertion will do it,
to get up all our huts before the end of this month.
I shall take a pride in this my last military duty, in
hutting the Division before any other one, notwithstanding they all have the rail except ourselves.   As
soon as all the huts are up, C. will, I suppose, go
away.   Bentinck being gone, C. is next in seniority to Simpson ; so that something remains for the
chapter of accidents.   If Simpson were taken suddenly worse, and forced to go, Lord Panmure would
be in a predicament.   Markham sick at home ;
Codrington covered, not with glory ; there is still
Eyre to put in command over C.  Lord Grey thinks
highly of him, and, I suppose, has some influence.

Still, chance and a fit of illness might, by possibility, place the best officer in the army at its head. You are to understand that S. often differs with C. about his plans; but no one I have seen can hold a candle to the latter as an officer; he is quite above all intrigue, and scorns meanness and idleness and shirking so fiercely and so openly, that all our fine highly-connected people both hate and fear him; he is also the man to make Lord Panmure afraid. If he were Commander-in-Chief, I am convinced he would not submit to manage his army under the dictation of the electric wires from the War-Office. It is reported that a message has come, beginning "Woe, woe," to all the Head-quarter Staff, if the army suffers this winter from the want of roads, or of any thing else. We have no information about the Russians. Our spies cannot get up on the plateau at Mackenzie's Farm; but I have no notion they mean to retire; nothing short of another army landed behind them can compel them to such a step. Another Battle of Alma fought in spring would do it; but speculation is vain. So many heads, so many secret cords pulled in different directions, leave our fate in a great measure to be decided by some accident; with which sad and too true conviction I bid you farewell.

## LETTER CXXIV.

Camp, Kamara,
15th October 1855.

WE have been excessively busy since we got the order to encamp here, in carrying up huts for winter barracks. The distance is not much less than five miles ; so you may fancy it is a job to carry hutting enough for 5000 men.

We have hired country-carts out here, and 1000 men go down every morning to load these carts. They then load themselves. The men carry their loads half-way, and are there met by another 1000, who bring the huts into camp. Then all the pieces are classified, and laid out in bundles for issuing ; meantime other men are levelling the ground, making roads, &c. I hope, if we work steadily, we may have the men hutted by the end of this month. On Saturday last, we got a sudden order to embark the Division and two batteries for Eupatoria, to act on the enemy's lines of communication.

This would have made our hutting impossible before the winter, and we should have had our old mud and misery.

To-day this expedition has been countermanded, partly because it was found that shipping would not be ready for some time to carry the 3700 animals necessary for our baggage and ammunition, and partly because Simpson has just had a message from Lord Stratford de Redcliffe, to the effect that he has heard from Berlin, that the Russians intended to hazard another battle. To tell you the truth, I do not think they will; but it is as well to be prepared. While it was thought we were going, a small discussion arose as to who would be in command, whether General d'Allonville or C.

In your letter to me, you speak of the trenches being crowded, as a fault of Simpson's. These crowds ought to have rushed out. In making a fresh assault, it would have been necessary to withdraw the first, which had been employed, and their reserves, before we could get our men into the advanced trenches.

Simpson's great fault, since he could not manage the details himself, was, to give the arrangements for the assault to an inexperienced man like Codrington. General Wetherall's son, who was a Captain in the Royals, is going to be made Quarter-Master General. The first thing he got was an appointment to the Guards, then a brevet Majority, then a Lieutenant-Colonelcy, then local rank of full Colonel, and Quarter-Master General to the Turkish Contingent. General Freeth, who is Quarter-Master General at the Horse Guards, is going to give up; and Airey gets that patent appointment. Colonel the Honourable A. Gordon, who began as Assistant Adjutant-General

G G

to the 1st Division, is made deputy Quarter-Master General at the Horse Guards. Great luck some people have, to be sure !

---

### LETTER CXXV.*

*To the Editor of the* Times.

Camp, Kamara,
19th October 1855.

Sir,—I have read with amazement a leading article in the *Times* of the 4th October, on the subject of the command of this army. The paragraph I wish to remark upon, is as follows; and I have italicised the parts I mean to touch upon : " A single year of warfare has disposed of the whole of these veterans, with the exception of *Sir Colin Campbell, who has been laid up in lavender all the winter with his Highlanders,* and whose military talents, if we may judge of them by *his exploits in the Punjab,* do not entitle him to aspire to a great command. We

---

* This Letter was published in the *Times* of Tuesday, November 13th, 1855. I think it just to the responsible Editor of the *Times* that I should state, that when the attack on Sir C. Campbell appeared, he was travelling in the Pyrenees; and that I have reason to know, that he was very sorry when he saw what his *locum tenens* had done. A. C. S.

have seen the result of sending a young army into the field almost entirely led by old chiefs, who owed their rank to seniority and brevet promotion; the best of them, however, have either fallen in battle, or sunk under disease; and those who remain are mere *obstructions to the real strength of the army.*"

The first assertion here is, that Sir Colin Campbell and his Highlanders were laid up in lavender during the winter. As I also was in lavender with them, I have better reason than the writer of this article to know what the fact was as to our comforts. The three regiments, the 42d, the 79th, and 93d, were united in front of Balaklava on the day after the so-called action of Balaklava. Their business was, aided by the Brigade of Royal Marines, consisting of some 1200 men, and several thousands of the poor Turks, who were driven out of the redoubts on the day of Balaklava, and who nearly all died during the winter of the cold and hardship, which the sturdy Scotchmen endured without a murmur, under the cheerful, noble, generous leading of Sir Colin Campbell;—their business, I say, was to finish the works on the heights, and to construct trenches, in mud and frost and snow; and when made, to guard them. The guarding consisted in the whole of the soldiers being fully accoutred all night and every night; one half of them lay every night in the trenches, and the other half in the muddy tents, from the 25th October to the 6th December, when the Russians retired across the Chernaya.

During this period, and for many weeks afterwards, they were never dry. Immediately on the enemy's retreat, the fatigue-parties to the front began ; on which subject I beg to introduce an extract of a letter written by Sir Colin Campbell to Major General Airey, dated January 29th, 1855 :

"During the last eight weeks the European troops under my command have been employed on fatigue to a very great extent. When I understood from the Artillery Officers here, that the progress of the siege would be assisted by my doing so, I employed of my own accord, and without any order, all the available soldiers in carrying to the park the following ordnance stores, besides a quantity of shot and shell, of which I have no account: viz.

| | |
|---|---|
| 33 platforms of 60 pieces, being a load for . | 3960 men. |
| 120 large platform sleepers . . . . | 1200 ,, |
| Iron shoes for platforms, in 90 packets . . | 90 ,, |
| 450 pickaxes . . . . . . . | 220 ,, |
| About 60 fascines . . . . . . | 120 ,, |
| About 30 cwt. of coals for platform stoves, &c. | 1236 ,, |
| | 6826 |

"Besides which, these men have carried to Lord Raglan's house nearly 4000 bags of biscuit, being above thirteen days' consumption for 25,000 men. Frequently 1300 Europeans, and from 300 to 500

Turks, have been thus employed. At the same time the troops had to carry up from Balaklava the whole of their rations, their regimental transport having been taken from them by the A. Q. M. G. of the 1st Division, and their public animals by the Commissary, the latter for the purpose of carrying the rations of the 1st Brigade of the 1st Division. During these fatigues, there frequently remained to protect the position merely the ordinary day guards and the cooks: these fatigues usually lasted from seven to eight hours daily, during which time the men were mid-leg in mud."

Until the 6th December, the small British force in the lines of Balaklava had 18 battalions of Russian infantry, and 24 guns in position, close overhanging them, and threatening an attack at any moment. The vigilance, the energy, and judgment displayed all this time by Sir Colin Campbell will be long remembered by those who witnessed the exhibition. That officer during the winter exposed himself to more cold and hardship than all the other Generals in the army and all their Staff-officers put together : always on parade, with all his officers and men, in rain and mud, before daylight, he slept in his clothes regularly for eight months ; and this is the lavender you write about.

The next point is a reference to Sir Colin Campbell's exploits in the Punjab, which can be called nothing but a depreciatory one, since the deduction drawn is, that they did not entitle him to a great command. I should like to know what does entitle a man to a great command? See Sir C. Napier's despatches, where he speaks of Sir Colin. The latter, when he left India, brought with him letters from Lord Dalhousie, containing the highest possible encomiums on his whole military conduct in the Punjab. His leading of the 61st Regiment at the battle of Chillianwallah decided the action and saved the British Army: the feat of this regiment on that day, under Sir Colin Campbell's leadership, was pronounced by the Duke of Wellington, as may be seen in his Grace's letter, preserved in the Orderly-room 61st Regiment, to have been one of the most brilliant exploits ever performed by the English Army. Sir Colin Campbell resigned the lucrative employment which he held at Peshawer, because he would not allow the Governor-General's political agents to dictate to him how he should fight; and the Governor-General preferred losing his services, which he acknowledged in the most flattering terms, rather than have an independent man fighting the battles of England with an energy and skill equalled by none, except Sir C. Napier. In Hart's Army List there are recorded some parts of Sir Colin's exploits; his early ones in the Peninsula may well be called so, as he commanded the storming party at Saint Sebastian's, and was twice wounded in the breach : but it is the fashion now to laugh at Peninsular heroes. Sir Colin commanded in India, and with constant success, against the enemy, from five to six batteries, as many cavalry regiments, and up to fourteen battalions ; besides which, at one time, he also held command of the Punjab Division, consisting of 54,000 men of all arms.

The third point is the sentence about old chiefs, who owe their rank to seniority and brevet promotion. It so happens, that Sir Colin was promoted to a company out of his regiment for distinguished conduct ; that he purchased his regimental Majority over another officer's head, and also purchased an unattached Lieutenant-Colonelcy ; his rank of Colonel he got by being made Queen's A. D. C., for his service in China ; and he was selected to be a Brigadier-General in this army on its formation. So that he never got a single step either by brevet or seniority.

The last point is the accusation implied of being a mere obstruction to the real strength of the army. This is very curious. I do not believe there are many men in the army who could outrun him now; and not one who could outride him, or endure more fatigue.

With all this great experience and practice in war, joined to a wonderful physical vigour, an untiring energy and will, a care and providence for his men not to be surpassed,—it seems to me that if any man could be selected more fit than another to command this army, that man is Sir Colin Campbell.

It is not a command to be wished for by a wise man, considering the tenure on which it must be held; it is the last thing which any friend of Sir Colin's would wish to see him accept: but that is no reason for allowing him to be assailed in your columns without a reply.

If you really have the honest wish to keep the English nation well informed as to facts concerning the officers out here, you will publish this letter. I pledge my honour to the truth, or to my belief in the truth, of them; and few people have better means of getting at the truth than I have had in this case. I have to assure you, that Sir C. Campbell has not seen this letter, nor does he know I am writing it.

I have the honour to be, Sir, &c.

(Signed)     A. C. STERLING, Lieut.-Col.,
Assistant Adjutant-General Highland Division.

## LETTER CXXVI.

Camp, Kamara,
22d October 1855.

THE *Morning Post* goes a little too far. My peak is very well; it was only a knock, not a knock

off. The curious of England seem to think it so odd
if a shot comes near any acquaintance. I only remarked, "That is a close shave;"—but bullets come
quite as close without touching, and one knows nothing about it. To call a peak of a cap shot off
shocking! What was shocking, I have described,
viz.: that the honour of England should have been
left in such hands, and that it should still be left
there. The people of England have given us up to
the Press; why does not the Press protect us? We
have a new hero set up now, Major-General Windham of the Guards, whose experience was limited to
what could be acquired in command of a company
of that corps. He came out of the Redan to ask for
supports. If he had had any experience, he would
have known that his leaving the spot would have
been, as it was, the signal for all the rest to follow.
An officer ought to stay with his men, and die with
his men. The Duke of Wellington once met an
officer, commanding a regiment which was engaged,
going to the rear for ammunition. He never would
see him again, and sent him back to Lisbon. All
the officers who were wounded did as well as Windham, with the exception of getting back unhurt. You
ask what the Redan is like, and what are traverses.
The inside of the Redan, when I saw it last, was filled
with broken gun-carriages, and strewed with dead men
and firelocks and clothes. Standing on the parapet,

you looked down on a deck, as you would standing
on a frigate's hammock nettings. Assaulting the
Redan was very much like boarding a frigate from
boats. A traverse is a mound of earth, usually about
seven feet high, joined at one end to the parapet of
the work. One use of it is, to get behind, or at that
side of it on which the shell about to burst has not
fallen; it is a protection to guns and to men against
shot falling into a work. I believe it was originally
invented to prevent ricochetting shot from dismounting guns; the shots stuck in the traverse, and there
remained. If I had nothing else to do than to write
about these warlike scenes, I dare say I could do it
well enough; but I have no time I can call my own,
and no newspaper would publish me. I am sure no
newspaper, or man in England, has had so much
truth written to them on this Crimean business as
has come from me to you. I doubt not at all, that a
bookmaker would construct a good article out of my
Letters.

---

## LETTER CXXVII.

Camp, Kamara,
27th October 1855.

WE continue working away, getting up huts; the
completion of which job, and the commencement of
the rains, will be the signal for our Hegira. We have

vague rumours of an intended promotion, founded on certain lists, which were called for by Simpson, from each General of Division. The *Times*, I observe, has begun to be satirical at the number of officers of the Guards, who have urgent private affairs. Poor young men! they have been accustomed all their lives to receive a certain portion of leave per annum.

------

## LETTER CXXVIII.

Camp, Kamara,
30th October 1855.

I HAVE moved myself into our new camp, about half a mile east of the old one, and have put up a wooden hut, which for the present I am occupying, while I am engaged in preparing the other huts and conveniences, in the way of kitchen, stables, &c., necessary for the *entourage* of a General Officer. The situation of the hut I am in, which is intended for C., is very beautiful, although exposed to all winds; it is surrounded by a gabionade, to keep off the blasts. Almost touching the hut, there is a very, very small chapel, with its wee cupola and cross; the inside of it is not more than six feet square. Who knows if we shall ever occupy these huts, which I am labouring at? It is certain that Simpson has sent in his resignation ; and the command may be offered to C. in such a manner that he will not be able to refuse it. The objections to his taking it are these : he was first damaged by Lord Raglan, who took the troops he had formed, and sent them to Kertsch under command of a junior officer, Sir John Campbell ; it afterwards became known in the army, that it had been intended to place first Codrington, and then Markham, in command over him. Codrington has swamped himself, I should think ; and Markham is gone home sick. Were the command now conferred on C., he would not be placed there in a fair position, but merely stuck in as a *pis aller*, which he does not choose to be. So that, I imagine, the resignation of Simpson will hurry C. in his own departure, as it is to be hoped we shall have all our men under cover in about ten days. On the other hand, if C. be compelled to assume the command, I am sure he will not submit for a moment to insolent messages from ——.

## LETTER CXXIX.

Camp, Kamara,
2d November 1855.

I HAVE applied for leave of absence, which I believe I am to obtain ; this is the first step to my resignation : once away, they cannot put their finger

on me again. C. goes off to-morrow : he will go
direct to London, and place his resignation in Hardinge's hands. We expect every day to hear the name
of Simpson's successor ; it might chance to be C., but
I do not believe it. He goes away to avoid the un-
pleasantness of having a junior officer put over his
head. If he were himself the man, I should remain
as his Military Secretary. I cannot take any appointment from the Horse Guards, after the way I have
been used ; and I am fairly driven out of the profession. There is good reason for believing that there
is a gazette of promotion on the tapis ; meantime the
army is undisciplined, and wants a General ; and a
precious job he will have of it. The probabilities are,
that I shall leave this place for Constantinople on
to-morrow week, the 10th November ; but I do not
know what I am going to do afterwards, feeling in a
sort of maze. All the things have to be sold off,
which is a troublesome affair. I deeply grieve at
leaving the army. All the old officers will go, who
have any spirit, and who are so treated : let us hope
the young ones are deserving of the way in which
they are pushed on, and that their great merits will
fully make up for the loss of the experienced people
who are expelled.

5th November.

I cannot tell you how much I regret leaving these
Highland soldiers, with whom I have been serving so

long ; they are so entirely different, and so superior, to any of the other Divisions, from the way in which they have been managed by C. ; there is that put into them, which will make the reputation of whatever officer has the good fortune to command them, when matters look murky ! Ah, me ! I am sick, and belong to the *classe dangereuse*. What else can an officer be, used as I have been? I declare I only wonder my brain is still sound.

---

## LETTER CXXX.

Camp, Kamara,
Monday, 5th November 1855.

I HAVE got my leave. C. sailed on Saturday ; I shall do so on Saturday next, for Constantinople and Malta. The weather, which has been very windy, is now beautiful again ; and I hope may continue so, at least till Wednesday, when my sale will take place. Regret at the departure of C. seems universal. We have, as yet, no news of the relieving General-in-Chief. It is expected hourly ; meantime a Russian Officer has deserted, and declares they are going to do something on the 7th : either to attack us or to retire. I do not believe a word of either. As I shall not embark till Friday at soonest, I shall have positive information on this point. The list is now to be made of things for my auction; such a collection of odds and ends, that I have been carrying about with me. Infinite trouble, but which is now at an end. Baggage is a great impediment ; and all the soldier servants seem to think, that the moment they come to a Staff-officer, they are also to carry baggage, which goes to load his mules. I am very sad and provoked, and know not where to go, nor what to do.

## LETTER CXXXI.

Malta, 20th November 1855.

AFTER a tedious voyage, I landed here yesterday. I find papers to the 11th ; and I see that I am made a substantive Lieutenant-Colonel, which they will pretend is according to the warrant : whereas the warrant says, if an officer shall have received brevet rank for distinguished service, he may afterwards be made substantive. Now I have not had any brevet rank conferred upon me, while —— is made a Colonel. On what pretence I am not to be promoted, is more than I can understand. The *Times*, I perceive, says, C. will be an irreparable loss. It is a pity they did not find that out sooner. The Editor then proceeds to objurgate him for not serving under a junior officer, ignoring the fact that Malta had been offered to him. It is not mentioned in the papers how Molesworth is to be replaced. Just as he had worked himself to the top of his profession, to be carried off, is a kind stroke of fate. No disappointments for him any more.

## LETTER CXXXII.

Malta, 29th November 1855.

I have been very much complimented here by many officers, on the score of my vindication of my chief. I do not think General Pennefather likes it; as I asserted that C. endured more hardships than any of the other Generals.

A letter from C. is just come, dated London. Lord Panmure had written to him on the 22d October, making an appeal to his patriotism of the strongest nature, so far as words go, to induce him to accept command under Codrington. Lord Panmure told him to take a copy of the letter with him, and make known his decision to Lord Hardinge for his information. C. then saw Lord Hardinge, and told him, neither the request of Lord Panmure nor of the whole body of Ministers would make him accede to this proposition. He is invited to Windsor on the 20th; if her Majesty asks him, I fear he cannot refuse, and I must follow his lead. The intention is to make him Commander of a Corps d'Armée of three Divisions. A mail from England is expected to-morrow,

bringing six days' later news. If C. is induced to
accept, I must go to England to get another fit-out,
all my things having been sold. "Jacob Omnium"
judged quite right in cutting out any parts of my
Letter which were offensive to the Editor of the
*Times;* the main point being to put C. right in the
same paper which traduced him. I hope they will not
meddle with us any more: " Nemo me impune la-
cessit." The explanation in Parliament for the necessity of putting Codrington over C. will be rather
curious. If he consents to serve, after being super-
seded by a junior officer, no one can doubt that I am
justified in doing so likewise, although it goes against
the grain. I am not surprised at your appreciation
of ——'s goodness, which I can believe in without
reading his book. Goodness, I think, is never without
some sort of talent; and clever people are always
good, so to speak : when they are bad, it is a mistake.
Fools are the only all-wicked; from them may the
Devil deliver me ! I am principally alluding to those
with the army; any where else I can keep them at
arm's-length, and the Devil as well. Most probably
the steamer which carries this letter will carry me ;
for I have a strong persuasion that the Queen will
persuade C., who will not say no to a woman, still
less to his Queen. Did I tell you Pelissier's last,
when he heard C. was gone ? " Je ne vois jamais cet
homme sans avoir envie de l'embrasser." Also, his

H H

getting hold of one of my French notes to Vinoy, and carrying it off as an autograph, it being signed C. C. Then I find it reported that he could not get on with the French.　Vinoy's remark was, " Ils renvoyent leur meilleur général, et leur plus brave soldat." The Spartans would have sent him their most beautiful maidens, to produce more Colins.　My own feeling now about our army is, that it is in a helpless state.　The General's first combat will be with his own officers.　I have therefore, independent of feeling that I have entered into a *lutte* in which I have been unsuccessful, a strong fear of further disaster and disgrace, from the incompetence of the selected.

2d December.

The mail is in up to the 26th, and brings a short letter from C.　The Queen proposed that he should return, in such a manner that he could not refuse. I am truly sorry; it puts him altogether in a false position.　It also deprives me of the power of retiring; for it may fairly be remarked, " If C. serves after having Codrington put over his head, you can have no pretence to refuse doing the same."　I am much vexed on account of C.　They first put the Court favourites at the top, and then employ the Queen to make the good officers serve under them; it is a shame of the first water.　I should think C. must be deeply disgusted; and I can scarcely believe so unnatural an arrangement will work for any time.

# EXTRACTS FROM LETTERS

AFTER MY RETURN TO THE CRIMEA.

---

Camp, Kamara,
17th February 1856.

THE old date ! how odd it seems !  We dined with the Ambassador at Constantinople, and I admired his house, which was built for him by the British Government.  I hear that Sir H. Seymour had been reprimanded from home for having allowed the Austrian propositions to be sent off with his signature, although the fifth article was not defined, and the Austrians were required to recall the document, which they objected to do, and began to threaten ; whereupon Lord Clarendon wrote a capital despatch, intimating that Great Britain would not be threatened at any price ; so I suppose the possibility of a hitch in the negotiation is still extant.  In truth, the question of peace or war turns upon the interior wish, or rather necessity, of Russia for peace.  Matters are very disgusting out here.  C. left England after receiving a clear intimation that he was to command a corps d'armée.  When he arrived in the Crimea, he found that no arrangements had been made to form a corps, and that Codrington was opposed to the system of corps; also, that Commander was disposed to leave C. in the air, with no command at all, till it should be seen whether it was to be peace or war. However, it was represented that his position by such a scheme would be a false one. He is now in orders to command a corps, the divisions to be named hereafter. This he also objects to ; and I believe the Highland Division is to be put in orders as part of his corps. The ostensible reasons put forward by Codrington are military ; but it is to be surmised that he does not wish to name divisions, because he could scarcely take them away again, which might interfere with comfortable arrangements for influential parties. If peace be made, I imagine C. will ask to go home immediately ; and I cannot think Codrington will wish to keep him. If it be war, we ought to go to Asia ; and a most difficult and formidable war it will be. I estimate two years as a period requisite to get a British army, with its supplies, from Trebizonde to Erzerum. It will be necessary to make roads, and form depots of provisions all along the road. However, I believe in peace, and expect to be home immediately.

22d February 1856.

Yours of the 8th is come, and I have papers of the 9th. As to politics, really do I care much about them ? Airey is coming here directly; most probably to collect facts for his defence. I cannot admit that when he found the Commissary could not, or would not, comply with his request, he was absolved. He ought to have then, *de son chef*, commenced some operation to procure the needful; besides, I do not think they pushed the Commissary half enough. Airey has now a patent office for life. What can they do to him ? It will all end in newspaper attacks, of which I see a severe one in the *Times*. You speak highly of Ruskin's remarks on the war. I suppose he knows nothing about war; I do know war, and I hate it; but I hate tyranny more, and would fight against that any day. As to my respect for the Russian Government, I only think it good for Russia, not for England, although Cromwell's despotism did very well there.

28th February 1856.

My cold is getting better. We have had some very heavy snow-storms; but I trust it is over now, and that fine weather will soon begin. I wrote explaining that our corps is not yet formed, and that at present I have a sinecure. We have heard privately that the Military Conference advises to attack by Eupatoria, which, as I remember, was always my plan. If peace be not made, we shall no doubt have a force to hold this position, and move some 60,000 men to Eupatoria, and direct their march upon Simpheropol. The result of which march must be, that the Russians on the north side of Sebastopol, for fear of being cut off, will retire on Simpheropol, and give us battle. The press and the public seem at last to have got their victim. A storm has burst upon Airey, which might sink any one. With Gordon they have nothing to do ; for he was a subordinate, and has been ill-advised in writing a letter. It is not every one who is capable of entering the arena with success against the regular gladiator. Lord Raglan was responsible for the appointment of Airey, as well as for that of his predecessor. In spite of the observations of the *Times*, I assert that the misery of the army generally was exaggerated. What misery there did exist, might no doubt have been diminished by men of more experience.

3d March 1856.

We have a sort of horrid day, not absolutely a down-pour of rain, but cloudy, windy, threatening, and snow still on the hills. *Hiawatha* I have not read. In truth, Longfellow is rather milky-watery for me, and is the very stuff for those who think Shelley no poet. Lucan's answer seems to clear him : he is a man of considerable ability ; but Cardigan was thought to be a favourite of Lord Raglan's. His Lordship always seemed disposed to put him in an unfair position towards Lord Lucan. I understand there is to be a Board of General Officers in Airey's case.

Some parts of the accusation against him he will dispose of, and, in the general scuffle, he will, I dare say, retain his place. Our armistice is still under negotiation; and I have full belief in an almost certain peace. The Russian officers, who came to meet ours, rode horses which seemed nearly starved; and I suspect those on the bleak Mackenzie heights must have been very badly off for more than forage. If we are disappointed in the terms of peace, depend upon it the Russians do not like them either. We cannot help it. The French and Russians being determined on stopping the affair, what can we do? You are quite right in doubting Rogers's wonderful wit. He was well placed to please many people, by entertaining, giving money, and saying ill-natured things. I am now in the possession of a perfect sinecure, which, with my intense activity, you may suppose, is no great catch. To-morrow, if the weather be tolerable, I am going, with C. and Vinoy, to breakfast with Marshal Pelissier, of which repast I shall send you an account.

7th March 1856.

Last night it rained, and now it is snowing again. My cold, however, is quite gone, in spite of feeling very cold in my feet and hands; this hut is so wretchedly thin, and full of splits. I do not consider it at all fair: last year we had no snow after the 20th February; it cannot, I trust, last very long now, as the sun has so much power. Our breakfast yester-dry with Marshal Pelissier did not take place ; the weather was so desperate, that we thought it out of the question. We gave our first dinner to-day to some officers, ten in number ; quite an undertaking with so few appliances. This peace we still have no news of ; you probably know by this time whether it is to be, or not to be. We have, however, the armis-tice, and are not allowed to go beyond the aqueduct. The engineers are tracing lines all round Balaklava, both east and west ; I believe this is only in anticipa-tion of no peace, to allow us to embark behind them, and enable the rear-guard to defend itself for forty-eight hours. I have been struck by the extreme bad English written by Codrington, with a good deal of ambitious attempt, too, at fine writing.

*12th March 1856.*

We are much amused by the Government trying their own commission before a court-martial. I see Roebuck proposes a resolution on the subject. He can scarcely hope to carry it, as that would upset the Ministry, who are safe from that event till peace be made. To-morrow our breakfast with Pelissier comes off. The weather has completely taken up, and is now most agreeable. I send a copy of a letter ; pro-bably Codrington would find it rather flat, after his own high-seasoned performances.

*General Sir Colin Campbell to the Editor of the*
Morning Chronicle.

Camp, Kamara, Crimea,
11th March 1856.

SIR,—I received yesterday, from Major-General Lord Rokeby, commanding the first Division, a printed slip, cut out of a newspaper, headed " Highlanders in the Crimea ;" " Sir Colin Campbell ;" dated Sebastopol, 3d February, and stated to be from "the Correspondent of the *Morning Chronicle*." As I am sure you would not willingly circulate unfounded statements, I have concluded that you will be glad of the opportunity of contradicting the assertions of the person who wrote the passages upon which I am about to remark. "When the Guards and Highlanders were brigaded together, Sir Colin, on more than one occasion, in his usual midnight inspection, found the Guards still under canvas ; and on those occasions he usually muttered forth his angry malediction in these, or something like these, terms : 'Oot on you, ye lazy Guards ! nae wonder ye wur surprised and licked at Inkermann.' I have to state that it is not true that I made *usual* midnight inspections ; I doubt if I ever made one midnight inspection. It is not true that I ever found the Guards under canvas when they ought to have been under arms. And the sentence in broad Scotch, imputed to me, bears its own evidence of falsehood; for I do not know how to speak broad Scotch, and I am told I have not even a Scotch accent; however, in Scotch or in English, I never said any thing of the kind. The Guards were quite as vigilant and as ready to turn out, when under my command, as any of the Highland Regiments. Your correspondent goes on to assert, that I was offered my choice between the command of the Guards and that of the Highlanders. This is not true; I never was offered any such choice. He gives an account of my reception by her Majesty: "How he was honoured by leading-in the Princess Royal; how the royal piper was stationed behind his chair at dinner;" and how, above all, "after dinner, the Queen summoned him to sit by her side on the sofa." I had not the honour of leading-in the Princess Royal; the royal piper was not stationed behind my chair at dinner; and her Majesty did not summon me to sit by her side on the sofa. Whether the person who wrote this account intended to injure me, I cannot tell; but I do feel that there may be many people not acquainted with me who might believe these idle and impertinent stories, the truth of which I emphatically repudiate.

(Signed)     C. CAMPBELL, General.

14th March 1856.

Yesterday we rode to General Vinoy's, picked him up, and then went on to the French head-quarters to breakfast with the Marshal. He has a large salon of reception, besides a great dining-room. The breakfast was funny: at 10 A.M. soup, then a turbot, then three or four dishes of meat, then vegetables, then *foie gras* and cheese, with claret and champagne. Marshal Pelissier is a little fat man, his hair snow-white and cut close to half an inch, eyebrows black, moustache and beard grizzled, sharp penetrating eyes, one smaller than the other, a great look of strong sense, perfect determination, a commander all over, considerable processes over the eyes, rather receding forehead. All about him seemed afraid of him, as he launched slight sarcasms in a low voice. The conversation did not become general till the *foie gras*, when I began to explain to my neighbour, that our philanthropic companies would prosecute people who made *foie gras*, for cruelty to animals. Pelissier pricked up his ears, and he began to compare the propriety of using geese so with that of fattening beeves, &c. &c.; he denied the cruelty: he said that when he was à young officer he was quartered at Strasburg; " he had an apartment—no, not an apartment, he was too poor to have an apartment, but a *chambre—chez une veuve* who reared geese for their livers." He said " they were only shut up in a small court, and *bourrés* with food *comme des ogres ;* in fact," said he, " the flesh of these geese is not so good as that of geese who are not destined to make *pâtés ;* and thus the poor profit, and buy their carcases, minus the liver, at a cheap rate." "So," I said, " we may deduce from that fact, that it becomes a charitable duty to eat *foie gras ;*" which finished the talk with a general laugh. It appears there were certain points in the armistice which were not agreed upon, and which were referred by the Russians. They have all been conceded ; and it is to be signed to-day at Traktir Bridge ; and I mean to be present, as there may be something to relate. Our position here, with respect to Codrington, continues very unpleasant. The officers named for the Commission are well selected. I dare say they will make a very fair and good report.* Lord Seaton is quite incapable of doing any thing dirty, and he has very good sense ; and General Peel is a man of perfect honour, and extremely shrewd.

17th March 1856.

On the 14th, I went to meet the Russians at Traktir Bridge : about twenty Russian officers came, in all sorts of uniforms ; all speaking French, many of them English. The escort was a small party of Don Cossacks, and some red Cossacks of the Em-

---

* Lord Seaton did not sit.

peror's Guard. The officers crossed the bridge, and
came to where there were two tents pitched ; one for
the three chiefs of the Staff—Windham, Martimpret,
and Timacheff—who were to sign. It was very odd
to find Russians, French, Sardinians, and English, all
mixed up together, smoking, and drinking champagne,
close to the spot where, last August, I saw many
hundred Russian corpses buried. The Russians were
very polite. On the hill just behind us a large collection of French soldiers made a capital background to
the picture. Yesterday I rode down to Traktir, and
from thence all along the valley of the Chernaya,
which river is now our boundary, keeping close to the
aqueduct. This course brought me by a long march
to the head of the harbour : the rocky cliffs at Inkermann, and on both sides of the river near the mouth,
are all perforated with caves, mostly natural, which
have been improved by stone walls, and even in some
places with ornamental architecture. Here, I have
heard, the poor old ancient Tartars used to dwell in
the good times of the Khans. Following on by the
margin of the harbour, and winding along its inlets,
there runs the dry canal, or aqueduct, which used to
give water to the town and shipping. This aqueduct
now does duty in some places for a road, and by it
and baddish pathways I rode clean into Sebastopol.
In many places before I came to the head of the
harbour, I saw small spots covered with remains of

uniforms, and human bones loosely scattered about, relics of dead and mortally-wounded Russians, left there in their retreat after the Battle of Inkermann. The weather here is now fine, but very cold; a bright sun and north wind. It freezes hard every night; my ink is now of the consistence of ice-cream; and a wood fire in my small stove seems to do nothing to raise the temperature of the hut, which is all full of yawning cracks, besides being made of very thin boards. It is impossible to believe that such severe weather can last much longer.

19th March 1856.

We remain still suspended here, with nothing to do but to shiver at the cold. The frost continues as intense as ever; at night the thermometer goes down to 14° Fahrenheit; by day a shamefully bright and impertinent sun, with a cutting north wind direct from the steppes, without an atom of caloric left in it. As to Sir De Lacy Evans, of whom you write, I see he has made an apology, which was quite right, if he thought he had said any thing which was incorrect. Many people may think the advice to Lord Raglan to change his position was sound. Evans denies *in toto* that he proposed embarking, and leaving guns, &c. The event proves nothing; and at last Lord Raglan was forced to tell Pelissier or Canrobert that if he did not take part of the English trenches, he (Lord R.) would be obliged to raise the siege. That

was in truth a change of position on the part of the
English.   As to the Military Commission, you are to
understand that military officers are never severe in
their decision upon other officers, unless some dis-
honourable action is proved against them.   Incompetence is no crime ; the crime is, to place incompetent men in critical positions ; they do not place
themselves there.   The honest verdict should run :
" These officers do not all appear to have been good
selections for the posts they filled ; perhaps they may,
nevertheless, have been the best that could be made
at the time.   They have erred, if at all, out of ignorance, and they did all they thought they were
empowered to do.   Where fault may be found with
them, that blame should fall on the shoulders of the
person who appointed them ; we do not know who
that was."   Whether the generals will have the courage and the wit to say this, we shall see.   Colonel
Gordon was an exceedingly hard-working and anxious
man ; his manner was very disagreeable, and often
almost insulting, and he was disliked accordingly ;
but he was not head of a department, and if that
head did not find fault with him, no one else had a
right to do so.   He was mistaken in writing that
letter to the *Times*.   I see it is said that Milnes is
to be a peer.   Lord Dicky will be very happy; and all
his friends, and he has many, will be glad to see him
happy.   I ought, if I was wise, to go out and ride ;

but I have no duty, and the wind is so cold, that I cannot make up my mind to face it. They have Crimean games on the plateau, which will go on without my presence. All the flowers which were coming out are nipped and gone, and I suppose the crocusses cannot bloom twice, however unreasonable the weather is.

Easter Monday, 23d March 1856.

I got your letter of the 6th just now. It was put into my hands about a quarter of an hour after my hut, with most of its contents, had been burned down. I left the habitation apparently all right at nine o'clock A.M., and went to breakfast in the next one. At ten o'clock, flames burst out, with no cause that I can suggest, and the wretched concern in about ten minutes was consumed with fire. Some of my things are saved, but many small odds and ends are gone " where the good niggers go." When I saw no one would be burned, I took heart of grace, and laughed immensely at the ridiculous scene. " So fiddled Nero when his Rome was burned." My bed is ashes ; my good sword, unlike his master, has lost his temper ; my few remaining cigars are dissolved into the elements ; all my boots are gone ; my favourite old dressing-gown ditto ;—and I shall send in a long bill to the Government, in the hope that I my receive compensation for what money cannot purchase here. My writing-desk is burned outside, but most of the

things inside are saved ; my Medal and Cross of the
Bath saved. Now I have got a bed from the hospital,
which is put up in C.'s tent. To-morrow I shall get
a marquee, and go under canvas.

27th March 1856.

I believe I told you we were to have races last
Monday (Easter Monday), the day after I was burned
out of house and home. My loss in effects amounts
to 200*l.* Many things gone which would have been
indispensable had the war continued. Now I have
got another hut, smaller and with no fire-place, so I
shall not be burned out again. All my remaining
goods are sadly scorched, including my whiskers and
beard. Well, as to the races ; the plain by the Chernaya, on the north side of the Feduchine heights,
was the ground selected. The links of the Chernaya
separated us from the Russians. On our side there
was about 20,000 people, and several thousand officers among them, all mounted. The Russians
thought it was a cavalry force, and they were surprised, as well they might be, at the condition of the
cattle. The day was lovely, and the whole scene lively
in every way, including colour. The first two races
were won by Frenchmen ; the pony-race by a little
gray Arab, ridden by I don't know whom ; the
steeple-chase by an English mare, bought from Lord
Burghersh, and admirably ridden by M. Le Baron
Talon, a sous-officier in the 4$^{me}$ Houssards. He is

I I

a rich man, well known in the French sporting circles, who I conclude entered the army for a lark when the war broke out. He rode most gallantly; and we were all very glad to see the fine young fellow come in a winner. You know I am not a sportsman; so I soon came away.

This morning when I woke with the full understanding that summer had begun, lo! there was a snow-storm and hard frost; only fancy what a take-in, and all my furs burned! The *Times* has an article on Codrington's rhetoric. You may easily see that, no corps having been formed, I have an absolute sinecure here, and that the situation is most disgusting. I cannot write very well, for my fingers are frozen, and there are six or seven carpenters at work at the other end of this hut, fixing it up for the two aides-de-camp; their hammering, and, above all, their swearing, is very distracting. The officers here are all speculating on their future prospects; many will be sent adrift who would wish to serve, and others will be compelled to serve who would be well contented to retire. Besides which, it is evident that the Commission consequent upon Evans's motion about purchase will alter every military man's fortune. I do not think it will make the least difference as to the class which will enter the army, but it will perhaps save some heartburnings among the very few who cannot muster cash enough to pay the regulation.

The true difficulty is, to restrain the current expenses of the officer's daily existence. A poor man living among rich ones is always in a false position; and a boy of eighteen, who perhaps lived at his father's in the most frugal manner, before he has been three months at the mess will be calling for claret and champagne, in imitation of his richer companions. It is the story of college-life with a red coat on its back. No one has been able to stop extravagance at college; in fact, credit for meat and drink is more easily obtained at college than in the army. In all well-regulated regiments the bills are paid every week, and the officers who exceed their means have to borrow money to pay their mess- and wine-bills; failing which payment, they come under the notice of the commanding officer.

31st March 1856.

Frost! sleet! rain! cold weather! Oh! oh! oh! The longer I am kept here waiting in this ridiculous position, the more annoying does it become, and the more do I grow out of sorts. Our armistice is prolonged till further orders; so decided, I conclude, by orders from the seat of Conference. If the weather would only become a little warm, one might ride and look about a bit; but I am too cold to do any thing of that sort, unless I had duty to perform, and duty does not exist for me.

5 P.M. I have just come in from a walk in the

woods, where I have been cutting sticks. The occupation is rather amusing, although fatiguing. One carries a hatchet and saw, and roots about in the coppices ; suddenly the eye hits on a straight stick, with some sort of a grotesque twist for a handle. The sticks, when brought home, are roasted over a fire to get the bark off, and are then put by ; they afterwards require dressing, filing, rasping, and polishing ; finally varnishing and a ferule, and the article is complete. You see how hard I am pushed for something to do.

3d April 1856.

The weather continues dreadful. At this moment there is a heavy snow-storm falling, and drifting into the hut and on my paper, and the water in my jug is frozen every night. It cannot last, one says every morning; but still it does last.

6th April 1856.

Yesterday I was looking over a plan of the battle of Chillianwallah, which was fought where Porus and Alexander fought. The country about there is full of Greek remains and remains of roads. The soldiers heard people talking about Alexander having made this or that; they saw the roads were very bad; at last they came to a broken bridge, and one fellow called out, "Well, that Alexander has a great deal to answer for." We hear that we are to have passes to go into the Russian lines. I shall at any rate go to

Bakchi-Serai, the old city of the Khans; it is about fifteen miles from here, up by the Mackenzie Farm Road. It will be curious for us to go up that road, which we descended last September year. What events have taken place since then, and how many good fellows in the prime of their lives have been laid under ground! You speak of the Hall and Cavendish affair. There is no conspiracy among officers to show-up their profession; it is the publicity now demanded by the nation which brings those and such matters to light. Lord Stratford is like to suffer more for not answering some letters, than if he had committed a crime: sometimes one does pay dearest for mistakes.

Engineer officers tell me that latterly our troops always behaved ill when attacked by night in the trenches, *i.e.* they did not stand. They were rallied by their officers, and retook the trenches, and their officers were rewarded. Whereas in the really well-regulated regiments, where the officers, instead of clustering together, and spending the night in smoking, drinking, and conversation, were continually circulating among the men, the first attack of the Russians was always repulsed with perfect ease. These officers were never noticed; there had been no loss; and rewards go with the butcher's bill, and in proportion to it. Just as at the battle of the Alma, we only lost 100 men killed and wounded, and those

who know nothing about the matter think the Highland Brigade did but little towards winning the day.

9th April 1856.

Yesterday I took a very long ride up the Mackenzie Road; when at the top, I turned to the left,
and went all the way to the North Fort, or Sever-
naia, then down to the harbour, and so back, up
the right bank of the river, to Traktir, about thirty
miles. The Russian huts are very wretched; and I
saw no stores, nor any signs of the abundance and
comfort in which our men revel. The Russians told
General Vinoy, who was of the party, that they were
surprised we did not go and take the north side after
the storm : but he pooh-pooh'd it ; he said, "The
French Emperor knew you could not stay there ; and
you see he was right, for you have been obliged to
ask for peace." They have evidently the "con-
signe" to be civil to the French, and cold to the
English, which Vinoy told them all the French could
see through.

13th April 1856.

On the 11th I saw the first swallow, or rather
swift, and the first butterfly. There are violets too,
and the various bulbs of this flowery land are pushing
out their green leaves, and preparing to paint the
bare soil. I have made several longish rides up the
gorges of the hills to the north-east. I have come

upon little Tartar villages, which seemed to have escaped in a great degree from the ravages of war; at
least the houses were inhabited, and not roofless; they
had only been put under the contribution of receiving Cossacks, who seem to have been billeted upon
them. The gardens and fruit-trees were intact; they
had been making up the fences; but the fields, alas,
were untilled! Magnificent groves of walnut-trees,
with an under-fringe of hazels, although leafless,
seemed beautiful, after this denuded neighbourhood.

16th April 1856.

Mounted at 6 A.M. for Bakchi-Serai. Our road
lay up to Mackenzie Farm; and it was interesting
to us, as we trotted along, to look at the changes
made along the sides of the road since we descended
from these heights last September twelvemonth, on
the day of the celebrated flank-march which made
us masters of Balaklava. Then the ground was
covered with thick coppices; the sides of the road
lined with good substantial trees, all now cut down
by the Russians, to deprive us of cover in the event
of our trying to take the heights from them. After we
had reached the top, a couple of miles' riding showed
us the interior of the country, and we could see
where Bakchi-Serai lay, about fifteen miles off. The
country is all volcanic, strange misshapen blocks of
granite rising in hillocks all round, and, as far as we

could see, the general soil chalky, and the roads also
of that material, which must have made them nearly
impassable in winter. After a long descent, we
reached the upper waters of the Belbek, a rapid moun-
tain-stream, fringed with oak and poplars, beyond
which a nearly level, but winding, track was seen
stretching itself along to the Katscha, a rather larger
river, on which there was a good-sized Turkish or
Tartar village, which at first we took for Bakchi-
Serai. Plenty of trees grew here ; four wersts further
on, we at last came to the beginning of Bakchi-Serai
itself, a considerable Turkish town, squeezed up in
a very narrow ravine, through which there flowed a
diminutive rivulet. In appearance this place differs
not at all from any Turkish town in Turkey : shops
open to the street, with the proprietors squatting
within them in busy idleness. The only pretty
things to buy as memorials were some silver ribbons,
with oxidised silver bosses and buckles and slides,
the work of the Caucasus, with ' Caucasus' imprinted
on them ; some silver plaited bracelets ; and silver
thimbles, all Caucasian, and enormously dear. We
were taken by our guide, a Turco-Polish officer, to
the house of a merchant, the interior of which had a
sort of Chinese look. The room we were introduced
into was wainscoted with pine unvarnished, the ceiling of the same, carved with some rude ornamental
battens running along the beams ; Chinese-looking

drawings and patterns, glazed, hung about the walls, and some of the windows had coloured glass in them. A divan ran round the room, and a small low table, about a foot high, was placed near the divan, at one end of the room. We were treated with excellent tea, the most delicious white bread, caviar, and honey in the comb. The only sight here is the old palace of the Khan, and the tombs of the Khans and Khanesses. The most famous, Kerim Garai, was stated to have died in 1185. There was also to be looked for the fountain of one Marie Potoska, which I do not believe we found; in the search, we came into a small kiosk, with a dried-up fountain, and on one side, on the divan, the corpse of a dead Russian soldier,—for the place is a hospital now; the principal diseases scurvy and low (not typhus) fever. The palace is far from splendid, although it has some rough coloured ornamentation outside, and one hall well enough wainscoted, and lighted with good coloured glass. The ride from Kamara to Bakchi-Serai and back is about forty-four miles, which we performed in twelve hours, including four hours' halt at Bakchi-Serai.

## PEACE !

### I.

Peace, Peace ! How soon shall we forget
    The friends, the loves who crumbling rest,
Whose fame has earn'd no coronet
    To deck the humble soldier's crest !

II.

Poor artisan or peasant lad,
   Beguiled by drink or glory's tale,
In worn red jacket meanly clad,
   Who died to win the peace we hail!

III.

In long gazettes his name was told,
   Dead, mangled, lost, for ever gone;
The wave of time is o'er him roll'd,
   His place is fill'd, his duty done.

IV.

The village wonder of a day,
   His sweetheart is another's now!
Bleak Tauris holds his lifeless clay,
   Without a cross its place to show.

V.

The blazon'd urn for lordly dead,
   The spurs, the stars for those that live,
The kiss of love, the bridal bed,—
   The country and the women give.

VI.

But who shall for plebeian weep,
   Of all who spell the warlike story?
The mothers only,—they will weep,
   When hearing of the nation's glory.

20th April 1856.

I sent by the last post a few lines about the poor dead soldiers; there are many who have never even been heard of, who never will be heard of. I have been reading an article in the *Westminster* about Kars.

It is curious to reflect on the consequences of a military appointment. Pelissier, of course, cared nothing about the Kars frontier; it was highly interesting to us. Our General, as we are told, took part with Pelissier in refusing to part with the Turkish troops, which Omar wanted to relieve Kars with. General Williams is made Military Commissioner in those parts, and, by the aid of the British Government apparently, he succeeded, in spite of the Turkish Government, in getting hold of the command, and then, in the teeth of the entreaties of the poor Turkish Cabinet, he kept the garrison at Kars till too late, and then let them all become prisoners of war. There has been a great review of the French and English, on the same day, for the benefit of Lüders and the Russians. They were surprised at the state of the horses, and imagined the troops were all picked men. One Russian said he saw porter and beefsteaks in all their figures. Pelissier says the Highlanders are the finest soldiers in the world. From what the Russians saw of the two armies, I have little doubt they will write to the Emperor to let him know he was very wise to make peace. Not that our army is really what it looks : both men and officers are undrilled. I do not believe in the least that Russia has abandoned or will abandon her policy ; she awaits a better opportunity, and I think will ultimately succeed, as perseverance usually does. The Turks will never submit to

be civilised, and to be made really strong and capable
of self-defence.   Omar is a quack, I should say; but
the Turkish soldiers believe in him.   We have got
rainy weather, which was much wanted; every thing
is parched, and the flowers cannot poke their heads
up easily through the hard crust.   General Vinoy has
got his orders to embark his division ; and will, I
suppose, be off in a very few days.   Would that our
turn were come!   The Artillery have a letter from
their own department, warning them to be ready.
The Russians are doing great politeness to all our
officers who go into their country ; I imagine their
policy is to try and persuade both English and French
that each of them has the preference in their affec-
tions.

24th April 1856.

Will you believe that we have frost still every
night ; sometimes the thermometer down to 23° ; but
it is generally fine and sunshiny by day.   Sir William
Eyre is ordered with six battalions to Canada ; this
will replace the usual force in that colony.   This is a
good appointment, as he had experience of a frontier
warfare in Africa, and was also with the 73d in the
Canadian rebellion.   I have heard that Lord Grey is
an admirer of his.   He will have local rank, which
will put him over the head of Major General Home,
late of the Guards, now commanding in Canada ; but
the case is very different of putting Eyre, with his

experience, over Home, who has none, from that of putting Codrington, with no experience and after a gross failure, over C., with his antecedents. A report has come of a new change of uniform. Really it is intolerable; a set of rascally men-milliners amusing themselves with dressing up the army, like girls with a doll; only the officers have to pay. Have you read St. Arnaud's letters? He was evidently a capital soldier; and if he had had another month's life in him, we should have taken Sebastopol at once; but it is not clear that Russia has not been more punished by the length of the siege than if she had been put out of pain by a short operation. I am disposed to think that Russia has exaggerated her losses, for the purpose of reconciling the war-party to making peace.

28th April 1856.

I send you the draft of the oration which C. means to make to the old Highland Brigade before he embarks; and shall be curious to hear how you like it.

*Speech of* SIR C. CAMPBELL *to the Highland Brigade, in taking leave of them; delivered on the 9th May* 1856.

"Soldiers of the 42d, 79th, and 93d! old Highland Brigade! with whom I passed the early and perilous part of this war! I have now to take leave of you; in a few hours I shall be on board ship, never to see you again as a body—a long farewell!

I am now old, and shall not be called to serve any more, and nothing will remain to me but the memory of my campaigns, and of the enduring, hardy, generous soldiers with whom I have been associated; whose name and whose glory will long be kept alive in the hearts of our countrymen. When you go home, as you gradually fulfil your term of service, each to his family and his cottage, you will tell the story of your immortal advance in that victorious *échelon* up the heights of Alma, and of the old Brigadier who led you, and who loved you so well; your children, and your children's children, will repeat the tale to other generations, when only a few lines of history will remain to record all the enthusiasm and discipline which have borne you so stoutly to the end of this war.

"Our native land will never forget the name of the Highland Brigade; and in some future war that nation will call for another one to equal this, which it can never surpass. Though I shall be gone, the thought of you will go with me wherever I may be, and cheer my old age with a glorious recollection of dangers affronted and of hardships endured. A pipe will never sound near me without carrying me back to those bright days when I was at your head, and wore the bonnet which you gained for me, and the honourable decorations on my breast, many of which I owe to your conduct. Brave soldiers! kind comrades! farewell!"

I hope your supposition will not come true, that I shall have to appear before the Commissioners; I doubt my having any thing to say; but I might submit my letter-book. I know we generally got our rations for our men, and that the hardships of war are great. When the English go to war again, it would save trouble if they would embark a Commission at once with the army. Lord Lucan, as you remark, is managing his affairs badly. The cavalry had a feeling against him, as they had also against Cardigan. Lord Raglan favoured the latter. What I personally saw of Lord Lucan was favourable to him. He was senior officer to C., and was always ready to take his advice. I know that C. stopped people's mouths in London, when they were going to abuse him. I sincerely congratulate you on the musical victory at Kensington Gardens of Sense over Dogmatism; it is getting the small end of the wedge in, and will bear fruit. I suppose I must plead guilty to not caring about the people as much as you do; but I have a strong wish to see them educated. That word, however, must be interpreted; for I do not consider the trick of reading and writing to be education; it is a tool. I am more for useful things; and cannot conceive that answering questions in geology is any use to a washerwoman. What I should like to see provided for the people would be leisure, and some rational amusement, instead of that damnable public-house, and beating their wives, who very often deserve it.

2d May 1856.

There is a large number of disconsolate officers here now, who are to be reduced on half- pay, and turned adrift from their regiments, which to many of them was their only home. Peace is not a blessing to every one. All the Tartars from Baidar and the great and small Miskomia are emigrating to Bulgaria ; Turkish Government vessels are come for them. The procession of wagons and entire families put me quite in mind of Herman and Dorothea ; Goethe evidently drew from nature. The Russians are glad to be rid of the Tartars, and will, I suppose, people the Crimea with German colonists. A clever Russian officer said the other day to a Frenchman, " You have given us a lesson, for which we thank you."

8th May 1856.

I have now to tell you that I shall embark at Kamish in the French packet which will convey this letter, on the 10th instant (Saturday). You will never, in all your life, receive another letter from Crim Tartary. That scene is now closed. The curtain is dropped, the tears dried up,—and to supper with what appetite we may !

THE END.